The Church,
Politics and Patronage
in the Fifteenth Century

The Church, Politics and Patronage in the Fifteenth Century

Edited by Barrie Dobson

ALAN SUTTON · Gloucester

ST. MARTIN'S PRESS · New York

1984

First published in Great Britain in 1984
Alan Sutton Publishing Limited
30 Brunswick Road
Gloucester GL1 1JJ

British Library Cataloguing in Publication Data

Church politics and patronage in the fifteenth
  century.
  1. Great Britain—Church history—
  Medieval period, 1066–1485   2. Great
  Britain—History—Lancaster and York,
  1399–1485
  I. Dobson, R.B.
  941.04   BR750

  ISBN 0-86299-041-6

First published in the United States of America in 1984
St. Martin's Press, Inc.,
175 Fifth Avenue,
New York, NY 10010

Library of Congress Cataloging in Publication Data
Main entry under title:

The Church politics and patronage in the fifteenth
  century.
    "Revised versions of those read to a colloquium . . .
at the University of York on 23–26 September 1982"—
Introd.
    Includes bibliographies and index.
    1. England—Church history—Medieval period,
1066–1485—Addresses, essays, lectures.   2. Church
and state—England—History—Addresses, essays,
lectures.   3. Patronage, Ecclesiastical—England—
History—Addresses, essays, lectures.   I. Dobson,
R.B. (Richard Barrie)
BR750.C48 1984   274.2'05   84-15102
ISBN 0-312-13481-9

Printed in Great Britain.

Contents

List of Abbreviations

Unless otherwise stated, the place of publication of cited works is London.

AFH	*Archivum Franciscanum Historicum*
BIHR	*Bulletin of the Institute of Historical Research*
BL	British Library, London
BRUC	A.B. Emden, A *Biographical Register of the University of Cambridge to 1500* (Cambridge, 1963)
BRUO	A.B. Emden, A *Biographical Register of the University of Oxford to 1540* (4 vols., Oxford, 1957–74)
CCR	*Calendar of Close Rolls*
CFR	*Calendar of Fine Rolls*
CPL	*Calendar of Papal Letters*
CPR	*Calendar of Patent Rolls*
CS	Camden Society
CYS	Canterbury and York Society
DNB	Dictionary of National Biography
EcHR	*Economic History Review*
EETS	Early English Text Society
EHR	*English Historical Review*
EWW	*The English Works of Wyclif Hitherto Unprinted*, ed. F.D. Matthew (EETS, OS 74, 1880)
HBC	*The Handbook of British Chronology*, ed. F.M. Powicke and E.B. Fryde (Royal Historical Society, 1961)
HMSO	Her Majesty's Stationery Office
JEH	*Journal of Ecclesiastical History*
PBA	*Proceedings of the British Academy*
PRO	Public Record Office
RC	Record Commission
RES	*Review of English Studies*
RP	*Rotuli Parliamentorum* (7 vols., RC, 1783–1832)
RS	Rolls Series
SCH	*Studies in Church History*
SEW	*Select English Works of John Wyclif*, ed. T. Arnold (3 vols., Oxford, 1869–71)
SR	*Statutes of the Realm* (11 vols., RC, 1810–28)

Test. Ebor. Testamenta Eboracensia (6 vols., Surtees Society, 1836–1902)
TRHS   *Transactions of the Royal Historical Society*
VCH   *Victoria History of the Counties of England*
WS   Wyclif Society

Introduction

The ten papers which comprise this volume are revised versions of those read to a colloquium of late medieval historians which took place at the University of York on 23–26 September 1982. That colloquium was itself the latest in a series of similar informal meetings held at periodic intervals in British universities during recent years: its most immediate predecessor was an Anglo-French Historical Colloquium which met at the University of Sheffield in September 1976 and whose own proceedings have since been published as *The Crown and Local Communities in England and France in the Fifteenth Century* (Gloucester, 1981) under the general editorship of Dr. J.R.L. Highfield and Dr. Robin Jeffs. Between 1976 and 1982 two other late medieval symposia were held at the Universities of Bristol (July 1978) and Swansea (July 1979) with the more specific object of encouraging younger scholars to make the results of their recent researches in fifteenth-century English history more widely available; and the papers delivered at those two symposia have also now been published by Alan Sutton Ltd. as *Patronage, Pedigree and Power in Later Medieval England* (Gloucester, 1979) and *Patronage, the Crown and the Provinces in Later Medieval England* (Gloucester, 1981), edited by Professors Charles Ross and Ralph Griffiths respectively. To an extent even the original sponsors of the first of these historical colloquia can hardly have anticipated, such occasional meetings of late medieval English – and sometimes French – historians seem to have proved an experiment well worth continuing. Less than a generation ago the fifteenth century was notoriously, in Professor S.B. Chrimes's phrase, 'the Cinderella of all the centuries of English history'.[1] To their slightly surprised pleasure most current practitioners of that century's history would probably concede that a fairy godmother has now rescued them from obscurity. Whatever the reasons, it could well be argued that few, if any, periods in this country's history seem to evoke so happy a combination of novel individual research and communal academic *esprit de corps*. In their very different ways the ten essays collected in this volume bear witness to both these qualities, as well as to their impact in beginning to revise some traditional historical impressions of pre-Reformation Britain.

Nor, perhaps, is there any need to justify – despite the inevitable ambiguities inherent in each of its three constituent elements – the choice of 'Church, Politics and Patronage' as an appropriate field of investigation for a colloquium of late medieval historians assembled at York in the autumn of 1982. Indeed, the very fact that both the political narrative and the patronage structures of fifteenth-century England have been subjected to unprecedently refined inter-pretation in a series of notable recent biographies, monographs and articles has made it all the more obvious that the ecclesiastical history of that same century still awaits similarly detailed scrutiny.[2] This is not of course to deny that the strengths and weaknesses of the pre-Reformation church have been the subject of perennial fascination, and often of acute controversy, ever since the Reformation itself. Indeed, if this volume had to be dedicated to the memory of any single historian, most late medievalists would probably find it easy to agree on the obvious candidate. During his years as Reader and then Professor of History at the University of Leeds between 1922 and 1939, the late Alexander Hamilton Thompson not only established an unrivalled knowledge of the administrative records of the province of York itself but also imposed an interpretative pattern on the institutional history of the late medieval English church which still stands remarkably and deservedly intact.[3] Nevertheless, no reader of this present volume can be left in any doubt that in their various fields all ten of its contributors have moved into areas of historical investigation considerably outside even Hamilton Thompson's magisterial ken. Such a development is indeed inevitable at a time when historical attention has inceasingly turned from the operations of the elaborately complex and abun-dantly well-documented ecclesiastical administration of late medieval Christen-dom towards a more 'global' investigation of church life in its myriad manifesta-tions. At the present stage of research it would be highly inopportune to anticipate the eventual outcome of much new work in progress. However, it seems at least conceivable that the essays printed in this volume may point towards the possibility of some future fundamental reassessment of the role of church in late medieval state and society.

Not, however, that all or even most of the contributors to this book would necessarily believe that such a fundamental reassessment was either attainable or desirable. In no sense is this volume intended either to promote a general thesis or to provide a comprehensive treatment of the immense subject matter implied by its title. Thanks to the learned attentions of Professors D.E.R. and J.A. Watt, the churches of fifteenth-century Scotland and Ireland are indeed properly represented in this collection; but to the justifiable criticism that the Welsh church may accordingly seem even more conspicuous for its absence from the following pages, one can only plead guilty and refer the complainant to the last chapters of Professor Glanmor Williams's monumental *The Welsh Church from Conquest to Reformation* which discuss issues highly relevant to this volume.[4] An equally obvious omission in the following pages is any account of the highly complex political relationship between English crown and papal curia in the fifteenth century; but in this case the omission was genuinely deliberate and due to the availability of Professor F.R.H. Du Boulay's short but incisive study of how during this period Anglo-papal relations 'reached the pass where compromise was the rule'.[5] Perhaps a more serious criticism still is that a volume with the title of *The Church, Politics and Patronage in the Fifteenth Century* should have paid more direct attention to the theme of ecclesiastical appointments, a sphere where in practice the late medieval English church was notoriously most subject to political pressures and patronage connections; here again, however, Dr. Robert Dunning's recently published study of 'Patronage and Promotion in the Late Medieval Church' provides an example of the rewards that lie in store for those who undertake research in this still much neglected field.[6] Not that such research will be at all certain to point in quite the same direction. As Professor Vauchez has recently been at pains to argue, and as the following papers themselves reveal, Christianity at the end of the middle ages was certainly not *'d'une seule pièce'*.[7] Readers of this volume will accordingly have no difficulty in detecting significant differences of emphasis within the collection, most obviously perhaps between Dr. Colin Richmond's arguments for a possible 'interiorisation of religion' in the case of at least some fifteenth-century English gentlemen and Mr. Peter Heath's inability to discover many 'traces of independent thoughts or even of independent emotion' among the wills of the late medieval inhabitants of Hull.

It need hardly be said that such differences of interpretation are themselves a reflection of the ambiguities of the original evidence available to the historians of the fifteenth-century church. Awareness that, in the words of Canon Etienne Delaruelle, 'we are better informed about the abuses of the fifteenth century than the virtues of the thirteenth' may help us to recognise those ambiguities but not altogether to circumvent them.[8] To adapt the late Mr. K.B. McFarlane's more recent and familiar formulation of the same difficulty, it may be ironical but is in some ways unavoidable 'that it is the very richness of their sources which has given the later middle ages a bad name.[9] However, the student of the fifteenth-century church in the British Isles is confronted with an additional and perhaps even more acute evidential problem still. As recently as 1969 the greatest of English monastic historians had no doubt that by contemporary European standards 'the fifteenth century in England is singularly barren of great men and genial (*sic*) ideas'.[10] Few contributors to this volume would be likely to endorse quite so stark and melancholy a view; but the late Dom David Knowles's dismissive judgement does call attention to the familiar dilemma that, despite the remarkable abundance of late medieval ecclesiastical records, comparatively few fifteenth-century Englishmen and Englishwomen successfully articulated their most personal religious ambitions and concerns to posterity. The inscrutability – to ourselves rather than themselves – of the late medieval clergy and laity should admittedly not be over-emphasised. The fifteenth century was, after

all, the age of Margery Kempe; and in her essay in this volume Dr. Margaret
Aston demonstrates, as she has done so often before, how evidence of religious
sensibility can be unearthed from voluminous literary material others have not
previously pondered quite intently enough. Similarly, and again not for the first
time, Dr. Colin Richmond here emerges from Paston territory with indications
of a more 'genial', and even congenial, religious atmosphere than that ever
detected by Dom David Knowles. Nevertheless that massive problems of
interpretation remain seems hard to deny. As Professor Hamilton Thompson
once pointed out in the case of the archiepiscopal registers of York itself,
fifteenth-century records can be large in scale but singularly devoid of illuminating content.[11] To an exceptional extent, even by the standards of earlier
medieval centuries, the religious predilections and prejudices of the period
usually have to be inferred from actions rather than from words. Dr. Helen
Jewell's essay in this collection is, for example, a sustained exercise in the
inevitability of such an approach even in the case of those members of the clergy,
the bishops of England themselves, who might have been expected to be among
the most articulate of all. Not only does the silent majority of fifteenth-century
England persist in remaining even more silent than such majorities usually are;
but its leaders and its critics, the literate and the learned, often appear to speak
to us in muted tones when indeed they speak to us at all.

Nowhere perhaps in the intellectual world of fifteenth-century England is this
silence more disconcerting than in the field of speculative thinking about the
political position of the church itself. It is one of the several virtues of M. Jean-
Philippe Genet's opening essay in this volume that it not only exposes a
notorious 'lack of vitality' in the 'political theology' of late medieval England but
provides some searching explanations for that deficiency. The comparative
quiescence of what we would now call ideological debate in fifteenth-century
England has most often been attributed to a disinclination to re-open the
perilous controversies associated with university speculation in the age of John
Wycliffe: after 1400, it can and has been argued, the leaders of the English
church were more careful than ever before to reduce the occasions for conflict
between alternative religious ideas and ideals.[12] By setting this major historical
problem in a wide chronological context, Jean-Philippe Genet persuades us to
look much deeper for its possible solution; the minor role played by members of
the English clerical intelligentsia in the Conciliar debates of the early fifteenth
century had been fore-shadowed by their predecessors' lack of involvement in
the 'enormous' development of political theology throughout much of Christendom two and three generations earlier. As with other centuries it may be a
French scholar who has an especially acute eye for what could be the most
distinctive features of the intellectual ethos on this side of the Channel. The
growth of the English vernacular and the emergence of a large politically
conscious audience which nevertheless found traditional political theology
largely irrelevant to its own concerns helped to lessen the demand for the

intellectual skills of the university-educated clerical polemicist; and the still somewhat bafflling disinclination of fifteenth-century English monarchs to patronise ambitious literary production among the clerks in their entourage stems at least in part from their lack of any urgent need for ideological propaganda on the French model. It follows that Sir John Fortescue can be firmly re-instated in his central position as the most interesting practitioner of what political theory in fifteenth-century England could actually be. Appropriately enough, this was the achievement not of a clerk but of a common lawyer who benefited from a specialised legal education which Dr. Eric Ives has recently extolled as 'perhaps the most significant cultural development in fifteenth-century England'.[13]

As M. Jean-Philippe Genet observes in the course of his argument, one of the more interesting features of much intellectual debate in late medieval England is its propensity to cluster around the familiar theme of evangelical poverty. For Dr. Margaret Aston too, 'the question of the poor' is inseparably linked to the vociferous and sometimes tortured controversies about clerical disendowment that form so striking a feature of observable religious attitudes in the decades immediately before and after 1400. Verbal assaults on 'Caim's Castles' were not of course a new phenomenon in the age of Wycliffe and the early Lollards; but in demonstrating the seriousness with which they were regarded at this period Dr. Aston provides us with a *locus classicus* of how arguments about religious and spiritual duties could develop an overtly political dimension. In many ways the Lollard disendowment bill of (almost certainly) 1410, with its intriguing provision for fifteen new universities as well as a hundred new almshouses, may be the most radical 'political' document produced in fifteenth-century England. It has now received the attention it deserves in a searching analysis of a complicated series of ideological cross-currents which may even take us back to an English Wycliffite work which was actually written by Wycliffe himself. Dr. Aston is surely justified in her advice to historians not to minimise unduly the importance of the political aspirations of the Lollard movement; and in her unravelling of some exceptionally tangled skeins of thought she reveals that it would be equally unwise to discount both the intellectual subtlety and the emotional passion with which the attacks on clerical possessioners and, especially, mendicants were pursued. Once again, as in much recent work by Dr. Anne Hudson and Dr. Aston herself, one can be left in no doubt of the high moral seriousness with which at least some members of early fifteenth-century English society could approach fundamental theological and political issues.[14] And if, as Dr. Aston herself admits, the call for clerical disendowment finally led to largely negative results in the political arena itself, her essay also reveals how little we yet know of the final stages of her story – what happened to that 'truly evangelical commitment to the poor' in the last generations of the pre-Reformation English church.[15]

Dr. Aston also reminds us that even before the fifteenth century began, John Wycliffe had pointed out that 'it is not strange for kings to correct clerks'.[16] In his novel treatment of a theme which must be central to any discussion of the relationship between church and national politics in late medieval England Professor R.L. Storey shows how limited could be the room for political manoeuvre even of an archbishop of Canterbury. The instability of royal fortunes in the fifteenth century notoriously presented the leaders of the English church with more than their usual share of difficult and often embarrassing political decisions; and of the various factors influencing those decisions the possibility that at least some ecclesiastical promoters of new kings believed they were thereby serving the wider interests of the *ecclesia Anglicana* has certainly been unfairly neglected. As Professor Storey implies, the common assumption that prelates like Archbishops Arundel and George Neville derived their political ambitions and attitudes exclusively from their own membership of the higher English nobility can beg some very important questions indeed. The sincerity with which Archbishop Arundel (in 1399) and Archbishop Bourchier (in 1460–1) believed that a change of dynasty might bring about a genuine change of heart in the crown's attitude to the grievances of the clergy may be hard to assess; but at least these constitutional crises seemed to afford those archbishops and their convocations with some bargaining power. It is central to Professor Storey's argument that by the 1460s such bargaining power was a good deal less than it had been two generations earlier. In the face of a parliamentary commons unsympathetic to the clergy's complaints, royal benevolence – even where it existed – was no longer enough. The arguments deployed here have obviously important implications for the inability of the English prelates to find a united or effective stance in the political bouleversements of the 1480s. More significantly still, the replacement of clergy by laymen in the crown's own administrative establishment may, in the words of one of Professor Storey's own recent papers, 'have helped to accentuate the distinction between civil and ecclesiastical institutions of government' in a positively fundamental manner.[17]

Such considerations were not, however, likely to be uppermost in the minds of the many Englishmen and Englishwomen who throughout the fifteenth century assiduously petitioned the papal 'well of Grace' for dispensations, pardons and favours. In the course of reviewing volume xiii of the *Calendar of Entries in the Papal Registers relating to Great Britain and Ireland (1471–84)*, the late Mr. K.B. McFarlane once observed that 'as far as the English church was concerned the pope's authority was mainly an authority to dispense'.[18] This judgement seems abundantly confirmed by Dr. John Thomson's careful study of the bewildering variety of successful English petitions recorded in the fifteenth-century papal registers. These cases have the particular attraction of throwing an unexpectedly vivid light on the personal aspirations and fears of many petitioners, not least their sensitivity to the dangers of committing matrimonial irregularities and disregarding religious vows. It is hard indeed to avoid Dr. Thomson's own conclusion that the seeking of such favours from the papal curia was usually motivated by an acutely personal 'desire for spiritual well-being'. A type of evidence so absolutely determined by the desires of particular individuals no doubt raises its own problems of interpretation; but it certainly seems significant that, with the exception of a decline in the number of indults to possess portable altars, Dr. Thomson fails to detect any major diminution in the number and range of papal dispensations during the course of the century. Eagerness for these favours bears little or no correlation to the political struggles between English crown and Roman curia; and the student of the fifteenth-century church has to accept the paradox that considerable anti-papal sentiment always co-existed with a recognition that the papacy itself was not only an extraordinary but a highly convenient institution. It is perhaps more ironical still that a system of dispensations so violently attacked as an abuse of papal power in the years after 1500 should in the previous century have cured the spiritual 'sores' of so many Englishmen who could afford the expense of the treatment.

One of the attractions of petitioning the Roman curia in the fifteenth century was no doubt that 'in the peculiar circumstances of the late medieval papacy, the line of least resistance meant first of all granting petitions instead of denying them'.[19] This not unfamiliar political problem seems to lie quite close to the surface of the tangled webs of the papacy's relationships with Scotland and Ireland in the fifteenth century. Professor Du Boulay once characterised Anglo-papal relations at the beginning of that century as the product of a 'desire for mutual support based unfruitfully on self-interest'.[20] In their respective surveys of two very different, and very differently documented, national experiences, Professors Donald and Jack Watt seem to leave no more favourable an impression. Like modern historians, so fifteenth-century papal administrators can perhaps be forgiven some bewilderment at the complexities of the political and ecclesiastical map of late medieval Ireland. However, as Professor Jack Watt points out, their propensity to muddy the waters, as when they appointed too many bishops of Down in the 1440s, hardly brought clarity to an already highly confused scene. Sometimes responsive and sometimes not to the complexities of the many diverse local situations forced upon its attention, the fifteenth-century papacy can hardly be expected to have displayed a consistent Irish ecclesiastical policy; if it had tried to do so, for instance by promoting an episcopal élite blatantly subservient to the English crown's political interests in Ireland, such an experiment would almost certainly have been foredoomed to failure. Even less could the papacy have hoped to restrict the operations of those Irish clerical dynasties, of whom the O'Loughrans are here taken as an example, who were to keep 'Gaelic Ulster Catholic through the Reformation'. By contrast it might be argued that in fifteenth-century Scotland the role of the 'political bishop' could be considerably more influential – though for very different reasons – than in either Ireland or England. To an exceptional extent in Christendom as a whole, it may even be that the kingdom of Scotland's allegiances during the Great Schism were determined by the preferences of the Scottish clergy themselves. Here again, moreover, Professor Donald Watt makes it clear that he sees the

Scottish evidence as pointing to the final conclusion that 'the popes of the fifteenth century emerge more as followers than leaders'. As in England, a harmonious *modus vivendi* between royal government and papal curia could never be maintained without some conscious effort on both sides; and by the end of the century the papacy's 'casual lack of concern' for the suitability of candidates for the Scottish episcopal bench was more uncomfortably evident than ever before.

Despite Thomas Gascoigne's embittered ruminations on the subject, quite what qualities made a clerk a 'suitable' bishop was an issue perhaps less often discussed in late medieval England than one might have had a reasonable right to expect. Some modern historians would still believe that the English bishops of the fifteenth century 'with few exceptions never measured up to their responsibilities' and were even guilty of a certain, no doubt involuntary, '*trahison des clercs*'[21]. However, in a powerful plea for their rehabilitation, or at least for a greater understanding of the realities of their position, Dr. Richard Davies has recently advised us to be wary of the 'invective against the later medieval episcopate handed down by contemporary critics and Protestant apologists'.[22] As Dr. Davies's survey of the English episcopal bench concentrated on the period between 1375 and 1461, it is all the more welcome that Dr. Helen Jewell's investigation of bishops as educational benefactors should be directed at the second half of the fifteenth century. That all but one (William Booth) of the forty-three bishops considered in Dr. Jewell's essay should themselves be 'university men' is the most obvious testimony to the critical influence of Oxford and Cambridge Universities in the formation of late medieval England's powerful ecclesiastical hierarchy. Less familiar is the way in which this 'essentially childless' élite, often in the fortunate position of actually having the financial means to make major endowments in this sphere, fulfilled its ill-defined responsibilities for educational provision. No doubt any precise assessment of the religious and pastoral qualities of the bishops of fifteenth-century England will always lie somewhat uncomfortably in the eye of the modern beholder. Nevertheless Dr. Jewell is able to detect genuine evidence of personal commitment to schools and scholars on the part of many members of the episcopal bench. Ironically enough, it is usually prelates like Waynflete, Rotherham, Alcock and Fox, most often interpreted as 'worldly careerists and busy politicians', who emerge as the really handsome benefactors of educational causes. Not unnaturally, patterns of educational patronage on the part of England's bishops often reflected the highly uneven income they derived from their respective dioceses; but Dr. Jewell's paper also leaves one in no doubt that the availability of educational opportunities in fifteenth-century English schools and universities was still largely determined by the personal and not at all predictable initiatives of a handful of wealthy prelates.

Dr. Jewell accordingly provides valuable new insights into one of the most frustrating of all problems facing the historian of church and politics in fifteenth-century England – that so remarkably little can be known for certain about the individual personalities of the seventeen men who at any one time presided over the judicial and administrative machines of the church. In stark contrast the operations of those machines themselves are abundantly, and at times almost overwhelmingly, well-documented. Nevertheless, Dr. Alison McHardy is surely justified in suggesting that clerical taxation in late medieval England has been undeservedly neglected both as a subject in its own right and as a central focus of relations between church and crown. Admittedly the exchequer records of the fifteenth-century English government can never be approached in an over-optimistic manner; and Dr. McHardy herself draws attention to serious miscalculation of clerical tax rates in the 1430s which possibly derived from popular misconceptions about the true income of chantry priests and other chaplains. As in the sphere of lay direct taxation, a period of strenuous but largely abortive experimentation with new forms of levy in the first half of the fifteenth century was apparently succeeded by a return to more traditional fiscal methods thereafter. Whether or not the royal government was ever as successful as it hoped in exploiting what it saw as the insufficiently tapped wealth of the clerical estate, its efforts in this direction certainly imposed some very considerable administrative as well as financial burdens on the English church. The records, where they survive, of fifteenth-century religious houses would seem to confirm Dr. McHardy's view that the collection of clerical taxes was the single most arduous duty many members of that church performed on behalf of the crown; and in this context too the bishops of England re-emerge, once again with little room for manoeuvre between the harassment of 'royal meddling' on the one side and the complaints of over-worked collectors of clerical subsidies on the other. Despite her revelations of these strains and tensions, Dr. McHardy's final conclusion is not however altogether melancholy. In emphasising the basic resilience of the clerical tax-collecting machinery, she draws attention in a not unimportant sphere to that 'solidité du système de la longue croissance' which made the fifteenth-century church considerably less feeble than its detractors have sometimes supposed.[23] And here even the recently much vilified clerical *bureaucrates* of late medieval Christendom appear in not unsympathetic guise, above all because they were the victims rather than the beneficiaries of the bureaucracy they serviced.[24]

Nor, in his very different and difficult search for what religion may have meant to the fifteenth-century English gentleman, does Dr. Colin Richmond discover immediate cause for gloom. He returns from his investigation of the Paston correspondence and other sources with the suggestion that its inhabitants were far from being 'oppressed by the so-called burdens of late medieval religion'. No doubt, as his own recent biography of John Hopton was at pains to demonstrate, it would always be dangerous to assume that the ambitions and attitudes of the Paston family were absolutely representative of those of other members of the fifteenth-century gentry.[25] Perhaps 'popular religion' (whatever quite that is) in late medieval England is likely to have comprised an even more varied and heterogeneous cluster of beliefs and fears than the religion of monks, friars and secular clerks. However, what does emerge most strikingly from Dr. Richmond's essay on this major theme is that the piety of the fifteenth-century gentleman can certainly not be interpreted as a pale and imitative reflection of that of contemporary ecclesiastical élites. For many of the Pastons and their peers, as well as for members of the English aristocracy too, the clerk they knew best was their private chaplain. Nor should the probability that many members of the gentry practised an 'uncomplicated' religion disguise the complexities as well as the strengths of the forces that had come to form their attitudes. In England, as elsewhere in Christendom, there is more than the occasional sign that by the fifteenth century the church had succeeded, in some ways almost too well, in convincing large numbers of laymen that religious salvation was primarily their own concern. For Dr. Richmond 'this privatization of religion for the gentry', compounded as it was by the socially divisive and anti-communal effects of increasing literacy and educational provision, not only led towards the English Reformation but made that Reformation largely what it was. Of all aspects of church history no doubt the so-called interiorisation of the religious life will, by its very nature, always be the most resistant to the modern historian; but here is one of several areas of fifteenth-century experience where it can be plausibly suggested that silence might sometimes be more eloquent than words.

By contrast the increasingly large numbers of late medieval historians who now hope to penetrate the world of popular religion by means of the evidence of probate registers can hardly complain of a lack of words. Here, however, as Mr. Peter Heath makes clear in the last essay in this collection, we may be confronted with source material which is 'as treacherous to use as it is beguiling to cite'. In the fifteenth century, as in more recent times, wills have the unusual fascination of being both the most personal and the most formal written documents to survive from large sections of the English population. Few sources available to the historian of the pre-Reformation English church would seem to lend themselves more readily to statistical treatment; yet few, if any, can be a more hazardous guide to the religious priorities of their age. Nevertheless Mr. Heath's study of the 355 wills produced by the inhabitants of the city of Hull between 1400 and 1529 proves how imperative it is not to look this gift-horse in the mouth to the extent of rejecting it completely. From this paper certain elements in the religious life of an important English town undoubtedly do emerge quite unambiguously, most obviously perhaps an intense communal loyalty – and generosity – to the two parish churches of Hull: here is evidence which adds some very considerable weight to the late Professor Hamilton Thompson's verdict that 'there is no period at which money was lavished so freely on English parish churches as in the fifteenth century'.[26] Nor perhaps can there ever have been a period when more testators (almost a half of the total in fifteenth-century Hull) made such copious monetary bequests for the commemoration of their souls. More interesting still perhaps are those supposedly familiar features of late medieval English religious life, like the cult of saints and the popularity of pilgrimages, which fail to leave many visible traces in the testamentary provisions of the inhabitants of Hull. In raising these and other issues Mr. Heath may be pointing to the possibility that the evidence of wills could be as important in questioning traditional assumptions as in producing a largely non-achievable definitive potrait of English religious attitudes as a whole. For some historians the strongest 'impression left by the majority of late medieval wills is one of insecurity only mitigated by religious benevolence';[27] but for Mr. Heath what characterises the fifteenth-century wills of Hull is less personal anxiety than a religion 'overlaid with civic pride and almost subsumed into civic ritual' – on the microcosmic urban scene an inextricable *mélange* of church, politics and patronage indeed.

However, not only Mr. Heath's concluding essay but this volume as a whole illustrates some of the ways in which both the opportunities and the problems presented by the study of the late medieval church in England and Britain seem considerably greater than they did even a generation ago. To adapt a recent phrase of Professor Francis Rapp, the history of the fifteenth-century church is beginning to appear, more than ever before, *'un domaine immense, une sorte de mare magnum parsemé de recifs'*.[28] Now that recent research has done so much (but perhaps still not enough?) to undermine the traditionally insidious tendency to interpret the ecclesiastical world of the fifteenth century exclusively in terms of its failure to anticipate the ethos of either the Protestant Reformation or of the Council of Trent, historians of that world are likely to be at the same time both more liberated and more uncertain in expressing general judgements. Despite its increasingly obvious inadequacies, the conventional predisposition to condemn the late medieval church for its supposed 'decline', 'dissolution', 'lassitude', 'spiritual rusticity' and 'ineffectiveness of its velleities for reform' did at least have the partial advantage of imposing a comparatively unified vision upon the religious experience of our fifteenth-century predecessors. The following essays seem to confirm Professor Francis Oakley's recent observation that no comparable unified vision now exists.[29] Even when utilised by its most skilful French practitioners, the concept of *'pre–Réforme'* appears to have engendered more heat than light as recently applied to the later medieval church:[30] nor will any readers of this book need to be reminded that in many areas of the religious life the clergy and the laity of the later middle ages were hardly complete masters of their own destinies.

Not perhaps that it could ever have been otherwise. In the familiar words with which Giles of Viterbo opened the Fifth Lateran Council in May 1512, *'Homines per sacra immutari fas est, non sacra per homines'*: 'Men must be changed by religion, not religion by men'.[31] There are few periods in the history of the Christian church when that admittedly somewhat ambiguous text is more likely to have been valid than the fifteenth century – with possibly explosive effects for the generations immediately thereafter. However, the contributors to this volume resist the temptation of supposing that an inordinate amount of the evidence they discuss points inevitably in the direction of the sixteenth-century Reformation. If anything, the cumulative effect of their essays may be to confirm the probability created by recent research, not least their own, that the religious history of late medieval Britain should be its own reward and is beginning to take on a genuinely novel, if as yet largely unresolved, complexion. Such was certainly the impression left in my own mind at the conclusion of the colloquium held at York in September 1982. For their most helpful advice and assistance during the preparation of that colloquium I am much indebted, among many others, to Dr. Christopher Allmand, Dr. Peter Biller, Professor John Bossy, Dr. Claire Cross, Professor Ralph Griffiths, Dr. Roger Highfield, Dr. Michael Jones, Mr. Peter Rycraft, Professor Charles Ross, Miss Brigette Vale, and, above all, to Dr. David Smith. To Dr. Smith's generous support this book too owes more than I can adequately say. My greatest thanks are inevitably due to the ten scholars whose volume this is, as well as to Mr. Alan Sutton, the publisher, for his encouragement and assistance at all stages of its production.

University of York, 1984   Barrie Dobson

Notes

1. *Fifteenth-century England, 1399–1509*, ed. S.B. Chrimes, C.D. Ross and R.A. Griffiths (Manchester, 1972), p. vii.
2. See the bibliographical review article, 'After McFarlane', by Dr. Colin Richmond in *History*, 68 (1983), 46–60. For the ecclesiastical policies and religious proclivities of fifteenth-century monarchs, a theme not considered in this volume, the following recent biographical studies are all indispensable: B. Wolffe, *Henry VI* (1981); R.A. Griffiths, *The Reign of King Henry VI* (1981); C. Ross, *Edward IV* (1974); C. Ross, *Richard III* (1981); and S.B. Chrimes, *Henry VII* (1972). An important statement of the case for a more 'dynamic religious ideology' on the part of the early Tudor kings is made by A. Goodman, 'Henry VII and Christian Renewal', *SCR*, 17, ed. K. Robbins (Oxford, 1981), 116–25.
3. A.H. Thompson, *The English Clergy and their Organization in the Later Middle Ages* (Oxford, 1947); cf. *An Address presented to Alexander Hamilton Thompson, with a Bibliography of his writings* (privately printed, Oxford, 1948).
4. 'The faith was accepted by Welshmen but dimly apprehended. Habit rather than conviction was its mainspring': G. Williams, *The Welsh Church from Conquest to Reformation* (Cardiff, 1962), 558.
5. F.R.H. Du Boulay, 'The Fifteenth Century', in *The English Church and the Papacy in the Middle Ages*, ed. C.H. Lawrence (1965), 240. Cf. R.G. Davies, 'Martin V and the English episcopate, with particular reference to his campaign for the repeal of the Statute of Provisors', *EHR*, 92 (1977), 309–44; and J.A.F. Thomson, *Popes and Princes, 1417–1517: Politics and Polity in the Late Medieval Church* (1980).
6. R.W. Dunning, 'Patronage and Promotion in the Late Medieval Church', in *Patronage, the Crown and the Provinces in Later Medieval England*, ed. R.A. Griffiths (Gloucester, 1981), 167–80. For the diagnosis of 'the deleterious system of lay patronage' as the most serious 'nettle which neither Catholic nor Protestant reformers ever had the moral courage to uproot', see J.R. Lander, *Government and Community: England 1450–1509* (1980), 137–8.
7. A. Vauchez, *Religion et Société dans l'Occident Médiéval* (Turin, 1980), 316.
8. E. Delaruelle, E.-R. Labande and P. Ourliac, *L'Église au temps du Grand Schisme et de la Crise Conciliaire, 1378–1449* (A. Fliche and V. Martin, *Histoire de L'Eglise depuis les origines jusqu'a nos jours*, 14 i (1962), p. xi.
9. K.B. McFarlane, *The Nobility of Later Medieval England* (Oxford, 1973), 114.
10. D. Knowles and D. Obolensky, *The Christian Centuries*, II: *The Middle Ages* (1969), 465.
11. A.H. Thompson, 'The Registers of the Archbishops of York', *Yorkshire Archaeological Journal*, xxxii (1935), 254.
12. More generally, a widespread desire to *'réduire les oppositions entre les théories ou les disciplines'* is seen as the most important single characteristic of the religious life of the fifteenth as opposed to the fourteenth century in F. Rapp, *L'Église et la Vie Religieuse en Occident à la fin du Moyen Age* (Paris, 1971), 365–6. The most familiar example of the fate that could befall a fifteenth-century English cleric who 'extolled the dictates of the human reason in many things' is best discussed by E.F. Jacob, 'Reynold Pecock, Bishop of Chichester', in *Essays in Later Medieval History* (Manchester, 1968), 1–34.
13. E.W. Ives, 'The Common Lawyers', in *Profession, Vocation and Culture in Later Medieval England*, ed. C.H. Clough (Liverpool, 1982), 209.
14. M. Aston, *Lollards and Reformers* (1983); *Selections from English Wycliffite Writings*, ed. A. Hudson (Cambridge, 1978); *English Wycliffite Sermons*, I, ed. A. Hudson (Oxford, 1983).
15. For an exceptionally well-documented case of old debating topics arousing new passions in

London during the second half of the fifteenth century see F.R.H. Du Boulay, 'The quarrel between the Carmelite friars and the secular clergy of London, 1464–1468', *JEH*, vi (1955), 156–74.

16. See below, p. 64.

17. R.L. Storey, 'Gentleman-Bureaucrats', in *Profession, Vocation and Culture*, ed. Clough, 91; cf. the same author's 'The Foundation and the Medieval College, 1379–1530', in *New College, Oxford: 1379–1979*, ed. J. Buxton and P. Williams (Oxford, 1979), 31–8.

18. *EHR*, lxxiii (1958), 677; cited by D. Hay, 'The Church of England in the later Middle Ages', *History*, liii (1968), 39.

19. R.E. Rhodes, Jr., *Ecclesiastical Administration in Medieval England: The Anglo-Saxons to the Reformation* (Notre Dame University, 1977), 172.

20. Du Boulay, 'The Fifteenth Century', 207.

21. A. Hamilton Thompson's strictures on the English bishops of the fifteenth century ('not a strong body of men': *The English Clergy*, 45) continue to carry considerable weight, not least because of their author's normal disinclination to moralise on the shortcomings of the late medieval church. Cf. Du Boulay, 'The Fifteenth Century', 213; A. Goodman, *A History of England from Edward II to James I* (1977), 340–6; C.S.L. Davies, *Peace, Print and Protestantism, 1450–1558* (1977), 138–9; R.J. Knecht, 'The Episcopate and the Wars of the Roses', *University of Birmingham Historical Journal*, vi (1958), 108–31; M.D. Knowles, *The Medieval Archbishops of York* (Oliver Sheldon Memorial Lecture, York, 1961), 16.

22. R.G. Davies, 'The Episcopate', in *Profession, Vocation and Culture*, ed. Clough, 51.

23. Cf. P. Chaunu, *Église, Culture et Société: Essais sur Réforme et Contre-Réforme, 1517–1620* (Paris, 1981), 70.

24. A similar conclusion emerges from perhaps the single most penetrating local study of the operations of clerical bureaucracy in late medieval Christendom: F. Rapp, *Réforme et Réformation a Strasbourg: Église et Société dans le diocèse de Strasbourg, 1450–1525* (Association des Publications près les Universités de Strasbourg: Collection de L'Institut des Hautes Etudes Alsaciennes, xxiii, Paris, 1974), 187–212.

25. C. Richmond, *John Hopton: A Fifteenth-Century Suffolk Gentleman* (Cambridge, 1981).

26. A.H. Thompson, *The English Clergy*, 128.

27. J.I. Kermode, 'The Merchants of three northern English towns', in *Profession, Vocation and Culture*, ed. Clough, 15, 23.

28. F. Rapp, 'Réflexions sur la Religion Populaire au Moyen Age', in *La Religion Populaire dans L'Occident Chrétien*, ed. B. Plongeron (Paris, 1976), 51.

29. F. Oakley, *The Western Church in the Later Middle Ages* (Cornell University Press. 1979), 15–21.

30. See the comments of D. Hay, *The Church in Italy in the Fifteenth Century* (Cambridge, 1977), 72–3; and A. Vauchez, *Religion et Société dans L'Occident Médiéval*, 311–16.

31. R.J. Schoek, 'The Fifth Lateran Council: its partial successes and its larger failures', in *Reform and Authority in the Medieval and Reformation Church*, ed. G.F. Lytle (Washington, D.C., 1981), 124–6.

1

Ecclesiastics and Political Theory in Late Medieval England: The End of a Monopoly

Jean-Philippe Genet
University of Paris I

The progressive laicisation of the ruling and intellectual strata of medieval society from the thirteenth century onwards is a well-established fact which requires no more demonstration today. The rise of the feudal monarchy, implying a dramatic increase in the number of professional administrators and law councillors;[1] the changes in the educational system with its decisive shift from the shadow of the cathedrals and of the monastic cloisters to the universities, not to speak – for England – of the Inns of Court for the teaching of the Common Law;[2] the gradual evolution of the place and functions filled by writing and by written documents in feudal society;[3] the blossoming of a written literature in vernacular, covering (after two centuries only) nearly all the departments of knowledge and literary activity:[4] these are all phenomena which have been abundantly described and studied. It is obvious that they all, each in its own way, affected the position of the church, and more precisely the monopoly it enjoyed in the production and control of ideology. The clerical *ordo* in some ways anticipated this evolution and adapted itself to the new state of things; but in certain areas evolution was slow and laicisation was only a difficult and disputed process. Understandably enough, this was so in the case of the part the lay element was reluctantly allowed to play in the writing of theological and devotional literature, as well as in religious life at large. But here, everything could be controlled by the church, and lay in the sphere of its jurisdiction.

However it is with another area of intellectual activity that we shall deal today, that which I have, in a bold generalization, described as political theory. It must be clear from the start that such a thing as political theory did not and could not exist in the fourteenth century. This concept has always been a source of misunderstanding: if we compare the lists of authorities quoted in their respective works by Brian Tierney,[5] Walter Ullmann,[6] Wilhelm Kleineke,[7] John Scattergood[8] or Janet Coleman,[9] we discover that these lists do not tally, to say the least. In fact, political theory is a purely modern category which does not fit with the categories of medieval culture: it could probably be argued that the emergence of the state was a prerequisite for the development of political theory as such. That is why, before trying to assess the part played by the church in the literature of politics, we must outline the limits of the territory we shall have to explore. In fact a study of such a subject can only be made when due attention is paid to the literary genre in which texts are moulded, to the language in which they are written, to the editions and diffusion of the manuscripts which contain them, as much as to the 'political ideas' themselves. It is an enormous task, and my purpose here is only a brief survey of the available evidence, with special regard to the English situation in the later middle ages.

Both history and politics lay largely outside the university cursus, and therefore outside the medieval system of sciences. Hugh of Saint Victor found room for the politica in his philosophia practica (described as publica and civilis, intended pro civium rectoribus), after the ethica and the oeconomica: but theologia as the first branch of the philosophia theorica stood at top of this tower of knowledge.[10] The introduction of Aristotle's works to the universities did not alter this pattern significantly: the notebook of a Catalan student at Paris University in 1245, though confined to the courses taught in the Faculty of Arts, opposes the philosophia practica to the philosophia naturalis (metaphysics, mathematics, physics) and to the philosophia rationalis (grammar, logic, rhetoric); the textbooks mentioned are the Liber Ethicorum, Plato's Timaeus and the Consolatio Philosophiae by Boethius;[11] later on, the curriculum of the arts course at Oxford in 1431 gives Aristotle's Ethics, Economics and Politics as the textbooks for moral philosophy.[12] Politics indeed occupied only a small place in the hierarchy of sciences in medieval universities, and then decidedly on the practical and moral side rather than soaring into the theoretical heights leading to theology and speculative thought.

This brings us to two further questions. If such was the situation of politics, what sort of literature could be developed in the field now so defined? Secondly, what is the status of the bulky literature devoted to the problem of the supremacy of either the imperial or the pontifical power, which is now usually considered as political but does not fit within the medieval definition?

As regards the first question, it is precisely in England that the answer must be sought. The remarkable achievements of Henry II rapidly confronted the church with the rise of the monarchical state, and several churchmen tried to cope with this new situation in both a practical and a moral way; it is accordingly understandable that Wilhelm Berges's catalogue of medieval Fürstenspiegel should start with John of Salisbury, though this is strictly a mistake, since the Policraticus is not at all a Miroir.[13] John, together with Peter of Blois, Gerald of

Wales and Walter Map tried to understand the extension of the royal power, to warn against tyranny and to analyze a new socio-political phenomenon, the royal court.[14] The full title of John's tract is significant: *Policratici sive de nugis curialium et vestigiis philosophorum Libri VIII.* This title may be in turn the source of Map's title for his own *De Nugis Curialium;* and it clearly reveals that John drew his inspiration from antiquity. His debt to Cicero is obvious throughout; and the *Institutio Trajani* of the Pseudo-Plutarch, be it a creation of John of Salisbury or a late classical work,[15] is built upon a pedagogic relation between the philosopher and his imperial pupil which is parallel to that between Aristotle and Alexander, made popular by the *Secreta Secretorum.* John's work, indeed, belongs to the spheres of rhetoric and moral philosophy rather than to that of practical theology.

There is another salient feature in the writings of the churchmen of the Plantagenet court: it is their taste for historical anecdotes and for history. Peter of Blois, in one of his epistles, tells us that his teacher at St Laumer of Blois ordered him to find the subject of his Latin poetries in histories rather than in *fabulae.*[16] If we turn our attention to Gerald of Wales, only the first *Distinction* of his *De Principis Instructione Liber* appears to deserve to be mentioned in Berges's list, each chapter being in fact only a catena of quotations chiefly from classical authors.[17] But the second and third *Distinctio* are merely a history of Henry II's reign, set out however for moral purposes in two contrasted parts, *Distinctio II* dealing with the successes of the king, *Distintio III* with his misfortunes. Ranulph Higden had therefore some valid reasons to quote the work under the following title: *Vita Regis Henrici Secundi sub triplici distinctione.*[18] But there can be no doubt about Gerald's own view of his book, though the first *Distinctio* was probably edited as an isolated work, before the author had had the leisure to complete the other two *Distinctiones*: his concluding remarks at the end of *Distinctio I* clearly announce the contents of the two following *Distinctiones.*[19] The same historical bias is obvious in John of Salisbury, who, when dealing with tyranny, cannot refrain from piling up references to a host of tyrants and the miserable ends they met; a brief comparison with Aquinas's treatment of the same subject in his *De Regno ad Regem Cypri* shows us that the Dominican, in addition to sixteen biblical quotations, uses only four historical *exempla,* which may be traced to Valerius Maximus (for Denys), Eusebius of Caesarea (for Tarquin and Domitian) and Flavius Josephus (for Archaelaus), but were most probably borrowed from Petrus Comestor, Vincent of Beauvais and Augustine.[20] The rhetorical use of history is by contrast one of the chief components of John of Salisbury's style.

On the whole, it seems reasonable to agree with Egbert Türk's verdict: starting from their own experience and from the works of Christian and pagan moralists, the Plantagenet churchmen helped to shape the traditional attitude towards the court and the courtiers, but they failed to provide a literature in keeping with the political reality of their time, because their philosophy was still entirely dominated by patristic and Augustinian ethics.[21] As a literary genre, this kind of moral denunciation was a dead end, thought it was by no means without posterity, as we shall see later. In fact, the task of providing a new political literature adapted to the rise of the monarchical state, still focused on the prince and on his moral virtues, but emphasizing his responsibilities for good govern-ance and the common good, was performed by the *Miroirs au Prince* proper. I have tried elsewhere to demonstrate that this new literary genre originated in Paris, under the influence of Paris University, to meet the needs of the Capetian court, and that it was chiefly the work of the friars;[22] the first French items in Berges's list are here misleading, since they bear the mark of the influence of the Plantagenet literature:– like the *De Regimine Principum* of Helinand of Froid-mont, which, from the quotations made from it by Vincent of Beauvais, seems to have been stuffed with excerpts from the *Policraticus*;[23] the *Karolinus* of Giles of Paris, which is predominantly historical; and the contemporary *De Principis Instructione* of Gerald of Wales.[24] However, the *Eruditio Regum* of the Franciscan Guibert of Tournai written for Louis IX, the *De Eruditione filiorum nobilium*[25] and the *De Moralis Principis Instructione* of the Dominican Vincent of Beauvais (the first tract being written for Queen Margaret, the second dedicated to both Louis IX and King Thibaud of Navarre), the *De Eruditione Principum* attributed to Guillaume Perrault but of Dominican origin, and finally the *De Regimine Principum* of Giles of Rome written for Philip IV all set the pattern of this type of literature. Here the genius of the mendicants for adapting their material to the needs and to the cultural equipment of the estate of society which they had selected as their target, their didactic abilities, were combined with an increasingly Aristotelian inspiration to give birth to a literature which may be termed political, even if it is still more practical than theoretical. It must be added, however, that this political literature, at least in the first stages of its development, is not English.[26]

And such is also the case with the other kind of literature which was referred to in the second question formulated a moment ago, and which therefore need not detain us long. The answer to this question is simple enough: we are dealing with theology, not with political literature. True, this theology concerns political matters, but the principles upon which the discussions are based, the technique of all such discussions, the authorities quoted, belong to the field of theology. It must be stressed that here too England stood apart from continental developments: the most obvious example of pure political theology associated with England is the work of the Norman Anonymous,[27] and the seriousness of the opinions expressed in his tracts is still a matter largely open to question. Moreover, they were written in Normandy!

To conclude this initial survey of political literature in the twelfth and thirteenth centuries, attention must be drawn to three points. First, little has been said about the literature of protest, i.e. what might be termed the active literature of politics. It existed in the thirteenth century, and the baron's war of the 1260s saw a considerable increase in its production and circulation. But its greater development belongs to the next period and it will be dealt with later.[28] Secondly, whereas another corpus of great political interest, the Roman Law, became more and more important in the intellectual history of the West and deeply penetrated political theology, often through canon law, England remained comparatively untouched thereby. True, common law could have performed the same role: but the speculative turn of mind and the intellectual creativity of the first English writers on Common Law, such as Bracton, soon vanished to leave the door open for an arid and purely technical literature, better suited to the immediate needs of legal practitioners.[29] Thirdly, that Aristotle's *Politics* was a rediscovery of the second half of the thirteenth century, through the translations of William of Moerbeke, the commentary by Aquinas and by Peter of Auvergne, and its vulgarization by the *Miroir au Prince* and particularly by Giles of Rome is indeed a scholarly view, but nothing more. Aristotle's political theory was in fact well known, because many (including Bacon and later Wycliffe) considered that it was contained in the pseudo-Aristotelian *Secreta Secretorum*, which was as popular in England as anywhere else.[30]

It is therefore obvious that if there was a monopoly of the church in the field of political theory, it was through political theology and through its vulgarisation by the *Miroir au Prince* literature. We have seen that the only effort to create a new corpus (the fact that this effort was also made by churchmen is not surprising given the cultural conditions of the twelfth century), that of John of Salisbury, had no immediate consequences: as Amnon Linder has shown, the work of John of Salisbury was later well known to the friars who used the *Policraticus* freely as a rich source of *exempla*, especially through the very influential collections of Johannes Wallensis.[31]

The development of political theology was indeed enormous in nearly all European countries. The struggle of the papacy versus the Empire had come to a standstill with the death of Frederick II but it was revived by Lewis IV; and new antagonisms between the papacy and the great lay powers, England and France, appeared with the problem of taxation. The courts of Philip IV of France[32] and of Lewis of Bavaria[33] were factories from which a seemingly endless string of libels and tracts poured out; and the papal curia, at least under Boniface VIII, matched them. It is most striking, especially if we make a comparison with France, that England should have stayed apart here too. There is no English John of Paris or Pierre Dubois. True, an Englishman played a prominent part in the pamphlet war which was raging through Europe: this was William of Ockham; but all the political works of Ockham were written abroad, and few of them came to be known in England. Only one of his political works, the *An princeps pro suo succursu scilicet guerrae, possit recipere bona ecclesiarum*,[34] was written in connection with an English problem and addressed to Edward III; it had no success, and today we have only an incomplete text subsisting in one manuscript. Among his other writings, only three (*Dialogus I*, with 25 manuscripts; *Dialogus III, Tractatus De Potestate et Juribus Romani imperii,* with 13 manuscripts; and the *Octo questiones de potestate papae,* with 14 manuscripts)[35] had a wide circulation; but few of these manuscripts are of English provenance. On the whole, the Italian Marsilius probably had a much greater influence on English political thought than the English Ockham.[36] The problem of the relations between the two powers had nevertheless some importance in fourteenth-century England, since on the Whitsunday of 1373, Brother John Mardisley, a Franciscan, preached on *Mitte gladium tuum in vaginam* in the presence of the king, to vindicate the claim for papal supremacy put forward by the Benedictine Uthred of Boldon in support of a papal demand for a subsidy in the realm.[37]

But ecclesiology was also part of political theology, as Brian Tierney and others have demonstrated.[38] The Schism and the conciliar crisis reinforced this trend. The universities took the lead: Paris University, as well as many newly founded German universities, took a prominent part in the debates, often in close relation with the princes and their councillors. Once more, England played only a minor part. Admittedly Oxford University wrote some important letters,[39] and several Englishmen composd tracts on the subject: John Colton, archbishop of Armagh (d. 1404),[40] the Carmelite Walter Diss,[41] the Franciscan Nicholas of Fakenham,[42] Thomas Palmer,[43] Richard Yonge,[44] Nicholas Radcliffe[45] and even John Wycliffe[46] all wrote more or less bulky works in support of one or other of the many remedies suggested to heal the wounds of the ecclesiastical institutions. But none of these works won an international reputation; none of them appear to have had a large circulation, judging from the small number of surviving manuscripts. Some (like Colton's tract) have even entirely disappeared. There was no D'Ailly, no Gerson, no Langenstein, no Zabarella in England!

Surprisingly enough, political theology in England concentrated on issues which, in the first stages of the controversies, were far from being predominantly political: I am thinking here of the debate on mendicant poverty which broadened into a major political controversy with the great works of Richard Fitz Ralph and John Wycliffe. The debate about evangelical poverty[47] was, from the very beginning of the existence of the mendicant orders, of fundamental concern to both the friars themselves and to their secular opponents. To the friars, Francis's poverty echoed Christ's poverty whereas their adversaries saw it as a false pretence as well as a threat to their own position. The first stages of the battle remained chiefly confined to purely theological discussions; but it may already be noted that several Englishmen played a prominent part in these. John Pecham wrote tracts in reply to William of Saint-Amour and Nicholas of Lisieux;[48] while Thomas of York composed one of the chief texts in the controversy, *Manus quae contra omnipotentem tenditur.*[49] It is however significant that a discrepancy should have soon appeared between the respective positions of the Dominicans and the Franciscans, well exemplified in England by the quarrel between Pecham himself and the Dominican Robert Kilwardby.[50] The bull *Exiit qui seminat* issued by Pope Nicholas III in August 1279 was intended to put an end to the argument by giving a moderate interpretation of the doctrine of poverty, borrowed from St. Bonaventura, admitting for the Friars an *usus facti* of all necessary goods, but reserving proprietary rights of these goods to the pope himself. At the same time, it banned all further discussion of the subject: from a purely ecclesiological point of view, the question seemed settled.

But the controversy acquired a new impetus and a much deeper significance when the opposition between conventuals and spirituals reached a climax at the council of Vienne: Richard of Conington wrote his *De Paupertate Evangelica*, and Ralph of Lockysley is credited by John Bale with a tract bearing the same title.[51] The conciliatory bull *Exivi de Paradiso* of Clement V and the activity of Michael of Cesena were not enough to bring peace to the order, and this prompted Pope John XXII to enter the battlefield.[52] Anxious to eradicate the seeds of heresy he recognized in the doctrines of the Sprirituals, drawing his inspiration from Aquinas and even from Aristotle's *Politics*,[53] he first organized a major confrontation of experts in March 1322, and then re-opened the debate ended by *Exiit qui seminat* with his own Bull *Quid nonnunquam*, destroying finally the 1279 compromise by refusing to admit the validity of the concept of use without property and suppressing the formal pontifical ownership in his bull *Ad Conditorem Canonum* of December 1322. It has been rightly pointed out that John's intervention must be understood in the difficult context of southern France. But, here too, it must be observed that the English brethren seem to have played an important part in the controversy. Robert of Leicester wrote between June 1322 and November 1323 a tract to defend the Franciscan position[54] and was supported by Walter of Chatton and Richard of Conington;[55] whereas one of the side-effects of the pontifical move against Michael of Cesena was to induce William of Ockham to throw in his lot with his discontented superior. Moreover the official answer of the Franciscans to the pope, which was prepared by the chapter which met at Perugia by the end of May 1323, was discussed in England and formally approved by the English theologians of the order.

Nevertheless, if the English church did play a prominent part in the mendicant controversy, it was mostly in its last stages, when Richard Fitz Ralph launched his violent and far-reaching attack against his Franciscan rivals in his diocese of Armagh. Katherine Walsh has recently demonstrated the extent to which the specific Irish conditions were responsible for the archbishop's action,[56] though some features of his later doctrines may already be detected in his *Summa de Quaestionibus Armenorum*.[57] Fitz Ralph shifted the emphasis in the debate from the problem of poverty to the problem of dominion: evangelical poverty is the subject of Book VII of the dialogue *De Pauperie Salvatoris*,[58] while the first five books, the best and the most coherent, discuss the question of *dominium*, the controversial decisions of John XXII being examined in Book VII which seems to have been added to the dialogue later; later still, a Book VIII was added, presumably at Avignon. That the quarrel over poverty was likely to raise the problem of the legitimacy of the endowment of the church [59] had been foreseen as early as 1322; however it was not from the earlier stages of the controversy that Fitz Ralph drew his material, but from the works of the leading Augustinian theologians working for the *curia*, Giles of Rome, Augustinus Triumphus and Giacomo da Viterbo.[60] From them he learnt that there was no power but that ordained from God: as the representative of Christ on earth, the pope held the *dominium* over the Christian community; all rights of property and possessions, from kingship to the smallest land-tenure, stemmed from God through the medium of the papacy. Indeed, this was a conclusive argument against lay rulers. But Fitz Ralph tried to turn it against the friars, since he felt that their doctrine of evangelical property was an attack against the institutional church. He made a clear-cut distinction between *dominium* such as it was at the original creation, before the fall of Adam, and what one could call 'civil dominion', under positive law. As Katherine Walsh puts it: 'Grace alone entitled a person to the exercise of lordship over temporal things and conferred upon all the just an equal right to their use'.[61] This statement conveys very accurately both the radicalism of Fitz Ralph's Augustinianism and its idealistic qualities; Fitz Ralph was not preaching an egalitarian creed.[62] In any case, grace alone authorised poverty, which *ipso facto* disqualified the friars. Indeed, who could claim to be sure of being vested with God's grace? Here was a potentially revolutionary element in Fitz Ralph's thought, even though he never considered that his doctrine could have practical consequences other than the abolition of the privileges of the mendicant orders.

In fact, the dangers inherent in Fitz Ralph's views were quickly perceived by his opponents. While Fitz Ralph had to defend them at Avignon, controversy raged; outstanding among the archbishop's opponents were Geoffrey Hardeby, another Austin Friar,[63] and Roger Conway, a Franciscan,[64] while his side was taken by the Dean of Saint Paul's, Richard Kilwington.[65] The death within a year of Fitz Ralph, Conway and Kilwington seems to have restored peace after 1360. But already a young Oxford master, John Wycliffe, was displaying his familiarity with Fitz Ralph's works, though his first precise reference to the dominium theory seems to date from 1373.[66] It would be foolish to pretend that Wycliffe's ecclesiology is merely a consequence of the evolution of the mendicant controversy in England; but it is true, nevertheless, that he derived his theory of dominion from Fitz Ralph, even if he, like Marx in the case of Hegel's dialectic, turned it upside down, against the Church in general and in favour of the lay power. Wycliffe's antisacerdotalism had other roots, and primarily his conception of the Bible. Gordon Leff has clearly shown how Wycliffe's ecclesiology and his political ideas (which were essentially a product of his ecclesiology) were dependent upon his metaphysics and his extreme doctrine of grace, though he may have minimized the importance of the part played by the theory of dominion in the whole system. In my view, Wycliffe's theory of dominion is important – and different from that of Fitz Ralph – because of the extreme Augustinianism of his theory of grace: whereas Fitz Ralph's caution in the handling of grace resulted in restricting the consequences of this doctrine to the kingdom of ideas, Wycliffe's extremism resulted in wiping out the visible church's power and substituting for it the power of the state, which may hardly be termed a conservative view.[67] With Wycliffe and his ablest opponents, English political theology had reached a point far ahead of the issues raised by conciliarists, since it implied the destruction of the church as an institution – and therefore the disappearance of its ideological power of control and constraint. But Wycliffe's views were condemned, his writings suppressed,[68] his followers, whether university or popular, condemned and tracked down. Whatever its merits, a century of rich political debate ended in a silence which was to be broken only in the sixteenth century.

It has long been said that the fear of a new outbreak of university reformist ideas was the main reason for the quiescence of intellectual life in fifteenth-century England. This statement needs to be qualified:[69] the condemnation of Wycliffe did not put an end to the controversies. There appeared a large number of orthodox answers to the heretic's challenge, his writings, and those of his supporters.[70] John Hynkeley,[71], Uthred of Boldon, [72] Roger Dymoke,[73] William Woodford,[74] Nicholas Radcliffe and Peter Stokes,[75] to mention only some of his most conspicuous adversaries, all wrote on the political issues discussed by Wycliffe. What put an end to the controversy may well have been the success of the work which was considered as offering the best answer, and hence became the official anti-Wycliffite statement: Thomas Netter's *Doctrinale Fidei Catholicae*;[76] but it was more probably, as Gordon Leff suggests, the effect of Archbishop Arundel's victory over the Oxford masters.[77] Thereafter, apart from Netter's tract, the only re-opening of the controversy was due to Reginald Pecock with his *Repressor of over much blaming the Clergy*, which was itself answered by John Bury's *Gladium Solomonis*.[78] The anti-mendicant controversy, too, dragged on, with some new if sporadic outbreaks:– Henry Crump, under Richard II;[79] Philip Norris in mid-fifteenth century Ireland;[80] and the London crisis of 1464–1468.[81] But, on the whole, everything seemed dead and finished by the end of the fifteenth century. Even if it had experienced a considerable amount of activity, English political theology had disappeared, leaving behind a desert: the only texts which still enjoyed a wide circulation were Richard Fitz Ralph's *Defensio Curatorum* and the imported *Dialogus inter militem et clericum*, translated for Thomas, Lord Berkeley, by John of Trevisa.[82]

The withdrawal of the church doctors from the field of political theology might have had a variety of consequences. One of them could have been to channel the energies of the clerical writers into other areas within the field of political literature. The obvious opportunity was the vulgarization of political theology by writing *Miroirs au Prince*. Nearly every late medieval English king received a political tract, from Edward III to Edward IV. Thus William de Pagula sent, before 1331, his *Epistle* to Edward III (a second edition of which was edited before 1333 by Archbishop Meopham);[83] and an Irish official may have been the author of a *Miroir* dedicated to Richard II – who also received an 'epistle' of advice from Philippe de Mézières.[84] Philip Repton wrote his Letter of Advice to Henry IV;[85] Thomas Hoccleve composed his *Regement of Princes* for Prince Henry, the future Henry V;[86] an anonymous author wrote a *De Regimine Principum ad Regem Henricum Sextum*,[87] and William of Worcester compiled his *Boke of Noblesse* for Edward IV;[88] while George Ashby produced his *Active Policy of a Prince*[89] for Prince Edward, son of Henry VI. But this is indeed a haphazard collection, and with the exception of the only successful work of the group, Hoccleve's *Regement*, none of these tracts is really a classical *Miroir*; not one was written by a friar, either, as far as we know. William de Pagula's epistle, though concerned with a practical problem, purveyance, is purely moral in tone and predominantly based on quotations from the Bible and the Fathers, very much like the more general *De Regimine Principum* for King Henry VI, with the addition in this last case of many Cistercian quotations. The tract dedicated to Richard II shares with Hoccleve's *Regement* a strong *Secreta Secretorum* flavour, whereas Ashby's tract is in fact combined with a collection of proverbs and *dicta* of ancient philosophers.[90] But the intention of conforming – at least superficially – to the pedagogic and moral overtones of the classical *Miroir* is obvious in all these texts, as it is also in the two tracts later dedicated to Henry VIII respectively by Edmund Dudley[91] and Stephen Barron[92] – the latter at least a Franciscan!

This heterogeneity may have been the result of a socio-linguistic factor. The kings, the court and the aristocracy were at first French-speaking; and they could, therefore, make use of the many French *Miroirs*. When in the fifteenth century French lost its position, it was easy to translate French *Miroirs* and political tracts: Giles of Rome himself was translated into English, as was a tract written for the duke of Normandy in 1347, the future King Jean II,[93] and the *Livre du Corps de Policie* by Christine de Pisan, which was translated later, possibly by Anthony Woodville, Earl Rivers.[94] Moreover several works by Alain Chartier were also translated.[95] We may also consider as an important text the *Secreta Secretorum* itself, which enjoyed great popularity in fifteenth-century England: there were several English translations.[96] One was a translation of the short version by Johannes Hispalensis, and is chiefly medical; but the longer Latin version, composed at the beginning of the thirteenth century by Philip of Tripoli from an Arabic text, was known in England very early since Roger Bacon used it. It was translated into French, one of these translations being made in the Pale by Geoffrey of Waterford. Seven prose translations were made, two directly from Philip of Tripoli's Latin text (one of these was commissioned by Sir Miles Stapleton from a Johannes de Caritate), and five from a shorter French version (among these five, one was by John Shirley and the last in date was the work of Robert Copland and printed in 1528). The Waterford version was translated by James Yonge. The text was also adapted in verse, the most faithful adaptations being those by John Lydgate and Benedict Burgh, and that by Sir William Forrest in the sixteenth century. But Hoccleve and Gower (in Book VII of his *Confessio Amantis*) also borrowed much from the *Secreta*.

Now if we try to explain this lack of vitality in the vulgarization of political theology, we have two types of problem to solve. First, this literature did not develop in England because there was not enough patronage for it. If we take the French case, such popularization was actively encouraged by the crown, as well as the production of entirely new works on matters of special interest to the king. Under Charles V and Charles VI, Aristotle was translated and commentaries in French were written,[97] St Augustine's *De Civitate Dei*[98] and John of Salisbury's *Policraticus*[99] were translated, while specially commissioned authors wrote about the relations between lay and ecclesiastical powers (the *Songe du Vergier*, perhaps written by Everard de Tremaugon)[100] or the meaning of the French coronation (Jean Golein's *Traité du Sacre*);[101] court poets, like Christine de Pisan, wrote vernacular verse tracts for the aristocratic public of the court.[102] Among these authors, there was a large majority of clerics, because their culture and aptitudes made them the most likely candidates to receive commissions to write such works, even though the culture of some lawyers[103] could have made the latter fit for the task. The royal example was followed by French princes,[104] most notoriously by the Valois Dukes of Burgundy.[105] But in England, nothing of the kind happened. Because of his realm's insularity the English monarch did not need to prove to his subjects that he was the king of the land. The French king had to do so: he played on the *redditus regni ad stirpem Karoli*,[106] he mustered Clovis[107] and the legend of the lilies,[108] he exploited the pleasant memories of Saint Louis. Against his English rival, he proved his legitimacy not so much through the vagaries of the Salic law but through the much more obvious and politically profitable fact that he *was* French, whereas his rival was a foreigner. The French court became a sponsor of a political mythology which could be useful to its cause.

This example was not followed by the English king. Perhaps there was no need for it. Perhaps his case was better forgotten than pleaded, as with Henry IV. In my view, it seems clear that the English kept, until late, a purely feudal view of international relations[109] because this suited them much better in the Hundred Years' War. Nationalism existed in England, but it was very much a strong and spontaneous popular feeling, which there was no need for the king to boost while it could not help him in his negotiations with the king of France. The English king, therefore, did not have to rely on propaganda and literary production: he preferred to pack the commons or exploit the opportunities of patronage to win his subjects' hearts. Only two kings could have developed courts on the French model: Richard II[110] and Henry VI;[111] both failed. Only when an English king became also king of France, did the English adhere to the French methods: John, Duke of Bedford, commissioned a French poet to justify

Henry VI's claim to both thrones,[112] and the Earl of Warwick had this poem translated by Lydgate in 1427.[113] At the same period precedents and chronicles were scoured, and memoirs on the king's rights were composed.[114]

Besides lack of patronage, there may also be another explanation: the lack of a receptive public. But this argument does not stand, and the very list of *Miroirs* and translations of *Miroirs* we have just established is here most revealing. It shows two things: first, it is clear that in time lay authors, all writing in English, grew more numerous; Hoccleve, Yonge, Ashby are outstanding examples. Then, even among tracts dedicated to the king, the English language became dominant from the fifteenth century onwards and, apart from translations, English verse rather than English prose. This suggests connections with another literary continent which has hitherto lain outside the scope of our exploration, an area which is not political theory, but which undoubtedly deals with politics; it contains what Janet Coleman calls 'literature of protest', and John Scattergood 'political poetry'. Very few of the authors of those pieces are known: some, like Langland and Lydgate, were ecclesiastics; others were laymen. In any case, it matters very little, because even if these writers were clerics, they had not the authority of the church behind them. Their status was not their distinctive feature which would have given more weight to what they said. Two other points must be stressed: first, this literature compares well – at least in quantity – with what we know of French poetry at the same time; secondly, what is striking in this political poetry is the importance of history and of historical anecdotes. Two good examples are Lydgate's *Troy Book* and his *Fall of Princes*, translated not from Boccaccio direct, but from Laurent de Premierfait's French version. In fact much of Scattergood's political poetry is made up of accounts of battles and of political events; all this points to a connection between political poetry and history rather than political theory. This may also be seen as a long-awaited posthumous revenge of John of Salisbury. As John himself would have probably admitted, the lessons of politics were better taught by experience; and the Roman historians and Boccaccio were both more useful and more entertaining than Giles of Rome.

This means that if there was an audience for English verse and for political subjects, this audience had but a limited taste for political theory as such, probably because neither political theology nor its popularized versions were up to their expectations. We know that in late medieval England there was a large (by the standards of the time) and cultivated public who had access to reading; the remarkable collection of essays dedicated to the late Professor Myers[115] provides us with many proofs of this. Historical production in the fifteenth century, though its technical quality may be questioned, was important and well-suited to the needs of a much larger public than the monastic chronicles: the many versions and continuations of the *Brut* and the London chronicles stand as outstanding testimonies of this evolution. But there are other facts which suggest a very high amount of political consciousness in fifteenth-century

England besides the working of the political system itself. Was it not an obligation for Parliament, at each opening session, to listen to a sermon by the royal chancellor, a sermon which was, more often than not, pure political theory?[116] And there were many other gatherings of important people (convocations, special meetings organized to deal with particular issues) which were the occasion for delivering political sermons or staging public *disputationes*. In which other European country at the time were the laws of the land, as arranged in the collections of Statutes (*Antiqua* and *Nova*) circulating in hundreds of manuscripts?[117] In fact, if political theology did not adapt itself to the new public, it is because something else was needed; and to create this something else was far from easy.

One author, at least, proved that it was possible and pointed in the new direction. He gave us what can be considered as political theory in fifteenth-century England; he was Sir John Fortescue.[118] First of all, it must be clear that he owed much to, and borrowed much from, political theology. He was able to understand the traditional Thomist-Aristotelian balance between the law of nature and positive law, and to use it as an element of his own system: this, in itself, was no mean achievement for a lawyer who had not followed the university cursus. It is moreover a good test of the intellectual abilities of the legal profession, the importance of which is repeatedly stressed but the culture of which remains difficult to assess, since we know so little about the Inns of Court in the fifteenth century; more generally it also proves that much of the contents of political theology was within reach of laymen. But Fortescue did much more than that: he was able to confront these elements of political theory both with his own legal knowledge and with the real situation of his time, and often by means of historical comparisons.[119] Here, too, his approach was not entirely new: the growing preoccupation of political theory with history has recently been emphasized by Brian Tierney. Nevertheless, the idea conveyed by Fortescue's writings was that a *politia* did not have to conform to some truth expressed once and for all, but that the function of a government was to adjust as well as possible to fluctuating conditions by what he called good governance and by law, in fact by what would be later called a constitutional system. The measure of Fortescue's achievement is seen by the success his works were to enjoy until the seventeenth century.[120] But we should not see him as ahead of his time in what he said, but only in the manner in which he said it:– to quote Professor Chrimes's words, 'in his attempt to array bare constitutional facts in the imposing raiment of political theory'.[121]

At the end of this survey, is it possible to qualify our rather enigmatic title? First of all, the monopoly was not taken away from the church, it was abandoned by it. It was abandoned, because its developments proved to be dangerous, and because no external stimulus, be it the international position of the English church in relation to the conciliar crisis, or the desire of English monarchy to use for its own advantages the intellectual expertise of the educated churchmen, helped to keep political theology and its popularised version alive. It was also abandoned because, well before the invention of the printing press, a new kind of relationship between readers and writers was developing: the number of those able to and wanting to read had increased, English had at last become the dominant language in the kingdom, and the price of manuscripts was going down whereas their number was going up.[122] In this new framework the traditional brand of political theology had no opportunities. What was needed was something new.

It is perhaps here that the English case is most interesting. Nowhere was this abandonment so complete; indeed, both in France and the Italian city-states, not only did political theology keep a much greater vitality but the state itself took into employment many of its best exponents. This did not happen in England: the crisis of the monarchy in the fifteenth century left the field empty, until Henry VIII chose the Reformation path. Between Archbishop Arundel's visitation of Oxford and Henry's divorce there was a unique situation, a blank page on which it was possible to write something new. That those who did so should have been close to the state itself is understandable: but they were not commissioned to do it.[123] The foundations of political theory, as independent speculation on the state and its relations to the citizens or to corporations such as, for instance, the church, were prepared in fifteenth-century England; but it was not an easy elaboration, only a gradual and dimly observable process. Nevertheless, the first steps in the right direction were taken in relating principles borrowed from law and political theology to history and to real life issues: a new ideology was slowly emerging.

Notes

1. For a general survey of these problems, see J.R. Strayer, *On the medieval origins of the modern State* (Princeton, 1970), and B. Guenée, *L'Occident aux XIVe et XVe siècles: Les Etats* (2nd edition, Paris, 1982). Precise data on the laicization of the English administration will be found in R.L. Storey, 'Gentleman-bureaucrats', in *Profession, Vocation and Culture in Later Medieval England*, ed. C.H. Clough (Liverpool, 1982), 90–129.

2. The most recent discussion of the early history of the Inns of Court is E.W. Ives, 'The Common Lawyers', in C.H. Clough, op. cit., 181–217.

3. M.T. Clanchy, *From Memory to Written Record: England 1066–1307* (1979).

4. This is well emphasized by J. Coleman, *English Literature in History, 1350–1400: Medieval Readers and Writers* (1981).

5. B. Tierney, *Religion, Law, and the Growth of Constitutional Thought* (Cambridge, 1982).

6. W. Ullmann, *Law and Politics in the Middle Ages: An Introduction to the Sources of Medieval Political Ideas* (1975).

7. W. Kleineke, *Englische Fürstenspiegel vom Policraticus Johannes von Salisbury bis zum Basilikon Doron König Jakobs I* (Halle, 1937).

8. V.J. Scattergood, *Politics and Poetry in the Fifteenth Century* (1971); see especially 264–297.

9. J. Coleman, op. cit., 58–156.

10. *Hugonis de Sancto Victore Didascalion de Studio Legendi*, ed. Ch. H. Buttimer (Washington, 1939), 23–47.

11. M. Grabmann, 'Eine Quaestionensammlung der Pariser Artistenfakultät aus der ersten Hälfte des 13 Jahrhunderts', *Revue de Néoscolastique*, xxxvi (1934), 211–229.

12. G. Leff, *Paris and Oxford Universities in the thirteenth and fourteenth centuries* (1968), 146.

13. W. Berges, *Die Fürstenspiegel des hohen und späten Mittelalters* (Stuttgart, 1938).

14. See E. Türk, *Nugae Curialium: Le régne d'Henri II Plantagenet (1154–1189) et l'éthique politique* (Geneva, 1977); to the works of these authors may be added the *Tractatus contra Curiales et Officiales Clericos* of Nigel Wireker, ed. A. Boutemy (Paris, 1959).

15. H. Liebeschütz, 'John of Salisbury and Pseudo-Plutarch', *Journal of the Warburg and Courtauld Institutes*, vi (1943), 33–49, and S. Desideri, *La Institutio Traiani* (Genoa, 1958) for conflicting views of this issue.

16. E. Türk, op. cit., 126, quoting *Epistola* 101: this would be the origin of Peter's knowledge of Trogus Pompaeus, Suetonius and Quintus Curcius.

17. *Giraldus Cambrensis De Principis Instructione Liber*, ed. G.F. Warner (Rolls Series, 1857).

18. Ibid., IX–X.

19. Ibid., 149: but the first *Distinctio* may have been written in Paris, before 1180.

20. John of Salisbury, *Policraticus sive de Nugis Curialium*, ed. C.C.J. Webb (Oxford, 1909, 2 vols), ii, 358–93 (Bk. VIII, chapters 19, 20, and 21). The easiest reference to Aquinas in this context is *St. Thomas Aquinas, on Kingship to the King of Cyprus*, ed. G.B. Phelan (Toronto, 1949), 23–29.

21. See E. Türk, op. cit.

22. See the introduction to *Four English Political Tracts of the Later Middle Ages*, ed. J.P. Genet (CS, 4th Series, xviii, London, 1977).

23. A. Linder, 'The Knowledge of John of Salisbury in the Later Middle Ages', *Studi Medievali*, xviii (1977), 315–66, quoting in support H. Hublocher, *Helinand von Froidmont und sein Verhältnis zu Johannes von Salisbury: ein Beitrag zur Geschichte des Plagiates in mittelalterlichen Literatur* (Ratisbon, 1913).

24. Cf. the edition by L.M. Colker, 'The 'Karolinus' of Egidius Parisiensis', *Traditio*, xxix (1973),

199–325; and for a discussion of some of its historical content A.W. Lewis, 'Dynastic Structures and Capetian Throne Right: the Views of Giles of Paris', ibid. xxxiii (1977), 225–52.

25. The importance of quotations from classical authors (Cicero, Seneca, Quintilian, Ovid) is reminiscent of Gerald of Wales's first *Distinctio*; but their number is matched by that of the quotations from patristic authors (chiefly Jerome, Augustine, Ambrose) and of later medieval writers (Hugh of St. Victor, St. Bernard, Gérard Ithier): see A. Steiner, *De Eruditione Filiorum Nobilium of Vincent de Beauvais* (Cambridge, Mass., 1938), xix–xxi.

26. Not much can be known about the *Abbreviatio de principatu regni* (or *De Tyrannide*)of Robert Grosseteste, a work mentioned in several sources about 1250–2 and the content of which may perhaps have found its way into some of the *Dicta*: see however W.A Pantin, 'Grosseteste's Relations with the Papacy and the Crown', in *Robert Grosseteste, Scholar and Bishop*, ed. D.A.P. Callus (Oxford, 1955), 212–13.

27. *Die Texte des Normanischen Anonymus*, ed. K. Pellens (Wiesbaden, 1966), on which see W. Ullmann, *Historische Zeitschrift*, ccvi (1968), 696–703; and K. Pellens and R. Nineham, *Der Kodex 415 des Corpus Christi College, Cambridge* (Wiesbaden, 1977). See W. Hartmann, 'Beziehungen des Normannischen Anonymus zu frühscholastischen Bildungszentren', *Deutsches Archiv*, xxx (1975), 108–142, who, confirming the traditional identification of the Anonymous with Archbishop William de Bona Anima, stresses the contrast between a conservative thought and an extremely modern scholastic technique; the ideas expressed in the manuscript must not be taken at face value, since they are virtuoso exercises in paradox rather than statements of a new theory, a fact nearly foreseen by E.H. Kantorowicz, *The King's Two Bodies* (Princeton, 1957).

28. See the songs and texts printed in *Political Songs of England*, ed. T. Wright (CS, old series, vi, 1839) and *Anglo-Norman Political Songs*, ed. I.S.T. Aspin (Anglo-Norman Text Society, xi, Oxford, 1953).

29. See J.P. Genet, 'Droit et Histoire en Angleterre: la 'préhistoire' de la Révolution Historique', *Annales de Bretagne et des Pays de l'Ouest*, lxxxvii (1980), 319–66.

30. H. Förster, 'Handschriften und Ausgaben des pseudo-aristotelischen Secretum Secretorum', *Centralblatt für Bibliothekswesen*, i (1889).

31. See A. Linder, op. cit.; on John of Wales, see B. Smalley, *English Friars and Antiquity in the early fourteenth century* (Oxford, 1960), 51–5.

32. R. Scholz, *Die Publizistik zur Zeit Philipps des Schönen und Bonifaz VIII* (Stuttgart, 1903); J. Rivière, *Le problème de l'Eglise et de l'Etat au temps de Philippe le Bel* (Paris, 1926); and G. Digeard, *Philippe le Bel et le Saint-Siège de 1295 à 1304* (Paris, 1936, 2 vols).

33. R. Scholz, *Unbekannte Kirchenpolitische Streitschriften aus der Zeit Ludwigs des Bayern, 1327–1354* (Rome, 1911–14, 2 vols); and S. Reizler, *Die literarischen Widersacher der Päpste zur Zeit Ludwigs des Baiern* (Leipzig, 1874), 230–271.

34. *Guillelmi de Ockham Opera Politica*, ed. J.G. Sikes (Manchester, 1940), i; see L. Baudry, *Guillaume d'Occam, sa vie, ses oeuvres, ses idées sociales et politiques* (Paris, 1950), i, 204–9 and 291.

35. This evaluation is based upon the lists printed in L. Baudry, op. cit., 288–94, with the addition of one manuscript for the *Octo Quaestiones*:– Koblenz Staatsarchiv Abt. 701, 230, described in *Marsile de Padoue, Oeuvres Mineures: Defensor Minor, De Translatione Imperii*, ed. C. Jeudy and J. Quillet (Paris, 1979), 83–5 (this manuscript was written for – and by – Heinrich Kalteisen, O.P., in 1437, during the Council of Basel).

36. This might be difficult to substantiate: among twenty-seven manuscripts of the *Defensor Pacis* listed in *Marsilius von Padua: Defensor Pacis*, ed. R. Scholz (Fontes Iuris Germanici Antiqui, Hanover, 1932) only four may have been in England in the middle ages, and only one has a known English owner: British Library Royal MS 10 A XV, owned by Thomas Gascoigne, who gave it to Lincoln College, Oxford. This manuscript also contains Ockham's *De Imperatorum et Pontificum Potestate*. The *Defensor* was translated into French by 1363, and into Italian in 1363, but into English only in 1534 by William Marshall, one of Cromwell's agents: on

Marsilius's influence on English political thought in the sixteenth century, see C.W. Previté-Orton, 'Marsilius of Padua', *PBA*, xxi (1935), 137–83, specially 163–5, and F. Le Van Baumer, *The Early Tudor Theory of Kingship* (New Haven, 1940), 53 with further bibliography.

37. On Mardisley, see *BRUO.*, ii, 1221 and M.E. Marcett, *Friar William Jordan and Piers Plowman* (New York, 1938). The atmosphere of the scene is vividly captured by the *Eulogium Historiarum*, ed. F.S. Haydon (RS, 1858), iii, 337–8: Mardisley is strikingly pre-Wycliffite ('. . . *narravit quomodo Bonifacius VIII statuit se dominum omnium regnorum et quomodo fuit repulsus in Francia et Anglia. Et quod Christus tradidit Petro vicariatum spiritualis regiminis non terrenae dominationis. Nam dixit quod in dominatione terrena papa non succedit Petro sed Constantino secundum Beatum Thomam. . .*'); Mardisley concluded against the papal claim, and with understandable nostalgia Archbishop Whittlesey remarked '*Bona consilia fuerunt in Anglia sine fratribus*'. The scene on the following day before the Black Prince, who presided over the meeting with Whittlesey, throws light on the possible causes of the reluctance of English ecclesiastics to tackle political problems when the English monarchy was so easily offended: the Black Prince asked Whittlesey to deliver his final verdict, since the meeting had been decided '*propter tuam fatuitatem*'; unable to decide between the royal and the papal claims, the unfortunate archbishop declined to do so, and the Black Prince answered '*Asine, responde; tu debes nos omnes informare*'. Is this an entirely fantastic story, as Perroy seems to think (op. cit. at note 39, p. 28)? See also below, p. 71, note 30.

38. B. Tierney, *Religion, Law, and the Growth of Constitutional Thought.*

39. See E. Perroy, *L'Angleterre et le Grand Schisme d'Occident* (Paris, 1933), 361 et seq; J.J.N. Palmer, 'England and the great western schism, 1388–1399', *EHR*, lxxxiii (1968), 516–22; and G. Ouy, 'Gerson et l'Angleterre: A propos d'un texte polémique retrouvé du chancelier de Paris contre l'Université d'Oxford, 1396', in *Humanism in France* (Manchester, 1970) 43–81.

40. *BRUC*, 150–1; his *De Causa justa ac remedio schismatis libri II* would have been, according to Leland, in the library of Westminster Abbey.

41. *BRUC*, 188; his *De Schismate* may have been a larger work than the *Carmen de Schismate Ecclesiae* in *Nicholai de Clemangiis Opera*, ed. J.M. Lydius (Leiden, 1613), iii, 31–4.

42. *BRUO*, ii, 664; his *Determinatio* is extant in five manuscripts and edited in F. Bleimetzrieder, 'Trakat des Minoritenprovinzials von England fr. Nikolaus de Fakenham', *AFH*, i (1908), 577–600 and ii (1909), 79–91.

43. *BRUO*, iii, 1421–2. His *Determinatio in materia schismatis* was also at Westminster Abbey (*Super facienda unione* according to Leland).

44. *BRUO*, iii, 2137–8 credits only Yonge, a doctor in civil and canon law, probably of Oxford, who became bishop of Rochester in 1404, with a letter to the *Curia* in 1407; but he is probably identical with the Richard Ingh who, according to Perroy, wrote the *Tractatus de Sedatione Scismatis* ('*editus in carceribus*') in Vatican MS. 4153, fos. 95–100 (E. Perroy, op. cit., 375).

45. *Questio de Schismate*, item 3 in British Library Royal MS. 6 D X; *BRUO*, iii, 1539.

46. *De dissensione paparum*, in *John Wyclif: Polemical Works in Latin*, ed. R. Buddensieg (1883) ii, 570 et seq.

47. M.D. Lambert, *Franciscan Poverty: The Doctrine of the absolute poverty of Christ and the apostles in the Franciscan order, 1210–1323* (1961) provides a good general survey of the question. See also D.L. Douie, *The Nature and the Effect of the heresy of the Fraticelli* (Manchester, 1932) especially pp. 202–8 for the English Franciscans.

48. See C.L. Kingsford, A.G. Little, F. Tocco, *Fratris Johannis Pecham . . . Tractatus Tres de Paupertate* (British Society of Franciscan Studies, ii, Aberdeen, 1910) which contains excerpts from Pecham's *Tractatus Pauperis*, an answer to the *Collectiones Catholicae* attributed to William of Saint-Amour; for editions of other parts of this tract, see J. Moorman, *A History of the Franciscan Order* (Oxford, 1968), 129. Pecham's *Utrum perfectio evangelica consistat in*

renuntiando vel carendo divitiis is edited by L. Oliger, *Franziskanische Studien*, iv (1917), 127–76.

49. For the attribution of this work to Thomas, see Moorman, op. cit., 129.

50. Pecham's tract against Kilwardby is edited in *Fratris Johannis Pecham . . .*, op. cit.; on the controversy irself, see D.L. Douie, *Archbishop Pecham* (Oxford, 1952), 39–40.

51. On Ralph of Lockisley, see *BRUO*, ii, 1155; on the Council of Vienne, see G. Leff, *Heresy in the Later Middle Ages* (Manchester, 1967), i, 139 et seq.; for Conington, see A. Heysse, 'Fr. Richard de Conington, O.F.M., Tractatus de Paupertate', *AFH*, xxiii (1930, 57–105 and 340–60, and V. Doucet, 'L'oeuvre scolastique de Richard de Conington', ibid, xxix (1936), 396–442 (especially p. 398 about the aforesaid edition).

52. See Moorman, op. cit., 307–38 and M.D. Lambert, 'The Franciscan Crisis under John XXII', *Franciscan Studies*,xxxii (1972), 123–42. See also F. Tocco, *La quistione della poverta nel secolo XIV* (Naples, 1910) and the useful introduction by J.G. Sikes to his edition of Hervaeus Natalis's *De Paupertate Christi et Apostolorum*, in *Archives d'Histoire Doctrinale et Littéraire du Moyen Age*, xii–xiii (1937–8), 209–97.

53. Lambert, 'The Franciscan Crisis'.

54. *BRUO*, ii, 1142; see C. Walmsley, 'Two Long Lost Works of William Woodford and Robert of Leicester', *AFH*, xlvi (1953), 458–70, which demonstrates that the *De Paupertate Domini* ascribed to Leicester by Leland is in fact the *Super Egenum et Pauperem Christum* in Cambridge University Library Add. MS. 3571.

55. These tracts are discussed in D.L. Douie, 'Three Treatises on evangelical poverty', *AFH*, xxiv (1931), 341–361, together with an anonymous Franciscan tract of the same period. Chatton's work purports to be an answer to a lost tract on the same subject by Nicholas Trevet, which may have been the *Scutum Veritatis contra Impugnantes Statum Perfectionis* mentioned in the catalogue of Urban V's library (Douie, 343)and for which he had received money from John XXII (Douie, *The Nature . . . Fraticelli*, 204). Moreover, four English Franciscans were arrested at the instance of the papal nuncio and sent to Avignon.

56. K. Walsh, *A Fourteenth Century Scholar and Primate: Richard Fitzralph in Oxford, Avignon and Armagh* (Oxford, 1981); on the specific situation in Ireland, see also R. Frame, *English Lordship in Ireland, 1318–1361* (Oxford, 1982).

57. K. Walsh, op. cit., 380, 384.

58. Bks. I–IV are edited in *John Wyclif, De dominio divino* ed. R. L. Poole (WS, 1890) 257–476; Books V–VII are edited in the unpublished thesis of R.O. Brock, *An edition of Richard Fitzralph's De Pauperie Salvatoris, Bks. V, VI, VII* (University of Colorado, Boulder, 1954); I have not made use of this and rely on K. Walsh's analysis of these last three books.

59. See. F. Tocco, op. cit., 34 et seq.

60. This has been established by A. Gwynn, *The English Austin Friars in the time of Wyclif* (1940), 35–73; see *Aegidius Romanus, De Ecclesiastica Potestate* ed. R. Scholz (Weimar, 1929); on Agostino Trionfo, see M. Wilks, *The Problem of Sovereignty in the Later Middle Ages* (Cambridge, 1963). On two other Augustinian masters, Alessandro da San Elpidio and Guglielmo Amidani da Cremona, see K. Walsh, op. cit., 382–3.

61. K. Walsh, op. cit., 404.

62. There has been much debate over the so-called 'revolutionary' character of Fitz Ralph's doctrine: for conflicting views, see R.R. Betts, 'Richard Fitz Ralph, Archbishop of Armagh, and the doctrine of Dominion', in *Essays in Czech History* (1969), 160–175 (hardly a Marxist interpretation, as K. Walsh thinks, though R.R. Betts may very well have been a Marxist); and M. Wilks, 'Predestination, property and power: Wyclif's theory of Dominion and Grace', SCH, ii (1965), 220–36. That Fitz Ralph was a conservative in his intellectual conceptions is amply demonstrated by G. Leff, *Richard Fitzralph, commentator of the Sentences* (Manchester, 1963): but the 'revolutionary' potentialities of his doctrines are not to be ignored.

63. Of great importance are chapters V and VI of the *De Vita Evangelica*, in which are discussed Fitz Ralph's theories of dominion of the community of temporal goods under natural law and

of the effects of mortal sin on dominion. See K. Walsh, 'The *De Vita Evangelica* of Geoffrey Hardeby (+ ca. 1385)', *Analecta Augustiniana*, xxxiii (1970) and xxxiv (1971), especially xxxiv, 6–11).

64. *BRUO*, ii, 1050–1. According to A. Gwynn, he might very well be the author of the tract *In Causa Domini Armachani* contained in Paris, Bibliothèque Nationale Latin MS. 3222.

65. *BRUO*, i, 479.

66. Most of the *De Pauperie Salvatoris* was composed at Avignon in 1350–1, but manuscripts of it were copied at Oxford at least from 1356–7 (cf. K. Walsh, op. cit., p. 389); according to Anne Hudson, the first precise reference to Wycliffe's theory of dominion is to be found in a 1373 sermon of William Rymyngton: P. Gradon, 'Langland and the Ideology of Dissent', *PBA* lxvi (1980), 179–205; quoting R. O'Brien, 'Two sermons at York Synod of William Rymyngton', *Citeaux*, xix (1968), 40–67. It is noteworthy that Rymyngton musters Becket's shadow in support of his denunciation: '*Si singulis annis huius decreti fieret exsecutio debita per episcopos, qui filius tenebrarum auderet per falsas prophetias et doctrinas subdolas informare principes seculares ad spoliandum sanctam ecclesiam de suis libertatibus et possessionibus, vel ad renovandum articulos pro quibus sanctus Thomas martyrium patiebatur?*' (loc. cit., 59).

67. G. Leff, *Heresy*, ii, 494–558.

68. See M. Aston, 'Lollardy and the Reformation: Survival or Revival?', *History*, xlix (1964), 149–70, for some Lollard texts which survived until the sixteenth century; and on the popular *Floretum* and its revised version, see C. Von Nolcken, 'Some alphabetical compendia and how preachers used them in fourteenth-century England', *Viator* (1981), 271–88; and A. Hudson, 'A Lollard compilation and the dissemination of Wycliffite Thought', *Journal of Theological Studies*, new series, 23 (1972), 65–81.

69. See for instance the unpublished Oxford University D.Phil. thesis of N.D. Hurnard, *Studies in intellectual life in England from the middle of the fifteenth century until the time of Colet* (1936), especially chapters V and VI.

70. On many of the authors who played a leading part during these years, see S.L. Forte, *A study of some Oxford schoolmen of the middle of the fourteenth century* (1947), an Oxford University B.Litt. dissertation.

71. *BRUO*, ii, 996; Hynkeley was an Austin friar, who wrote against Wycliffe a *De Potestate Ecclesiae* in three books.

72. *BRUO* i, 212–13.

73. *BRUO*, i, 617.

74. *BRUO*, iii, 2081–2; see E. Doyle,' William Woodford's *De dominio civili clericorum* against John Wyclif', *AFH*, lxvi (1973), 49–109.

75. *BRUO*, iii, 1539, for Radcliffe, on whom also see Perroy (op. cit., 371–2) for his *quaestio* (*Utrum pro scandalo scismatice pravitatis cedando, dominus papa Bonifacius una cum antepapa cedere teneatur*). His chief work against Wycliffe deals more especially with political problems: it is a dialogue between 'Nicholas' and 'Peter' on several topics (1. *De immortalitate primi hominis*; 2. *De dominio naturali*; 3. *De obedienciali dominio*; 4. *De dominio regali et judiciali*; 5. and 6. *De potestate Petri apostoli et successorum*). See also E.F. Jacob, 'Some English Documents of the Conciliar Movement', *Bulletin of the John Rylands Library*, (1931), 358–94, especially 367–71, and *Essays in the Conciliar Epoch* (Manchester, 1953), 65–8. On Stokes, see *BRUO*, iii, 1783–4.

76. *BRUO*, ii, 1343–4; see also Kingsford's article in the *DNB*. The three books of the work were officially presented to Pope Martin V by English Carmelites, and they were then edited in various places until the last complete edition of 1757 in Venice. A fourth book planned by Netter does not seem to have been written.

77. On Arundel's action against the Oxford Wycliffites, see G. Leff, *Heresy*, ii, 570–4.

78. *BRUO*, i, 239; extracts of the *Gladium* are printed in Reginald Pecock, *The repressor of over much blaming of the clergy*, ed. C. Babington (RS, 1860), ii, 575–613.

79. Crump was an adversary of both Wycliffe (who answered a sermon preached by him in his *De*

Civili Dominio) and the mendicants. He was condemned twice, in 1384 and 1392, and was an Irish (yet again) Cistercian: *BRUO*, i, 524–5, and R.L. Poole's article in *DNB*.

80.   Bale credits Norris with a *Contra Mendicitatem Validam*: a canon of St. Patrick's, Dublin, he was condemned by the pope in 1440; *BRUO*, ii, 1365–6.

81.   See F.R.H. Du Boulay, 'The Quarrel between the Carmelite Friars and the Secular Clergy in London, 1464–1468', *JEH*, vi (1955), 156–74.

82.   The fact that Trevisa was interested in political theory (or that his patron Lord Berkeley was) is proved by his translation of Giles of Rome's *De Regimine Principum*; why he selected for translation an anonymous tract written some time before 1302 is obscure. On the Latin text, see T. Renna, 'Kingship in the Disputatio inter clericum et militem', *Speculum*, xlviii (1973), 675–93. For Trevisa, see *BRUO*, iii, 1903–4; D.C. Fowler, 'New light on John Trevisa', *Traditio*, xvii (1962), 289–317, and 'More about Trevisa', *Modern Language Quarterly*, xxxii (1971), 243–54; also *Dialogus inter Militem et Clericum*, ed. A.J. Perry (EETS, OS 167, 1925).

83.   *De Speculo Regis Edwardi III*, ed. A. Moisant (Paris, 1891). For the ascription and related problems, see the excellent article of L.E. Boyle, 'The *Oculus sacerdotis* and some other works of William of Pagula', *TRHS*, 5th. series, v (1955), 81–110, especially 107–8.

84.   *Four English Political Tracts*, 27–30; however, R.G. Davies has proposed as a possible author Thomas Rushook in *Profession, Vocation and Culture*, ed. Clough, 87. See also Philippe de Mézières, *Letter to King Richard II*, ed. G.W. Coopland (Liverpool, 1975).

85.   Repton's letter survives in several manuscripts, all of different nature, e.g. letter-collections and chronicles. It is found for instance in BL. Royal MS 10 B ix, fo. 35 in a fragment chiefly devoted to treatises and models of dictamen; and in BL. Stowe MS 67, a longer version of a short chronicle found in at least four other manuscripts. The letter also occurs in Adam of Usk's *Chronicle* and in Beckington's *Correspondence* and has been printed with both. Although this does not make a high total of manuscripts, such diversity may be the proof of a wider circulation.

86.   Thomas Hoccleve, *The Regement of Princes and Fourteen Minor Poems*, ed. F.J. Furnivall (EETS, ES. lxxii, 1897); J. Mitchell, *Thomas Hoccleve* (Chicago-Urbana, 1968).

87.   *Four English Political Tracts*, 40–173; for new proposals about date and authorship, see B.P. Wolffe, *Henry VI* (1981), 14–15.

88.   W. of Worcester, *The Boke of Noblesse*, ed. J.G. Nichols (Roxburghe Club, lxxvii, London, 1860); see 'William Worcester: a preliminary survey', in K.B. McFarlane, *England in the Fifteenth Century: Collected Essays* (1981) 199–224.

89.   George Asbhy, *Poems*, ed. M. Bateson (EETS, ES. lxxvi, 1899).

90.   This view, based upon the Latin envoi to the *Active Policy*, is proposed by V.J. Scattergood, *Politics and Poetry*, 285–6.

91.   E. Dudley, *The Tree of Commonwealth*, ed. D.M. Brodie (Cambridge, 1948).

92.   *De Regimine Principum ad serenissimum regem Anglie Henricum Octavum* (Short Title Catalogue 1497).

93.   *Four English Political Tracts*, 174–219. Another manuscript must be added to those quoted in the edition: BL. Royal MS F ii, a copy prepared perhaps for Prince Arthur, maybe by Bernard André (ex inf. G. Labory).

94.   *The Middle English Translation of Christine de Pisan's Livre du Corps de Policie*, ed. D. Bornstein (Heidelberg, 1977).

95.   *Fifteenth Century English Translations of Alain Chartier's Le Traité de l'Espérance and le Quadrilogue Invectif*, ed. M.S. Blayney (EETS, OS 270 and 281, 1974 and 1980). Another text of Chartier with political implications is *Le Curial*, translated by Caxton in 1484.

96.   See M.A. Manzalaoui, *The Secretum Secretorum in English Thought and Literature from the fourteenth to the seventeenth century*, unpublished diss., Oxford University, 1954, and *Secretum Secretorum: Nine English Versions* (EETS, OS 276, London, 1977).

97.   N. Oresme, *Le livre de Politiques d'Aristote*, ed. A. Menut (Transactions of the American

Philosophical Society, new series, lx, pt. 6, 1970) and *Le Livre de Ethiques d'Aristote* (New York, 1940).

98. On Charles V and his councillors in the field of political theory, see A. Coville, in E. Lavisse, *Histoire de France* (Paris, 1902) iv, 182–217.

99. Translated for Charles V by the Franciscan Denis Foulechat: see L. Delisle, *Recherches sur la bibliothèque de Charles V* (Paris, 1907), 73–85.

100. M. Schnerb-Lièvre, 'Evrart de Trémaugon et le Songe du Vergier' *Romania*, 101 (1980), 527–30 and *Le songe du Vergier*, ed. M. Schnerb-Lièvre (Paris, 1982).

101. Paris, B.N. MS. Français 437; see the comments of R. Cazelles, *Société Politique, Noblesse et Couronne sous Jean le Bon et Charles V* (Geneva, Paris, 1982), 507.

102. On Christine de Pisan, see S. Solente, 'Christine de Pisan', in *Histoire Littéraire de la France*, xl (Paris, 1974), 335–422; J. Krynen, *Idèal du Prince et Pouvoir Royal en France à la fin du Moyen Age (1380–1440)* (Paris 1982), 62–8; and more especially Cl. Gauvard, 'Christine de Pisan a-t-elle eu une pensée politique?', *Revue Historique*, 240 (1973), 417–31.

103. See F. Autrand, 'Culture et mentalité: les librairies des gens du Parlement sous Charles VI', *Annales E.S.C.*, xxviii (1973), 1219–44; an interesting article on the culture and mentality of the court jurists and councillors is H. Boockmann, 'Zur Mentalität Spätmittelalterlicher Gelehrter Räte', *Historische Zeitschrift*, 233 (1981), 295–316.

104. For instance, Jacques Legrand wrote his *Livre des Bonnes Moeurs* for John, duke of Berry.

105. This is not entirely true, in so much as there was even before the Valois Dukes a real taste for *Miroirs* in the Low Countries courts: see, for instance, the *De Regimine Principum* of Jean d'Anneux for Count William I of Hainault (No. 31 in Berges, op. cit.); the *Speculum Morale* of Johannes Calligator (No. 37 in Berges) for Duke Wenceslas of Bribant; the *De Cura Rei Publicae* of Philip of Leyden for Count William V of Holland (no. 38 in Berges), on which see the introduction of R. Feenstra to his reprint of the 1516 edition (Amsterdam, 1971). Among the authors who wrote for the Valois Dukes of Burgundy are Ghillebert de Lannoy and Georges Chastellain.

106. G.M. Spiegel, 'The Reditus Regni ad Stirpem Karoli Magni. A new look', *French Historical Studies*, vii (1971), 145–74; B. Guenée, 'Les généalogies entre l'histoire et la politique: la fierté d'être Capétien, en France, au Moyen Age', reprinted in *Politique et Histoire au Moyen Age* (Paris, 1981) 341–68.

107. See C. Beaune, 'Saint Clovis: Histoire, Religion Royale et Sentiment National en France à la fin du Moyen Age', in B. Guenée, *Le Métier d'historien au Moyen Age* (Paris, 1977), 139–56.

108. See the forthcoming *thèse de doctorat d'Etat* by C. Beaune. The best analysis of the divergent attitudes of the French and of the English monarchies is the short essay by Peter Lewis, 'War-propaganda and historiography in Fifteenth Century France and England'; *TRHS*, 5th series, xv (1965), 1–21. See also his *Later Medieval France: The Polity* (1968).

109. See my forthcoming article: 'Thomas Polton and the expression of English Nationalism at the Council of Constance'.

110. G. Matthew, *The Court of Richard II* (1968).

111. This is especially true of the period of the De La Pole and Margaret of Anjou's ascendancy.

112. See B.J.H. Rowe, 'Henry VI's claim to France in picture and poem', *The Library*, 4th series, xiii (1932–3), 77–88; and J.W. McKenna, 'Henry VI and the dual monarchy: aspects of royal political propaganda', *Journal of the Warburg and Courtauld Institutes*, xxviii (1965), 145–62.

113. V.J. Scattergood, op. cit., 71–2.

114. See P. Lewis, 'War-propaganda', on the works of Jean de Rinel, William of Worcester and Thomas Beckington.

115. See note 1 above.

116. On this literature, see S.B. Chrimes, *English Constitutional Ideas in the Fifteenth Century* (Cambridge 1936).

117. J.-Ph. Genet, 'Droit et Histoire en Angleterre: la préhistoire de la "révolution historique"', *Annales de Bretagne et des Pays de l'Ouest*, lxxxvii (1980), 319–66.

118. S.B. Chrimes, 'Sir John Fortescue and his theory of dominion', *TRHS*, 4th series, xvii (1934), 117–47, and J.-Ph. Genet, 'Les Idées sociales de Sir John Fortescue', in *Economies et Sociétés au Moyen Age: Mélanges offerts à Edouard Perroy* (Paris, 1973), 446–61.

119. A good example of this method is chapter IX of the *Governance of England*, ed. C. Plummer (Oxford, 1885), 127–30.

120. C.A.J. Skeel, 'The influence of the writings of Sir John Fortescue', *TRHS*, 3rd series, x (1916), 77–114.

121. Chrimes, 'Sir John Fortescue', 147.

122. This estimate is based upon a parallel with France, on which see the pioneering study of C. Bozzolo and E. Ornato, *Pour une histoire du livre manuscrit au Moyen Age: trois essais de codicologie quantitative* (Paris, 1980).

123. This statement is somewhat ambiguous as regards Fortescue: but neither for Dudley nor for Christopher Saint-German, a little later.

2

'Caim's Castles': Poverty, Politics, and Disendowment*

Margaret Aston

'. . . *pars sacrilegii est rem pauperum dare non pauperibus . . .*'[1]

'*Isti autem sunt stultificati idiotae . . . nescientes inter paupertatem et mendicationem distinguere . . .*'[2]

In the early fifteenth century, *Jack Upland's* comprehensive invective against the friars included the following charge. 'These ben cockers in convents and covetous in markets, marrers of matrimony and Caym's castle-makers'. 'Jack', returned Friar Daw (whose reply to the sexual accusation was less than comprehensive),

> 'Jack, thou sayest that we bilden the castles of Caym,
> It is God's house, old shrew, that we ben about'.[3]

These exchanges relate to a piece of Wycliffite typology that by this time was commonplace. The adaptation of Middle English legends of Cain (or Caim, as usage then also had it) to help damn the mendicant orders became prominent about 1382, and the extended currency of the term 'Caim's Castles' can be attributed to Wycliffe. I have chosen this phrase as a useful point of entry into an aspect of disendowment politics that seems to be important, though it is not usually put first: namely the bearing on them of the controversy over mendicant poverty, which was still very alive in the fifteenth century.

The attributes of Cain in late medieval literature and art were various – and all bad. Cain was of course the prototype murderer, a fratricide at that. He also stood for possession – false possession – and indeed his name is associated with the Hebrew word meaning to acquire or get.[4] In addition, by a process of association, Cain came to be thought of as a heretic. Thanks to a fusion accomplished in early exegesis, the passage in Genesis 4 describing the offerings of Cain and Abel became linked with the parable of the sower's wheat and tares in Matthew 13. In fact Genesis tells of Cain offering fruits of the ground while Abel offered the firstlings of his flock, but they came to be seen in terms of true and false offerers of tithe – Abel rendering his best beast, or sometimes pure wheat; Cain giving wheat mixed with tares.[5] '*Caim cum lolio*': these words were placed over Cain's head in a twelfth-century sculpture that clearly depicts the weeds among the wheat. From here it was not a long step to the association of Matthew 13 – the heretical cockle in the clean corn.[6] To call the friars Cainites was therefore to blacken them with a cluster of damning qualities, most useful for some controversialists from the 1380s. Moreover Genesis used a phrase to describe cursed Cain that seemed perfectly fitted to the wandering mendicant. The condemned brother, 'a fugitive and a vagabond in the earth', was identifiable as the vagrant friar.[7]

Wycliffe made use of this typing in several of his works. In *De mandatis divinis* (of the mid 1370s), when discussing different sorts of theft under the seventh commandment, he turned to the sin of Cain and his avaricious cheating over tithes. Wycliffe called the 'heresiarch Caym' the initiator of injustice in the Old Testament, while Judas played the same role in the New Testament.

> 'So, just as the heresiarch Caym was the first plainly unjust in the old law, the beginning of injustice in the secular arm, so Scarioth was by the same avarice the first plainly unjust heresiarch in the time of the law of grace, and the beginning [of injustice] in the name of clerks'.[8]

In the section of his *Trialogus* which was written after the so-called Earthquake Council of 1382, where the four orders of friars had played such a prominent part in condemning his heresies, Wycliffe included a discussion of the origin of the different mendicant orders. He accused the friars of the most mendacious claims in their quest for antiquity, the Austins asserting that they were founded by St. Augustine, the Carmelites romancing about their origin on Mount Carmel in the time of Elisha. Such claimants were the true descendants of the father of lies. And there are some, Wycliffe went on, who seeing this tide of lying

> 'make out that these four orders took their beginning in CAYM, and so the voice of his brother Abel cried to the Lord from the ground to shape the malice of these friars. In witness of which the four letters of this name CAIM give the initials of these four orders, according to the sequence in which the friars pretend they originated. . .'

i.e. C. for Carmelites with their bogus Old Testament claim; A. for the Austins – moving on many centuries to the time of Augustine; J. for Jacobites, or Dominicans; and M. for Minorites, looking respectively (and more respectably) to St. Dominic and St. Francis.[9]

This anti-fraternal acrostic may have made its popular appearance in the flow of exchanges that took place after the Blackfriars Council in May 1382. An English poem against the friars, which has been dated to this time (though on inconclusive grounds), versifies the C-A-I-M acronym to illustrate the truth 'that men say of them/in many divers land', that the friars' origin lay with 'that caitiff cursed Caym'.

> 'thus grounded caym these four orders,
> that fillen the world full of errors & of hypocrisy'.[10]

Who coined this acrostic? It could have been Wycliffe, though given the long-standing controversies surrounding the mendicant orders he could equally well have borrowed this word-play. I have not been able to trace an earlier usage, and Wycliffe might have been referring to himself when, in a sermon, he alluded to the remarks of a certain 'someone' on this topic. Speaking there of the friars as having lie-stained lips and blood-stained hands, he wrote: 'and thus (as someone says – ut quidam dicit) these homicides of the race of Caym are figured in the four-letter name' – C. for Carmelites etc.[11] At any rate and whoever invented the acrostic, the extended use of this Caimite vocabulary in the later fourteenth century certainly owed much to Wycliffe.

'Caim's Castles' was of the same currency. In the text appended to the Trialogus on the endowment of the church, Wycliffe returned to the topic of the friars, their houses and churches. Why should they build themselves such towers and monstrous edifices at the expense of the kingdom? It was the devil working in them the avarice of Cain. 'It would be to the advantage of kingdoms', he wrote, 'were the expenses of which friars despoil kingdoms to be distributed to the poor for the building of humble houses'.[12] There is an implicit contrast here between the tall and sumptuous buildings of the mendicants and the lowly dwellings of the poor. The contrast appears again in one of Wycliffe's last writings (De fundacione sectarum, datable to the third quarter of 1383), where he attacks the blasphemous excesses of mendicant convents, all built of thefts from deprived Christians and completely incongruous with any imitation of Christ. Thus, he wrote, they fraudulently despoil the destitute to make their 'Caimitical castles' (castella caimitica).[13]

'Caim's castles' proved a useful shorthand for the unacceptable face of mendicant possession. It appears in a number of English Wycliffite texts, where its usage always advertizes a Lollard viewpoint, even if there was not exact consistency of meaning. It is worthwhile spending a moment on this changing usage, since it may tell us something about Lollard development.

In the seven or so Lollard texts in print that use the term 'Caim's castles', most apply it as Wycliffe did to the buildings of the four mendicant orders: 'a Caim's castle of friars', 'Caim's castles of the new orders', 'by this spoiling they builden Caim's castles', and so on.[14] Others show the phrase taking on a wider meaning. It parts company from the mendicant acrostic to be used against all

unjustifiable non-parochial church buildings. 'What advantage shall a poor man
have that he suffers against his will his alms to be borne to caim's castle to feed a
flock of antichrists?' The author who asked this question (in the vernacular 'De
officio pastorali') had in mind not only friary churches, but also cathedrals and
royal chapels and colleges of studies to which parish churches were damagingly
appropriated. He warned any member of a religious order with a cure of souls
deputed to a vicar, to be sure to 'live in poverty as baptist did, not in high castles
of caim and lustful [of] food as boars in sty'.[15] Another English text, on the
papacy, seems also to have been attacking religious foundations in general when
it alluded to the alms collected by antichrist to make 'such caim's castles'.

> 'Truly in the old law was Solomon's temple a figure of the church in the new
> law, but not that the church should be such, but free and large under the cope
> of heaven, and stand in virtues of man's soul; but antichrist will close it now
> in cold stones that must perish'.[16]

'Caim's castles' implied the duality of Cain and Abel: the murderer and the
murdered. It was not only a question of rich churches being wrong in
themselves; they were built out of the proceeds of misappropriated alms. The
grandiose edifices of all religious foundations (monasteries and colleges as well as
friaries) could be proscribed with this term. It sums up the apposition between
the unapostolic display of such 'costly churches' and (as one of these authors put
it) 'old parish churches that were ordained by Christ's apostles'.[17]

Given our inability to date English Lollard texts, it is impossible to build a
semantic chronology on these few references.[18] But we do have one dated
example which seems to show 'Caim's castles' being used with a still wider
meaning. In the year 1393 Anne Palmer and six other Northampton Lollards
(two of them chaplains) were accused by Bishop Buckingham of holding the
following belief.

> 'Item, that it suffices every Christian to serve God's commandments in his
> chamber or to worship God secretly in the field, without paying heed to public
> prayers in a material building, lest conforming to the pharisees he is
> accounted a hypocrite; neither is the material church building held among
> them as holy church, but rather every such materially built house is called by
> them 'caym' castle.[19]

Caim's castles are here clearly associated with the rejection of material churches,
suggestive of sectarian developments among the heretics.

Two other points in the charges listed against this cell of Northampton
Lollards indicate that Anne Palmer and her associates may have had some grasp
of Wycliffe's case against church temporalities. They were accused of regarding
the endowment of the church by Pope Sylvester as poisoning it – a favourite
theme of Wycliffe and others long before him, who recited the story of the
angelic voice heard saying at the donation of Constantine, 'today poison is

poured into the holy church of God'.[20] The other matter concerned almsgiving to the poor.

> 'Item, they are reported to say', ran this article, 'that it is vain to give alms to any beggar except only to the lame and crooked and blind who are weak or lying paralysed, and that all who give such alms are supporting and sustaining such mendicants in their sins, and whoever gives such alms serves the devil'.[21]

I have more to say later on the question of poverty and alms. For the moment there are two points worth noticing about this accusation. First, that the criterion for almsgiving was the distinction between the able-bodied and the several categories of beggars. Second, and all-important, is the gospel text that lies behind these words. They derived from the parable of the great supper in Luke 14, when the places of the recalcitrant guests were filled by those brought in from the highways and hedges. The *claudis et curvis et cecis que sunt debiles* of Buckingham's bill echo the Vulgate's *voca pauperes, debiles, claudos, et caecos*. This passage became a *locus classicus* for Lollards, as it had been a gospel focus for Wycliffe; and as it is important to my argument I shall quote the Wycliffite Bible's version of it.

> 'But whanne thou makist a feeste, clepe pore men, feble men, crokid, and blynde, and thou schalt be blessid; for thei han not, wher of to yelde to thee, forsoth it schal be yeldun to thee in the rising agen of iuste men . . . Go out soone in to grete stretis and smale streetis of the citee, and brynge in hidur poor men, and feble, and blynde, and crokid'.[22]

Lollard attacks on Caim's castles remind us that the heresy was polemical as well as pastoral. But the case against the friars – which was nearly as old as the orders themselves – always remained attached to the serious reconsideration of evangelical life and Christian service. The new-style mendicants' pursuit of 'voluntary poverty and . . . other simple and virtuous living' (as William Thorpe put it)[23] was to place them at odds with old-style professional mendicants, and this perpetuation and revival of the ancient controversy bore closely on the politics of disendowment. Let us now turn to that question.

For roughly a hundred years, from the 1350s to the 1450s (concentrated particularly in the middle of that period), a variety of schemes were floated and ideas sounded for removing some of the temporal possessions of the church. Some were threatening verbal squibs. Others, most notably the Lollard plan of (probably) 1410, were more elaborate programmes. They had different objectives and a variety of results.

Broadly we can see that these ideas surfaced in a period conspicuous for the exigencies of war and war financing, and clearly it is no coincidence that the most daring of these projects appeared in times that produced outstanding new expedients for royal taxation, as well as social unrest and popular heresy. At the same time such proposals, however serviceable they might be (or seem to be) in the political arena, started out as arguments about religion and spiritual duties. Their idealistic content was not necessarily at risk in unsuccessful brushes with politics.

The bill of 1410 marks the climax of this intermittent sequence, but before considering it we ought to look at its precedents. We must start, therefore, in the later 1350s, at the peak of Archbishop FitzRalph's controversy with the friars. On 26 March of a year we do not know for certain, but quite likely 1358, a letter was addressed to FitzRalph by the chancellor and regent masters of Oxford. The university authorities wanted the archbishop (who was then at the curia) to help them by informing the pope about a recent scandal in the schools. The full horrors of the affair, including the rumpus caused in the faculty of theology, were left to be reported by the bearer of the letter, but the outline was set down in writing. An unnamed scholar (as they wrote)

'at the devil's own prompting publicly determined in the schools against the possessions of the church, damnably asserting it to be lawful for founders of churches to take away goods dedicated to God and the church on account of the abuses of clerics, and to transfer and apply them directly to seculars and knights. Also that church tithes are due more to mendicant friars than to curates'.

For this dreadful offence the disputant was suspended, and was not going to be allowed to resume any scholastic activity until he showed himself duly contrite. The trouble was (FitzRalph was told) that 'we cannot compel him to a public revocation, or to any other punishment, on account of the confidence he has in the magnates of the realm, who, he says, wish to support him in this matter'.[24]

It seems probable that this offender was the 'frater Johannes' who, on Sunday 21 October 1358, had publicly to recant in St. Mary's, Oxford, after the university sermon, the same views as those described in the letter. His offence was very serious – witness his punishment and the presence at his revocation of the chancellor and proctors and the superiors of his order (the name of which is unfortunately not known). Friar John had maintained in the schools that tithes belonged to the friars more than to rectors and curates of churches; that the king and temporal lords had the right to deprive evil-living clergy of their possessions, and that the university was a school of heresy. He was fined 100 shillings and was never to lecture again without permission from the chancellor, proctors and regent doctors of theology.[25]

This incident (which so far as we know remained a purely academic affair) sets the stage for later events in several ways. There is the mendicant initiative; there is the alleged interest of secular lords: and there is the linking of tithes with temporal endowments.

The next occasion when disendowment was openly mooted was more public and is better known. This was at the parliament of 1371, when there was urgent need of funds for the French war and the tide was running high against ecclesiastical administrators. It was in the context of parliament's effort to shunt half the burden of this session's taxation on to the clergy that two Austin friars argued the case for sharing ecclesiastical possessions. One of these spokesmen was John Bankin, an Oxford theologian. We do not know the name of the other, though Thomas Ashborne is a possible candidate.[26]

The two friars mustered ecclesiastical law and patristic precedent to demonstrate that the 'common need of the whole realm' overrode all claims to clerical privilege and exemption. Gratian's *Decretum* and the natural law were cited to suggest that all possessions, ecclesiastical and otherwise, were held in common and in critical circumstances individual right must yield to general need.[27] All the temporal possessions of the church (leaving aside first fruits and tithes) had come to it from king and lords for the service of God and relief of the poor, and in the event of necessity the original donors could properly call on these endowments to help defend the realm. This was an argument calculated to go down well with secular founders, and according to a report of Wycliffe, one lord declared that 'if war is waged against us we must take back from the endowed clergy temporal possessions which belong in common to us and the whole kingdom'.[28] Edging into this case are hints of the idea voiced earlier at Oxford of the conditional nature of church possessions: that clerical endowment was premised on clerical probity as well as the performance of certain services, and in the event of failure expropriation was justifiable. A patristic quotation appended to the friars' articles, which referred to the sacrilege of not giving to the poor the goods of the poor, raised the issue of superfluous clerical possessions.[29] Those who redressed the clergy's charitable lapses by diminishing their wealth, might be blessed by God.

Only two years after this – after Whitsun 1373, if we follow Jeremy Catto's rehabilitation of a story in the continuation of the *Eulogium Historiarum* – two friars were once again propounding arguments against temporal dominion in the church. The circumstances were different. The meeting was a great council, not a parliament, and papal, not royal taxation was at issue. But some of the underlying questions were the same, and it is possible that one of the disputants may have been at both meetings, for John Mardisley (Franciscan), the main spokesman against the temporal claims of the pope, was supported by the Austin, Thomas Ashborne.[30]

It was, therefore, specially thanks to the activity of friars that politics and church temporalities got mixed as they did in the early 1370s. That mix was not initially altered by Wycliffe's contribution to the question, though he brought to the topic new prominence, more publicity, and the edge of a fresh theoretical basis.[31] This is not the place to explore Wycliffe's views, but it is clear that what he wrote and said on church ownership had much to do with the winning and losing of his allies, and that in turn reflected back on the politics of disendowment.[32] He presented the pattern of the true church, which had failed its apostolic origin ever since the Donation of Constantine. The secular powers who were called to reform, while not without expected benefits for themselves, were invoked to complete a spiritual task – not merely to resolve a financial crisis. And the failings in temporal possessions afflicted every order of the church, prelates, parish clergy, religious orders, mendicants. Apostolic poverty was always central for Wycliffe, but anti-mendicancy only became a dominant strain during his last years, partly as the direct result of some dramatic changes.

Among the twenty-four heresies and errors in Wycliffe's writings condemned at the Blackfriars Council in May 1382, two consecutive errors dealt with temporalities and tithes.[33] They should be considered together: namely;

'That temporal lords may at will take away temporal goods from habitually offending churchmen';[34]

'That tithes are pure alms, and parishioners may, on account of the sins of their curates, withhold them and freely confer them on others'.[35]

In the list of mendicant doctors who subscribed to this proscription were the two Austins, Thomas Ashborne and John Bankin.[36] Their presence must have been particularly galling to Wycliffe, given their earlier championing of a cause so near his heart. The great doctor was furious. Damning allusions to mendicant idiocy at the council were dashed into the work then on his desk – the *Trialogus*. The friars were as good as making Christ a heretic, let alone trying to make heretics of the king and lords of England, by their denial of the secular right to withdraw temporalities.[37] The point was echoed in English tracts.

'Tell we how friars deceived late our realm at London, in the council; they would deceive our bishops, and also lords and commons that dwell in this realm. They said as belief, that [it] is an heresy to say that [for] men of the church [to] have temporal possessions is against holy writ, whosoever affirms it'.[38]

The bitter recriminations against the friars for this miserable *volte-face* were expressed in Latin and English, prose and verse. And, as contemporaries took note, there was also a new thrust in anti-mendicant arguments – on which more later.

Parliamentary lobbying for disendowment continued for many years after 1382, but it now had to contend with the heretical associations of the case. Also, since the friars were now aligned on the other side, the question of mendicant possessions presented itself more conspicuously. An English tract that marks a stage in this development was addressed to parliament some time after 1382. This text petitioned King Richard, the duke of Lancaster, and 'other great men of the realm, both . . . seculars and men of holy church, that are gathered in the parliament', to support four articles. Two of them concerned clerical possessions. The second defended the legal right of king and lords to remove the temporalities of delinquent clergy – with special reference to offending bishops and abbots. The third article dealt with tithe. If priests sinned and tithes were not used for the purposes for which they were ordained, argued this paper, parishioners could withhold them and divert them to better uses: particularly in question were appropriated churches, from which revenues were siphoned off to pay for luxuries like fat horses, gay saddles and jingling bridles for men who already had overmuch, whereas 'the tithes and offerings should be given to poor needy men'. This case was attached to lengthy pleading against the friars, with specific reference to certain friars of Coventry, who had condemned as heretical the right of secular lords to withdraw temporalities from the church. 'See lords, see and understand, with what punishment they deserve to be chastized, who thus unwarily and wrongfully have damned you for heretics'.[39]

There were several occasions in the last fifteen years of the fourteenth century when disendowment – in one form or another – seems to have come within range of parliament. According to Walsingham (who never failed on spicy stories of threats to his own house), anger about taxation in the parliament of 1385 led to anticlerical moves by the commons. The laity's grant of a fifteenth was made conditional on a clerical grant. Archbishop Courtenay rose in defence of the church and the consent of convocation. Whereupon (relates the chronicler) the enraged knights of the shire, together with some of the lords, furiously threatened the removal of temporalities, asserting that the clergy were too domineering. Such action, they suggested, might improve churchmen's commitment to charity and almsgiving. Walsingham then adds an interesting detail. The proposal was submitted to the king in a short text (*in scriptis brevibus*), which Richard – with proper loyalty to the church – ordered to be destroyed.[40]

Ten years later parliament was again reminded, albeit indirectly, of the role it might play in church reform. The twelve conclusions posted up on the doors of Westminster Hall when parliament was in session in 1395, were presented in the name of 'poor men, treasurers of Christ and his apostles', denouncing to the lords and commons the state of the English church as 'blind and leprous many years by maintenance of the proud prelacy, borne up with flattering of private religion'. Temporal endowment topped the listed articles.

> 'When the church of England began to dote in temporality after her stepmother the great church of Rome, and churches were slain by appropriation to diverse places; faith, hope and charity began for to flee out of our church . . .'[41]

The text that follows, however, does not elucidate this question, though the sixth conclusion dealt with prelates holding secular office and the seventh with special prayers for the dead. Still, we can deduce something about the desired remedies from other sources, as will be seen shortly.

One of Walsingham's most powerful reports of a proposed parliamentary disendowment was assigned by him to the Coventry Parliament of 1404 – the idea being that the king should take over church temporalities for at least one year. There are difficulties about this story, including the fact that Sir John Cheyne, to whom a leading role was attributed, was not (as Walsingham stated in one of his versions of these events) speaker of this parliament. B.P. Wolffe has argued that the chronicler has here telescoped events, and suggests that this incident should be put back five years into the first parliament of Henry IV.[42] We know that Cheyne was elected speaker in that parliament but withdrew, the day after his election, officially for reasons of ill-health. It seems likely that the real reason for his resignation was the suspicion entertained of him as a dangerous critic of the church, who would not be afraid to speak his mind in parliament. According to Walsingham's report of the proceedings of convocation in October 1399, Archbishop Arundel was fearful of moves that might be made in the commons under Cheyne's guidance. In anticipation of this he apparently advised – which is worth noticing – that the commons' anticlericalism might be forestalled by action against pluralism and non-residence.[43] Clearly the archbishop was anxious to take a firm stand at the beginning of the new regime against any Lollard demonstration. But it remains possible, despite some muddled reporting, that clerical disendowment was proposed alongside a resumption of crown lands in 1404.[44]

We come now to the fullest of all these paper plans – the Lollard disendowment bill assigned respectively to 1407 or 1410, the latter date seeming the more probable.[45] Kingsford thought that this bill, though composed as a petition of 'all the true commons' to king and lords 'of this present parliament' should be regarded as 'rather a manifesto meant for a popular audience than a serious attempt at legislation'.[46] We have no evidence of any formal parliamentary notice, though the silence of the parliament rolls cannot be taken as conclusive.

When we look at the contents of the bill it is clear that it was intended to have much more than popular appeal. The beneficiaries of disendowment were to include king, lords, knights, and squires, as well as the poor and needy, and provision was also made for ordinary priests and clerks and the learned. The detailed arithmetic (which, as had often been pointed out, does not add up) is less interesting than the detailed objectives. The confiscation seems to have been designed to net the revenues of all the English bishops as well as both archbishops,[47] together with seventy-five or so abbeys and religious houses, mainly Benedictine but also some Cistercian, and some of Augustinian Canons. The friaries were not included. Even if (as Anne Hudson has suggested) this is explicable by virtue of mendicant property being vested in the holy see, we still have to square it with a good deal else, including specific proposals by Wycliffe for mulcting the mendicants, parliamentary levies on the exempt religious,[48] and the strong force of Lollard anti-mendicancy. But the case for true mendicants did not go by default in the bill.

The positive proposals were threefold. First was the provision for the new secular endowments of fifteen earls, 1,500 knights, and 6,200 squires, together with enlarged royal revenues. This was linked with the defence of the realm, and places this part of the scheme in line with ideas mooted in 1371 and (probably) 1385 and 1399/1404. The needs of defence (and taxation) were obviously of central interest in the parliamentary context – hence this leading position. Alongside this comes the idea for 100 new almshouses, which is joined with remarks about worldly clerks and the misuse of funds intended for the poor. These new almshouses seem to have been intended as additions to the existing foundations (estimated by one historian at over six hundred), and it was stipulated that the income of 100 marks assigned to each for feeding 'needful poor men' was not, as in times past, to be dissipated by proud priests and worldly clerks, but to be adminstered by good and true secular persons.[49] Thirdly, there is the plan to increase the numbers of universities and secular clerks. The proposed foundation of fifteen new universities is mentioned almost as an aside – though to Kingsford it redeemed the entire scheme 'from any charge of sordid or socialist intention'.[50] Whatever we may think about the sort of institution that was intended, this item of the bill must be seen as having some bearing on the interests of its backers. So also do the fifteen thousand priests and clerks, sufficiently endowed by 'temporal alms' to fulfil their pastoral office. As glossed in one version, these would be 'good priests and perfect clerks to preach the word of god without flattering or begging or worldly reward to seek therefore'.[51]

Provision for the poor, true curates ('true men', i.e. Lollard sympathisers) and needy beggars, repeats itself in the bill, consorting rather uneasily with the secular endowments sandwiched in between. Priests and prelates were henceforth to live off spiritual revenues, since they had conspicuously failed in their duty to 'help the poor commons with their lordships', and the past lusts and ease of the great had been extorted from 'profits that should come to true men'.[52]

The 100 almshouses constitute an important clue that makes it possible to trace the 1410 scheme back to at least the 1390s. The 'one hundred almshouses for the bedridden (decumbentibus)' appeared, with other details of the 1410 plan, in the extracts of John Purvey's heresies listed by Richard Lavenham. This summary cannot be exactly dated, but its allusion to another 'special tract' explaining details of the plans for distributing church possessions, tells of the existence of some document specifically devoted to the disendowment plan.[53] We do not know what this special tract amounted to. But something of the kind seems to have been available by 1395. For the seventh of the twelve conclusions of that year ended with the statement that;

'it was proved in a book that the king heard [i.e. it had been read aloud to Richard II] that an hundred of alms houses sufficed to all the realm, and thereof should fall the greatest increase possible to [the] temporal part'.[54]

Here, we may notice, it was *only* a hundred almshouses, not a hundred *additional* almshouses, the concern being to reduce the wrong sorts of foundation.

This seventh conclusion of the 'manifesto' concentrated on the point that special prayers for the dead amounted to simony and were the negation of true charity and almsgiving. The merchandise for such prayers for souls, 'made to mendicants and possessioners and other soul priests', was said to be a great burden to the realm. If we set this conclusion beside Purvey's reference to the bedridden, the implication is that prayers for the dead were an impediment to serving the needs of the impotent poor. And Roger Dymoke's reply shows that the needs of the poor (though not mentioned in this seventh clause) were an assumed part of the heretics' case, for he argued that the more colleges and hospitals that were founded, the more people there were to assist the poor.[55]

A careful reading of Dymoke's long book against the 'manifesto' shows how the case for evangelical poverty lay behind the 1395 conclusions. He concentrated his answer to the first point (the church's 'doting' in temporalities) on two matters: first, the necessity of papal government; second, the irrelevance of apostolic poverty to the needs of the church after the period of conversion. Ecclesiastical possessions were necessary for church discipline, 'for the people', said Dymoke (and it reads like a direct dig at the Lollards), 'take no account of the poor and impotent, however just in themselves or in their rule, either to honour or obey them'.[56] Poverty and authority could not be married.

It is interesting too, that Dymoke's arguments against the recommended 100 almshouses suggest he knew more of this idea than conclusion seven alone. He talks about the dangerous suggestion made to parliament (*parliamento suggerebant*) 'that the English church should be despoiled, and that lands and tenements seized from churchmen could fall into the king's power'. No such statement was made in the twelve conclusions. Dymoke also read into this conclusion a deduction about the endowment of knighthood which, on the face of it, he had no reason to think up for the benefit of his own argument. It would be contrary to the king's coronation oath, he wrote, 'if he were to destroy so many churches and colleges, and distribute their goods among knights, as they [the Lollards] seem to recommend by this assertion'. And again, were the Lollards, he asked, so blinded by avarice that they thought 'to enrich knighthood out of church possessions?'[57] Was this Dymoke's own understanding of the expected gain to the 'temporal part', or did he have some other guide to Lollard plans?

A clause that was attached to the almshouse foundations in the bill of 1410, gives us another pointer that links this proposal with long-standing Lollard interests. It ran;

'and also for to ordain that every town throughout the realm should keep all poor men and beggars which may not travail for their sustenance, after the statute made at Cambridge, and, in case at the foresaid commons might not extend for to sustain them, then the foresaid houses of alms might help them'.[58]

The act of the Cambridge Parliament of 1388 here referred to had laid down regulations for the treatment of able-bodied and impotent beggars. The former (in line with the 1349 Ordinance of Labourers) were forbidden alms and to be kept in their place of work, subject to punishment. The impotent, who were allowed to beg, had to remain in their place of residence at the time of the act, or to return to their place of birth.[59] This legislation was of the utmost interest to Lollards, since it accorded with their continuous insistence on the scriptural duty of almsgiving to the truly poor[60] – who were to be assisted by the 100 almshouses. A great deal was said and written by the heretics on this topic, and they turned to their own use the canon law theory that alms should not be given to the able-bodied. They set the whole question in a new context. To explain will be to recapitulate.

One of the challenging questions put by 'Jack Upland' – with whom we started – concerned the friars' slander that Christ begged other men's goods as they did. 'Friar, since in God's law such clamorous begging is utterly forbidden, on what law do you ground you thus for to beg, and namely of [those] poorer than you are yourself?' Friar Daw, in his answer to this important point (mustering his doctors with the help of the Latin he had picked up as manciple of Merton) cited biblical examples in support of the lawfulness of 'clamorous begging', including the blind beggar who called out to Christ and was healed in Luke 18, and the example of Lazarus (Luke 16; 20–22) who 'cried loud' at the rich man's gate to catch his alms.[61]

This rather peculiar phrase, 'clamorous begging', amounted to a technical term. It was explained in the section on begging (*mendicacio*) in the popular Lollard alphabetical repertory, the *Rosarium Theologie*, the full Latin text of which, the *Floretum*, was compiled between 1384 and 1396: the various versions of these compilations were used thereafter well into the fifteenth century. The *Rosarium* classified begging according to a threefold division: *innuitiva*, *insinuativa*, and *declamatoria*, innuitive, insinuative, and declamatory, englished alternatively as 'tokening', 'showing', and 'crying' or 'clamorous' begging. These scholastic terms conveyed the differences between legitimate and illegitimate begging. Innuitive begging – that of Christ – was the direct manifestation, through his visible condition, of 'any poor man and needy'. Insinuative begging included verbal asking, as well as showing. 'It is definitively asking by a needy man for bodily alms', but solely in order to relieve his need. Such asking was lawful for those in true need. The third category, 'clamorous begging' (not glossed but implying persistent crying or pleading) was lawful in two conditions: when a man was in extreme necessity, or when a 'strong man' lacked labour or means to support himself. It was unlawful when it was done voluntarily and habitually, and by 'strong men' not driven by need. Unlawful begging of this kind was to be avoided at all costs.[62]

These distinctions had formed part of Wycliffe's attack on the friars in the *Trialogus*. In Book IV of that work, Phronesis (the 'subtle and mature theologian' who settles the truth) expounds to the conveniently questioning Alithia (speaking for sound philosophy) the blasphemous heresies of the friars. Phronesis deals with three points: the sacrament of the altar, the mendicancy of Christ, and letters of fraternity. The section on mendicancy explains how the begging of the friars is quite unscriptural and emphatically not that of Christ. Wycliffe drew a clear distinction between the innuitive begging of Christ, 'without petition and vocal insinuation', and the friars' vehement begging from the people, 'clamorously' and 'onerously'. He showed that a major part of these mendicants' offence was their begging as 'strong men', 'strong beggars', not driven by genuine need. The phrase *personis validis, mendicos validos* recurs in this discussion. Moreover, the point was pressed home that the *valide mendicans* was taking alms from the very people who were in need of them, from the poor themselves – from the poor blind, needy and feeble of Luke 14.[63]

The *Trialogus* discussion makes plain that this was not the first exposition of this question. In the course of their dialogue Phronesis three times refers Alithia to his vernacular treatment of the blasphemies of the friars. 'Three blasphemies out of many I showed to the people concerning these friars in the vernacular'; and 'I am glad to say about this in Latin what I formerly expressed in English'. At another point he seems to suggest that he is condensing the arguments scored against the friars' defence of mendicancy in his previous work.[64]

As it happens, there survives an English text that exactly fits this description. Thomas Arnold printed in 1871 (from Bodley MS. 647, which was the only copy he had found), a vernacular tract that expounds these same three blasphemies of the friars, entitling it (after Bale) *De Blasphemia, contra Fratres*.[65] The English version does not read like a translation. It uses its sources differently, sometimes changes the order, and introduces fresh illustrative material.[66] But the vernacular tract does make use of the same scriptural passages (with less citation of chapter and verse than the Latin), covers the same ground, and has some close verbal echoes. (For example, the same rather unusual image, 'each knot of a stree' or straw, *nodulum straminis*, is used in either case for comparison with the worshipped host).[67]

Could this text possibly be a rarely authenticated English work by Wycliffe? The thin disguise of Phronesis in the dialogue perhaps allowed for some enhanced freedom of speech, and Wycliffe (though not prone to caution) knew how to hedge his words. Extreme hesitancy is always in order before putting a name – or a date – to Wycliffite vernacular tracts. This is probably as near as we can hope to get to an authorial claim by the evangelical doctor himself, and that is not something to pass over, though it needs more detailed assessment than is possible here.[68] Quite apart from the question of authorship, the relationship of the two texts suggests that the English version may have originated before the meeting of the Blackfriars Council,[69] and the priority of an English over a Latin text is noteworthy.

Thomas Netter, who quotes the English tract (in Latin), took it as Wycliffe's and refers to it alongside the *Trialogus*. He used it to rebuke Wycliffe for his attempt to put a wedge between the begging of the friars and the begging of Christ.[70] The vernacular text pursued even more insistently than the Latin the argument that the friars' begging was not that of Christ because it was clamorous and they were strong beggars. 'To know frauds and falseness of friars, must we know what is begging, and manner of begging'. 'Some beggen of men in word, and some beggen in deed . . . and some cry by word after temporal goods in evil manner, after more than they should have . . . if he wilfully [voluntarily] beg, and has no need, he is a cursed beggar, reproved of God'.[71] Christ was poor and needy and a beggar, but he never asked help in words, vocally.

When the friars turned the tables on Wycliffe, he turned the law of the gospel back on them. He took the accepted canonical distinction between true poor and strong beggars, and placed the friars firmly on the wrong side of the gospel law. There are several contemporary (or near-contemporary) notices of this strategy. The author of the continuation of the *Eulogium Historiarum*, himself very probably a Franciscan, described Wycliffe's determining at Oxford in 1382 against the religious orders, including the argument that 'the begging of able-bodied friars is unlawful, and they should labour for their sustenance . . .'[72] This year Wycliffe's supporters were preaching on the same lines, including Nicholas Hereford at Oxford and William Swinderby at Leicester.

A summary of Hereford's famous sermon, delivered at St. Frideswide's, Oxford, on Ascension Day 1382, survives in an official notarial record. Even this condemnatory report conveys a sense of his impassioned pleading against the temporal failings of all orders in the church, special attention being directed against the acquisitiveness of the religious orders and mendicants. Hereford was at pains to show how founders' wishes were being contravened by the life style (lordly equipages, high houses, and great churches) of the religious, whose excess revenues should be used to help the poor, not spent on the rich and powerful – an abuse of *bona pauperum*. He slated the begging and extortions of the mendicants (particularly those in the university) and the folly of giving money for prayers to intercessors who could only invoke the anger of God. Possessioners and mendicants alike threatened the peace of the realm, and they would never be humbled until their possessions and mendicancy were dealt with. The preacher invoked the community to undertake this task with outstretched hands. If the king were to remove the possessions and riches of these orders as he should, he would not need to tax the poor commons. The sermon ended with a lament that the realm lacked justices (*iusticiarii*) to execute this supreme justice, and so it was left to faithful Christians to take up the work – as Hereford trusted they would – and so perform God's will.[73]

We do not know if William Swinderby used such rousing words. In the sermon he delivered on Palm Sunday, 1382, in Leicester, he certainly attacked the friars, reportedly maintaining that begging by the able-bodied was forbidden in secular law and nowhere sanctioned in evangelical law, that Christ never ordered anyone to beg, and that nobody should give alms to a person better clothed or housed than himself.[74] From this time on, anti-mendicancy was firmly entrenched in Lollard teaching.[75]

Almsgiving was, of course, linked with tithes, and we cannot leave this topic without considering them. It is clear, from the instances I have cited, how often the case against church endowment was associated with tithes. Temporalities and spiritualities were viewed together. The right of temporal lords to remove lands from offending prelates was paired with the right of parishioners to withhold tithes from offending curates. Reginald Pecock later seized on this double issue when, in the third part of his *Repressor*, he set about justifying, at some length, the church's endowments. Two arguments, Pecock saw, had to be answered together: first, that bishops and other clerks who did not live virtuously 'may justly be unpossessed, (that is to say, may justly be put out of possession of the same goods)'; and secondly, the idea that if any clerk failed to fulfil his spiritual office, then the people 'may justly withdraw the tithes and offerings' and all other dues.[76] These were the twin remedies Wycliffe had advocated to cure the church of its ills: the king and secular lords should remove temporalities from offending prelates; the people, 'poor subjects', should withdraw offerings and tithes from offending parish clergy.[77] Behind both recommendations lay the idea of the pristine purity of the evangelical church, combined with the belief that divergence from that state had disinherited Christ's true poor.

At some unknown date Wycliffe addressed himself to a series of eight 'difficult questions' about tithes that had been put to him by a 'distinguished friend'. They included: 'in what land and for what reason were tithes given to knights?'; 'whether before the time of Gregory X Christians were allowed to pay predial and other tithes to the most indigent poor?'; and 'whether it is a sin to give things of the poor to those who are not poor, since, tithes being the tribute of the poor, it seems sacrilege to pay tithes to offending curates?'. Wycliffe fudged his reply to the first question. His answer to the others is more illuminating, and it is worth noting that the last of these three questions is related to the quotation cited by Bankin in 1371 – which goes back to a letter of Jerome. Wycliffe affirmed that tithes are the goods of the poor. Rectors should use them to relieve their people, receiving themselves (the criterion here was 1 Timothy 6;8) sufficient sustenance in food and clothing. But, Wycliffe added, it often happened that poor parishioners thought their curate could live more economically, especially if he laboured like poor laymen and made the most of his temporalities (though that might endanger his pastoral work). There might be a case then, for thinking it 'permissible and meritorious to withdraw tithes from a curate abusing them and to spend them on other pious uses'.[78]

After Wycliffe others were more explicit in saying that tithes could be paid direct to the poor. 'Dymes or tithes are alms or goods of poor men, truly for to be offered', opened the section on this topic in the *Rosarium Theologie*, which ended with a note stating that it was Gregory X who had ordered tithes to be paid to parish churches, instead of being freely disposed of by the payer.[79] There were a number of vernacular texts which made quite clear that the proper destination of tithes was Christ's poor. 'I cannot see by God's law but that tithes may be divided among Christ's poor men, the which Christ tells in the gospel, as poor feeble, and poor lame and poor blind' – categories (those of Luke 14) which should include priests among the foremost.[80] The implication was that the clergy received tithe by virtue of being poor, instead of the poor receiving tithe through the ministry of the clergy. There would seem to have been some justice in bishops accusing Lollards of saying 'that no man is holden to tithe in manner now used of the church, but such tithes and offerings by the law of God should be given to poor needy men'. The prevaricating defence put up against this point argued that if curates were themselves poor and needy, assigning tithes as they should to other poor people, then there would be no harm in rendering such dues to them.[81]

The canon law provision that a proportion of tithes (in England generally accepted as a third, though the initial division was fourfold) should be given to the poor did, of course, provide some genuine basis for these claims. There was, moreover, a body of opinion in early Christian sources which maintained that church property belonged to God and the poor, to be dispensed by churchmen for all those in need. On this theory the clergy's role was that of steward, and there are some early examples of tithes being paid direct to the poor.[82]

There were Lollards who, though not conversant with the whole of the early church precedent, were sure of their ground. Nor were they alone in their persuasion: witness the long-drawn out proceedings against William Russell, warden of the London Greyfriars, who preached publicly in the capital in 1425 'that personal tithes do not fall under the commandment of God's law', and so, 'if custom were not to the contrary, it would be lawful to Christ's people to dispose of them to uses of pity to poor men'.[83]

Poverty was a continuous theme – if not an obsession – in Lollard writings. Naturally it was presented in Gospel terms. The poor man is the only true image of Christ, and the 'wrongs and extortions of poor men'[84] are premised, as Piers Plowman's vision was premised, on a passionate concern for biblical justice. But the hurts of contemporary life were not all described in scriptural terms. Some are sharp with the reality of direct experience. 'I see thine image gone in cold and in heat in clothes all to broken with outen shoon and hosen, an hungered and a thirst': 'poor men wander in storms and sleep with the swine': 'poor needy men that have naked sides and torn sleeves and their children starve for cold': 'poor bedridden men that may not go'[85] – to take a sample of quotations from four different texts. It was this world that the poor preachers professed to share and that, as 'poor men, treasurers of Christ and his apostles', they aspired to reform.

The admissions of their opponents, who repeatedly adverted to Matthew 7 ('beware of false prophets') made it plain that the Lollards, or enough of them to be noticeable, really did present an evangelical appearance. The consensus on this, from a variety of hostile witnesses, is fairly impressive. 'They have nothing more', wrote Dymoke, 'than a certain appearance of humility of posture, in lowering of the head, abandonment of clothing, and pretence of fasting, they pretend simplicity in words, affirming themselves to be burning with love of God and neighbour'.[86] A preacher who, not long after 1390, was able to capitalize on a recently recanted Oxford Wycliffite, glossed the usual verse of Matthew; take heed, said Christ, 'of false prophets, yea, false Lollards, that come to you in clothing of meekness and holy living, for to teach or preach you'. The fact (he went on) that they go 'to-ragged and to-rent and show outward' was no guide to their true hearts.[87] Even Walsingham, writing about the sorry end of Oldcastle's followers, admitted the ostensible 'modesty, patience, humility, and charity, of speech and appearance' which so belied the inner depravity of such men.[88] The likelihood is that this constant harping on the deceptiveness of externals was necessary because the preachers' poverty really did look convincing – and attractive.

Concern for the poor – the truly evangelical poor, not the pseudo-poor – powered the anti-mendicant case. 'For Christ', wrote Wycliffe, 'instituted that men should bodily help the poor and weak, poor and halt, poor and blind, which these sects withdraw by their false inventions baselessly introduced'.[89] The mendicant friars, who were so overburdened with great houses and valuable possessions, maintained that the alms which belonged to the poor feeble men, poor crooked men, poor blind men and poor bedridden men should be given to these hypocrites. The constant criterion was the passage from Luke 14 which I quoted at the beginning, used not only to define the proper recipients of alms, but also to exclude others, distinguishing true beggars from strong beggars – i.e. friars.[90] Thomas Netter, who devoted a chapter of the Doctrinale to this abuse of these verses in Luke's gospel, attacked Wycliffe for the misconstructions he placed on these words. 'Consider O Wycliffe', he wrote, 'how here, no less than elsewhere, you have erred in the gospel of Jesus Christ, by thus promoting the common poor before the holy poor of Christ, namely friars and monks, in taking alms'.[91]

The worst of it – from the Lollards' point of view – was that in failing to imitate the poverty of Christ, these strong beggars expected the poor to support their expensive faults. To be sure, there was plenty to be said about the gross life-style of monks and bishops. But their misuse of temporal possessions seemed to impinge less directly on the poor and more on the upper ranks of society, the well-to-do lords and gentry. If friars 'increase begging with great cry', the chief sufferers were those who could least afford almsgiving, and if 'poor men are defrauded of livelihood, then the friars are much worse than other religious, and are blasphemers against Christ, and are mankillers of poor men, both in bodies and souls'. Friars were to ordinary people what monks and chantrists and collegiate clergy were to gentry – blasphemous despoilers.

> 'Certis it seemeth by open reason and works, visibly, that as religious possessioners destroy knights and squires by amortising of secular lordships, so friars destroy the commons by subtle and needless begging'.[92]

The attack on church ownership was two-pronged. At one level were the temporal endowments of bishoprics, monasteries and colleges, whose lordly estates could only be remedied by lordly means – centrally, with the help of parliament. On another, local level, humble people, by withholding alms and tithes, could take steps towards reforming the mendicants and parish clergy.

Because the idea of parliamentary disendowment had so little positive effect and left no trace in official records, historians have tended to discount such Lollard political aspirations.[93] This seems mistaken. Opponents, as well as supporters, gave serious (sometimes fearful) consideration to disendowment projects;[94] and we can point to several spheres in which statute law and legislation might have encouraged Lollard hopes of parliamentary action.

The examples of the Templars and the alien priories were not missed by Wycliffe and others who mulled over the idea of secularizing church property. When it came to the theory of the case, the idea that all ecclesiastical endowment was conditional, and ultimately secular in origin, was something laymen were not reluctant to believe, and its application could be both general and particular. The rights of lay founders over their religious foundations could seem to lead in a fairly straight line towards the argument that clerical shortcomings were open to correction by responsible laymen.

Founders' rights were safeguarded in law, to the extent that endowments might be reclaimed from a church that was negligent in performing contracted services. Wycliffe insisted on the legal rights of founders, and pointed to the legislation of Edward I. The second Statute of Westminster (1285) made it possible for founders or their heirs to sue by writ of *cessavit* in the lay courts for recovery of lands held by religious houses, in the event of stipulated services not being carried out.

> 'But if the land so given for a chantry, light, feeding the poor, or for the support and doing of other alms, be not alienated but such alms be withdrawn for the space of two years, an action shall lie with the donor or his heir to seek the land so given in demesne, as it is ordained in the Statute of Gloucester . . .'[95]

An example of such an action is that taken in 1341 by Margaret de Roos, who regained lands granted to the abbey of Creake in Norfolk, because the abbot had failed to provide the services specified in the endowment charter – including singing masses in the chapel of Margaret's foundation and daily liveries of bread to the poor.[96] Another such case was that brought in 1387 against the abbot of St Osyth in Essex by Robert Hotot, for recovery of sixty acres of land, on the grounds that for two years the abbey had failed to find a chaplain to celebrate commemorative masses in a chapel in Stowmarket, Suffolk. This foundation was already over a century old, having been established by Herlwin Hotot in the time of Henry III, and six generations of Hotots lay between Herlwin and his heir who brought this action in the King's Bench under Richard II.[97] Time was no bar to the sense of property in founders' heirs – witness pleas voiced at the dissolution. And those who were so conscious of their rights over individual religious houses might have been persuaded to think in terms of correcting offending institutions as a class.

Bishops' temporalities (the 'great manors, castles, and . . . great lordships of baronies', as Pecock defined them)[98] clearly presented an easy target for secular resumption. Their post-reformation history shows the eventual implementation of such a policy. It was advocated long before. The Lollard tacticians who thought of episcopal confiscation in 1410 and (perhaps) 1404, were enlarging on suggestions of Wycliffe, who in several works indicated the advantages of such disendowment. 'The king', he pointed out, 'often took into his hands the temporalities of his clergy'. 'It is not strange for kings to correct clerks'.[99] Not only was the king able to remove temporal possessions, movable and immovable, from clergy who were guilty of treason or other crimes. He was also in a position to retain during pleasure the temporalities of bishops when these came into his hands in the normal course of events. Wycliffe explained more than once that a means to the gradual reconquest of antichrist would be for the king to retain such temporal lordships permanently, thereby preventing them from ever returning to mortmain. The live hand (*manus viva*) could thus eventually cheat the dead hand (*manus mortua*).[100] This, moreover, should be through action in parliament. Among the examples of such contemporary parliamentary forfeiture, one that must have brought special satisfaction to Lollards was the case of Henry Despenser, whose temporalities were taken into the king's hands for two years after the failure of his much vilified crusade.[101]

Another matter on which it was reasonable to seek parliamentary remedy was appropriation. The damage done to parochial almsgiving by the appropriation of benefices, on which Lollard writers harped so insistently, was also a topic of parliamentary concern. Petitions about this were presented on a number of occasions; and one of 1391, alleging the loss of charity, hospitality, and other aid to poor parishioners caused by appropriations, had some effect. It resulted in a statute providing that when licences were issued in chancery for appropriating parish churches, the diocesan should allocate an annual proportion of the revenues in aid of 'the poor parishioners of the said churches', as well as making adequate endowment for the vicar.[102] Complaints continued thereafter, but there were clearly grounds for looking hopefully to lords and commons for support over this problem, and this parliamentary record ought to be placed beside the 1395 conclusions and Archbishop Arundel's reported diversionary reforms of 1399.

Concern for the plight of the poor – even in parliamentary legislation – was not motivated only by fears of 'perturbation of the realm'.[103] Alongside the rights of king, patrons, founders, and benefice holders over church endowments, there floated another continent of claimants – not necessarily unrepresented. If it was possible for Lollards to regard the statute of 1388 as constructive legislation for the poor, there were many others whose desire to help the deprived was in no way tangled with heresy.

For those touched by Lollard evangelism, service to Christ's poor was a call that rose above the hostile skirmishings against friars and possessioners. Christ taught, Wycliffe admonished, referring yet again to that well-worked passage in Luke, 'how we ought to give bodily alms to the poor blind, the poor halt, and the poor feeble, and as a result to oblige other strong beggars to work . . . But how can the universal and perpetual endowment of the church consort with this rule of Christ?'[104] The overall endowment of the church may not have been much affected, but we know of a number of almsgivers and payers of tithe who acted on such teaching.

Sir Thomas Latimer (followed by his wife Anne) showed concern in his will for the triple categories of gospel poor, the feeble, blind, and crooked – Wycliffe's 'trinity of the poor',[105] as Netter disparagingly dubbed it. Neither husband nor wife made any bequests to any religious, or requests for prayers for their souls.[106] Two other fifteenth-century knights who were Lollard sympathizers, Sir Thomas Broke of Holditch in Devon and his son, another Thomas, were also mindful of the 'poor, blind or lame man or woman' – likewise to the exclusion of soul masses and gifts to mendicants.[107] Humbler believers in these priorities included Anne Palmer, encountered earlier.[108] And among those who helped to spread the view that tithes might legitimately be transferred from possessioner clergy to indigent poor was William White, in the diocese of Norwich. He admitted in 1428 to having taught that tithes could be withdrawn, providing this was done prudently, since from Christ's passion until Gregory X the people only gave tithes to the poor – which meant proper beggars, since mendicant friars were not then in existence. A certain Thomas Plowman, shipman of Sizewell in Suffolk, seems to have taken this teaching to heart. He confessed in 1430 that he had been giving his tithes to the poor in the belief that this was lawful.[109]

Though the issues and motives for disendowing the church were mixed, the question of the poor was visible throughout. Poverty was a theme that truly transcended the divergence between secular and religious – and for that matter the mutual mistrust between clerical and lay, orthodox and heterodox. It was one of the moving debates of the time. There are periods when poverty is in vogue, and the manner of being poor is also subject to the constraints of fashion. Whereas the eleventh century had seen (as Michel Mollat puts it) a sort of 'exaltation of the dignity of the poor',[110] the late fourteenth and fifteenth centuries witnessed impassioned pleading on behalf of the miseries of the poor. Evangelical poverty was now as much a criterion for redressing social injustice as for imitating Christ, and mendicancy promoted a revaluation of poverty. The contemporary poor were held up as a mirror for would-be imitators of Christ. Poverty was still holy, but far too much of it seemed to be the result of the most unholy misappropriation and neglect.

Revulsion against the temporal possessions of the English church in the fifteenth century existed on many levels, and manifested itself in various ways and places. It reached the political arena by both stealth and direct assault, with largely negative results. The broad appeal of the issue ensured both the continuity of these efforts and, paradoxically, their ultimate failure. The parliamentary approach was pushed off course by the popular one. The call to disendow – Caim's Castles and monastic nests alike – was heard more widely than a mere survey of paper projects and parliamentary gestures might suggest.[111]

Let me end with the planning of a great feast, that pulls some of these different strands together.

On 1 August 1424, a great reception was ordered to take place in the hall of the bishop's palace at Lincoln. Four hundred poor people from the area were to be brought in, given meals of varying quality, sums of money of between 20d and 4d, and a pair of shoes each. Another hundred 'most needy' poor were to be given clothing as well as all the rest. This largesse to the indigent poor of Lincolnshire owed nothing to the reigning bishop, Richard Fleming. Indeed one may wonder how he viewed this projected invasion of his residence. It was ordained as funeral ceremony by the will of Fleming's predecessor, Philip Repingdon, or Repton, the sometime Wycliffite, who four years earlier had taken the extraordinary step of resigning his see.[112]

When he came to make his will, Repton's mind turned back with some remorse to his days of prelatical dignity. He wanted this ceremony at Lincoln to be (as he put it) 'in remission of the sins of worldly vanity committed by me in that place'. Concern for the poor was virtually the sole preoccupation of Repton's will, which contains not a word about masses for his soul after death, gave not a mite to any religious order or foundation. All his worldly goods, down to the last penny, halfpenny, and farthing, were allocated to the poor of Lincoln.[113]

In making this will Repton could have taken as his blue-print a sermon of Wycliffe's on the gospel of the *Missa pro defunctis*, which had explained how burial of the dead was, or could be, one of the seven corporal works of mercy. To be so it should avoid elaborate exequies, sumptuous burial, and fulsome sermonizing for the dead, bequests to friars for soul masses, and to religious houses in perpetual alms. Such spending as there was on funeral feasts should be modelled on Christ's words in Luke 14; 'call not thy friends, neither thy brethren, neither thy kinsmen, nor thy rich neighbours . . . but call poor men and feeble and blind and crooked', distributing largesse to the most needy. Could executors, asked Wycliffe, do better than follow the law of God?[114]

Did Repton's executors carry out his wishes? I do not know. Repton himself, committing this funeral feast of the poor to a trusted group of friends, acknowledged that works of charity met with many obstacles and setbacks.[115] The events of his lifetime had proved that, witness all the proposed schemes to redistribute the wealth of Caim's castles. But the fact that they got nowhere should not be allowed to obscure the genuinely idealistic charitable aims that were present, together with materialistic interests, in these proposals. Behind the stream of polemic and discontinuities of politics lay a truly evangelical commitment to the poor. Philip Repton was not alone in showing that there were more ways of championing Christ against Cain than petitioning parliament.

Notes

*   I am grateful for the contributions made at the delivery of this paper, not all of which could be acknowledged below. I also thank Anne Hudson for her comments and suggestions, and for sending me manuscript material.

1. St. Jerome, Epist. 66, §8; *Corpus Scriptorum Ecclesiasticorum Latinorum*, liv (Vienna & Leipzig, 1910), 657.

2. *Joannis Wiclif Trialogus*, ed. G. Lechler (Oxford, 1869), 348–9.

3. *Jack Upland, Friar Daw's Reply, and Upland's Rejoinder*, ed. P.L. Heyworth (Oxford, 1968), 57–8, 76. On the development of allegations of friars' seduction (spiritual and physical) see A. Williams, 'Chaucer and the Friars', *Speculum*, xxviii (1953), 511–13; E.D. McShane, *A Critical Appraisal of the Antimendicantism of John Wyclif* (Rome, 1950), 32.

4. *The Wycliffe Bible Commentary*, ed. C.F. Pfeiffer and E.F. Harrison (London & Edinburgh, 1963), 9. For typical remarks on the cupidity of Cain see FitzRalph's *De Pauperie Salvatoris*, ed. R.L. Poole (WS, 1890), 328, 369, 399; *EWW* , 374, 'cayme, that is possession . . .' This tract against clerical property, here citing a sermon of Odo of Cheriton, links Cain's false possession with the poisoning of the church by Constantine (see below note 20), interpreting 'Am I my brother's keeper?' (Gen. 4;9) as 'What charge is to me of the souls, so that I have well ordained for the temporal goods'. Jude 1:11, commonly cited in this context, coupled Cain with Balaam in the avarice/false possession stakes; *The Lanterne of Li3t*, ed. L.M. Swinburn (EETS, OS 151, 1917), 16, 132; cf. Reginald Pecock, *The Repressor of Over Much Blaming of the Clergy*, ed. C. Babington (RS, 1860), ii, 480.

5. A theme made familiar in plays of Cain; e.g. *The Chester Mystery Cycle*, ed. R.M. Lumiansky and D. Mills (EETS, SS 3, 1974), 33–41; in *The Towneley Plays*, ed. G. England and A.W. Pollard (EETS, ES 71, 1897), 14–17, Abel's 'trussell' which burns so easily is contrasted with Cain's sheaves containing 'thistles and briars' which only smoked.

6. This paragraph owes much to Pearl F. Braude, '"Cokkel in oure Clene Corn": Some Implications of Cain's Sacrifice', in *No Graven Images: Studies in Art and the Hebrew Bible*, ed. J. Gutmann (New York, 1971), 559–599, reprinted from *Gesta*, vii (1968), 15–28, which shows how both brothers' sacrifices came to be represented by bundles of wheat (adulterated and pure), whereas earlier images more accurately portrayed a sheaf and a lamb. Cf. also O.F. Emerson, 'Legends of Cain, especially in Old and Middle English', *Pubs. of the Modern Language Assn. of America*, xxi (1906), 831–929; *Middle English Dictionary*, ed. H. Kurath and S.M. Kuhn (Ann Arbor, 1954–), *s.v.* 'Caim'.

7. 'vagus et profugus eris super terram'; Gen. 4:12 (cf. *Chester Mystery Cycle*, 38 'idell and wandringe as an theyfe'). For this association see P.R. Szittya, 'The antifraternal Tradition in Middle English Literature', *Speculum*, lii (1977), 312; Wycliffe, *Trialogus*, 437.

8. *Tractatus de Mandatis Divinis*, ed. J. Loserth and F.D. Matthew (WS, 1922), 372. On Judas as the epitome of venality see J. A. Yunck, *The Lineage of Lady Meed* (Notre Dame, Ind., 1963), 3, 26, 35, 100–1, 125–6, 136, 243–4, 259, 267.

9. *Trialogus*, 361–2. (The historical element in this criticism deserves notice). Cf. 306 for Wycliffe's use of the term 'Caymitica institutio' to describe the wrong (covetous) sort of clerical possession. The term Jacobites for the Dominicans (derived from the Paris convent of St. Jacques) was established usage; W.R. Thomson, 'The Image of the Mendicants in the Chronicles of Matthew Paris', *AFH*, lxx (1977), 16; A.G. Rigg, 'Two Latin Poems against the Friars', *Mediaeval Studies*, xxx (1968), 111–12.

10. *Historical Poems of the XIVth and XVth Centuries*, ed. R.H. Robbins (New York, 1959), 160,

333. The ascribed date is based on the Latin poem (cited in note 73 below) that precedes this in the manuscript, and which describes the Earthquake Council. As these are not paired poems the deduction is doubtful. Another poem that uses the acrostic is *Mum and the Sothsegger*, ed. M. Day and R. Steele (EETS, OS 199, 1936), 41–2. This is interesting in that it attributes the acrostic to FitzRalph, and (losing sight of Wycliffe's historical criticism of mendicant foundations) uses the four initials to signify vices (crooked Carmelites, amorous Austins, Judas-like Jacobites, 'monsyd' = cursed-working Minorities). As the editors point out (115), there is no support for the attribution to FitzRalph. For a systematic attack on the four orders of friars which impugns their false foundation claims see *Pierce the Ploughmans Crede*, ed. W.W. Skeat (EETS, OS 30, 1867), 3, 10, 12, 15.

11. *Sermones*, ed. J. Loserth (WS, 1887–90), ii, 84, quoted by McShane, op. cit., 15. For Wycliffe referring to himself as *quidam fidelis* see A. Hudson, 'A Lollard sect vocabulary?', in *So meny people longages and tonges: philological essays*, ed. M. Benskin and M.L. Samuels (Edinburgh, 1981), 17; *Polemical Works*, ed. R. Buddensieg (WS, 1883), ii, 692, cf. 671 and below note 89. For another allusion to the acrostic see the fiercely antimendicant letter *'De fratribus ad scholares'* in *Opera Minora*, ed. J. Loserth (WS, 1913), 15 ('. . . *nomine Caym quatuor Fratum ordines in se continens*. . .'). There are two questions here; who first applied Cain's false possession specifically to the friars, and who devised the acrostic to emphasize this? I have not found FitzRalph doing either, but the origin of this Caimite antimendicant vocabulary is elusive and all that can be said with certainty is that it was after 1382 that it became prominent, and acquired heretical associations. Wycliffe's laboured play on the letters and syllables of C-A-R-D-I-N-A-L-I-S in *De Blasphemia*, ed. M.H. Dziewicki (WS, 1893), 65–80, is on the same lines as the C-A-I-M device. Both Thomas Netter (a Carmelite) and William Woodford (a Franciscan) attacked Wycliffe for his fatuous Caim acrostic, pointing out that Cain not Caim was the proper ancient form (and, as Netter indicated, the N belonged to the Hebrew word for acquisition). Wycliffe did in fact use both forms (cf. *Supplementum Trialogi* in *Trialogus*, 437, 444). See Thomas Netter, *Doctrinale*, ed. B. Blanciotti (Venice, 1757-9), i. cols. 614–16; *Fasciculus Rerum Expetendarum et Fugiendarum*, ed. E. Brown (London, 1690), i. 264–5.

12. '. . . *ad aedificationem domorum humilium pauperibus sint dispersae*'; *Supplementum Trialogi*, 444–5.

13. *Polemical Works*, i, 39–40, cf. 194–5. *Castrum caymiticum* and *castra caimitica* also appear in *Opus Evangelicum*, ed. J. Loserth (WS, 1895–6), i, 349, and *Tractatus de Officio Pastorali*, ed. G.V. Lechler (Leipzig, 1863), 38. Cf. Netter, *Doctrinale*, i, cols. 614–16 on Wycliffe's use of the term, including the objection that Caim built a city (Gen. 4:17), not castles. Wycliffe said as much himself (*Supplementum Trialogi*, 444). Cf. Augustine, *De Civitate Dei*, Lib. xv, cap. 1, and for the Cain-and-Abel prototyping of the two cities passing into the Apocalyptic doctrine of the two churches see R. Bauckham, *Tudor Apocalypse* (Appleford, 1978), 55–62.

14. *SEW*, iii, 398–9, 241, 348, (cf. 353 on friars' foundation claims).

15. *EWW*, 419–20, 425, cf. 448–9. On Chapter 9 of this text (where this first quotation appears) cf. Netter, op. cit., i, col. 614, citing Wycliffe's *'de cura Pastorali'*, cap. ix. Netter's citation – though the order is different – is much closer to the English text than anything I have found in the Latin *De Officio Pastorali*.

16. *EWW*, 478 ('De Papa'); cf. 129 ('Of clerks possessioners'), and 211 ('How Satan and his children') for other instances.

17. Ibid., 448 ('De officio pastorali'); cf. 14, 'parish churches fall down for default' while false religious 'make new churches as castles without need'; 322 ('Tractatus de pseudo-freris') friars' church buildings ('castle of the fiend') 'destroy holier old places'; *SEW*, iii, 369, 'great cloisters and costly, as Caim's Castles' (friary churches).

18. There are some indications that the phrase was used to condemn non-parochial churches before 1380. Lechler thought that *De Officio Pastorali* was written before then, and the English work of that title says (*EWW*, 457) 'the pope dwelleth in Avignon' (which places it

before 1378), and the English tract 'De papa' (ibid., 461) refers to 'division of these popes that is now late fallen'.

19. A.K. McHardy, 'Bishop Buckingham and the Lollards of Lincoln Diocese', *SCH*, ix (1972), 143. Cf. the view abjured by John Skilly of Flixton (Suffolk) in 1429; 'that material churches be but of little avail and ought to be but of little reputation, for every man's prayer said in the field is as good as the prayer said in the church': *Heresy Trials in the Diocese of Norwich*, ed. N.P. Tanner (CS, 4th Series, 20, 1977), 58, cf. 53.

20. McHardy, art. cit., 141,143–4. On the legend of the poisoning of the church (which goes back to the thirteenth century, if not earlier) see W. Farr, *John Wyclif as Legal Reformer* (Leiden, 1974), 48–9; P. Gradon 'Langland and the Ideology of Dissent', *PBA*, lxvi (1980), 185. (My paper, which was written before I had read this most valuable lecture, overlaps with its arguments on several points).

21. McHardy, art. cit., 144–5.

22. Luke 14; 13, 21. 'Sed cum facis convivium, voca pauperes, debiles, claudos, et caecos . . . Exi cito in plateas et vicos civitatis, et pauperes ac debiles, et caecos et claudos introduc huc'. *The Holy Bible*, ed. J. Forshall and F. Madden (Oxford, 1850), iv, 196–7. As I show below (pp. 62, 65) the use (or as others thought, abuse) of this passage made and makes it a clue pointing to Lollard sympathies – not necessarily at all the same as heresy. This may be specially clear from the wording – though the biblical allusion has often passed unrecognized by modern editors. For where Luke might seem to indicate *four* classes of poor, feeble, lame, and blind, a frequent (not invariable) Wycliffite reading was *three* different classes of poor: poor feeble, poor lame, and poor blind. 'Christ hath limited in his law who should have such alms, – poor men and blind, poor men and lame, poor men and feeble' (*SEW*, iii, 170, cf. 293, 372); 'Christ biddeth men thus to do alms to poor feeble and lame and blind' (*EWW*, 421, cf. 27); cf. *Jack Upland*, 59, 121; *Selections from English Wycliffite Writings*, ed. A. Hudson (Cambridge, 1978), 95, 1. 75: and see below notes 91, 105. The dominical gospels glossed in York Chapter MS XVI.D.2 include a long commentary on these verses of Luke 14 (second Sunday after Trinity, fos. 141ᵛ–143ᵛ) which is moderate in tone and keeps the fourfold division of 'poor men, and feeble and blind and crooked', while making it clear that the rich were excluded and the poor were the chosen. 'God chesith hem, which the world dispiseth . . . for syk men and dispisid in this world bi so myche heren hastiliere the vois of god' (fo. 142ᵛ). The 'simple servant' sent to bid men to the supper (with its resurrection implications – 'the supper that is at the end of the world'), is here interpreted as none but 'the order of preachers'. Cf. the three categories in the text for this day in the Wycliffite sermon-cycle: '*and bring into this feast* these three manner of men: *poor feeble men, poor blind men and poor lame men* – these three are God's prisoners that both God and man help with alms'. *English Wycliffite Sermons*, ed. Anne Hudson, i (Oxford, 1983), 230.

23. *Selections*, ed. Hudson, 31.

24. 'Hinc est ut dolentes vobis referimus quiddam nuper accidit a fundamentis universitatis hactenus insuetum quod expressam altissimi sapit iniuriam ecclesie preiudicium manifestis-sime comminatur ac etiam ecclesiastice libertati notabiliter est adversum. Insurrexit enim quidam qui suadente diabolo in scolis puplice determinavit contra possessiones ecclesie dampnabiliter invehendo licere quibuscunque ecclesiarum fundatoribus propter clericorum abusus bona deo et ecclesie dedicata auferre et eadem secularibus et militibus conferre et simpliciter applicare. Secundo quod decime ecclesie magis debentur fratribus mendicantibus quam curatis que quidem ex rumore vulgari et clamore communi scolarium theologie ac etiam ex notorietate clara facti concepimus prout lator presencium vestram reverenciam poterit plenius informare . . . nec possumus eum compellere ad revocacionem publicam, nec ad aliquam aliam penam propter confidenciam quam habet in magnatibus de regno, quos dicit velle se defendere in hac causa . . .' Sidney Sussex College, Cambridge, MS 64, fo. 126ᵛ. See K. Walsh, *A Fourteenth-Century Scholar and Primate. Richard FitzRalph in Oxford, Avignon and Armagh* (Oxford, 1981), 436, to which I owe knowledge of this source. Walsh

says the disputant advocated the abolition of tithes, but this seems to be a slip. For the story that the 1409 bull, *Regnans in excelsis*, granted friars the right to tithes see F.X. Martin, 'An Irish Augustinian disputes at Oxford: Adam Payn, 1402', in *Scientia Augustiniana. Studien über Augustinus, den Augustinismus und den Augustinerorden. Festschrift . . . Adolar Zumkeller*, ed. C.P. Mayer (Würzburg, 1975), 306; cf. *SEW*, iii, 175; 'friars . . . would that these dimes were given unto them'.

25.   *Munimenta Academica*, ed. H. Anstey (RS, 1868), i, 208–11; Walsh, op. cit., 436–7; A.G. Little, *The Grey Friars in Oxford* (Oxford Historical Society, xx, 1891), 81–2. John was said to have propounded these views in his winter lectures this year (*'in quadam determinatione sua hyemali'*), which presumably means late 1357 or early 1358 and would fit with the March 1358 date for the letter to FitzRalph.

26.   V.H. Galbraith, 'Articles laid before the Parliament of 1371', *EHR*, xxxiv (1919), 579–82; A. Gwynn, *The English Austin Friars in the time of Wyclif* (Oxford, 1940), 212–16 (proposing Ashborne as the unnamed friar); K.B. McFarlane, *John Wycliffe and the Beginnings of English Nonconformity* (1952), 45–6, 59–60; J.H. Dahmus, *The Prosecution of John Wyclyf* (New Haven, Conn., 1970), 8–9; Gradon, art. cit., 187–9. On Bankin and Ashborne see *BRUO*, i, 54, 104.

27.   The well-known passage from St. Ambrose (Galbraith, art. cit., 581) on selling chalices and church ornaments to redeem prisoners of war was exploited by Wycliffe in the same context; *De Civili Dominio*, ii, ed. J. Loserth (WS, 1900), 28–9; cf. Gratian's *Decretum*, Pt I, Dist. 86, c.xviii, in *Corpus Iuris Canonici*, ed. E. Friedberg (Leipzig, 1879–81), i, col. 302. See B. Tierney, *Medieval Poor Law. A Sketch of Canonical Theory and its Application in England* (Berkeley and Los Angeles, 1959), 32–3, for the influential *Glossa ordinaria* of Joannes Teutonicus explaining the statement 'according to natural law all things are common', by reference to the obligation of charity; 'that is they are to be shared in time of necessity'.

28.   *De Civili Dominio*, ii, 7; McFarlane, op. cit., 46; cf. T.J. Hanrahan, 'John Wyclif's Political Activity', *Mediaeval Studies*, xx (1958), 157–8 (arguing that this remark could equally well be applied to the parliament of Jan. 1377). Cf. *Opera Minora*, 424–5 (Wycliffe's reply to William Binham of (?) late 1373) on views of the right to withdraw temporalities which *'olim fuissent in parlamento dominorum Anglie ventilata'*, and on the arguments used *'in quodam consilio a dominis secularibus'*. These remarks (which show Wycliffe in close touch with events at Westminster) might be related either to the parliament of 1371 or the council of 1373.

29.   For the remark about sacrilege and the poor, originally Jerome's, see note 1 above, and below p. 60. This, and other remarks of Jerome incorporated in the *Decretum* on the clergy's duty to be content with food and clothing (1 Tim. 6:8), and that 'whatever the clergy has belongs to the poor' were 'almost proverbial among the canonists'; Tierney, op. cit., 76; *Corpus Iuris Canonici*, i, cols. 677–8 (*Decretum*, Pt. II, causa 12, quest. 1, ccv–vii). Cf. Wycliffe, *De Civili Dominio*, i, ed. R.L. Poole (WS, 1885), 353; *'nemo potest donare quidquam ecclesie nisi sub condicione ut serviat Deo in gracia'* – a condition that was broken by the abuse of *bona pauperum*.

30.   J.I. Catto, 'An alleged Great Council of 1374', *EHR*, lxxxii (1967), 764–771; *Eulogium Historiarum*, ed. F.S. Haydon (RS, 1858–63), iii, 337–9. On Mardisley see Little, *Grey Friars in Oxford*, 242; idem, *Studies in English Franciscan History* (Manchester, 1917), 53–4; and see above, p. 39 (note 37).

31.   Wycliffe's view that the king and temporal lords could justly remove goods from an offending church was attacked, well before the papal condemnation of 1377, by the two Benedictines Uthred of Boldon and William Binham. These texts do not survive but we have Wycliffe's reply (above note 28) called the 'Determinatio' (*Opera Minora*, 405–30). McFarlane, op. cit., 62–3 dated this controversy 1372–3; G.A. Holmes, *The Good Parliament* (Oxford, 1975), 168, cf. 14, puts Wycliffe's reply in the latter part of 1373. For Thomas Brinton referring in a sermon of probably April 1375 to the view that goods of churches and monasteries could be removed see *Sermons of Thomas Brinton*, ed. M.A. Devlin (CS, 3rd series, lxxxv, 1954), 48.

Cf. also Gwynn, op cit., 72; Dahmus, op. cit., 22–3; Gradon, art. cit., 182; *Fasciculi Zizaniorum*, ed. W.W. Shirley (RS, 1858), 241.

32. G. Leff, 'John Wyclif: The Path to Dissent', *PBA*, lii (1966), 162–3, 169, 171–3; Cf. M. Wilks, '*Reformatio regni*: Wyclif and Hus as leaders of religious protest movements', *SCH*, ix (1972), 118, on 'Wyclif's obsessive demands for the confiscation of clerical wealth', which have been considered in many other works.

33. Temporalities were a matter of heresy, as well as error, and these two errors (nos. 17 and 18) follow on the heresy (no. 10) of asserting it to be against scripture for men of church to have temporal possessions. Clause 17 also includes the secular correlative 'that the people can at will correct offending lords' (on which see Wycliffe's comments in *Trialogus*, 377). Thomas Walsingham, *Historia Anglicana*, ed. H.T. Riley (RS, 1863–4), ii, 58–9; *Fasc. Ziz.*, 279–81, 494–6; *Concilia*, iii, 157–8; trans. in Workman, op. cit., ii, 416–17.

34. For the points concerning temporalities condemned in the 1377 bulls, including no. 6; 'If God is, temporal lords may legitimately and meritoriously remove goods of fortune from an offending church', see *Chronicon Angliae*, ed. E.M. Thompson (RS, 1874), 182; and for Wycliffe's defence of them, ibid., 186, 188–9; *Fasc. Ziz.*, 248–9, 254–6. Clause 6 was taken from Bk. I, cap. xxxvii of *De Civili Dominio*, i, 267, cf. ii, 5 *et seq.*

35. Cf. ibid., i, 340–1. In this part of Bk. I, caps. xli–xlii, Wycliffe was mainly concerned with the use of excommunication as a sanction for tithes. See *Sermones*, iii, 471; *Selections*, ed. Hudson, 147; and below, p. 60.

36. *Fasc. Ziz.*, 286.

37. *Trialogus*, 377; for other condemnations of the council see 339, 374–6, 445, 447; cf. *Fasc. Ziz.*, 283–5. The fact that these allusions only appear in Bk. IV (and the *Supplementum Trialogi*) helps to indicate the stages of the book's composition.

38. *SEW*, iii, 233–4; cf. 175 (attacking the council's view of tithes), and *Pierce the Ploughmans Crede*, 20. Of course eucharistic differences were also critical.

39. *SEW*, iii, 508–23 (quoted at 508, 519, 515). For the Latin version attributed to Wycliffe see I. H. Stein, 'The Wyclif Manuscript in Florence', *Speculum*, v (1930), 97; idem, 'The Latin Text of Wyclif's *Complaint*', *Speculum*, vii (1932), 87–94 (at 88, 91, 93). This text has been linked with the seven *imprecaciones* in *De Blasphemia*, 270–1 – heads of reforming proposals which Walsingham set in the parliament of May 1382; *Historia Anglicana*, ii, 51–2; Workman, op. cit., ii, 250–2; *DNB*, *s.n.* Wycliffe. The grounds for connecting these texts are extremely slim, as they overlap on only one point (confiscation of temporalities), and the dating of the four-point address remains conjectural.

40. *Historia Anglicana*, ii, 139–40; J. Dahmus, *William Courtenay* (University Park and London, 1966), 166–7.

41. *Rogeri Dymmok Liber Contra XII Errores et Hereses Lollardorum*, ed. H.S. Cronin (WS, 1922), 25, 30; *Selections*, ed Hudson, 24. Dymoke's reply to the first conclusion (cf. below. p. 56) says nothing about appropriated churches, which one might read as central to this grievance, given the repeated complaints in Lollard texts about the loss of charity and pastoral care through appropriation. See above pp. 48, 53; *SEW*, iii, 215–16; *EWW*, 223; *Selections*, ed. Hudson, 65–6, 172–3; *Remonstrance against Romish Corruptions in the Church*, ed. J. Forshall (London, 1851), 10–12, 93; Workman, *Wyclif*, ii, 95–6, 410. The phrase in the preamble, 'poor men treasurers of Christ', was taken up in the papal letters of Sept. 1395; *CPL*, iv, 515. Of the five conclusions singled out for papal condemnation, one was the view that founding prayers for the dead was false alms.

42. B.P. Wolffe, *The Royal Demesne in English History* (1971), 76–86, Appendix 'B', 245–7; cf. J.S. Roskell, 'Sir John Cheyne of Beckford', *Trans. Bristol and Gloucs. Arch. Soc.*, lxxv (1956), 58–60, 64–7; idem, *The Commons and their Speakers in English Parliaments, 1376–1523* (Manchester, 1965), 136–7, 354–5; *Rot Parl.*, iii, 424b.

43. *Annales Ricardi Secundi et Henrici Quarti*, ed. H.T. Riley (RS, 1866), 290, 391–4. Cf. (in support of Walsingham's report of this convocation) *Concilia*, iii, 242, somewhat misreading

Reg. Arundel (Lambeth), i, fo. 53ᵛ, ii, fo. 5ʳ which reports the clergy's petition against illicit intentions among the laity who, reportedly spurred on by Lollards, 'intendant contra prelatos et alios viros ecclesiasticos in presenti parliamento novas constitutiones seu statuta facere, edere, et introducere, contra ecclesie libertatem que non constituciones sed pocius destituciones immo destrucciones merito dici possunt': *Historia Anglicana*, ii, 239 et seq., 265–7. Relevant to the continuing debate is Richard Ullerston's *Defensorium Dotacionis Ecclesie*, dated 1401 in the surviving manuscripts, which mentioned the question 'utrum omnes clerici corpore validi ad laborem manuum obligantur': Anne Hudson, 'The Debate on Bible Translation, Oxford 1401', *EHR*, xc (1975), 10.

44. Did the release this year of several Lollard suspects from prison (where Cheyne had also been) have some effect on this stand? (cf. my 'Lollardy and Sedition' in *Peasants, Knights and Heretics*, ed. R.H. Hilton [Cambridge, 1976], 294–5). While the circumstances of 1399 (on which see Professor Storey below, p. 89) might have circumscribed any such manoeuvres, a proposed resumption (as some saw it) of clerical temporalities would have arisen naturally in 1404. It should be pointed out, too, that though he made some slips in the *Annales*, it was only in his condensed restrospective account in the *Historia Anglicana* that Walsingham (now omitting the 1399 convocation report), switched his tale of Cheyne's anticlericalism to 1404. It may be that his memory faulted him in thus combining two events because of the similarity of the two occasions: i.e. talk of clerical deprivation (not a rare parliamentary occurrence!) possibly occurred in both 1399 and 1404. (There is no evidence of Cheyne being a member of the Coventry Parliament; cf. Roskell, art. cit., 65).

45. For this text and its various versions see *Selections*, ed. Hudson, 135–7, 203–7; modernized in *English Historical Documents, IV, 1327–1485*, ed. A.R. Myers (1969), 668–70. The variants in the different versions, especially the garbled place-names and discrepancies in the arithmetic, indicate that we only have imperfect transcriptions.

46. *Chronicles of London*, ed. C.L. Kingsford (Oxford, 1905), xxv, 65; *Selections*, ed. Hudson, 135. For an attempt to make sense of the arithmetic see Kingsford's notes, 295–6.

47. If we suppose that the bishop of 'Chestre' means Coventry and Lichfield, all seventeen bishoprics of England are named; the only Welsh one listed is St. Davids. The Latin text in *The St. Albans Chronicle 1406–1420*, ed. V. H. Galbraith (Oxford, 1937), 54, makes it clear that Carlisle, Chichester, and Rochester are listed as bishoprics; cf. *Selections*, ed. Hudson, 136 and note on 11. 77–8.

48. Ibid., 204–5, 207. Wycliffe's calculation that the friars cost the realm £40,000 (or 60,000 marks) *per annum* appears in several of his works, and in *De Quattuor Sectis Novellis* he proposed an annual levy on them by the king of 1000 marks or more; *Polemical Works*, i, 255–6, cf. 28, 192–3, 244; *Trialogus*, 369. On the taxing of exempt religious see *Jack Upland*, 10.

49. Tierney, *Medieval Poor Law*, 86, 155; *Selections*, ed. Hudson, 135, 137, 205; 'and c houses of almesse mo thanne he hath now at this tyme. . .' Dymoke's estimate of the colleges and hospices which had care of souls and the poor was 'perhaps more than one or two thousand'; *Rogeri Dymmok Liber*, 175.

50. *Chronicles of London*, xxxviii. The universities do not feature in Fabian's version, or in that attached (wrongly, according to Anne Hudson) to the 1431 rebellion; *Selections*, 204, and cf. 206 on 1. 68. The *St. Albans Chronicle*, 54–5, mentions only five universities and implies that the 15,000 priests and clerks were to be provided for there (i.e. in study).

51. *Selections*, ed. Hudson, 136 and 206, note on 1, 64. However, this comes from a late version and (see previous note) there is an ambiguity about this suggestion, which perhaps belongs with Lollard ideas on schooling preachers.

52. Ibid., 137: Hudson, 'A Lollard sect vocabulary?' (note 11 above), 20–21.

53. *Fasc. Ziz.*, 393 (reporting that Purvey invoked king, lords, and commons to implement these proposals). On the problem of dating this source see *Selections*, ed. Hudson, 204; A. Hudson, 'John Purvey: A Reconsideration of the evidence for his life and writings', *Viator*, xii (1981), 361–2, 368–9, 379.

54. *Rogeri Dymmok Liber*, 160, cf. 306: *Selections*, ed. Hudson, 26, cf. 29 – which leaves it uncertain whether the book in which the twelve conclusions were 'longly declared' was this or another text. *Fasc. Ziz.*, 364 has 'in uno libro quem rex *habuit*' for Dymoke's 'quem rex *audivit*' (my italics), presumably from a misreading of 'herd[e]' as 'had'. Could the text the king heard conceivably be that which he had ordered to be destroyed in 1385? (above p. 53)

55. *Dymmok*, loc. cit.; *Selections*, 26 and notes, pp. 153 (ll. 90–92), 205 (l. 16 *et seq*).

56. *Dymmok*, 47; cf. 213 on the lack of coercive powers of '*prelati pauperes*' in the early church. (Of course it has to be remembered that Dymoke's book may be read as a refutation of Wycliffe's writings, as much or more than as a specific redress of the Lollard case. And this does not apply only to the most obvious topic, the eucharist and the *Trialogus* quoted in conclusion 4).

57. *Dymmok*, 177–8, 175 *et seq*. Cf. Dymoke's arguments (172–3) justifying prayers for founders' souls; whether saved, damned, or in purgatory, and the 31st of Wycliffe's 33 Conclusions (*Opera Minora*, 66–8); 'Whether the defunct progenitors of surviving lords are in heaven, in purgatory, or in hell, it would be expedient in cases where almsdoers abuse their alms for these to be withdrawn and converted to other pious uses'.

58. *Selections*, ed. Hudson, 135; *St. Albans Chronicle*, 53.

59. *SR*, ii, 58, cf. 56; 12 Ric. II, cap. vii, cf. cap. iii; *SR*, i, 308; 23 Ed. III, cap. vii. On this legislation see J.A. Tuck, 'The Cambridge Parliament, 1388', *EHR*, lxxxiv (1969), 225–43; Tierney, op. cit., 128–9; B.H. Putnam, *The Enforcement of the Statute of Labourers* (Columbia, 1908), 71–2, 77–9. Tierney points out that 'the canonists had quite consistently held that able–bodied beggars were to be denied alms in order that they should not be encouraged in idleness', and the prior claims on alms of those suffering from bodily weakness (the old and infirm) were set out in the *Decretum: Corpus Iuris Canonici*, ed. Friedberg, i, cols. 299, 301 (Part 1, Dist. 86, cc. vi, xvi, xvii); Tierney, op. cit., 56–61, 118–19, quoted at 130.

60. Lollards would not have faulted 'lez voegles, lepers, et couchantz sur litz en maladie' as a definition of impotent beggars in the common petition behind the statute, but the act also explicitly excepted the religious from the provisions about the able-bodied poor. *The Westminster Chronicle, 1381–1394*, ed. L.C. Hector and B.F. Harvey (Oxford, 1982), 362–3. (This must surely mean blind and lepers, not 'blind lepers').

61. *Jack Upland*, 66, 94; cf. *Polemical Works*, i, 196.

62. Gonville and Caius College, Cambridge, MS. 354/581, fos. 75ᵛ–76ʳ; the Latin version of this passage is in Gonville and Caius College, MS 232/118, fos. 205ᵛ–208ʳ. See *The Middle English Translation of the Rosarium Theologie*, ed. C. von Nolcken (Heidelberg, 1979), for the dating of this work and selections (not including this passage) from the former manuscript. In the fuller section on *Mendicitas* in BL. MS. Harl. 401 copy of the *Floretum* (I am grateful to Anne Hudson for sending me a copy of this) the distinctions of begging are pursued at less length and do not form the starting-point of the discussion. The *Rosetum* entry harps on the unlawfulness of begging by 'strong men', and alludes to the prohibition of this in '*Codic. de mendicantibus valid. L. unica*' – a citation of Justinian which could have come from any number of intermediate sources, including Aquinas, William of St. Amour (Williams, art. cit., [above, note 3], 506, n. 28); and cf. John Pecham, *Tractatus tres de Paupertate*, ed. C.L. Kingsford, A.G. Little, F. Tocco (British Society of Franciscan Studies, ii, Aberdeen, 1910), 177, 185. The *Rosarium* ends its comment on begging with an allusion to the supper of Christ (in Luke 14) to which there came 'but beggars, feeble men, halting and blind'. See *An Apology for Lollard Doctrines*, ed. J.H. Todd (Camden Society, xx 1842), 108–13, for an exposition of the thesis that 'it is not lawful to religious to beg', which draws on some of the same sources as the *Rosarium*, and also expounds the 'divers manners' of begging 'by sign or by token or by express voice', as manifesting need 'by word or work or token'. Christ begged by 'showing' his need. But 'wilful [i.e. voluntary] begging of stalwart men' was forbidden to Christians, and 'the alms of the poor shall not be given to them that are sufficient and mighty to travail'.

63. *Trialogus*, 38, 338 *et seq.* at 341–2, 343–4; cf. also Wycliffe's letter 'De fratribus ad scholares' (of about the same date as the *Trialogus*) which attacks the friars as 'validi mendicantes' (*Opera Minora*, 18); *Polemical Works*, i, 312; and for friars begging not 'innuitive vel insinuative . . . sed clamorose ac eciam importune', *Sermones*, iv, 13; *Pol. Works*, i, 187–8, 366–7 *et seq.* I have not found any helpful discussion of the development of this terminology, as employed by Wycliffe or anyone else. Cf. St. Thomas's distinctions of licit and illicit begging; *Summa Theologiae*, II–II, Quaest. clxxxvii, Art. V ('utrum religiosis liceat mendicare'), which cites the civil code's punishment of strong beggars, who begged neither for utility (i.e. justifiable causes) nor of necessity; and, on Christ's voluntary poverty III, Quaest. xl, Art. III. It is possible to trace the radical change in Wycliffe's views on this issue. In the *Trialogus* he turned on their head arguments he had used earlier in defence of the friars; cf. *De Civili Dominio*, iii, 7–10, where he mentions the threefold kinds of asking in order to support the legitimacy of friars' begging. Cf. *De Apostasia*, ed. M.H. Dziewicki (WS, 1889), 31–2, for a condemnation of inordinate begging of friars and reference to 'clamorous begging'.

64. *Trialogus*, 338, 349; cf. 341–2 ('Dixi alias in lingua multiplici, quomodo mendicatio est satis aequivoca, sicut oratio . . . alias descripsi mendicationem . . . Feci hoc in vulgari multiplices rationes').

65. *SEW*, iii, 402–29; cf. *Trialogus*, 338–53 *et seq.*; J. Bale, *Scriptorum illustrium maioris Brytannie Catalogus* (Basel, 1557–9), Cent. sexta, 453. Arnold, (*SEW*, iii, 402), followed by Workman (*Wyclif*, i, 330), compared this tract with Wycliffe's Latin *De Blasphemia*. The only person who seems to have noticed the link between these texts is A.G. Little, *Grey Friars in Oxford*, 82, n. 3.

66. FitzRalph is cited in the English (*SEW*, iii, 412), but not the Latin version, on the begging of Christ. FitzRalph's arguments against the voluntary begging of the friars were undoubtedly a valuable precedent, but the case was carried further under Wycliffite impetus. Mendicancy had not been a central topic in FitzRalph's *De Pauperie Salvatoris*, but came to the fore in 1356–7 and seems to have been at the centre of controversy thereafter: 'Defensio Curatorum' in *Trevisa's Dialogus*, ed. A.J. Perry (EETS, OS 167, 1925), 80 *et seq.*; and see K. Walsh, 'The "De Vita Evangelica" of Geoffrey Hardeby, O.E.S.A. (c. 1320 – c. 1385): A Study in the Mendicant Controversies of the Fourteenth Century', *Analecta Augustiniana*, xxxiii (1970), 151–261, xxxiv (1971), 5–83, especially pt. 1, 255 and pt. 2, 21–3, 74 *et seq.* for some of the lines on which Wycliffe parted company from FitzRalph, and on how the Wycliffite attack concentrated attention on the issue of evangelical poverty. (Cf. also above note 63 and below note 91). I am aware that I have only nibbled at the edges of this large subject.

67. Some of the passages cited (without specific references in the English) were biblical commonplaces (e.g. the woman of Samaria in John 4:7; cf. the sermon on mendicancy in *Selections*, ed. Hudson, 94), but the overall interrelationship of matter seems too extensive to be accounted for by this. There is not room to present this case properly here, since it calls for an analysis of style as well as content. *Trialogus*, Bk. IV, caps. 27–30 (338–53) has the same three divisions as the English, the two central chapters being devoted to mendicancy. There are correspondences between the English text, 415–29, and passages in the *Trialogus* down to cap. 38, not at all in the same order. In addition, the English text 403–6 on the eucharist is related to *Trialogus*, Bk. IV, caps. ii–v (247–61). Wycliffe himself (Phronesis) tells us (339) to turn back to this earlier passage, and we find there (248) another reference to a previous vernacular discussion. 'Sunt autem in materia de quiddicate hujus sensibilis sacramenti errores multiplices . . . contra quos multipliciter invexi alias tam scholastice quam etiam in vulgari . . .' The passage about the eucharistic worship and 'iche knotte of a stree', which comes in the summing up in English (*SEW*, iii, 428), appears in the middle of *Trial*. Bk. IV, cap. 27 (339). As an example of the kind of version one would not expect of a straight translator cf. the passage quoted above, p. 45, note 2. 'Isti autem sunt stultificati idiotae, qui nescientes inter paupertatem et mendicationem distinguere, primam, quae perfectionem sonaret, dimittunt,

et secundam cupide ut Ischarioth amplectuntur' (*Trial.*, 348–9): 'Bot thes blynde blas-
phemes con not depart beggynge fro povert, for bothe acorden sumwhat' (*SEW*, iii, 415).

68. For other hints by Wycliffe on this question see *Opera Minora*, ii, 74; *De Veritate Sacrae
Scripturae*, ed. R. Buddensieg (WS, 1905–7), i, 349–50. As Anne Hudson has recently
pointed out in 'Lollardy: the English Heresy?', SCH, xviii (1982), 264–5, there is small
evidence for Wycliffe's interest in the vernacular before the last years of his life, and (270 *et
seq.*) it was some time after the adverse publicity of 1382 before definite repressive steps were
taken against the use of the vernacular. But after May 1382, openly to claim authorship of a
vernacular tract expounding points of lately prohibited teaching might well have seemed
inadvisable.

69. The English *De Blasphemia*, unlike the corresponding chapters of the *Trialogus*, makes no
mention of the Blackfriars Council.

70. Netter, *Doctrinale*, i, Bk. IV, cap. iii, col. 829; 'Dixit enim in libello *de blasphemiis*, cap. ii,
secundae blasphemiae: et idem habet ubi supra in *Trial.* lib. IV. cap. xxvii'; Netter then gives
a Latin version of *SEW*, iii, 412, 11. 3–12, 16–19 (cf. *Trial.* cap. 28, 341–2). Netter (using
the example of the woman of Samaria in John 4) was here arguing the case that Christ did
himself beg vocally, and attacking Wycliffe's 'Judaic' idea of 'nodding' (innuitive) begging.
Wycliffe corrected William of St. Amour, who had denied that Christ ever begged, since he
recognized that Scripture said otherwise, but he also wanted to exclude the friars and so
produced the argument that Christ begged, 'sed insinuative, et non clamose cum Fratribus . . .
assignat Christo mendicitatem tantum per nutus . . .' – an idea, Netter indicated (830)
specifically Wycliffe's own. While, however, showing Wycliffe's contribution to the antimendicant argument, Netter saw Wycliffites as *Amoraei*, continuing the tradition of William of
St. Amour and 'his son' FitzRalph: op. cit., cols. 842, 846, 850–1, 855, 895 etc.

71. *SEW*, iii, 410–11.

72. This year too, he added, Wycliffe's followers withdrew alms from the friars, saying
mendicants ought to work and preached only for gain, attacking them and their errors in
English tracts: *Eulogium Historiarum*, iii, 354–5. This report, though perhaps written (like
Knighton's) a good many years later (see Catto, art. cit., 766) is worth notice, not only for its
retrospective view of the importance of this year in the attack on the mendicants, but also for
what it says about Wycliffe's disciples working at the compilation of sermons, travelling
throughout England to preach Wycliffe's doctrine to 'nobilibus et literatis' as well as lay
people. (See Hudson, 'Lollardy: The English Heresy?', 271). For William Woodford on
Wycliffe attacking the mendicants after their condemnation of his eucharistic doctrine in
1381 see *Fasc. Ziz.*, 517–18; Workman, op. cit., i, 186. The Blackfriars Council perhaps led
contemporaries to over-emphasize the importance of 1382, and its last two articles
condemned the views that friars should get their sustenance by manual labour, not begging,
and that almsgivers to friars were excommunicate. But the split between Wycliffe and the
friars was in the making from 1378, and from our point of view the question is when the case
against mendicants as strong beggars began to be publicized. This remains uncertain, though
Nicholas Hereford's preaching (see next note) suggests that this was being done at least by
Feb. 1382. McShane, op. cit., 2–6; E. Doyle. 'William Woodford, O.F.M., and John
Wyclif's *De Religione*', *Speculum*, lii (1977), 329–36.

73. *Fasc. Ziz.*, 296, 303, 305; MS. Bodley 240, pp. 848–50 (I am extremely grateful to Anne
Hudson for sending me a transcript of this); Gradon, art. cit., 182; cf. Little, *Grey Friars in
Oxford*, 91, n. 8. For arguments used by Hereford before 18 Feb. 1382 representing friars'
mendicancy as spoliation of the poor, and for his and Repton's replies to the 24 Conclusions
on this question, see *Fasc. Ziz.*, 292–5, 305, 324–5. For a defence of mendicancy against
these attacks see the Latin verses in *Monumenta Franciscana*, i, ed. J.S. Brewer (RS, 1858),
598–9.

74. *Chronicon Henrici Knighton*, ed. J.R. Lumby (RS, 1889–95), ii, 174–5; McFarlane, op. cit.,
122; J. Crompton, 'Leicestershire Lollards', *Trans. Leics. Archaeol. and Hist. Soc.*, xliv

(1968–9), 20–22. Swinderby also maintained that tithes were pure alms and could be withheld from priests of evil life.

75. For questions about religious orders, including whether friars ought to labour with their hands rather than beg, in the questionnaire of (probably) 1428, see A. Hudson, 'The Examination of Lollards', *BIHR*, xlvi (1973), 154–5. For Richard Wyche's view of friars' begging as unlawful, '*spontanea clamosa*', see *Fasc. Ziz.*, 380–1, 502, 504–5; F.D. Matthew, 'The Trial of Richard Wyche', *EHR*, v (1890), 531. The case against friars as 'clamorous' able–bodied beggars can be traced in various texts, witnessing to the Wycliffite contribution to antimendicant literature: e.g. *Pierce the Ploughmans Crede*, 23 ('Whereto beggen these men and been not so feeble . . . Withouten any travail untruly they liveth./They be not maimed men, nor no meat lacketh'), 4 ('With sterne staves and strong they over land straketh'); *Laterne of Liʒt*, 54 (against almsgiving to 'strong staff-beggars and strikers over the land, and groaners without cause').

76. Pecock, *Repressor*, ii, 380–1. Cf. *Remonstrance*, ed. Forshall, 14–16; for Purvey's and Swinderby's pairing of these two issues see *Fasc. Ziz.*, 394, and *Registrum Johannis Trefnant*, ed. W.W. Capes (CYS, xx, 1916), 240, 263–6, and for two defendants who in 1430 renounced the view that tithes and temporalities should be withdrawn for the benefit of the poor see *Norwich Heresy Trials*, ed. Tanner, 141, 147 and below p. 65. Of course tithes were an intrinsic part of the case for disendowment in the supposition that a properly evangelical ministry would subsist on tithes and offerings.

77. *Opus Evangelicum*, ii, 363. Cf. *De Simonia*, ed. H.-Fränkel and M.H. Dziewicki (WS, 1898), 93–4 for three remedies for dealing with the endowed orders (number one, the miracle that God would enlighten the pope, scarcely counted); *Opera Minora*, 45–6 (no. 19 of the 33 Conclusions '*de paupertate Christi*') on how the elemosinary failings of rectors and curates should be corrected by patrons of churches withdrawing endowments, just as the king should correct negligent prelates by removing their temporalities.

78. *Opera Minora*, 12–15 (ending with a passage on why the law of the church/antichrist judged otherwise). On 1 Tim 6:8, frequently cited as the criterion for the acceptable reception of tithe, see *Trialogus*, 419; for Wycliffe's view of tithes as *bona pauperum*, and Augustine's 'tithes are the tribute of needy souls', *De Blasphemia*, 34–5; *De Civili Dominio*, i, 320, 338, 340, 345, 353 etc.; see notes 29, 35, above.

79. *Rosarium Theologie*, ed. von Nolcken, 62–3, 109–10. This misapprehension about Gregory X was repeated elsewhere (see below, p. 65) and derived from the Polychronicon. It was, as Selden pointed out, wholly mistaken to suppose that the parochial right to tithe started at the Council of Lyons in 1274. See *Polychronicon Ranulphi Higden*, viii, ed. J.R. Lumby (RS, 1882), 256–7; J. Selden, *The Historie of Tithes* (London, 1618), 147; and for William Thorpe's use of this source, including the argument that Christ taught payment not of tithes, but of alms to 'poor needy men',*Fifteenth Century Prose and Verse*, ed. A.W. Pollard (Westminster, 1903), 143–4.

80. *EWW*, 431–2; cf. 415, 421 ('De officio pastorali'); 132 ('Of clerks possessioners'); *SEW*, iii, 175.

81. *Selections*, ed. Hudson, 19, 21 (no. 3), and notes pp. 146–7; cf. Thorpe, loc. cit., 145. Cf. also on the right to withhold tithe Swinderby's views in *Reg. Trefnant*, 239–41, 263–4, 280, and the devious logic of *Remonstrance*, ed. Forshall, 12–18, which moved via documented 'corollaries' from the position that Christians should give support to faithful curates, to the proposition that tithes and offerings should be withdrawn from sinful curates.

82. Gelasius in 494 ruled a quadripartite division of tithes (between bishop, clergy, church fabric, and poor), but this came to be superseded by a threefold one (between clergy, church fabric, and poor). See R.A.R. Hartridge, *A History of Vicarages in the Middle Ages* (Cambridge, 1930), 1–2; G. Constable, *Monastic Tithes from their Origins to the Twelfth Century* (Cambridge, 1964), 11, 21–3, 43, 49–56; Tierney, *Medieval Poor Law*, 21, 40–1, 43, 70, 73–4, 148. Cf. *Mum and the Sothsegger*, 45–7 on the threefold division and the claims of the poor.

83. *Register of Henry Chichele*, ed. E.F. Jacob (CYS, xlii, xlv–xlvii, 1938–47), i, cxxxv–cxxxvi, iii, 118–57, 173–9 (quoted at 152); trans. in *Eng. Hist. Docts.*, IV, ed. Myers, 707–9; *Munimenta Academica*, ed. Anstey, ii, 374, 376, cf. i, 270, n. 1; C.L. Kingsford, *The Grey Friars of London* (Aberdeen, 1915), 57–8; Little, *Grey Friars in Oxford*, 85–6, 257–9; idem, 'Personal Tithes', *EHR*, lx (1945), 67. *BRUO*, iii, 1611–12, indicates that Little was wrong to suppose that Russell had studied at Oxford. Cf. ibid., ii, 1258, and Little, op. cit., 259 for the case of William de Melton, another Franciscan and an Oxford doctor, who in 1427 caused the university to seek the aid of Duke Humphrey and the council against his itinerant preaching against tithes.

84. *Selections*, ed. Hudson, 88.

85. *The Praier and complaynte of the ploweman unto Christe* (Antwerp, 1531), sig. CVr; *EWW*, 211 (cf. 210), 14; *SEW*, iii, 383.

86. *Rogeri Dymmok Liber*, 307, cf. 6, 314; and on the 'treasurers of Christ' claim, 25, 28, 92, 226, 228, 311. Both friars and Lollards were accused of wearing russet (a coarse cloth, originally grey or brown in color) 'that betokeneth travail upon earth', as a kind of poverty costume. *Pierce the Ploughmans Crede*, 27; *Trialogus*, 337; *Jack Upland*, 85, 151; *Norwich Heresy Trials*, 75; H.L. Cannon, 'The Poor Priests; a study in the rise of English Lollardry', *Annual Rept. of the Am. Hist. Assn. for 1899* (Washington, 1900), i, 451–82; G. F. Jones, 'Sartorial symbols in mediaeval literature', *Medium Aevum*, xxv (1956), 63–70.

87. *Three Middle English Sermons*, ed. D.M. Grisdale (Leeds School of English Language, Texts and Monographs, v, 1939), 65–6. (Of course the 'false prophets' of the sermon on the mount was applied just as often by Wycliffites to the friars: e.g. *English Wycliffite Sermons*, ed. Hudson, i, 253 – alluding to the three offences of the *Trialogus*, 'of the sacred host, of begging of Christ, of letters of their brotherhood').

88. *St. Albans Chronicle*, 80; cf. *Historia Anglicana*, ii, 299–300. As it has already been treated elsewhere I have not attempted here to consider the effect of Oldcastle's rising on the politics of disendowment. But even in the 1450s the aims of 1414 may not have been entirely dead. In the short–lived rising of John Wilkins in Kent in May 1452 some rebels had ideas of clerical dispossession and looked to Lord Cobham to support their plans. As reported in one charge these sound authentically Lollard:– 'that priests throughout England should have no possessions or chattels except a chair and a candlestick for studying their books': R. Virgoe, 'Some Ancient Indictments in the King's Bench referring to Kent, 1450–1452', in *Kent Records*, ed. F.R.H. Du Boulay (Kent Arch. Soc., xviii, 1964), 257–9. Cf. *EWW*, 380 against clerical possession on how '. . . a chair, and a candlestick . . . ben according to a studier or a contemplative man' (= 2 Kings 4; 10).

89. *Polemical Works*, i, 47. This is one of many instances (see note 22 above) in Wycliffe's and Lollard writings where the allusion to Luke 14 has gone unnoticed. For some other examples of Wycliffe's use of this passage see ibid., i, 308, 311; *Trialogus*, 305, 343–4, 354; *De Ecclesia*, ed. J. Loserth (WS. 1886), 286; *De Officio Pastorali*, i, 18–19; *Sermones*, i, 230 (expounding four categories), cf. ii, 186; iii. 500; iv, 19, 105. For Wycliffe referring to himself in 1383/4 as '*debilis et claudus*' see *Pol. Works*, ii, 543, 556.

90. *EWW*, 27, 387, 421.

91. Netter, *Doctrinale*, i, Bk, IV, cap. x, col. 861. Cf. col. 860 for Netter's objection that Wycliffe abused the gospel text by taking '*pauperes*' as an adjectival description of '*debiles, caecos, et claudos*', thereby making three categories out of what should be the fourfold '*pauperes et debiles, caecos, et claudos*'. FitzRalph seems to have given the lead here, arguing (against the begging of friars) that the 'feast of beggars' of Luke 14 excluded poor men who were stalwart and strong, just as much as rich men who were feeble, halt, or blind: 'Defensio Curatorum' in *Trevisa's Dialogus*, 88.

92. *Remonstrance*, ed. Forshall, 95, 97; cf. *SEW*, iii, 372.

93. E.g. May McKisack, *The Fourteenth Century* (Oxford, 1959), 291; Cronin in *Rogeri Dymmok*

Liber, xxxi ff.; W.T. Waugh, 'Sir John Oldcastle', *EHR*, xx (1905), 440–1; Kingsford, above p. 54. Cf. Myers in *Eng. Hist. docts.*, IV, 629.

94. Dymoke, for instance, talking about the suggestions made to parliament for spoiling the church (above, p. 56) adds that 'as yet, thank God, no lord has agreed with them' ('*nullus . . . adhuc assensit*'; *Dymmok Liber*, 178). While doubtless meant as a warning this *adhuc* implies an open-ended situation. Trevisa's *Dialogus inter Militem et Clericum* (Trevisa's *Dialogus*, 1–38) with its arguments (comparable to those used in 1371) that common need of the realm overrode clerical privilege and that restoration was in order when founders' wishes for works of charity were neglected, shows the currency of such ideas. See also A. Hudson, 'A Lollard Quaternion', *RES*, NS xxiii (1971), 441, and idem, *Selections*, Text 26. For B.L. Egerton MS 2820, a fine copy of a variant version of *The Clergy may not hold Property* which was evidently made for a well-to-do owner, see *Selections*, 185–6; *English Wycliffite Sermons*, i, 194.

95. *SR*, i, 92; 13 Ed. I, cap. 41. E. Tatnall, 'John Wyclif and *Ecclesia Anglicana*', *JEH*, xx (1969), 30; Farr, op cit., (above n. 20) 104–5; Wycliffe, *De Civili Dominio*, ii, 39–41, and for statements of the rights of founders and their heirs *Opera Minora*, 42–5, 63–4 (nos. 18 and 30 of the 33 Conclusions). For Lollards on the role of founders in correcting endowments see *Fasc. Ziz.*, 394 (Purvey); *EWW*, 392; *Remonstrance*, ed. Forshall, 91–2.

96. Farr, op. cit., 106–7.

97. *Year Books of Richard II. 11 Richard II 1387–1388*, ed. I.D. Thornley (1937), xxxi, 72–5. The outcome of this case is not known.

98. Pecock, *Repressor*, ii, 400.

99. *Polemical Works*, i, 283; *Opera Minora*, 409.

100. *Polemical Works*, i, 281–3; cf. *Trialogus*, 313; *De Ecclesia*, 331–2; *Opera Minora*, 41–2; *De Apostasia*, 88; H. Kaminsky, 'Wyclifism as Ideology of Revolution', *Church History*, xxxii (1963), 67 and n. 82; Farr, op. cit.,152, n. 85; Gradon, art. cit., 187; Tatnall, art. cit., 31– 4. On royal exploitation of episcopal vacancies in the thirteenth century and the question of whether Henry III and Edward I deliberately prolonged vacancies for financial reasons, see M. Howell, *Regalian Right in Medieval England* (1962), p. 167 and Chapter V.

101. *Rot. Parl.*, iii, 156b; *Historia Anglicana*, ii, 109, 141, cf. 128; *Westminster Chronicle*, 52–3; Workman, op. cit., ii, 69.

102. *Rot. Parl.*, iii, 293b–294a; cf. ii, 284a, iii, 645; *SR*, ii, 80, 15 Ric. II, cap. vi, cf. 136, 4 Hen. IV, cap. xii; Hartridge, op. cit., 157–8, 198–9; Tierney, op.cit., 128–9.

103. *EWW*, 27.

104. *Trialogus*, 305–6; cf. *Polemical Works*, i, 47, 312.

105. Netter, *Doctrinale*, i, col. 862; cf. col. 859, *illos tres pauperes*'. Cf. Wycliffe in *Trialogus*, 305 ('Oportet enim quod in Christi regula sit paupertas in triplici sequenti particula tripliciter intellecta . . .'); *Sermones*, iv, 105 ('. . . oportet pauperes in verbis sequentibus triplicare . . .'); *Lanterne of Liзt*, 86, ostensibly translating Luke 14, 'bring in to thine house these three manner of people, poor feeble, poor blind, and poor crooked'. See notes 22, 89, 91 above.

106. *The Ancestor*, x (1904), 19–21 ('poor and feeble, poor and blind, poor and crooked', 20). Thomas Latimer's will was dated 13 Sept. 1401 and proved 20 April 1402, Anne Latimer's dated 13 July 1402 and proved 27 Oct. 1402. See K.B. McFarlane, *Lancastrian Kings and Lollard Knights* (Oxford, 1972), 214; A. Hudson, 'The Debate on Bible Translation, Oxford, 1401', *EHR*, xc (1975), 12.

107. *The Fifty Earliest English Wills*, ed. F.J. Furnivall (EETS, OS 78, 1882), 26–8, 129–30 (1415, proved 1418, and 1439); McFarlane, op. cit., 216. The elder Sir Thomas was MP for Somerset in the parliaments of 1395, 1399 and 1410 discussed above. The younger Sir Thomas married Joan Braybrooke, heiress of Oldcastle's wife, Lady Cobham. He took part in the rising of 1414 and was the father of Edward Broke, Lord Cobham, who was looked to by the Kent rebels of 1452 (above note 88). McFarlane (ibid., 207 *et seq.*) who pointed to the

expressions of unworthiness, revulsion towards the flesh, and rejection of funeral pomp as characteristics of Lollard wills, did not analyse this other feature. It likewise (probably more so) reflects an aspect of the evangelical movement that was not in itself unorthodox (ibid., 225), though the terminology used – the triple classes of poor – may indicate a link with suspect sources.

108. Above, p. 48. Cf. the case of William Mundy of Wokingham (1412) in *The Register of Robert Hallum*, ed. J.M. Horn (CYS, lxxii, 1982), 219.

109. *Fasc. Ziz.*, 428; *Norwich Heresy Trials*, 103, and above note 76.

110. *Études sur l'Histoire de la Pauvreté*, ed. M. Mollat (Paris, 1974), i, 27.

111. Did the case against the possessioners have any long-term traceable effects on charitable bequests? This important question (posed by Professor Barrie Dobson) is hard to answer. Undoubtedly people of all classes continued to make bequests to the friars throughout the fifteenth century. Figures (statistically a small sample) cited in Little, *Grey Friars in Oxford*, 101–2 ff., suggest a decline in the proportion of wills that included such bequests from the late fourteenth to the early sixteenth century. On Franciscan failure in charitable works (echoing Wycliffe – 'They confounded mendicancy with poverty') and the shift of lay piety to other sorts of foundation, see idem, *Studies in English Franciscan History*, 78, 89–91; J. Moorman, *A History of the Franciscan Order* (Oxford, 1968), 364, cf. 514. Colin Richmond, *John Hopton* (Cambridge, 1981), 203–4, cites the will of John Tasburgh, who in 1473 left a house and land for poor people to live in, with no provision for prayers for his soul – an informal small secular almshouse. Perhaps further analysis of wills will eventually make it possible to see whether almsgiving in general moved in the direction Lollards had signposted: away from established orders and soul-masses, towards the needy (secular) poor.

112. *Reg. Chichele*, ii, 285–7; McFarlane, op. cit., 217–18; *DNB*, s.n. Repington. Repton's will is undated; it was proved 1 August 1424. Richard Fleming at this moment had other things on his mind: R.G. Davies, 'Martin V and the English episcopate', *EHR*, xcii (1977), 322–4, 326–7. Contrary to his request, Repton was buried in Lincoln Cathedral with an inscribed gravestone.

113. 'in remissionem peccatorum meorum in seculi vanitate per me miserum peccatorem ibidem commissorum'; *Reg. Chichele*, ii, 286. He granted the bare courtesies (sums of 20s to the clergy and 6s 8d to the ringers) to those celebrating his obsequies at St. Margaret's, Lincoln. Margery Kempe's pleased report of Repton's daily charity dispensed to thirteen poor men, shows that he had benefited the poor of Lincoln as bishop: *The Book of Margery Kempe*, ed. S.B. Meech and H.E. Allen (EETS, OS 212, 1940), 34. There are other features of Repton's will that suggest trace-elements of Lollardy: his reiterated anxiety that the bell-ringing at his obsequies should not be loud and clamorous with secular pomp; his request for his body to be committed naked to the earth, *outside* the church, without coffin or tomb (the equivalent of a poor man's burial). Another unusual feature is his thrice stated wish that his funeral service should, if possible, take place while he was still alive. Cf. K.B. McFarlane, 'At the deathbed of Cardinal Beaufort', *England in the Fifteenth Century*, introd. G.L. Harriss (London, 1981), 118–19 (a reference I owe to a reminder of Dr. J.A.F. Thomson). For other indications that Repton did not lose all sympathy for Lollardy see *Selections*, ed. Hudson, 158.

114. *Sermones*, iv, 17–20 (on John 11.21: cf. 104–7 on feeding the poor and Luke 14). '. . . omnes tales exequie vel consuetudines quantumcunque sumptuose fuerint non prosunt defunctis . . . Non enim videtur racio quare mundo dives tam sumptuose et sollempniter sepelitur nisi propter mundanam gloriam servandam in genere vel propter solacia in viventibus conservanda'; cf. Repton; 'funeralis mea non pomposa vel sumptuose que magis vivorum solacia vel nugancium spectacula quam subsidia mortuorum. . .': Wycliffe; 'sed melius foret quod . . . magis egentibus forent talia distributa'; Repton; 'centum pauperes ad hoc electi maxime indigentes. . .' Cf. *Sermones*, ii, 185–6. Of course there was nothing unorthodox in such

views. For other examples of the wish to avoid funeral excesses, combined with conventional pieties, see *The Register of Edmund Stafford*, ed. F.C. Hingeston-Randolph (London, 1886), 389–90, 410, 412.

115. 'opera caritatis multa paciuntur impedimenta et adversa'; *Reg. Chichele*, ii, 285. If the executors failed over his burial would they have succeeded better with the *pastus pauperum*?

3

Episcopal King-Makers in the Fifteenth Century

R.L. Storey
University of Nottingham

'The identification of the church with the whole of organized society is the fundamental feature which distinguishes the Middle Ages from earlier and later periods of history'.[1] This aphorism should influence every analysis of the nature of the medieval body politic. Heretics apart, all the inhabitants of a kingdom were members of its church, their minds and behaviour constantly influenced by the religion and laws of the Church universal through the ministry and jurisdiction of the national clergy. For this reason the involvement of leaders of that clergy in secular politics had a larger importance than is often appreciated. It is not enough to consider episcopal figures prominent in the theatre of medieval politics as individuals with personal records in temporal affairs, so that their participation may be explained in the same terms as are adduced for the lay actors. Such interpretation of the conduct of bishops and archbishops in constitutional crises arises from a presumption that the causes of those crises were of a secular nature. The grievances of baronial militants whose rebellion brought about the deposition of a king are obviously of first importance in any assessment of the causes of his downfall, but it must be asked why and how others assented to the results of the coup d'état. In late medieval England, the brutal facts of revolt, deposition and usurpation were legitimized by constitutional devices and propaganda enshrined in the rolls of parliament. A small number of prelates had key roles in these processes of kingmaking. Their part in councils and parliaments, as spokesmen in other assemblies, is acknowledged in recent descriptions and analyses of these constitutional crises, but never, to my knowledge, with any discussion of even the possibility that these leaders of the English church may have believed themselves to be serving its interests by promoting new kings. For the opening and close of the Lancastrian regime, ecclesiastical records overlooked by constitutional historians from Gaillard Lapsley onward permit some consideration of this neglected question.

No account of Richard II's deposition can overlook the prominence of Thomas Arundel, archbishop of Canterbury, in bringing about Richard's capture and abdication, in the acceptance of Henry IV's title in a pseudo-parliamentary forum, and, subsequently, after crowning the new king, acting as his spokesman and principal councillor in the first parliament of the reign.[2] Nor is it difficult to suggest why Thomas Arundel should have been willing to act as stage-manager for the Lancastrian usurpation. According to the continuator of the *Eulogium*, when the captive Richard was brought before Duke Henry and Archbishop Thomas, the latter broke into a bitter tirade against the king, firstly denouncing his perfidy in executing the Earl of Arundel and, again in breach of his promises, exiling Thomas and depriving him of his archbishopric. He then went on to accuse Richard of misgovernment and vicious life until the catalogue of iniquities was cut short by Henry's '*sufficit*' – 'that's enough!'[3] That curt stopping of the flood of archiepiscopal invective gives an authentic touch to a scene which the chronicler could easily have invented. In the deposition articles, Arundel's exile was first noticed briefly as another example of Richard II's illegal acts, and then again at length, with much circumstantial detail, as the last article, and thus possibly a late addition at Arundel's instance. None of the other charges provides such a closely-focussed report of Richard in action, practising his cruel deceptions on the strangely gullible archbishop.[4] Chancery records from 19 August 1399 describe Arundel as archbishop, but his title was hardly canonical.[5] The pope had translated him to St. Andrews at Richard's bidding, and in his stead provided Roger Walden, who had been consecrated as archbishop in 1398. Canterbury, as the chronicler Usk observed, now had two heads, Roger by right, and Thomas in fact, 'by the secular power which everywhere prevails'.[6] Recovery of his archbishopric was another strong induce-ment for Thomas Arundel to be a kingmaker.

Two prelates qualify for this description at the other end of the Lancastrian monarchy. They are Thomas Bourchier, archbishop of Canterbury, and George Neville, bishop of Exeter and chancellor of England since the Yorkist victory at Northampton in July 1460. In the following December, after the duke of York had set out for his fateful encounter with Queen Margaret's forces, the council left in charge at London signed a letter to the duke of Milan. The five signatories were the archbishop and his brothers Henry, Viscount Bourchier, and John, Lord Berners, as well as Bishop Neville and his brother, the earl of Warwick.[7] The archbishop, George Neville and Richard Beauchamp, bishop of Salisbury, were three of the eight known members of the junta which decided, on 3 March 1461, that Edward of York should assume the crown.[8] Like Thomas Arundel, Thomas Bourchier and George Neville were cadets of the higher aristocracy. All three had been designated for ecclesiastical careers by their parents, and sent to

Oxford for the education appropriate for this chosen profession; through their families' influence with the crown, they were provided to their first bishoprics when in their twenties, a canonical irregularity which required, and received, papal dispensation.[9] It might seem reasonable to suppose that from their precocious entry into parliaments and councils as lords spiritual, these prelates would have inclined to associate with their fathers and brothers on political and social issues. Arundel's exile and deprivation in 1397 resulted from his active participation in the regime of the Lords Appellant, of whom one was his brother the earl and another the future King Henry IV.

George Neville had likewise been implicated in the politics of faction from an early stage of his career and consequently had a cause of personal grievance against the regime of Henry VI. In June 1453, when he was elected as chancellor of Oxford University at the age of 21, the Nevilles were still valued champions of the Lancastrian court.[10] One result of their subsequent alliance with the duke of York was George's provision to the bishopric of Exeter in 1456. The young bishop chose to remain in Oxford. Beside his genuine intellectual interests, he obviously derived satisfaction from his office as the university's chief governor, and to conscientious application he added the Neville flair for the exercise of good lordship. His popularity with the Oxford masters was attested by his re-election at the end of his two-year term, and again in April 1457. Ten weeks later he resigned, but it may be suspected that his resignation was not voluntary. It followed soon after a royal visit to Oxford, and can be associated with other indications that the court suspected the university's loyalty.[11] Just as Thomas Arundel's restoration to Canterbury was assured by Henry IV's usurpation, so did the Yorkist triumph lead to George Neville's return to office as chancellor of Oxford University; he was its first chancellor elected for life. Neville's partnership with his brother Warwick was later to achieve the restoration of Henry VI. He survived its collapse, but his persisting addiction to treasonable conspiracy caused Edward IV to order Oxford to remove him from the chancellorship in 1472.[12] This intervention, and similar action by Richard III against Lionel Woodville in 1483, emphasise the crown's concern that the government of the university should be in politically reliable hands.[13]

If Arundel, Bourchier and Neville had confined their recorded public activity to the stage of national politics in 1399 and 1460-61, it would be hard to deny that their involvement arose from their membership of the higher aristocracy. Indeed one would be able to accept Professor Du Boulay's conclusion that Thomas Bourchier was a reluctant Yorkist partisan if his record in secular business was the only evidence.[14] He certainly never achieved an eminence in Edward IV's council and government equal to that of Thomas Arundel in the reign of Henry IV. In Arundel's case also, however, modern scholarship has concluded that the most pressing concern in the archbishop's mind was his responsibility for the welfare of the church; he consequently regarded political involvement as an unwelcome distraction.[15] It was Bourchier's happier fortune to escape much of that distraction because George Neville, and then others, were sufficiently ambitious and capable to be the crown's leading clerical ministers. The two archbishops held the same sense of prior responsibility to their ecclesiastical office; this can be demonstrated from a suggestive parallel in their *acta* as primates in the national crises which established and dethroned the Lancastrian dynasty.

The first recognition under the great seal that Thomas Arundel was again archbishop of Canterbury was his writ of summons to a parliament to be held on 30 September issued on 19 August 1399.[16] There was a brief period of pretence that the see was vacant, perhaps to avoid offence to canonical purists. Roger Walden was deprived of the temporalities by a royal order made on 5 September with the advice of the duke of Lancaster and assent of the so-called king's council.[17] It was presumably at this juncture that an envoy was sent to Rome to obtain the pope's ratification of Arundel's restoration. Two days earlier, on 3 September, a mandate was issued under the name of the prior and chapter of Christ Church as keepers of the spirituality of Canterbury, convoking the prelates, dignitaries and elected proctors of the clergy of the province to assemble in St. Paul's cathedral on 6 October.[18] Somewhat unusually, the mandate did not quote a royal writ ordering a convocation to be held for the purpose of attending to business of national concern, which normally meant granting a subsidy to the king. This time the initiative purported to come from the prior and chapter, but that was another transparent fiction. The mandate was dated from London where the convent's seal was not available; this failure was remedied by applying the seal of Master John Barnet, official of the court of Canterbury, whose connection with Arundel went back to the beginning of his episcopate at Ely.[19] No doubt Barnet was present at that undated meeting of 'doctors, bishops and others' reported by Adam Usk as called to determine how Richard II might be deposed. It may have been a committee of ecclesiastical lawyers only, and thus probably summoned by Arundel, because its single pronouncement of expert opinion recorded is that a chapter of the Sext was applicable to Richard's case. The committee advised that 'for greater security, Richard should be deposed by authority of the clergy and people, who were being called for that purpose'.[20] The mandate itself gives the reasons for convocation's summons as 'newly arising business concerning the common weal and the defence of the laws and liberties of the church and kingdom'. The meeting was to be held under the presidency of either the prior and chapter of Christ Church or an unnamed archbishop or his commissaries.

In the event, Arundel fully resumed his authority in spiritualities on the day after Henry IV was accepted as king.[21] On 6 October the bishop of London's certificate that the mandate to cite convocation had been executed was addressed to Archbishop Thomas or his deputies, and it referred to the vacancy as being past. Another fiction was devised on the temporal side. The judgement against Arundel in 1397 was reversed by Henry's first parliament, and when his goods and estates were restored by letters patent dated 21 October, it was stated that the temporalities of Canterbury had been in the king's hands since the forfeiture in 1397.[22] There was no mention of Roger Walden, nor of Arundel's translation to St. Andrews. Stubbs observed that Henry's restoration of Arundel revealed that, despite his orthodoxy, the new king had no intention of being servile to Rome.[23] The tenth charge in Richard's deposition described his application for papal letters confirming the statutes of the parliament of 1397–8 as contrary to the long-established freedom of the crown and kingdom from the pope and all other external powers.[24] Boniface IX had been sent a message to inform him that Arundel was to be reinstated at Canterbury; he cannot have known of the events at Westminster on 30 September when, on 19 October, he responded to this message by cancelling Arundel's translation to St. Andrews and Walden's provision to Canterbury. The papal letters declared that the translation was void because it had been made without Arundel's consent, a detail which Boniface had doubtless already learnt from Arundel's own lips in 1398.[25] The archbishop was obviously relieved to have papal authority to resume office: a copy of the bull was the first entry in his register for 1399, although it was followed by notices of *acta* before the bull could have arrived in England towards the end of November.[26]

By that time the convocation of Canterbury had already been held under Arundel's presidency. The opening session on 6 October was adjourned because the archbishop was preaching at the opening of parliament on the text 'It is our duty to ordain for the kingdom'.[27] For the preacher to convocation on the following day, Arundel had appointed his immediate suffragan, the bishop of Rochester. His text, 'My heart rejoices in the governors of Israel', is from chapter V (v.9) of Judges, but the theme was drawn from the fourth chapter which tells of the downfall of Sisera after his oppression of the chosen people for a period of twenty years, the same length as Richard's reign. No doubt Henry of Lancaster was compared with Barak, and Arundel with Deborah, the judge of Israel who had urged Barak to raise an army to overthrow Sisera. The Song of Deborah refers to delivery 'from the noise of archers', another topical allusion which the preacher was unlikely to have omitted.[28] Formal business followed the sermon, and next a visit by envoys from the king. For this mission Henry had chosen his two earliest magnate supporters, the earls of Northumberland and Westmorland, and the Lancastrian knight Thomas Erpingham. Northumberland was spokesman. He told the clergy that the king had not sent him to ask for money, as so many of his predecessors had done: indeed, Henry was unwilling to take taxes from any of his subjects. Instead he asked the prelates and clergy to pray for him, and he assured them that he intended to defend the liberties of the church and do his utmost to destroy heresy. The archbishop then replied to the earl on behalf of the prelates and all the clergy, with copious thanks to the king '*pro benevolencia sua*'.

It is quite obvious that Archbishop Arundel had called this convocation for the purpose of enlisting clerical support for the monarchy of Henry IV.[29] In contrast, the convocation over which Thomas Bourchier presided in 1460 was called in response to a royal mandate. On 12 February letters close ordered both archbishops to convoke their clergy in all haste to attend to urgent business of national concern: this was a routine formula. Sixteen days later, Bourchier decided that 6 May was early enough for his convocation to receive the king's request for a subsidy.[30] The government's need for financial aid was desperate. In mid-January, the Yorkist raid on Sandwich had captured the royal fleet; another had to be formed and put to sea to prevent a major invasion from Calais and Ireland, where Warwick was visiting the duke of York. Commissions were appointed to raise loans; in March, five bishops and thirteen abbots and priors lent a total of £1,790, with assignment on a future clerical subsidy as one of the promised methods of repayment.[31] The grant of this subsidy, however, was not given priority in the convocation's agenda. The king's representatives, among them the treasurer of England, were not heard until 11 May. On the first day, 6 May, the preacher was William Say, doctor of theology and dean of St Paul's. He had been dean of the chapel in the king's household for the previous ten years, but he was to continue in that office under Edward IV.[32] His convocation sermon was clearly not Lancastrian propaganda. The text was 'Take heed therefore to yourselves, and to all the flock over which the Holy Ghost hath made you overseers' from St Paul's charge to the elders of Ephesus, an appropriate choice for a call to reform disorders in the English church.[33] The lower house had a lengthy and far-ranging series of discussions which eventually resulted in articles on procurations payable at visitations, the calling of banns for marriage, clerical dress, and issues of similar import. A case of alleged heresy, and the arrest of a clerical proctor by the sheriffs of London, provided further distraction from the king's financial problems; while the archbishop's uncertain health, and the absence of some bishops attending the king at Coventry, also impeded the flow of business. On 20 June a letter from the king was read but, unfortunately, not recorded: one need not 'marvel greatly' as to its contents. The archbishop returned to his bed, and no more progress was made for a week.[34] It was then too late to make any financial provision for Henry VI. On 2 July London opened its gates to the earls of March, Salisbury and Warwick, and the next day they were in St. Paul's, announcing to convocation their reasons for resorting to arms, and swearing on the cross of Canterbury that their intentions were compatible with their allegiance to the king.[35]

Both these meetings of the Canterbury convocation thus provided platforms for the propaganda of secular factions, by the archbishop's own design in 1399, and possibly by accident in 1460, although some of the prelates at the later meeting must have been anticipating the Yorkist advance from Calais: Bishops Grey of Ely and Neville of Exeter went, with armed escorts, to meet it outside London.[36] Despite their association with lay political interests, however, these bishops promoted other causes with their colleagues. Neville submitted an article intended to ensure higher educational standards among parochial incumbents, a proposal which must have been devised to benefit his clients, the regent masters of Oxford; they had written to ask this convocation to increase the promotion of scholars to benefices.[37]

In contrast to 1460, Arundel's register shows that in 1399 a convocation could be efficiently managed. Its first full meeting was on 7 October, the last on the sixteenth. To avoid difficulties, the archbishop appointed a committee of five ecclesiastical lawyers to draw up the articles from the two houses of prelates and lower clergy. The official record indicates the nature of the articles expected by the archbishop: they would be complaints of injuries to the church and clergy ('*super quibus pretendunt ecclesiam et se gravatos*').[38] It was perhaps then that Arundel made the speech reported by Usk, on how the temporal power had no scruple in violating the liberties of the English church, particularly by the seizure, imprisonment and judgement of bishops as if they were laymen.[39] The clergy's *gravamina* asserted that some of their members had also suffered at the hands of lay officials. A score of their articles instanced various forms of exaction and oppression. The activities of church courts had been impeded by improper use of writs of prohibition, and royal judges had disregarded established procedures for these writs. Royal officials had arrested clergy while they were performing services in cathedrals and churches; it might have been added that such arrests had been forbidden by statute in 1376 and 1377.[40] Clerks and even priests had been maliciously indicted and convicted in lay courts, and then been denied benefit of clergy and hanged like lay felons because their indictments had included charges of general notoriety.[41] Obviously the examples of these and the other violations of ecclesiastical rights in the minds of convocation in October 1399 had occurred in the reign of Richard II. The deposition articles had quoted two others, purveyance of monastic property and signet letters stopping actions in church courts. Some individual clergy were to claim that they had been ousted from their benefices.[42] The initiative for these acts of spoliation lay with the king's clerks who had obtained Richard's letters of presentation, just as blame for the other alleged malpractices properly belonged to common law judges and royal officials, and to individuals who had successfully petitioned the king or 'laboured' juries to assist their prosecution of suits against clergy. This was why the convocation of October 1399 wanted Henry IV to confirm all the privileges and rights granted to the prelates and clergy, and particularly those in Magna Carta, the statute (*sic*) of *Circumspecte Agatis* and Edward II's letters patent *pro clero*.[43]

Following this well-organized expression of clerical grievances, Arundel made a statement claiming that the English church had been in grave peril in Richard's reign. In mandates issued on the last day of convocation, he referred to England's recent afflictions. God's people had been oppressed by unprecedented wrongs and justice had been denied. The church had been crushed by rapacity, the inheritance of Christ trampled down, and God himself despised in the treatment given to his ministers. But, the order continued, in his wisdom the Eternal Judge had sought to save England from the final destruction of peace, justice and divine worship, by calling on Henry, now king, like another Maccabeus, to rule his people and lead them back into the paths of righteousness. From his own knowledge, Arundel testified that in all his doings, King Henry walked in the fear of the Lord, and he would not spare himself in the defence of the church and the salvation of his people.[44]

This was far more useful propaganda for Henry IV's usurpation than any number of doctored accounts of Richard's supposed abdication or of the proceedings at Westminster on 29 September.[45] The archbishop's interpretation of the political upheaval would have been distributed throughout the province of Canterbury, through his suffragans to their archdeacons, to heads of religious houses and rural deans, and finally to the parochial clergy. It appeared in an order for clergy and people to take part in processions and prayers that God would bless and favour Henry of Lancaster. This was Arundel's response to Henry's message asking for prayers, a means of communication which had been used for the last hundred years by royal governments anxious to win public support for their policies.[46] Congregations of parishes were accustomed to being taught, in the 'Great Curse', that rebellion was a grievous sin, incurring *ipso facto* sentence of excommunication.[47] Through Archbishop Arundel's message, however, they were assured that the rebellion against Richard II was entirely justified, and that they could now owe full loyalty to Henry IV as their divinely-chosen king. The archbishop doubtless presumed that the willing co-operation of the clergy in this exercise of indoctrination had been secured by their persuasion, if they needed it, at the recent convocation, that the church's liberties were being destroyed by Richard II and would be preserved by Henry IV. Henry had indeed newly given the clergy reassuring proof of his orthodoxy by causing Sir John Cheyne to withdraw from his election as speaker of the Commons, after the archbishop had told convocation that Cheyne was a notorious enemy of the Church.[48] Despite his obvious personal interest in the success of the political revolution, it need not be denied that Arundel himself sincerely believed that he was serving the church by acting as a kingmaker.[49]

The same conclusion may be made about the conduct of Thomas Bourchier. The protracted course of his convocation in 1460 was not wholly, if at all, deliberately contrived for the benefit of the Yorkist faction. This was the first convocation since he had become archbishop in January 1455, and he must have had ample reason to call on his clergy to correct defects in their ministry and conduct. Grievances also were expressed. At the sixth session, on 14 May, written articles from the bishops asked that two categories of people should be declared excommunicate: sheriffs, other officials and juries who caused priests to be indicted on false charges; and secondly, those who cited clergy to secular courts by writs of *premunire facias* and '*alia injusta brevia*'.[50] Neither complaint was new. False indictments of clergy had appeared yet again in *gravamina* of the convocation of Canterbury in 1421.[51] Defendants in ecclesiastical causes, in diocesan courts as well as the Roman curia, resorted to process under the statutes of *premunire* on the alleged grounds that the matters at issue should properly have been tried in common law courts; as a result, the plaintiffs in these causes, together with their proctors and sometimes also the officials of church courts, were cited to King's Bench under threat of outlawry and confiscation, and might be condemned to pay damages if juries pronounced against them.[52] The anti-clerical animus of certain judges and juries could weigh the scales against those answering to process by *premunire*. Benefit generally preserved clergy from execution, although not from arrest or trial, or outlawry consequent to indictment.[53] From 1434, at the latest, convocations of Canterbury and York expressed their fears about both forms of judicial harassment, and petitioned parliaments for remedy.[54] In 1449, it was conceded that individual priests maliciously indicted of rape might have the king's letters of pardon, but even this limited relief was bought by convocation's grant to the king of a poll-tax on chaplains normally exempt from taxation.[55] The clergy's pleas otherwise fell upon deaf ears. The renewed attention to these two serious grievances in 1460 further explains why that convocation was unwilling to give any priority to Henry VI's request for a subsidy.[56] For nearly thirty years his government had allowed clergy to be persecuted by false indictments and the jurisdiction of their courts to be hampered by *premunires*. On this count it might well have been argued that the king had failed to honour his coronation oath to protect the church and its rights and privileges.[57] To adapt a familiar quotation, it may be said that Archbishop Bourchier and some of his suffragans attached themselves to the house of York because they were unable to rescue the church from the consequences of Henry VI's inanity by any other means.[58]

Edward IV, like Thomas Arundel on Henry IV's behalf, invoked divine sanction for his assumption of the throne. On 6 March 1461, two days after his enthronement, he issued a proclamation which began:

> 'He that directeth the hertes of all princes, by whoos disposicion we ben born the verrey enheriter of the corones and roiall astate of the reaumes of Englond and of Fraunce and lordshipp of Irland, hathe putte in oure remembraunce the lamentable state and ruyne of this reaume of Englonde.'[59]

The declaration of Edward's title in his first parliament developed the thesis that England's recent tribulations were God's doom for the Lancastrian usurpation.[60] In the following year he issued another statement about monstrous calamities in years just passed; but on this occasion the foremost cause of divine punishment, Edward professed to believe, was that for many years the prelates and ministers of the English church had not been permitted to enjoy their liberties. As a Christian prince called to the throne by divine grace, Edward intended to honour the canons of the holy fathers and save his people from the censures of the church. Again, this was clearly propaganda designed to recruit clerical enthusiasm for the new political order, but the words and sentiments had been put into Edward's mouth by the episcopal authors of a petition which was promulgated as a royal charter to the clergy of England.[61] George Neville had declared the articles of Edward's title to the crown in St. John's Fields on 1 March 1461, and had preached at St. Paul's Cross on the morning of the enthronement three days later.[62] As chancellor of England he would also have supervised the preparation of these three declarations of Yorkist theology.

Although Henry IV and Edward IV gained early benefits from the convocations held at the beginnings of their reigns, neither acted promptly to remedy the grievances articulated in those meetings. The plea by the convocation of October 1399 that the king should confirm various instruments beneficial to the clergy finally bore fruit in a statute three years later.[63] There is no reference to this request and its associated grievances in the record of the convocation held by Arundel early in 1401: its principal business was the trials of the Lollard William Sawtre and two others, but it also made a grant of three half-tenths to the king in recognition of his gracious protection of the clergy and in particular for his defence of the orthodox faith.[64] This statement in the archbishop's certificate of the grant suggests that the clergy had agreed to their subsidy on 11 March because a simultaneous parliament had assented to their petition against unlicensed preachers and approved of the burning of Sawtre.[65] Arundel's next mandate, in 1402, began with an apology that urgent business compelled him to call a convocation despite his resolve to preserve his prelates and clergy from wearisome and costly vexations. On the opening day, 21 October, the king's envoys arrived so promptly that they had to listen to the sermon and routine business before the earl of Worcester could explain why another subsidy was required. This time, convocation took advantage of the king's financial difficulties to gain some concessions of substance. Arundel advised the clergy to appoint another committee to list their grievances, and they chose twelve 'good men and true' ('*probos et excellentes*'), surely a Freudian revelation that they were preoccupied with their treatment by courts of common law. Henry IV's third parliament was then in session. Arundel and his suffragans, claiming to speak for all the clergy of the realm, petitioned the king to provide a remedy with parliament's assent against the practice of common law courts in denying benefit to clergy indicted in novel, general terms. The archbishop's concern about this form of prosecution had been heightened a few months earlier when a member of his entourage, the chronicler Adam Usk, had been the victim of a false indictment which added that Usk was a notorious thief.[66] The petition was granted and enacted as a statute, as were confirmations of all extant chartered and statutory liberties of the clergy. A third statute extended the common law remedy available for incumbents expelled by royal presentations.[67] The parliament was dissolved on 25 November, but the Canterbury convocation had its final session two days later, when it granted the king three more half-tenths.[68]

The legislation of 1402 did not make any addition to the legal privileges which protected the clerical estate; the clergy's petition against novel generalities in indictments was amended so that the prohibition would benefit all subjects.[69] It thus seems strange that Arundel and his convocation adopted the expedient of withholding assent to a subsidy until these statutes were enacted. They were obviously expecting opposition to their limited requests from the house of commons. The majority of its members, as orthodox believers, were ready enough to approve legislation against heretics, as in 1401 and again in 1414, but the wealth and privileges of the church attracted much hostile comment.[70] Any parliamentary bill seeking some enhancement of the clergy's legal immunities was unlikely to receive the commons' necessary support. Henry IV granted a charter to Oxford University in 1406; it was criticized in all the later parliaments of his reign, and the university consequently failed to secure the new privilege it had conferred.[71] Occasionally the commons petitioned for the reform of alleged ecclesiastical abuses, but Henry acted as protector of the church by either refusing these bills or referring them to the episcopate; his successors dealt with anti-clerical commons' petitions in the same way, 'so that the church shall have his freedoms and liberties'.[72] Henry IV's commons did not adopt any of the radical schemes being proposed for plundering the church's endowments, but they did insist that when parliaments were asked for subsidies, the clergy should make at least a matching contribution to the king's relief.[73] In 1402, the southern convocation's grant was more generous than parliament's single lay subsidy. This was the price for the last legislation by any fifteenth-century parliament in response to petitions from the clergy seeking relief for their order.[74] Thomas Arundel's leadership of convocation, when he was fully conscious of his king's need for money, confirms that, for him, responsibility for the church was his paramount consideration.

Archbishop Bourchier was constrained to resort to similar tactics. The same convocation which failed to give Henry VI financial support reassembled in 1461 and granted Edward IV a tenth, after the archbishop and others had undertaken to ask the king to remedy the clergy's complaints.[75] No remedy had been provided when the next convocation met twelve months later, at Edward's request. By now the king had held a parliament, and the clergy's leaders had accepted that they could not obtain a remedial statute. They therefore applied for a royal charter, possibly at the suggestion of George Neville: in 1461, shortly after his re-election as chancellor of Oxford, he had induced Edward to grant a charter confirming, and even slightly amplifying, all previous royal grants of privilege to the university.[76] In its sessions in the summer of 1462, the convocation of Canterbury presumably agreed to the terms of a petition for a charter and agreed in principle that the king might have a clerical tenth. Edward gave his consent to the clergy's bill on 2 November, a week before a much reduced convocation reassembled and confirmed the subsidy.[77] The clergy of the northern province likewise delayed their grant of a subsidy until the petition had been granted.[78] The charter promised to relieve all clergy in holy orders from the two perils which had threatened them throughout Henry VI's reign. It offered a radical solution for the long-standing complaint about malicious indictments, because it forbad all common law prosecutions of ordained clergy; they would be triable only in church courts. Process by *premunire facias* against judges and parties in English church courts was also forbidden.[79]

It seems appropriate that a royal grant of clerical immunity from common law jurisdiction which would have satisfied Thomas Becket should be conveyed by charter. This was a very antiquated instrument for conferring rights on an extensive group of subjects. For that purpose, common law judges regarded royal charters as less authoritative than statute; in their opinion, the king could not give legal rights to a particular section of subjects which would impair the rights of the remainder of his subjects: only statute could do that.[80] The convocation of Canterbury seemingly appreciated this distinction at its next meeting after the grant of the charter, in July 1463. It learned that clergy were still being indicted and arrested. It appointed a committee to ascertain, before the next parliament, how the charter might be better observed, and it granted a charitable subsidy to the archbishop and George Neville, who was still chancellor of England; this was probably intended to meet the costs of promoting a parliamentary bill.[81] No statute for the clergy emerged from the next or any other of the parliaments of Edward IV. In their desperation, the two primates and their clergy sued a bull from Sixtus IV, in 1476, which forbad the arrest and trial of their members by secular authorities under pains of excommunication and anathema; but in 1481 Bourchier was still being asked by convocation to urge the king to restrain his judges and officers.[82] In 1484, Canterbury made another attempt to win statutory recognition of Edward's concessions; in return for two clerical tenths, Richard III confirmed his brother's charter, but his parliament yielded nothing.[83]

Edward IV's charter of 1462 was an expression of royal benevolence, but the king's sympathetic intentions, however genuine, did not stop his subjects' vexatious litigation against clergy, or his judges from hearing their suits.[84] The public disregard of the charter emphasises the impotence of the crown to introduce legal change without parliamentary support. It suggests also that Archbishop Bourchier and his suffragans in the early 1460s were politically naive if they held Henry VI personally responsible for their clergy's tribulations and put their faith in a new king providing a remedy. This inference is not unreasonable given their aristocratic and academic backgrounds, and Gascoigne's contention that bishops were out of touch with their people.[85] Certainly personal experience in the daily routine of royal government was as rare among the episcopate of 1460 as it had been common in Arundel's lifetime. Since then the crown's administrative establishment at Westminster had come to be staffed almost entirely by laymen: unlike their predecessors in the fourteenth century, civil servants were generally no longer ordained and consequently promoted to benefices, sometimes to bishoprics. The disappearance of 'king's clerks' from the bureaucracy reduced the representation of the church establishment in government, while more widely in southern England the declining numbers of ordinands to the secular priesthood reflected the growth of popular anticlericalism.[86] The common elements in the records of the prelates who furthered depositions of kings in 1399 and 1461 indicate that the defence of ecclesiastical interests did have some part in directing their conduct in national politics. The contrast in their achievements is no less significant: Thomas Arundel was the last medieval archbishop of Canterbury to win any parliamentary enactment intended to protect the clerical estate; the ineffectual Yorkist charter was buried with Richard III.[87]

Notes

1. R.W. Southern, *Western Society and the Church in the Middle Ages* (1970), 16.
2. G. Lapsley, *Crown, Community and Parliament* (Oxford, 1951), 273–373, reprints his articles of 1934 and 1938 which began modern revision of Henry IV's 'parliamentary title'. The latest contribution is G.O. Sayles, 'The deposition of Richard II: three Lancastrian narratives', *BIHR*, liv (1981), 257–70.
3. *Eulogium Historiarum sive Temporis*, ed. F.S. Haydon (RS, 1858–63), iii, 382.
4. *Rotuli Parliamentorum* (1783), iii, 421–2. See also *Historia Vitae et Regni Ricardi Secundi*, ed. G.B. Stow (University of Pennsylvania Press, 1977), 139–41; *The Kirkstall Abbey Chronicles*, ed. J. Taylor (Thoresby Society, 1952), 83; *Eulogium*, iii, 376; T. Walsingham, *Historia Anglicana*, ed. H.T. Riley (RS, 1863–4), ii, 224–6; *Johannis de Trokelowe et Henrici de Blaneforde Chronica et Annales*, ed. H.T. Riley (RS, 1865), 210–13; A.L. Brown, 'The Latin letters in MS. All Souls 182', *EHR*, lxxxvii (1972), 568–71; R.G. Davies, 'Richard II and the Church in the years of "tyranny"', *Journal of Medieval History*, 1 (1975), 338–42. According to K.B. McFarlane, *Lancastrian Kings and Lollard Knights* (Oxford, 1972), 51–2, Arundel was duped by Henry of Lancaster in 1399; cf. the hostile Dieulacres chronicler, who regarded them as partners in perjury (M.V. Clarke and V.H. Galbraith, 'The Deposition of Richard II', *Bulletin of the John Rylands Library*, 14 (1930), 52.
5. *CCR, 1396–99*, 520, 522–3; *CPR, 1396–99*, 589, 591; *Eulogium*, iii, 381.
6. *Chronicon Adae de Usk*, ed. E.M. Thompson (1904), 38, 193.
7. *Calendar of State Papers: Milan*, ed. A.B. Hinds (H.M.S.O., 1913), i, 36.
8. *Wars of the English in France*, ed. J. Stevenson (RS, 1861–4), ii, part 2, 999. For Beauchamp, see notes 58–9 below.
9. *BRUO*, i, 51–3, 230–2; ii, 1347–9.
10. R.L. Storey, *The End of the House of Lancaster* (1966), 113–15, 130, 133–5.
11. *CPR, 1452–61*, 352; *Registrum Cancellarii Oxoniensis, 1434–1469*, ed. H.E. Salter (Oxford Historical Society, 1932), i, 400: *The Register of Congregation, 1448–1463*, ed. W.A. Pantin and W.T. Mitchell (Oxford Hist. Soc., 1972), 357–8; *Epistolae Academicae Oxon.*, ed. H. Anstey (Oxford Hist. Soc., 1898), ii, 350. See also G.I. Keir, 'The ecclesiastical career of George Neville, 1432–1476' (unpublished B.Litt. thesis, Oxford, 1970), and my contribution to the forthcoming *History of Oxford University*, ii.
12. Corpus Christi College, Cambridge: MS. 423, pp. 37–8 (which refers to Neville's election for life); cf. *BRUO*, ii, 1347.
13. *Epistolae Acad. Oxon.*, ii, 489–90; *BRUO*, iii, 2083–4.
14. *Registrum Thome Bourgchier*, ed. F.R.H. Du Boulay (CYS, liv, 1957), p. xx; cf. R.J. Knecht, 'The Episcopate and the Wars of the Roses', *University of Birmingham Historical Journal*, 6 (1957–8), 111.
15. M. Aston, *Thomas Arundel* (Oxford, 1967), 2–4, 375–7; R.G. Davies, 'Thomas Arundel as Archbishop of Canterbury, 1396–1414', *JEH*, xxiv (1973), 9–21; for his reluctance to become chancellor in 1407, see *St. Albans' Chronicle 1406–20*, ed. V.H. Galbraith (Oxford, 1927), 10.
16. *CCR, 1396–99*, 520.
17. *CPR, 1396–99*, 590, 594; for Roger, 'late archbishop', etc., see ibid. 597; *CCR, 1396–99*, 523.
18. Lambeth Palace Library: archiepiscopal register of Thomas Arundel, i, fo. 51; *Wykeham's Register*, ed. T.F. Kirby (Hampshire Record Society, 1896–9), ii, 490: omitted from the record of this convocation in *Concilia Magnae Britanniae et Hiberniae*, ed. D. Wilkins (1737), iii, 238–45.
19. Aston, 210–11, 318; *BRUO*, i, 113–14.
20. *Chron. Usk*, 29–30, 181–2, 181 n. 2.

21. Reg. Arundel, i, fos. 93, 262 (memorandum of institution on 1 October by the archbishop 'post exilium suum ad Angliam reversus').

22. Rot. Parl., iii, 425–7; CPR, 1399–1401, 28–9; cf. CFR, 1391–99, 244–5.

23. W. Stubbs, The Constitutional History of England (Oxford, 1903), iii, 25–6.

24. Rot. Parl., iii, 419; cf. CPL, v, 259–60; Walsingham, Hist. Angl., ii, 227.

25. Concilia, iii, 246; Wykeham's Reg., ii, 492–3; Literae Cantuarienses, ed. J.B. Sheppard (RS, 1887–9), iii, 71.

26. Reg. Arundel, i, fo. 51.

27. I. Maccabees, vi. 57; Rot. Parl., iii, 415. Note Arundel's allusion to Maccabeus above, p. 89.

28. I am indebted to the Rt. Revd. E.W. Kemp for the identification of these biblical references. From after this point Wilkins printed the record from Arundel's register (Concilia, iii, 238–45). Cf. Trokelowe, 289.

29. Presumption that the initiative was Arundel's is strengthened by the lack of any record that a convocation of York was held at this time (HBC, 558; D.B. Weske, Convocation of the Clergy (1937), 270. In fact, Archbishop Scrope of York was active at Westminster then (Rot. Parl., iii, 416–17).

30. CCR, 1454–61, 422; Reg. Bourgchier, 78–80. For the convocation of York, see note 75, below.

31. C.L. Scofield, The Life and Reign of Edward the Fourth (1923), i, 51–64; PRO: Exchequer, Receipt rolls (E.401), nos. 867–70.

32. Reg. Bourgchier, 84, 81; BRUO, iii, 1649–50.

33. Acts, xx.28.

34. Reg. Bourgchier, 82–92.

35. An English Chronicle of the reigns of Richard II, Henry IV, Henry V and Henry VI, ed. J.S. Davies (CS, old series, lxiv, 1856), 95.

36. Scofield, i, 78–80.

37. Reg. Bourgchier, 86; Epistolae Acad. Oxon., ii, 359–61 (a letter misdated 1471 by the editor although signed by John Farley who died in 1464: BRUO, ii, 667).

38. Concilia, iii, 329.

39. Chron. Usk, 44, 204.

40. SR, i, 398; ii, 5.

41. Concilia, iii, 243–5 (nos. 44–63).

42. Rot. Parl., iii, 420–1, 430, 438, 444; CPR, 1399–1401, 32, 120, 129, 311; Anglo-Norman Letters and Petitions, ed. M.D. Legge (Anglo-Norman Text Society, 1941), 28–9, 327–8.

43. Concilia, iii, 243 (nos. 44–5); Trokelowe, 290–1. Davies, 'Richard II and the Church', concentrates on Richard's relations with the papacy and episcopate in 1396–9.

44. Wykeham's Reg., ii, 491–2.

45. See note 2, above.

46. W.R. Jones, 'The English Church and Royal Propaganda during the Hundred Years War', Journal of British Studies, xix (1980), 18–30. Wykeham's Reg. shows that bishop as particularly interested in the events of 1399 (see notes 18, 25, 44). On 19 July, when he would have known of Henry's advance, Wykeham ordered processions in his diocese that God would direct Richard 'per suorum semitas mandatorum' (ii, 490).

47. John Myrc, Instructions for Parish Priests (EETS, OS 31, 1868), 21–2; Register of Henry Chichele, ed. E.F. Jacob (CYS, 1937–47) i, cxxviii–ix.

48. J.S. Roskell, The Commons and their Speakers in English Parliaments, 1376–1523 (Manchester, 1965), 68–9, 136–7.

49. On 10 Jan. 1400, he wrote to Christ Church, Canterbury, about his escape from ambush by the earls plotting Henry's death; there is no expression of regret or piety in his account of the deaths of these 'sceleris auctores'. Both here and in an order for processions soon afterwards, Arundel attributed his escape to divine intervention (Lit. Cantuar., iii, 73–5; Concilia, iii, 246–7). The notion that Richard received divinely-ordained punishment also appears in Mum and the Sothsegger, ed. M. Day and R. Steele (EETS, OS 199, 1936), 22–3; 'The Chronicle of

Thomas Otterbourne', *Duo rerum Anglicarum Scriptores*, ed. T. Hearne (Oxford, 1732), i, 201; *Trokelowe*, 240; John Gower, *The Major Latin Works*, trans. E.W. Stockton (Washington, 1962), 311–25.

50. *Reg. Bourgchier*, xxix, 85–6.
51. *Reg. Chichele*, iii, 77–8.
52. R.L. Storey, 'Clergy and common law in the reign of Henry IV', *Medieval Legal Records*, ed. R.F. Hunnisett and J.B. Post (H.M.S.O., 1978), 346–8.
53. L.C. Gabel, *Benefit of Clergy in England in the Later Middle Ages* (1928–9, reprinted New York, 1969), 30–60; R.L. Storey, *Diocesan Administration in Fifteenth-Century England* (Borthwick Papers, 16, York, 1972), 25–7.
54. *Reg. Chichele*, i, cxxviii–ix; ii, 256–7, 282–6; *Concilia*, iii, 540, 555–6; E.F. Jacob, 'Archbishop John Stafford', *TRHS*, 5th series, 12 (1962), 16–17.
55. *Rot. Parl.*, v. 152–3; *SR*, ii, 352.
56. The Receipt Roll (E.401/871) records only two loans by members of convocation while it was sitting , of 100 marks each by the bishop of Worcester and abbot of Ramsey, on 15 and 26 May (cf. p. 87 above).
57. The 'Yorkist' manifesto addressed to Archbishop Bourchier and all the commons, apparently in June 1460, cited the oppression of the church and its ministers as the first, but briefest, reason for disaffection with Henry VI's rule (*English Chron.*, 86).
58. K.B. McFarlane, 'The Wars of the Roses', *PBA*, l (1965), 97. Bishop Richard Beauchamp of Salisbury had been the king's envoy to the duke of York in 1459, and was his spokesman to ask convocation for a subsidy in 1460; he may have been a boyhood companion of the king, because in 1428 his father, Sir Walter Beauchamp of Powick, had been appointed one of the young king's attendants (*BRUO*, i, 137–8; *Reg. Bourgchier*, 84; Roskell, *Speakers*, 348–50; cf. p.83 above). Thomas Kemp of London had been sued by *praemunire facias* in 1448, when the duke of Suffolk was blocking his provision to the see (*BRUO*, ii, 1032; *Yearbooks* (1679), 27 Hen. VI, Mich. no. 35; Knecht, 'Episcopate', 110).
59. PRO: Chancery, Close rolls (C.54), no. 312, m. 38d.; *CCR*, 1461–68, 54–5. After the battle of Towton, Beauchamp wrote of Edward as a saviour sent by God (*Cal. S.P. Milan*, i, 64).
60. *Rot. Parl.*, v, 463–4.
61. See p. 92 above.
62. Scofield, i, 150–1.
63. *Concilia*, iii, 243 (nos. 44–5).
64. Ibid.iii, 254–63, prints part of the record in Reg. Arundel, ii, fos. 178–86; *CFR*, 1399–1405, 123.
65. *Rot. Parl.*, iii, 473; *SR*, ii, 125–8 (unusually, the text of the statute is in Latin, confirming its explicit origin from the convocation). The parliament ended one day earlier; Sawtre was burnt on 2 March.
66. Storey, 'Clergy and common law', 343, 362–3. A dozen friars and other clergy had been executed earlier that year, for treason, which (convocation's petition shows) was not clergiable (ibid., 343).
67. *Rot. Parl.*, iii, 494, 507; *SR*, ii, 132–3.
68. Reg. Arundel, i, fos. 54–5v. (*Concilia*, iii, 270, gives part of this record); *CFR*, 1399–1405, 197.
69. Another point noted in the king's reply to the petition was an undertaking by Arundel and his bishops to observe a provincial constitution of 1352 concerning the imprisonment of convicted clerks (*Concilia*, iii, 13–14, 272; *Rot. Parl.*, iii, 494). Arundel ordered its observation at the last session of convocation (Reg., i, fo.55v.).
70. *Rot. Parl.*, iii, 583–4; iv, 2; *SR*, ii, 181–2.
71. *Medieval Archives of the University of Oxford*, ed. H.E. Salter (Oxford Hist. Soc., 1920–1), i, 231–4; *Calendar of Charter Rolls*, v, 430–1; *Rot. Parl.*, iii, 613, 638, 660–1; *SR*, ii, 166.

72. Storey, *Diocesan Administration*, 19–20.
73. Walsingham, *Hist. Angl.*, ii, 259, 265–7, 272; *St. Albans' Chron.*, 52–6; E.F. Jacob, 'The Canterbury Convocation of 1406', *Essays in Medieval History presented to B. Wilkinson*, ed. T.A. Sandquist and M.R. Powicke (Toronto, 1969), 345–53; A. Rogers, 'Clerical Taxation under Henry IV', *BIHR*, xlvi (1973), 123–44.
74. There were two limited exceptions: an act of 1429 which gave members of convocations the same immunity from arrest as members of parliaments (*Rot. Parl.*, iv, 347; *Stat. Realm*, ii, 238); and the pardon in 1449 (p. 90 above).
75. *Reg. Bourgchier*, 93–4. The convocation of York also granted Edward a tenth, on 23 March 1462, the final session of an assembly opened on 30 April 1460; it is not known to have made any grant to Henry VI (*CFR, 1461–71*, 89–90).
76. *Medieval Archives of Univ. Oxford*, i, 247–52, esp. 249.
77. Bourchier's register has no record of this convocation. For his mandate of citation, quoting the king's writ of 4 June, see Hants Records Office, Winchester: episcopal register of William Waynflete, i, fo. 72 (second foliation). The petition for the charter must have been written before John Kingescote was consecrated as bishop of Carlisle on 24 October, because his name is interlined after those of other bishops. The bill is written in an unmistakable 'Chancery hand', evidence of George Neville's part in its promotion. After Edward's sign-manual had been applied, it was a warrant for the great seal (PRO: C.81, file 149, no. 49).
    CFR, 1461–71, 81–8, shows that the Canterbury convocation met on 21 July–2 August and 8–25 November. The terms of the subsidy required earlier payment by listed absentees from the November meeting, also at St. Paul's, on the alleged grounds that they had been spared the expense of attendance. The heads of 130 religious houses shown as absent, however, were those of the wealthier houses (e.g. Westminster!). It is possible that poorer houses had also been excused but were spared the earlier payment. Seven bishops and forty one dignitaries were also absent. It seems improbable that the November rump could have assented to the subsidy on behalf of all the clergy: at this date, a full convocation would have had nearly 450 members (E.W. Kemp, *Counsel and Consent* [1961], 119–20).
78. Also after a writ of 4 June, Archbishop Booth called a York convocation for 1 September; how long it sat is not known, but Booth did not certify the king until 3 August 1463 that a half-tenth would be paid on 2 February 1464 (*Concilia*, iii, 580; *CFR, 1461–71*, 119–20).
79. *Concilia*, iii, 583–5; *Reg. Bourgchier*, 102–7. Also conceded was that church courts might try tithe-suits on trees over twenty years old, on which Canterbury convocation had vainly sued in 1444 (*Concilia*, iii, 540). See also Gabel, 122–3; C.B. Firth, 'Benefit of clergy in the time of Edward IV', *EHR*, xxxii (1917), 175–91.
80. *Yearbooks*, 8 Hen. VI, Hil. no. 6; T.F.T. Plucknett, 'The Lancastrian Constitution', in *Tudor Studies*, ed. R.W. Seton-Watson (1924), 168-9, 173–80.
81. *Reg. Bourgchier*, 102, 107–9, 111–12; F. R.H. Du Boulay, 'Charitable subsidies granted to the archbishop of Canterbury, 1300–1489', *BIHR*, xxiii (1950), 157, 160–1.
82. *Concilia*, iii, 608–9 (cf. *Reg Bourgchier*, xxxv, n.3), 609–10; *CPL*, xiii, part ii, 506; *Reg. Bourgchier*, 134–5.
83. *Concilia*, iii, 614, 616; *CFR, 1471–85*, 278–80.
84. Storey, 'Clergy and common law', 348. For specific evidence of disregard of the charter, see K.B. Klesh, 'Edward IV's Charter to the Clergy' (unpublished M.Phil. thesis, Nottingham, 1981).
85. *Loci e Libro Veritatum*, ed. J.E.T. Rogers (Oxford, 1881), 39, 41–3.
86. R.L. Storey, 'Gentleman-Bureaucrats', in *Profession, Vocation and Culture in Later Medieval England*, ed. C.H. Clough (Liverpool, 1982), 97–109; and 'Recruitment of English Clergy in the Period of the Conciliar Movement', *Annuarium Historiae Conciliorum*, 7 (1975), 309–13.
87. It was not confirmed by Henry VII, whose council initiated prosecutions under the statutes of *Praemunire* (Storey, *Diocesan Administration*, 30–2).

4

'The Well of Grace': Englishmen and Rome in the Fifteenth Century[1]

John A.F. Thomson
University of Glasgow

On 22 November 1473 Sir John Paston wrote in a letter to his brother:

> Ye prayed me also to sende yow tydynges how I spedde in my materis, and in cheff of Mestresse Anne Hault. I have answer ageyn fro Roome that there is the welle of grace and salve sufficient for suche a soore, and that I may be dyspencyd with; nevertheless my proctore there axith a m[1] docatys, as he demythe. But Master Lacy, another Rome renner heer, whyche knowyth my seyde proctor theer, as he seythe, as weell as Bernard knewe hys sheeld, seythe that he menyth byt a C. docates or CC. at the most; wherffor afftre thys comythe moor. He wrote to me also, *quod Papa hoc facit hodiernis diebus multociens..*[2]

The evidence of this extract for the character of Anglo-papal relations in the fifteenth century is all the more revealing because it is a private letter, referring to negotiations for a dispensation, and is free from the propaganda which is contained in such sources as the preambles to statutes for regulating relations between England and Rome. It touches on church life rather than on church government, and the historian should take care to distinguish between the two.[3]

From all that one knows of his career, Sir John Paston was a fairly typical upper class Englishman of the period, whose views on the papacy would have been echoed by many of his contemporaries. Unfortunately for the historian, explicit statements about the papacy are rare in surviving letters of the period; in the Paston correspondence it is mentioned only in connection with obtaining a grace which Rome alone could provide or with the settlement of a legal matter which was reserved for papal decision. In 1466, for instance, there is a note of a payment for bringing a pardon from Rome, 'to pray for alle our frends sowles'; and in a letter of about 1479-80 mention is made of a friar who is seeking letters from Rome to some bishop in England 'to amend his mater'.[4] Other fifteenth-century letter writers seem similarly indifferent to the papacy. It is not mentioned in the Stonor correspondence, and in the letters of the Plumptons the only pre-Reformation allusion to the pope is a note in 1516 of the arrival of a legate in England to bring full powers to Cardinal Wolsey.[5] Had it not been for the close association of the Cely family with Sir John Weston, the master of the knights of St. John of Jerusalem in England, one may doubt whether their correspondence would have mentioned the pope at all; as it is, there is only a single reference in 1481 in which Weston informed George Cely of a meeting which he had had with the pope.[6]

Narrative sources for the period are equally sparse in allusions to the papacy, and might again leave an impression of indifference to it, at least after the time of the council of Constance. The latter was described at some length by the St. Albans chronicler;[7] and various London sources comment briefly on the restoration of unity after the schism.[8] Thereafter, however, the only London writer who provides more than the occasional passing comment is the conti-nuator of *Gregory's Chronicle*, who was probably a churchman himself.[9] He stresses similar matters to those mentioned in the letter sources, a papal indulgence, recourse to Rome for an authoritative decision in the dispute between the secular clergy of the city and the Carmelite friars, and the visit of a legate.[10] Slightly out of the ordinary is the mention of a bull of 1468 against the making of piked shoes, from which the cordwainers had secured royal exemption by privy seal. Such papal interference provoked some public hostility; '. . . sum men sayd that they wolde were longe pykys whethyr Pope wylle or nylle, for they sayd the Popys curse wolde not kylle a flye'. This sentiment clearly annoyed the chronicler, who added the pious postscript, 'God amend thys' to his narrative.[11] Other London sources mention papal indulgences, or their suspension during the year of Jubilee in Rome in 1500, and describe, although primarily as occasions of civic pageantry, visits of papal emissaries when caps of maintenance were conferred on English kings.[12] It is clear, however, that there was a basic loyalty to the pope; when the news of Julius II's election reached London, the mayor and his brethren went to St. Paul's to hear the *Te deum* sung in honour of the occasion.[13]

It is hardly surprising that the monastic continuator of the Croyland chronicle showed a wider interest in ecclesiastical affairs than the London writers. He gave a graphic description of the Turkish capture of Constantinople and described Pius II's failure to organize a crusade against the Ottoman threat, mentioning, in this context, a tax to be levied on the English Church.[14] It was probably the same man, or another monk, who wrote an obituary of Abbot John Wisbech, praising him, among other things, for obtaining a papal bull dispensing the monks to eat meat at Septuagesima.[15] The 'civil service' continuator of the chronicle alludes to the Papacy twice, both times in connection with its dispensing power. In the context of allegations that Richard III was planning to marry his niece, the chronicler notes that assertions were made that the pope did not have the power to grant a dispensation in such a case of consanguinity. Later, he records the dispensation for Henry VII's marriage to Elizabeth of York.[16]

The chroniclers' comparative indifference to the papacy might suggest that it made little impression on Englishmen, but such a conclusion cannot be justified. The study of papal letters reveals numerous ties between individual Englishmen and Rome, and that these persisted irrespective of tensions in the political relationships between the papacy and the English Crown. Unfortunately, the historian of the fifteenth-century English Church does not possess the advantages of his Scottish counterpart in having easy access to a mass of supplication material, either published or in a manuscript calendar with available microfilms. A similar calendar of English supplications would be of considerable value to historians. For the present, however, one may note that the letters issued by the papacy conferring graces on English recipients frequently stress that they had originated in response to an individual's petition, which is related in the bull. Indeed it is fair to say that *motu proprio* grants by the popes comprise a very small part of the letters issued, and are principally concerned with reservations and provisions of benefices to Englishmen who held posts at the curia.[17] Even where the eventual papal letters make no mention of a petition, it is clear from their subject matter that the papacy could have been made aware of the need for the grace only by the request of the eventual beneficiary.

The background to these supplications was essentially three-fold. Men might petition the pope to be dispensed from some proviso of canon law in order to take some action in the future, or they might be seeking a pardon for some past action so that it would not be to their disadvantage, either in this world or in eternity. Men were concerned that their actions should accord with the laws of both God and man, and it is noteworthy that a considerable number of petitions state that the request was prompted by scruples of conscience on the part of the petitioner, even although there was no public knowledge of the sin which had caused the sense of guilt. Thirdly, there were certain favours which the pope could grant, which might give the individual the opportunity to lead a fuller spiritual life. Both clergy and laity might want grants in all three of these groups, dispensations, pardons, and favours.

The power to dispense from the provisions of canon law was a recognised right of the pope, and one which was noted in varying tones by two major English scholars of the century, the detached canonist William Lyndwood and the atrabilious theologian Thomas Gascoigne. Gasgoigne saw the dispensing power essentially as an abuse, particularly in cases affecting ecclesiastical organization and discipline; although he admitted that in positive law a papal dispensation could supersede a human prohibition, he stressed also that it must remain within the law of God.[18] He appealed to the pope, using all the rhetoric he could muster, to see that dispensations did not give rise to causes of scandal and offence.[19] Where Gascoigne declaimed, Lyndwood analysed, noting the circumstances in which papal dispensations were required. A man of illegitimate birth whose parents were both lay could be ordained to holy orders only with a papal dispensation, unless he entered religion, because an episcopal dispensation for illegitimacy sufficed only for minor orders.[20] Other irregularities from which only the pope could dispense a man for ordination were being in a state of excommunication or suspension at the time of ordination, defect of body,[21] guilt of an avoidable homicide,[22] simony[23] or bigamy.[24] Further dispensations might be required in cases where the man concerned was not only illegitimate but was also the son of a priest. The complexity of canon law, and the determination of the lawyers to provide for every eventuality, is shown by Lyndwood's consideration of the position of a man who had been conceived, perhaps in lawful wedlock, but who had not been born until his father was ordained.[25]

Not all these cases which Lyndwood considers actually appear in the dispensations recorded in the papal registers, although many of them do. Perhaps the greatest single group of dispensations was that of licences to men to hold incompatible benefices, a practice incidentally which was violently attacked by Gascoigne.[26] A quick glance at the index of subjects in any volume of the *Calendar of Papal Letters* makes this abundantly clear. Men who were illegitimately born could be dispensed to receive orders, holy as well as minor.[27] In order to meet the precise requirements of the law, the circumstances of their illegitimacy were set out. The range of these can be seen in three cases from 1418 which appear close together in the register: Alexander Sparwe or Herbard of Bucknell, Oxfordshire, was the son of an unmarried man and an unmarried woman, as was John Dalton, rector of St. Ebbe's, Oxford, with the further complication that his parents were within the fourth degree of kinship; while Lewis Coychurche or ap Howell, presumably a man of Welsh origin although residing in the diocese of London where he was an officer of the consistory court, was the son of a priest and an unmarried woman.[28] In the same year John Arondel, also from this diocese, who was still only in his seventeenth year, was dispensed to hold benefices, admittedly only compatible ones, although he was the son of a married knight and a woman married to someone else.[29] The procedure for men who were holding benefices in plurality seems to have been to present their papal letters to the bishop or his vicar-general when they were seeking institution, and it is likely that other letters of dispensation were produced in the same way.[30] They could also be produced at a later date; in the court of audience of Bishop Atwater of Lincoln in the early sixteenth century there are records of a number of men cited for non-residence, who then produced their dispensations to hold more than one benefice.[31] Nuns too could be dispensed for promotion to offices in their houses despite illegitimacy. Thomasina Warde, an Augustinian nun of Burnham, and the daughter of a priest and a nun, was licensed to hold dignities below that of abbess (1418); but Alice Burton (1432), a Benedictine of Broomhall and the daughter of an unmarried nobleman and an unmarried noblewoman, as well as Joan Burton (1444), of the Fontevrault house of Nuneaton and the daughter of a priest and a widow, were given full dispensations to hold any dignities within their houses.[32]

Another possible bar to ordination, or to the exercise of powers pertaining to orders if a man had been ordained previously, was physical defect. But even if a priest suffered from such a defect, he could obtain permission to continue fulfilling sacerdotal functions. In the cases of a canon of Warter (1456), who had been accidentally blinded in one eye,[33] and of John Manyngham, vicar of St. Margaret, Lowestoft (1472), who suffered from a deformity of his left shoulder, arm and hand,[34] both of whom were ordained to the priesthood with these defects, no responsibility could be attached to the party concerned for the imperfection involved; but two cases are recorded of men who were dispensed to continue ministering in their orders despite having castrated themselves in order to live more chastely.[35]

A well known limitation on the priesthood was that its members should not be involved in the shedding of blood, with, conversely, protection against having its own blood shed. Commission of a crime involving bloodshed could involve penalties for those already in orders, and might also be a barrier to ordination, but these restrictions could also be set aside by dispensation. Master Hugh Martill, rector of Tollerton in the diocese of York, was permitted (1400) to resume celebration of divine services, from which he had voluntarily abstained after the accidental homicide of John Smytheman in self-defence in a quarrel over lands belonging to the church.[36] Richard Norman, a monk, who had before entering religion accidentally killed a priest whose servant he was, and who had gone on pilgrimage to Rome and been absolved from this, was further dispensed (1435) for promotion to holy orders or to monastic dignities.[37] Robert Porte, a priest, who had committed a homicide in self-defence, and possibly had contributed to the accidental death of another man, was suspended (1482) for a year before rehabilitation;[38] and a penance was imposed in the more surprising case of John Degre (1482), who abandoned his priestly habit and went for three years to fight as a mercenary for the duke of Burgundy, taking part in a fight in which men were slain, although he himself did not kill nor wound anyone.[39]

Men might, however, feel guilt for more indirect involvement in bloodshed. There are cases of men seeking ordination who had earlier in their lives performed duties which had led to men's deaths. For example, Roger Huswyfe (1429), as a judge in the royal court at Lincoln, had pronounced sentences of death and mutilation; and John Stafford (1437), as scribe to the sheriffs of London, had written accusations against various robbers, several of whom were executed. Both were dispensed to receive holy orders, but with certain restrictions; Roger was not to proceed beyond deacon's orders, and John's ordination to the priesthood was not to take place until a year had elapsed from the date of the dispensation.[40] Possibly later in the century the rules were slightly relaxed: John Haxey (1456) was dispensed to proceed to all orders, despite participation as a coroner in proceedings involving capital sentences; and Richard Cavood (1488) who, while in the service of a secular judge, had selected jurors who had found a murderer guilty and delivered him to capital punishment, was dispensed for irregularity in receiving deacon's orders in ignorance of the impediment, and was permitted to proceed to the priesthood.[41]

The most striking case, however, of a man who felt guilty for indirect involvement in bloodshed was that of a future bishop of London, Robert Gilbert. In 1435, as dean of York, he received a dispensation in response to his own petition, which related that he had gone to France as dean of Henry V's chapel, and had several times been present at battles. He had not borne arms, nor had he killed or wounded anybody, but he was troubled in his conscience because he had rejoiced when the king's men gained the victory and lamented when they were defeated. Gilbert did not say when he began to feel these qualms; they may have been prompted by the horrors of war as he saw it, or he may have been led to have doubts about the justice of the English cause by the protracted and inconclusive warfare of the 1420s and the English reverses of the early 1430s.[42]

Canon law, however, did not apply only to churchmen, and there were certain offences which might be committed by laymen from which only the pope or his legate could grant absolution. These included the use of violence against clerks, the burning of a church, forgery of papal bulls (or the use knowingly of forged bulls), and participation, either in a religious service or in a criminal act, with someone whom the pope had excommunicated.[43] Most commonly of all, a layman might be involved with the provisions of canon law for the regulation of marriage, if a dispensation was required from its strict letter. 'Strict', indeed, is the right word; in theory marriage was forbidden on grounds of consanguinity to those within the fourth degree of kindred, namely those descended from a common great-great-grandparent. The rules of affinity complicated matters further, restricting marriage with those who were kindred of anyone with whom an individual had become 'one flesh', either licitly or illicitly. A man could not lawfully marry a woman if he had previously married or committed fornication with her sister, or her first, second or third cousin. In addition there was the complication of spiritual relationships, when a tie was established between a godparent and a godchild at baptism or confirmation.[44] When one considers the small size of some communities, the fact that in many marriages both parties came from the same parish,[45] and the high rate of mortality and remarriage, one can see that literal enforcement of the law could have led to almost impossible problems. In the upper reaches of society, the tendency of landed families to intermarry could also make it essential for a dispensation to be obtained. This presumably was the problem which Sir John Paston was facing in the extract quoted at the beginning of this paper.

The papal registers show clearly how many English men and women sought dispensations to regularize their marital status. Equally, it is certain that those responsible for upholding church law were more concerned with a pastoral responsibility to their subjects than with the letter of the rules. Where the parties concerned were aware that they had broken the regulations, a penance would normally be imposed as a condition for obtaining the dispensation. In 1418 John Aburham and Isabelle Boydelle of the diocese of Lichfield, who had married 'not in ignorance of an impediment arising from their being related in the third and third degrees of affinity', were enjoined to do penance and separate temporarily, but were then dispensed to contract marriage anew.[46] In the case of John Kupping and Margery Lomnoure of the diocese of Norwich in 1429 there was a different impediment, in that they had committed adultery during the lifetime of Margery's former husband and had exchanged a promise to marry after he died, although they were both innocent of his death. They too had to do penance and be temporarily separated; but they were also dispensed to remain in a marriage which they had contracted, the offspring of it being declared legitimate.[47]

The two barriers of adultery and affinity were united in the case of William Soper and Joan Chamberlayn of London in 1438, with the further complication of a surreptitious marriage. Joan was related to William's first wife Isabel in the second and third degrees of kindred, and had lived in their house during her cousin's lifetime. During that time she had had sexual relations with William, these falling into the class of incest, and after Isabel's death they had married without calling of banns, and consummated the marriage. They had to perform penance, but were dispensed to remain married, their offspring being declared legitimate, even if they had exchanged a promise during Isabel's lifetime to marry after her death provided that they, or one of them, had not encompassed it.[48] One further point about this case is worth stressing. In the petition for the dispensation, William and Joan stated that little or nothing of the circumstances had become known. If this was true, and one can certainly not say that it was not, the couple must have sought the dispensation not because of public notoriety but to secure relief from personal feelings of guilt. The desire for a grant from the papacy lay as much in the psychological needs of individuals as in legal requirements. The feeling that Rome could provide such relief established a strong tie between the individual Christian and the central organisation of the Church.

When a marriage had been contracted without knowledge of an existing impediment, no penance might be imposed on the parties, although the papacy does not seem to have had any clear policy in such cases. In 1418 Robert Clerck and Elena Wryght of the diocese of York did not have to perform penance before the validation of their marriage, despite the fact that Robert's first wife had been godmother to a child of Elena by an earlier husband.[49] On the other hand, in 1424 a penance was imposed on Ralph de Andirton and Ellen de Asshurst of

Lichfield diocese, when they were dispensed to contract marriage anew, after having originally wed in ignorance of their being in the third degree of affinity.[50] Possibly they may have persisted in a marriage, contracted in the assumption that it was valid, after discovering that the impediment existed. This certainly was the case of Nicholas Asgard and Isabel Vernon, also from Lichfield, in 1475. They had married unaware that Isabel's former husband was related to Nicholas, but after discovering the impediment, they had continued in the marriage with sexual relations for seven years. The penance imposed on them may again have been due to persistence in the marriage rather than to the original contracting of it.[51]

Papal grants did not only rectify breaches of canon law; they could also be sought in anticipation of a marriage to ensure that it would be lawful from the start. This presumably was the background to Sir John Paston's quest for a grace from Rome, although in fact his marriage plan never came to fruition and no dispensation was recorded. Among the landed classes, family alliances might be cemented by intermarriage, and in such cases one can see licences being sought in advance, as in 1442 when dispensations were granted for two marriages between members of the Harrington and Pilkington families, the parties concerned being related in the second and third degrees of kinship.[52] The most scrupulous would seek a dispensation even if they were uncertain that the impediment existed. In 1445 Thomas Gray and Alice de Elwyk were dispensed to contract marriage despite Alice's mother having been godmother to one of the twin sons of Thomas's mother, although the parties concerned did not know if the godson had been Thomas himself or his brother.[53]

The papal dispensing power could of course be exercised in other matters than marital ones. It could also release those who had taken incautious vows, possibly under highly emotional circumstances. This was particularly true of women who had vowed not to remarry after their husband's deaths. On his deathbed John Clerck had begged his wife Edeynna never to take another husband, and she had agreed. In her petition (1419), she stated that she had made this promise because if she had not given John, who loved her tenderly, this consolation, he might have died in a state of sin because of excessive grief, or, if he had recovered, might have loved her less and less every day. Because she was still young and desired to have children, she sought and obtained release from her vow, although she had to do penance for her incautious oath.[54] Alice, widow of William Hoton, had taken a vow of continence on the death of her husband, when she was still only in her twenty-seventh year; but she too secured release from her vow (1449–50), because she wished to marry and thought that she might find it difficult to resist attempts to ravish her.[55] As with some of the marriage dispensations, one sees pastoral concern for the individual petitioner in the permission granted to disregard a vow.

There were circumstances too in which vows of pilgrimage could be set aside. Robert de Wylby (1440), who had actually set out for the Holy Sepulchre, had been captured and imprisoned in Germany, where he had been held to ransom. He was afraid that he could not recover his liberty without very great loss, and that if he made a fresh attempt to carry out his vow, the losses might become intolerable. He was absolved from the vow.[56] No reason was given for Richard Lessi seeking release from a vow of pilgrimage (1481), but he was able to secure this by paying 100 ducats to crusading funds.[57] Where a pilgrimage was associated with an indulgence, it was possible to secure the benefits of the latter without making the journey. Henry VI's shield-bearer, Richard Tunstall, had resolved to go to Rome, but had not taken any oath to do so. He seems to have felt some moral compunction about not going, and was able to secure a release from any obligation to do so. At the king's request he was granted (1451) the benefits of the jubilee indulgence in return for small gifts to the poor and a promise to visit St. Paul's Cathedral and Westminster Abbey on three successive days.[58] On other occasions pilgrimage provided a pretext for temporary release from another kind of vow, that of enclosure. William Lucas, a priest anchorite at All Hallows, London, received such permission in 1478;[59] but a more interesting case dates from the end of the fourteenth century when a London woman, Catherine Kelsey, who had taken a vow of enclosure in Rome and had promised to live on alms alone, was permitted to leave her place of residence near St. Peter's and go on pilgrimage or to visit relatives and friends and then return.[60] It reflects the emotional appeal which Rome had to Christians that an Englishwoman should settle there as an anchoress; and the same attraction can be seen in the endowment of chaplains there. Rome remained a place which drew pilgrims; one knows that Margery Kempe spent considerable time there, and the records of the English hospital of St. Thomas in Rome from the first decade of the sixteenth century give the names of 489 visitors in the two and a half years between November 1504 and May 1507.[61] It is true that devotion to the shrines of the apostles did not necessarily involve affection for the papacy; but it is probable that the latter still gained something from the reflected glory of the early Church.

This issue is a digression from the main theme, but one which may help us to put the dispensing power into perspective. To return to it, perhaps the most unusual case of seeking release from a hasty vow was that of a priest of the diocese of Exeter, John Chiellod, in 1458, who had sworn that if he did not pronounce the words of his offices distinctly, he would resign his benefices and enter the Carthusian order. With perhaps excess scrupulosity, he feared that he had incurred irregularity after pronouncing the words of a benediction indistinctly. Here, clearly, one sees an individual being impelled by his conscience to seek an absolution, which was in fact granted.[62]

Another obligation from which individuals might seek release was that of fasting. This seems to have been willingly granted on grounds of health when observance of the Church's rules could be deleterious to the party concerned;[63] but a dispensation could also be forthcoming if fasting might harm the work which an individual had to perform, as in the case of the Hospitaller John Styllynflete (1441), who not only pleaded that the eating of fish was harmful to him, but also claimed that it prevented him from performing duties which he had to undertake for his order.[64] Those exempted from fasting had to perform works of piety or almsgiving instead.

Recourse to Rome, however, was not prompted simply by the search for dispensations. Time does not permit discussion of legal cases taken to Rome on appeal from English church courts, although one certainly finds a number of these, particularly in matrimonial and testamentary suits. More striking is the way in which local communities might appeal to Rome to solve practical difficulties in their religious observance. In a far-flung parish, small villages might be remote from the church to which their inhabitants owed obligations of attendance, and at seasons when the weather was bad, the roads between them and it might become impassable. In 1418 the inhabitants of Swynfelt (Swinefleet) on the Yorkshire Ouse stated that they were four miles distant from their parish church and two miles from another parish church at Whitgift, where their dead had been buried. Floods and bad roads made it difficult for them to go to either for mass or other offices, and they had built a chapel where mass was celebrated, *submissa voce*, by a chaplain. The pope granted their petition to have a font and for mass to be celebrated solemnly by the chaplain.[65] One sees similar activity by a community within a parish when, in 1456, the inhabitants of Great Dunmow in Essex were granted permission to have a priest in a chapel which they had erected, and to which they had given books, a chalice, vestments and ornaments. The priest was to be allowed to celebrate mass and other offices for them when the weather was too inclement for them to visit the parish church.[66] The papacy could, however, also safeguard existing parochial rights; when in 1430 the inhabitants of Senane (Sennen) in Cornwall were permitted to have a cemetery at the chapel of St. Senan, it was stipulated that this should not prejudice the parish church of St. Buryan, which was presumably still to receive the various dues payable at the time of burial.[67] A judicious balance was maintained between preserving existing rights and ensuring that services were available for the faithful.

In other circumstances lay petitioners might seek papal support to maintain the existing parish organisation, and expected to have justice from the pope even against churchmen. In 1426 the parishioners of West Hoathly, Patcham and Ditchling, in the diocese of Chichester, secured a papal mandate to the archbishop of Canterbury to investigate, and if need be to revoke, the appropriation of these churches because the appropriator, the prior of Lewes, had diminished worship there.[68] Similarly in 1481 the parishioners of Barnaby in the diocese of Norwich petitioned successfully that their parish church should not be united to another, nor to a monastery, without their consent, provided that they contributed enough annually to enable the rector to maintain himself.[69]

Papal grants could also affect the spiritual lives of individuals as well as the corporate worship of communities. This is most obvious in the indults to possess portable altars, on which the beneficiaries could celebrate mass if they were priests, or have it celebrated for them if they were laymen, or to choose one's own confessor, who could in certain circumstances grant plenary remission. There are literally hundreds of these grants scattered through the registers, although my impression is that there was some decrease in numbers in the latter part of the century. One cannot give precise figues for these grants, because the diocese of the recipient is not always mentioned and the registers also contain Scottish and Irish material which lies beyond the scope of this paper. Furthermore some such graces might come from Rome only indirectly, as papal agents in England could be empowered to grant them without a petition being sent to the pope.[70]

It is noteworthy that the majority of beneficiaries from such indults were laymen. During Martin V's pontificate, not less than 890 indults to possess portable altars were granted to English recipients. Churchmen received 432 of these, and 4 were granted to nuns; married couples were granted 318, individual laymen 103, and laywomen 33.[71] Of the 429 indults from the same period to choose a confessor who could grant plenary remission, 156 went to churchmen, 11 to nuns, 143 to married couples, 55 to laymen and 64 to laywomen.[72] When one remembers that during this pontificate there occurred the sharpest single conflict between the papacy and England after the end of the Great Schism and before the start of the Reformation,[73] it is striking that no apparent barrier was put on men seeking favours from Rome; nor was the pope reluctant to confer them. In many ways the operation of ecclesiastical life could be almost completely detached from questions of competing authority between the secular and spiritual powers.

The recipients of these grants included a wide cross-section of those members of English society who could afford to petition Rome for them. They included the highest in the land; in 1477 Edward IV himself received an indult to choose a confessor who could grant him plenary remission.[74] But many of the grants were made to obscure men and women, in both town and countryside; and when indults were conferred on corporate bodies such as guilds the members who benefitted may have been drawn from an even wider section of the population. In 1450 the guild of St. Christopher at York was permitted to choose a confessor who could grant plenary remission; and a similar indult was conferred on the Holy Trinity guild at King's Lynn in 1467.[75] Nor were guilds with purely religious functions the only such beneficiaries. In 1480 the wardens of the Mercers' guild in London received an indult that they and their wives, present and future, should have a portable altar on which mass might be celebrated by their own or another fit priest in presence of themselves and their household servants.[76]

One final point to be stressed is the value which was attached to securing a grant from Rome rather than from any other source. This was particularly true of dispensations, and some cases are recorded where parties who had already secured a grant went to the expense of securing its confirmation in Rome. This was true (in 1423) of Philip Courtenay and Elizabeth Hungerford, who had been dispensed to marry, despite relationship in the third and fourth degrees, by Henry Beaufort, bishop of Winchester, authorized by a faculty to give such dispensations.[77] Even a dispensation by a papal penitentiary did not give assurance to Thomas Damet, a priest who doubted if he could hold a benefice without apostolic dispensation, because before his fourteenth year he had, under duress, made profession as a Cistercian before subsequently returning to the world.[78] Lastly another priest, Robert Porte, who had shed blood in self-defence, had doubts whether or not a friar in London and a penitentiary at Santiago had, as they claimed, faculty from the holy see to grant him absolution, so he sought, and secured, it from the pope.[79]

The seeking of favours from Rome was therefore prompted by the desire for spiritual well-being. Sometimes individuals were concerned with a technical problem of canon law, sometimes with the desire to live a more active spiritual life, and sometimes with the wish to be freed from some burden of sin and guilt. Some dispensations were intended to prevent a future breach of canon law, others to rectify irregularities incurred by some past offence against it. One may suspect that the strongest force behind this pursuit of favours was the thought of the four last things, heaven, hell, death and judgment, and the hope of salvation in eternity. Because the papacy was, in Sir John Paston's words, 'the well of grace', it possessed an authority over men's minds, though not necessarily a hold on their affections. Pilgrimages may suggest that there was some emotional attachment to the holy city, but how far this was transferred to the institution of the papacy is hard to judge. The latter's authority, however, could survive, untouched by any political or administrative struggles between the popes and the secular powers of Europe.

There are two implications of this which can provide a conclusion to this paper. Firstly, the connections between England and Rome which can be traced in the papal registers show how the latter's role as a source of graces was taken for granted by the vast majority of Englishmen; and any criticism of the papacy must be seen in the perspective of this acceptance of its essential role on the part of most people.[80] More work on the registers will be required to discover how far attitudes remained static during the century. It may point to a decline in loyalty to the pope that the number of individuals seeking indults to have portable altars seems to have declined during the century; but it is not clear if there was any significant change in the total number of dispensations. Secondly, the fact that the papacy was seen as fulfilling a necessary role may explain why there was still an attachment to old ways in the Reformation period, and why perhaps it was only with the emergence of a new theology, of a doctrine of justification by faith, which made this role superfluous, that these spiritual ties between England and Rome could be broken, and a political breach between Henry VIII and the pope could develop into a deeper and more lasting division in the Church.

Notes

1. I am grateful to Professor R.B. Dobson and Dr. M.T. Clanchy for reading an earlier draft of this paper and for their suggestions.
2. *The Paston Letters*, ed. J. Gairdner (Library Edition, 1904), v, 198.
3. For an admirable study of Anglo-papal relations at the level of church government, see F.R.H. Du Boulay, 'The Fifteenth Century', in C.H. Lawrence, ed., *The English Church and the Papacy in the Middle Ages*, (1965), 197–242. For an examination of the English church's awareness of its own identity, see D. Hay, 'The Church of England in the Later Middle Ages', *History*, liii (1968), 35–50.
4. *The Paston Letters*, iv, 321; vi, 35.
5. *Plumpton Correspondence*, ed. T. Stapleton (CS, old series, iv, 1839), 217.
6. *The Cely Letters 1472–1488*, ed. A. Hanham (EETS, 273, 1975), 116.
7. *St. Albans Chronicle 1406–1420*, ed. V.H. Galbraith (Oxford, 1937), 104–9.
8. *The Great Chronicle of London*, ed. A.H. Thomas and I.D. Thornley (1938), 96; *Chronicles of London*, ed. C.L. Kingsford (Oxford, 1905), 72, 126; *Historical Collections of a London Citizen*, ed. J. Gairdner (CS, 2nd series, xvii, 1876), 116.
9. J.A.F. Thomson, 'The Continuation of "Gregory's Chronicle" – a possible Author?', *British Museum Quarterly*, 36 (1971–2), 93–4. The arguments advanced there that the author was a clerk appear overwhelming, but my suggestion that he might have been Thomas Eborall is perhaps rather less convincing. It has been pointed out that the association of the original chronicle with Gregory (the basis of the Eborall suggestion) is doubtful, because of the date of the indulgence to which the chronicler alludes. See W.E. Lunt, *Financial Relations of the Papacy with England 1327–1534* (Cambridge, Mass., 1962), 575, 578.
10. *Historical Collections of a London Citizen*, 197, 230–2, 235–6.
11. Ibid., 238.
12. *The Great Chronicle of London*, 274, 292, 329, 379; *Chronicles of London*, 147, 228–9.
13. *The Great Chronicle of London*, 327.
14. W. Fulman, *Rerum Anglicarum Scriptorum Veterum* (Oxford, 1684), i, 528–9, 533–4.
15. Ibid., 560. Although this note appears in the later continuation of the chronicle, generally attributed to a royal official, the text probably incorporates some material, including this, from a monastic source.
16. Ibid., 572, 577.
17. *CPL*, vi, 454; vii, 286; x, 4.
18. T. Gascoigne, *Loci e libro veritatum*, ed. J.E.T. Rogers (Oxford, 1881), 92, 94, 97.
19. Ibid., 173.
20. W. Lyndwood, *Provinciale* (Oxford, 1679), 26b, gloss c *Non Legitimo*.
21. Ibid., 28b–29a, gloss r (28b) *Dispensare poterint*.
22. Ibid., 29b, gloss g *Homicidas*.
23. Ibid., 30a, gloss a *Simoniacos*.
24. Ibid., 31a, gloss d *Bigamos*; 130b, gloss p *Ingerentes*.
25. Ibid., 45b–46a, gloss p (45b) *Ministrarunt*.
26. *Loci e libro veritatum*, 14.
27. It was perhaps because of the need for dispensations for illegitimacy that the records of men being elected to certain ecclesiastical offices state that they were legitimately born, the implication being that in their cases no dispensation need be sought. See Wiltshire Record Office, Reg(ister of Thomas) Langton (Sarum), pt. ii, fos. 10v, 14 for the examples of the dean of Salisbury and abbot of Reading.

28. *CPL*, vii, 56–7.
29. *CPL*, vii, 80–1, 87–8.
30. *Calendar of the Register of Robert Waldby, Archbishop of York*, ed. D.M. Smith (Borthwick Texts and Calendars 2, York, 1974), 28. *Registers of Oliver King and Hadrian de Castello*, ed. H. Maxwell-Lyte (Somerset Record Society, 54, 1939), 137–8. A bull of dispensation to William Ayleward to receive a benefice, despite being under age, and not to reside in it is entered in the register of Bishop Langton of Salisbury immediately before the record of his institution to the vicarage of Pedelton (*CPL*, xv, 513–4 (No. 942), Reg. Langton (Sarum), pt. i, fos. 40v–1). There is no obvious reason why some dispensations are entered in the bishops' registers and others are not. Even if the dispensation was not entered in full, a note might be made that it existed. When in 1496, John Shipton, a Cistercian monk of Beaulieu, was admitted to the parish of Wodditon, the record of his institution mentioned that he had been sufficiently dispensed to receive a benefice (Hampshire Record Office, Register of Thomas Langton (Winton), fo. 7).
31. *An Episcopal Court-Book for the Diocese of Lincoln 1514–1520*, ed. M. Bowker (Lincoln Record Society, lxi, 1967), 26, 35.
32. *CPL*, vii, 68; viii, 43; ix, 421.
33. *CPL*, xi, 186–7.
34. *CPL*, xiii, 20–1.
35. *CPL*, ix, 494; x, 401.
36. The bull is not printed in the *CPL*, but has been preserved in Archbishop Scrope's register: see *Calendar of the Register of Richard Scrope, Archbishop of York*, ed. R.N. Swanson (Borthwick Texts and Calendars 8, York, 1981), i, 74.
37. *CPL*, viii, 453. In the *Book of Margery Kempe*, there is a reference to a man having to obtain a dispensation from Rome to be ordained after having been guilty of wounding another person: it is accordingly likely that the existence of this impediment was well known (*Book of Margery Kempe*, ed. S.B. Meech and H.E. Allen, EETS, OS 212, 1940, 55–6).
38. *CPL*, xiii, 147–8.
39. *CPL*, xiii, 783.
40. *CPL*, viii, 88, 648.
41. *CPL*, xi, 110–1; xv, 131.
42. *CPL*, viii, 532.
43. *Provinciale*, 329b–30a, gloss t (329b) *Solus papa*. The pope could, however, for special cause shown, dispense an individual to communicate with someone who was excommunicated. Ibid., 352a, gloss k *Cum excommunicatis*.
44. R.H. Helmholz, *Marriage Litigation in Medieval England* (Cambridge, 1974), 78.
45. Ibid., 80–1.
46. *CPL*, vii, 87.
47. *CPL*, viii, 80.
48. *CPL*, viii, 579–80. In a case in 1477 the petitioners admitted that they had been committing adultery for some three years during the lifetime of the woman's former husband, but asserted that they had neither compassed the latter's death nor promised each other that they would marry after it (*CPL*, xiii, 237).
49. *CPL*, vii, 87.
50. *CPL*, vii, 363. A further complication might arise when a dispensation had been granted for one impediment and a further one came to light. After William Goteson and Matilda Lange had received a dispensation to marry despite being within the fourth degree of affinity, they had doubts abouts its validity because William had also had sexual relations with a woman related to Matilda in the third and fourth degrees of consanguinity. In this case of 1396 the papal penitentiary commissioned the vicar-general of the diocese to declare the earlier dispensation valid as if mention had then been made of the relationship in the third degree (*Register of Robert Waldby*, 5).

51. CPL, xiii, 404–5. A dispensation could also be granted for a marriage when the parties were aware that a spiritual relationship existed, but were ignorant that it was an impediment. William Wodisgane and Catherine Wrang were dispensed to remain married (1438), although William's mother had been Catherine's godmother (CPL, ix, 9). It is easy to see how such impediments could arise when neighbours were friendly and provided sponsors for each other's children. In 1459 the pope instructed the archbishop of Canterbury to dispense James Borne and Joan Chyrche to marry, despite the fact that James's father had been Joan's godfather and Joan's father James's godfather. (CPL, xii, 50).

52. William Harrington was to marry Elizabeth Pilkington, and Thomas Pilkington to marry Margaret Harrington. (CPL, ix, 182).

53. CPL, ix, 562.

54. CPL, vii, 120.

55. CPL, x, 55. A variation on this theme may be found in the case of Robert and Margaret Singleton (1482). She had taken a vow of chastity after the death of her first husband, but contracted marriage as the lesser evil when she feared that she could not keep the vow. She still, however, continued to wear the habit of a widow. Matters were complicated by the fact that Robert had had sexual relations with a daughter of Margaret by her first husband. Both had to do penance, but they appear to have been allowed to remain in the marriage: CPL, xiii, 835–6. One should, however, note that requests to be dispensed from such vows of chastity were relatively few in relation to the numbers who took it. In the printed register of Archbishop Rotherham of York, for the years 1480–1500, there are twenty-six commissions, mostly to the archbishop's suffragan, William, bishop of Dromore, to veil widows within the diocese. The register also records one veiling by the archbishop personally as well as a licence to receive the veil, the ratification of the veiling of a woman from the diocese by a suffragan of the bishop of Lincoln, and letters testimonial to the bishop of Coventry and Lichfield of the veiling of a woman from his diocese. See Register of Thomas Rotherham, ed. E.E. Barker, (CYS, 69, 1976), i, 2, 20–21, 28–29,31, 33, 40, 42, 48, 57–8, 62, 67, 77, 82, 191, 193, 201, 205, 213–5, 219, 225, 233, 237, 245. The motives behind the vow were well expressed in a certification by the suffragan of Bishop Langton of Winchester that he had given the ring of perpetual widowhood and chastity with the customary solemnity of mass and obsequies to Agnes Salmon, widow of Southampton, 'que pompas et vanitates seculi huius transitorii totaliter dimittere et soli domino virtutum sub vita et habitu perpetue viduale castitatis ut asseruit vivere intendit in dies residuos vite sue ipsi domino offerat.' Reg. Langton (Winton), fo. 63v.

56. CPL, ix, 84. Germany could prove a hazardous place for Englishmen travelling to or from Rome. In 1470 the pope ordered the bishop of Basel to absolve five men who had robbed a canon of York and held him to ransom, once they had made restitution to their victim and a payment to the papal Camera: CPL, xii, 353–4. The London tithe dispute in the 1450s was protracted when the city's emissaries were detained at Cologne: J.A.F. Thomson, 'Tithe Disputes in Medieval London', EHR, lxxviii (1963), 5–6; and a Durham monk was imprisoned and held to ransom in 1468, also at Cologne: R.B. Dobson, Durham Priory, 1400–1450 (Cambridge, 1973), 211, n.2. The pope might grant favours to the victims of such violence; in 1462 an indulgence was granted to all penitents who gave alms for the support of a certain John Hildreth who, while en route to Rome to obtain indulgences, had been plundered and despoiled by armed men and now had no means of support: CPL, xi, 607–8.

57. CPL, xiii, 102. The cost of obtaining dispensations is an obscure subject, and it is only occasionally that there are indications, as here, of how much an individual might have to pay. The comments of Sir John Paston (see above, p. 99) suggest that expenses may well have varied according to the demands of individual proctors. The fees payable at the curia, however, seem to have been fixed for each particular kind of dispensation. Tables of the tariffs charged at the end of the fifteenth and the beginning of the sixteenth century are printed in L. Celier, Les dataires du XVe siècle et les origines de la daterie apostolique (Bibliothèque des écoles francaises

d'Athènes et de Rome, 103; Paris, 1910), 152–64. There is little doubt that the system of dispensations was elaborated and the level of fees increased for fiscal reasons in the latter part of the fifteenth century: see J.A.F. Thomson, *Popes and Princes 1417–1517* (1980), 89. For the activities of curial proctors in general, see E.F. Jacob, *Essays in Later Medieval History* (Manchester, 1968), 60–72.

58. *CPL*, x, 102–3.
59. *CPL*, xiii, 625.
60. *CPL*, v, 249.
61. *Book of Margery Kempe*, 80–91. By her will of 1386, proved in 1400, Joan Maykyn of London endowed a chaplain for a year in the church of St. John Lateran. See *Calendar of Wills proved and enrolled in the Court of Husting, London*, ed. R.R. Sharpe (London, 1890), ii, 343; P.R.O., Roman Transcripts, 31/10/8.
62. *CPL*, xi, 366.
63. *CPL*, viii, 26 (Bishop Fleming of Lincoln); 503 (Humphrey, duke of Gloucester).
64. *CPL*, ix, 210.
65. *CPL*, vii, 57. Cf. *Book of Margery Kempe*, 59, for another reference to a local community seeking a font for a chapel.
66. *CPL*, xi, 92.
67. *CPL*, viii, 173.
68. *CPL*, vii, 445–6.
69. *CPL*, xiii, 778.
70. In 1436 and 1439 Piero da Monte was empowered to grant indults to have a portable altar to ten and twelve persons respectively (*CPL*, viii, 254–5, 290–1); and in 1451 no fewer than nineteen bulls were granted to a papal legate listing the graces which he could confer (*CPL*, x, 223–6).
71. *CPL*, vii, viii, *passim*.
72. One cannot always classify grants precisely in these categories, as they were sometimes conferred on unusual family groups, e.g. a widow and her two daughters; a man and his sisters; a priest, his mother and two sisters; and two brothers, their mother, and the wife of one of them (*CPL*, ix, 300, 310, 318; xi, 19).
73. R.G. Davies, 'Martin V and the English episcopate, with particular reference to his campaign for the repeal of the Statute of Provisors', *EHR*, xcii (1977), 309–44, gives the fullest and most up to date account of this.
74. *CPL*, xiii, 239. The confessor was also empowered to commute vows of pilgrimage and abstinence but not of chastity. One hardly imagines that this king would have taken that particular vow!
75. *CPL*, x, 485; xii, 618.
76. *CPL*, xiii, 270.
77. *CPL*, vii, 379.
78. *CPL*, xii, 66–7.
79. *CPL*, xiii, 147–8.
80. The development of royal influence over the English church under the reserve powers of the Statutes of Provisors and Praemunire served to push political anti-papalism into the background in the fifteenth century: see M.H. Keen, *England in the Later Middle Ages*, (1973), 211–14. The most vocal popular antipapalism occurred in some of the utterances of the Lollards (J.A.F. Thomson, *The Later Lollards 1414–1520*, Oxford, 1965, 71, 80, 128); but their beliefs should not be regarded as more than the views of a very small minority of the English population as a whole. The number of heretics executed in the course of the century was much smaller than the number of individuals who sought graces from Rome in any single year.

5

The Papacy and Scotland in the Fifteenth Century

D.E.R. Watt
University of St. Andrews

The opening of the fifteenth century came in the middle of the Great Schism, and it should be noted immediately that it was the pope at Avignon (not yet, of course, styled an anti-pope) who enjoyed recognition in Scotland. It is true that in the year 1400 itself Pope Benedict XIII was not very accessible, for he was then a virtual prisoner in the papal palace, and for the time being he was recognised just by Aragon and Scotland. This was the stage in the forty years of schism when France had led the way in trying to force both popes to resign by withdrawing obedience in 1398 from the line of popes whom she had recognised since 1378. But Scotland had not followed suit, even if individual Scots then at the University of Paris had been in favour of the French royal policy.[1] Scotland in 1400 therefore was behaving independently, almost idiosyncratically, in remaining loyal to the pope at Avignon. This is the starting point for the fifteenth-century story.

It is generally assumed that Scotland had chosen in 1378-80 to recognize Pope Clement VII because her ally France invited her to do so. Certainly in 1379 we know of envoys from King Charles V as well as from Clement coming to Scotland in search of support,[2] and we do not know of any envoys from Pope Urban VI. It is curious, however, that there is no evidence of King Robert II calling a parliament or an ecclesiastical provincial council to advise him on this matter; and in fact we do not know when or why he decided to adhere to Clement. It may well be that a political or diplomatic motive was not uppermost. As early as February 1379 while Clement was still in Italy, the Scottish chancellor (Bishop John de Peblis of Dunkeld) was negotiating with him for a second consecration as bishop, on the grounds that his earlier consecration by authority of Urban VI before the schism was now questionable; and by July 1379 in his other capacity as papal collector in Scotland some funds which Peblis had collected were being paid into the papal treasury at Avignon rather than at Rome.[3] It is probable that the moving spirit was his colleague Bishop Walter de Wardlaw of Glasgow, who had been employed at the curia in the early 1370s before the schism and had certainly known Clement as Cardinal Robert of Geneva there. Wardlaw in his turn was to be made the first ever Scottish cardinal by this pope in December 1383.[4] It is likely therefore that it was the preference of such leading clergy in favour of Clement rather than Urban that decided the issue in Scotland. It was not long before the whole Scottish episcopate was populated by bishops who owed their promotion to Clement or from 1394 his successor Benedict XIII.[5] Only in Galloway and the Isles were there some complications raised by the presence of alternative bishops loyal to the Roman pope: these problems were solved by the expulsion to England of the Romanist claimant to Galloway, and by the effective splitting of the Isles diocese into Romanist and Avignonese halves. Otherwise there was for forty years a steady supply of bishops loyal only to Avignon in the kingdom of Scotland. Besides Cardinal Wardlaw two successive bishops of St. Andrews were particularly concerned over a long period to keep the Avignonese connection going – Walter Trayl, who came back to Scotland in 1386 after employment in Pope Clement's chancery and served until 1401;[6] and Henry de Wardlaw (the cardinal's nephew) who, on returning to the country as bishop in 1403 after long years of study at Avignon, held office until 1440.[7] Bishop Gilbert de Grenlaw of Aberdeen (1390–1421), who was chancellor of Scotland for more than twenty-four years from 1397, seems to have been another steadying influence for a long time.[8] With such committed episcopal leaders, the Scottish government remained unwaveringly loyal to Benedict XIII right through the years of withdrawal of obedience and the councils of Pisa and Constance until at last it grudgingly offered recognition to Martin V in July–August 1419.[9]

This independent line contrasts with that taken in most other countries. While political considerations everywhere had some part in shaping attitudes to the schism, in Scotland they did not have much influence. It was much more a matter of clerical preference and convenience. This stage in Scoto-papal relations has to be set in the context of the previous 200 years, during which the ecclesia Scoticana had been officially and uniquely regarded collectively as a 'special daughter' of the pope, with ten equal bishops and no archbishop.[10] This could have the comparatively simple implication that the pope regarded himself as metropolitan for Scotland.[11] But obviously he was no ordinary metropolitan. From one point of view his authority was weak, for the Scottish bishops and other prelates from 1225 met periodically in provincial council, and delegated authority between meetings to one of their number as conservator,[12] so that a degree of uniformity in practice and of discipline was achieved by self-help within the kingdom without reference to or interference from the Roman court.

But from another point of view papal power in Scotland was unusually effective, for when the pope was brought into things he was no mere metropolitan: indeed the Universal Ordinary and Vicar of Christ was one stage in the hierarchy more accessible to Scottish clergy and laity than in most other countries. Recourse to Avignon in person or through an agent had become familiar to most leading Scots during the fourteenth century, with no impediments such as the politics of the Hundred Years' War or statutes of provisors to get in the way. Every advantage was taken of the complex procedures which led to the issue of papal letters of grace on a wide range of business concerning benefices, dispensations, privileges, and justice.[13] Certainly on the benefice front there were by the end of the fourteenth century few of the cathedral or the more substantial parochial benefices in ecclesiastical patronage where it was not customary for would-be incumbents to seek a papal title by way of a bull of provision. And there was frequently keen rivalry and litigation up to the level of the Roman court between claimants with papal titles of a contradictory character. In such circumstances there was a need to keep in with the pope who was generally recognized in Scotland; and two printed volumes of papal letters issued by Clement VII and Benedict XIII in favour of Scots have recently been published, which give a vivid (if incomplete) picture of the regularity and complexity of papal business concerning Scotland right through the schism. It is no wonder that the Scots did not want to abandon the popes who were so accessible and so useful to them. Indeed they could not face switching to Alexander V or John XXIII after the council of Pisa, and had very little to do with the council of Constance – occasional envoys travelled between the council and Scotland, but no official participants were sent.[14] This had the effect of making the final desertion of Benedict XIII in favour of Martin V all the more traumatic. In the end it was the masters of the university of St. Andrews who took a lead in pushing the country in the direction of submitting to the pope who was now universally acknowledged; and typically they made it their business to ensure that Scotland's final act of adherence was accompanied by Martin's confirmation of the status of their university along the lines of the privileges granted by Benedict in 1413.[15]

The transition from one pope to the other was not an easy one. Martin was elected at Constance in November 1417; but until as late as January 1419 some Scots were still obtaining letters of grace from Benedict at Peñiscola in Aragon, often with the backing of the Duke of Albany who was then governor of Scotland.[16] In parallel with this, however, there were others who from as early as January 1418 onwards were anticipating the government's change of allegiance by frequenting the curia of Martin at Constance, Geneva, Mantua or Florence.[17] Some of these had the backing of the Earl of Douglas, who was a political opponent of the Duke of Albany at home: others were sponsored by the young King James I, then a prisoner in England, who chose to adhere formally to Martin in July 1418, a whole year before the official adherence of the Albany government.[18] A consequence was that candidates were provided by both popes for some important benefices such as the bishopric of Ross, the priorship of St. Andrews, or the archdeaconry of Teviotdate in Glasgow.[19] It was an unsettling and disputacious period, as the different political factions in Scotland sought to help their followers by latching on to different popes. This unprecedented period of confusion lasted well into the 1420s, and was still raising tricky problems after King James returned from captivity in 1424. So far as Scotland is concerned, it can be argued that the greatest evils arising from the Great Schism came after it had in the eyes of most of Europe been ended.

Another period of unfortunate confusion came in the early 1440s as a result of the 'Little Schism'[20] created in 1439 by the council of Basel. Scotland had changed her attitude to general councils after adhering to Martin V. A large official delegation was sent to the council which met at Pavia and Siena, though only three members in fact reached it in time to join in some anti-English deliberations for about ten days just before the council was dissolved in March 1424.[21] They were said to have been briefed on the various ways in which the church in Scotland was suffering interference from temporal lords in its rights and jurisdiction; but presumably it was Murdoch Duke of Albany, the governor, and his advisers who thought it worthwhile to send such official representatives. King James I took the same view of the council of Basel in its turn, and from mid-1433 onwards maintained an official delegation there, which for some considerable time included his chancellor, Bishop John Cameron of Glasgow.[22] Some twenty-eight other Scottish clergy also took part in this council's affairs during its most active period, February 1434–February 1437. It is no wonder that in 1436 Pope Eugenius IV was willing to send the first papal legate that Scotland had seen for nearly 200 years to try to establish a concordat with even so distant and comparatively petty a king.[23] The assassination of the king in February 1437, however, introduced a period of faction politics in Scotland during the long minority of James II, and this was matched in time by the split between the council and the pope. Though at least Bishop James Kennedy of Dunkeld did attend the pope at the council of Florence in July 1439 when the famous union of the eastern and western churches was proclaimed,[24] and though the majority of lay and clerical leaders in Scotland continued to support Eugenius after the remaining councillors at Basel had indulged in the Little Schism by electing Pope Felix V in November 1439, the Livingston-Douglas faction who dominated the Scottish government in the 1440s took the chance of adhering to the alternative pope for internal political reasons, and so caused even more disruption in the Scottish church than had ever been experienced during the Great Schism or its aftermath.[25]. Thomas Livingston, Abbot of Dundrennan, was now a leading member of the rump council at Basel,[26] and Scots supporting his family's faction appeared there and at the curia of Felix to obtain alternative papal titles to many bishoprics and lesser benefices in Scotland.[27] This had the dire effect of attaching new vested interests to the factions in Scotland, which survived the death of the Earl of Douglas in March 1443 and held out in many cases until after 1449, when on the one hand the Livingstons were ousted from power, and on the other western Christendom as a whole accepted one pope again in the person of Nicholas V. At the same time King James II was old enough to take a grip of things in Scotland. But the unfortunate coincidence of the papal schism and a royal minority had for about a decade a critically divisive and harmful effect on Scottish affairs. Conciliarist ideas must clearly have been much bandied about in Scotland in the 1430s and 1440s, and not merely in academic circles;[28] and for her own internal reasons the country was taken into the European swim in a way that Governor Albany had not permitted at the time of Pisa and Constance. But since it was the pro-papal rather than the pro-conciliar faction which won locally in the end, it turned out that it was respect for co-operation with the papacy rather than hostility to it which in Scotland as elsewhere was to govern later fifteenth-century attitudes.

Co-operation between pope and king had, of course, long been the normal situation. This was common enough elsewhere, but was particularly evident in a country whose church came directly under Rome and which produced no Anselm, Becket, Langton or Winchelsey. Nowadays we are escaping from the historical tradition of taking papal propagandists at face value and realize that church liberties in any era exist only insofar as the state is prepared to allow them. The organized church in later medieval Scotland is therefore best approached as the greatest of the jurisdictional franchises in the country. The king normally sent his representatives to sit with the prelates when they met in provincial council;[29] and he could be quite direct in giving them instructions about a piece of local legislation which he wanted them to accept. This was exemplified in July 1427 when an act was passed in parliament on a matter of procedure in the church courts, the intention being to make things quicker and less expensive for lay plaintiffs against clerical defendants: the provincial council, which was also meeting at Perth at the same time, was simply expected to put this royal act into effect by adding its own authority to it.[30] It is true that this example comes from a time when the young James I, just back from eighteen years of captivity in England, was particularly active in a review of many interlocking aspects of the administration of Scotland; but the main point is that the prelates co-operated with him and were prepared to work with him as a reformer.

This king took a personal interest also in institutions purely ecclesiastical. In 1425 he urged in parliament that the abbots and priors of the Benedictine and Augustinian orders in Scotland should hold general chapters to achieve a revival of the religious life to its pristine state:

'He appeared to cherish and favour equally all churches and religious orders for the quality of their life, praising highly men of religion and their way of life as he heard of it. And if he found anything less than praiseworthy among them (during his frequent visits to monasteries), he discussed it charitably without pretending to be embarrassed, quietly persisting until by some convenient way they might be turned back to the normal way of life.'[31]

This is the man who founded a monastery for Carthusians at his capital at Perth in 1429.[32] King James also took a close interest in the new university at St. Andrews which was developing very slowly and contentiously. After threatening to move it to Perth, he stirred up sufficient constructive response for him to feel able to agree in 1432 to confirming the privileges which he had originally given to the university community – but only at the cost of their accepting his interference in their internal affairs thereafter. He seems to have imposed his own man (Laurence de Lindores) as perpetual dean of arts, and laid down the law on such matters as how the dean was to conduct himself, how the students were to be disciplined, and how the masters were to develop a healthy corporate life.[33] Whether therefore it was church justice, the monastic life, or university organisation, it was the king who set the standards. He thought it his responsibility to supervise positively the franchise jurisdictions within his kingdom. In all these examples there is no mention of the pope. It was just royal authority which was being accepted in matters internal to the *ecclesia Scoticana*, and no one seems to have wanted to bring in the pope.

Royal authority could, however, be exercised more debatably in the traditional delicate borderline territory between church and state, as happened in 1450 when the young James II was in his turn being assertive in the royal interest. He then made a solemn parliamentary definition on a series of matters related to the property and rights of bishoprics in the interval between the decease or demission of one bishop and the admission of his successor.[34] Such matters had been in contention between conflicting interests in most countries for centuries, and now in Scotland we find emerging from discussions between the king and his prelates the kind of balanced definition that was meant to be lasting. On the one hand bishops were to be allowed to dispose of their movable goods by testament (a practice which both kings and popes had from time to time sought to prevent). Then the general point was made that during the vacancy spiritualities were to be administered by a vicar-general accountable to the next bishop, while temporalities were to be at the king's disposal. Lastly the patronage of benefices in the bishop's gift was to be exercised by the crown. It is quite likely that at this date the main weight was put on the last of these four defiinitions.[35] It was not in itself new, but a series of explanatory acts of provincial council and of parliament over the rest of the century makes it clear that the main intention was to assert royal right not against local ecclesiastical patrons, but against competing papal claims to provide to the benefices in question under general or special reservations.[36] We can see therefore that in just this one category of church patronage king and clergy in Scotland were combining to exclude the papal interest in favour of regalian right. In practice this was a major interference with the usual flow from Rome of confident letters of provision; and since it was governed by unforeseeable circumstances, it must have been a vexatious complication for clerical benefice-hunters who throughout the century were still eagerly 'playing the system' of papal provisions.

But the act of 1450 was not a statute of provisors. And this brings us to the papal reaction to these Scottish kings who were so confidently setting their own limits to the liberty of the Scottish church. The story has sometimes been told in terms of a 'prolonged trial of strength';[37] but there are dangers in adopting a framework for discussion in terms of 'struggle' and ultimate 'victory' for the crown. Since both sides had as usual much to gain from co-operation, any periods of dispute should be examined in terms of the special circumstances which brought them about, rather than used as the basis of generalisations about overall trends. If we first consider Pope Martin V, we find that as part of his commitment to re-establishing papal authority after the Great Schism he ran a curia that was most attentive to providing many services to Scottish laymen and clerics; but he was hardly in a position to seek a showdown with the Scottish government. He was remarkably helpful in the early 1420s to ambitious and litigious clerics, who seem to have been all too willing to commit themselves to paying substantial fees by way of annates to the papal treasury in return for papal provisions of various complicated kinds.[38] Not only were dispensations for pluralism freely granted, but the convenient device of allowing one claimant to a benefice to buy off the claims of another by settling a pension on him from the revenues of the benefice was sometimes approved.[39] When James I came on the scene, he reacted to this situation by a series of acts of parliament in 1424, 1427 and 1428 that was aimed at stopping this practice of 'purchasing pensions' and more generally at controlling the flow of clerics or their agents to the Roman court.[40] There is interesting mention of a nefarious practice to which the word 'barratry' was attached. This expression was derived from a root meaning 'to deceive', and a 'barrator' was a cleric who was considered to have used underhand means to obtain a benefice which properly belonged to another.[41] The introduction of such a pejorative term into royal legislation at this time is an instructive indication of the way in which the pope's easy generosity was being regarded by those who felt responsible for the health of the Scottish church. In practice this legislation was unworkable and not generally enforced; but Martin did for a time in 1429–30 take seriously certain accusations made by the Scottish cleric William Croyser (who was an active barrator by any standards) against Bishop John Cameron of Glasgow, the king's chancellor, who was said to have been chiefly responsible for these parliamentary statutes, which were in papal eyes 'against ecclesiastical liberty and the rights of the Roman church'.[42] The bishop was cited to Rome under threat of deprivation; but no great crisis followed; the king just sent his envoys to arrange for the exoneration of Cameron, on the vague understanding that he might sometime try to arrange for the offending statutes to be repealed. It was in effect an agreement not to define the rights of pope and king too clearly. Perhaps the affair is more noteworthy for the king's patience with some of the inconvenience which arose from papal openness towards barrators than for any serious interest in principles on the pope's part. Certainly James for his part did pursue Croyser for a time, not just for barratry, but for treason;[43] and this ever-resourceful cleric was to take another chance which came his way in June 1434 at the council of Basel to retaliate by accusing the king of anti-papal acts:

> 'The king himself disposes of ecclesiastical benefices as he likes against the pope's decisions; many clerics and priests with papal letters have been killed in the kingdom; and those coming to the Roman court are being deprived of their goods, etc.'[44]

But this was very much an *ex parte* statement: the council did not take the matter up. It is true that as part of continuing protection for Croyser Pope Eugenius IV in 1436 raised again the matter of the Scottish legislation which was designed to restrict the free access of Scottish clerics to the curia;[45] but the legislation remained on the books and, so far as most people were concerned, unenforced. Perhaps the issue might have been pressed further from the papal side if the visit of the legate to Scotland in 1437 had not been made abortive by the murder of the king. It may be argued that neither Martin nor Eugenius had been much worried by the Scottish apparently hostile legislation. Their protests seem to have been forced out of them mainly by the litigious William Croyser, whose benefice-hunting activities at the curia both king and bishops at home wanted to curtail. From his self-seeking point of view he wanted Scottish clerics to be free to benefit from the facilities offered at the papal curia; but the occasional declarations of principle which two popes were prepared to make on his behalf were just so many words on parchment. Croyser was no Becket.

It can accordingly be argued that Scoto-papal relations in this period were dominated by the personal rivalries of individual clerics playing politics as they tried their best to use the system to their own advantage, and that no one was much interested in principles. Yet some financial aspects of these relations did have an important general influence. The pope needed all the fees which he could extract from the beneficiaries of papal graces; ambitious clerics in Scotland thought it worth their while to pay these fees; but the government took the view that the cost of these papal services to the Scottish church was unsuitably high, and made efforts to control the flow of money from the country in this connection. Ranald Nicholson puts it rather well: 'James I, who fully shared the mercantilist outlook, looked askance at any flow of bullion from his kingdom, particularly one that brought in return not an import of goods but merely a re-allocation of Scottish benefices, sometimes to the disadvantage of the crown.'[46]

It was a similar sense of duty about the need to protect the rights of the crown which lay behind the legislation of James II in 1450 with respect to the exercise of ecclesiastical patronage at times of episcopal vacancies. For the rest of the century the crown was quite firm in continuing to assert its rights in the face of papal counter-claims. The need for repeated legislation on this matter, however, shows that the pope kept interfering in particular cases. This was traditional enough, and suggests simply that the complexity of the system for papal control of church patronage was too great for the curia to be willing to incorporate eccentric local variations into its procedures. The distance and time factors were always a major problem for the papacy in trying to deal with matters of detail pertaining to a country so far away as Scotland. Financial pressures and bureaucratic inertia therefore both had a part to play in keeping a certain tension going throughout the century between Rome and Scotland. These provide a background against which should be set the actions of individual clerics such as Croyser and his kind.

This background has to be borne in mind too when we examine the fundamental change in the constitutional position of the Scottish church which was approved by the papacy in 1472, namely the erection of the bishopric of St. Andrews into a metropolitan see.[47] This act makes general sense within the political trend of the time, when there was a need to adjust the definition of *ecclesia Scoticana* to fit better with current political theory that young King James III had 'full jurisdiction and free empire within his realm'.[48] By this date the country had its own two universities at St. Andrews (from 1410) and Glasgow (from 1451). The religious orders such as the Franciscans (both Observant and Conventual) and the Dominicans were being organised for the first time into separate Scottish provinces.[49] It was therefore logical for the pope to take account of political reality and detach the diocese of Galloway from the province of York and the dioceses of the Isles and Orkney from the province of Trondheim. In the first two of these cases the change was long overdue: so far as Orkney was concerned this was papal acknowledgement of a royal ambition to hold on to the Northern Isles, which had only very recently been transferred to Scotland from the kingdom of Denmark and Norway as a pledge for an unpaid dowry for the queen.[50] But why in 1472 did the pope add to this territorial adjustment a rejection of the 'special daughter' arrangements which were of nearly 300 years' standing, and of the unifying provincial council of prelates (which seems to have been in good running order)? We may take Ranald Nicholson as a recent exponent of a long historical tradition about this remarkable change of papal policy.[51] He presents us with a picture in 1471 of the ambitious James III emerging from his minority and using parliament as James I and James II had done to pass acts warning the pope against unwelcome interference in Scotland, discouraging traffic with the curia, and once again emphasizing the financial loss involved in the papal connection. It is then suggested that the new pope, Sixtus IV, reacted to this situation by taking up the ambitious personal plans of a favoured Scottish cleric at the Roman court, namely Bishop Patrick Graham of St. Andrews, that his see should become a metropolitan one. The pope is seen as taking the initiative quite suddenly and without consulting the king or the other Scottish bishops. If this is the true explanation for what happened, it was surely an astonishing break with the normal conventions of papal diplomacy over the centuries, and certainly Sixtus would have been doing something much more drastic for Patrick Graham than either Martin V or Eugenius IV ever did for William Croyser. But even Nicholson has to admit that nothing in the bull of erection alluded to what he argues was the leading cause of controversy – the disputed control of ecclesiastical patronage. Indeed this traditional explanation does not hold water in my view; and here I am in the good company of the late David McRoberts, who observed that the circumstances whereby the change of 1472 came about form 'one of the more intractable problems of Scottish history'.[52]

It is possible to suggest a novel solution to this problem. The bull of erection itself[53] emphasizes the inconvenience and expense to which inhabitants of Scotland are put in having to come to the Roman court when appealing against actions of their bishops; it claims that as a consequence some cases have been taken instead to a 'forbidden forum' (perhaps parliament is meant); and it asserts that some bishops have been taking advantage of their distance from Rome to exceed their proper powers, so that it will be advantageous for them to be subjected to a metropolitan for their transgressions to be punished. This language hardly suggests that the Scottish provincial council of prelates as a body had helped to draft the petition to the pope which (though now lost) must have provided at least some basic material for the subsequent bull. But this language could well have emanated from the king and his advisers as, following the troubles of his minority, they sought to arrange with the pope for a more tightly organised *ecclesia Scoticana* and sent Bishop Graham to Rome to negotiate a revised settlement. It would be attractive to the government to have co-extensive boundaries for church and state, to lessen the traffic in appeals to Rome, to have church cases properly adjudged in church courts, and to have one trusted leading prelate in Scotland to discipline the others. This all makes more sense than the theory of a sudden papal initiative to impose a new organisation on an unwilling king.

This new interpretation is offered in full awareness that the hopes which lay behind the bull of erection were not to be realized in their entirety. In the long run, however, it did bring some advantages to Scotland. The setting up of a metropolitan court under the official of St. Andrews did help with all of the objectives set out in the bull. We know from the recent work of Simon Ollivant on such records as survive from the mid-sixteenth century that this court became a very busy one, which probably did attract business away from civil courts because of the better standard of justice it offered, and which certainly helped to control the activities of the suffragan bishops by reviewing cases from their courts which were brought to it on appeal.[54] But the pull of the Roman Court for litigation over ecclesiastical benefices remained until the Reformation. Though it is only recently that James Robertson has started work on the records left in

Rome by this litigation, it already seems clear that benefice cases continued to be rare in the local ecclesiastical courts in Scotland and were still normally taken to Rome by those who could afford it.[55] The setting up of a metropolitan court therefore did not end the most complex category of traffic to the curia, even if it offered local remedies for other categories of business. It must surely, however, have done something to keep the circulation of money for legal costs within the country.

In the years immediately following 1472 there was some delay in putting the new arrangements into effect as a consequence of what I take to be the wholly unexpected mental deterioration of Patrick Graham.[56] He was of royal blood and a nephew of James Kennedy, his predecessor as bishop of St. Andrews and a dominant political figure in Scotland for a time during the minority of James III. Graham was made bishop of Brechin in 1463 and translated to St. Andrews in 1465 on his uncle's death, when still aged about thirty. His ambition to hold a monastic abbacy or priorship *in commendam* along with his see soon aroused opposition of a general kind in parliament as well as from his rivals,[57] though this may well have been politically motivated while the Boyd faction was in power during the later sixties. We should reserve judgment on whether his motives were pastoral with an eye to monastic reform or merely financial with an eye to an increased income, though at this date the latter motive is quite likely.[58] There seems to be no good reason to deny the possibility that the young James III, once he had rid himself of the Boyd faction in November 1469, saw in Graham a suitable ally to help in putting the Scottish church under firmer control. It is more likely than not that it was with the king's backing that he went off to Rome to negotiate the bull of erection which was eventually granted on 17 August 1472.[59] It was more than a year after that before he returned to Scotland, and this delay has traditionally been explained by the suggestion that there was already an outcry there, with both king and clergy up in arms against the whole plan for a metropolitan see.[60] But this interpretation of events rests mainly on the assertions of historians writing a hundred years after these events, whose views are not supported by contemporary evidence. We should do better to note the fact that Graham in February 1473 was appointed by the pope to the office of legate *a latere* in Scotland with duties which included raising support for a crusade against the Turks and reforming all the monasteries in the country.[61] Such unpopular responsibilities may well have been imposed on him by the pope as a quid pro quo for agreeing to the bull of erection, and it is possible that by now Graham was beginning to feel the pressure of his double duty to king and pope (though of course mental illness need not have any external cause at all). At any rate by August 1473 (while he was still no nearer home than Bruges) we get the first hints that the king had learned something of the confusion which was overtaking the poor man, presumably progressively.[62] Here was a problem that was unexpected and embarrassing. The general council of the kingdom was consulted at about the end of the year over what was to be done about the archbishop,[63] who seems to have returned to Scotland about then. We know of no solemn celebrations at St. Andrews to mark his new status: instead we can trace a series of measures designed to protect the rights of king and pope until the situation could be clarified.[64] An old acquaintance (or possibly a friend) from his student days at St. Andrews University in the 1450s (when the two of them were members of an Arts class of about a dozen) was now brought into the picture, apparently with the king's support, in these frustrating circumstances while the future of Graham's mental condition was unknowable. This was William Scheves.[65] It seems to have been with Graham's help that he became archdeacon of St. Andrews by early 1474,[66] then vicar-general for the presumably incapacitated archbishop by June 1475,[67] and then with the blessing of both king and pope coadjutor in the metropolitan office in September 1476.[68] A papal enquiry established formally the delusions of poor Graham, and in January 1478 he was eased out of office into suitable confinement and Scheves was confirmed by the pope as archbishop in his stead.[69] Only now was it possible to put the policy of the bull of erection of 1472 into effect. There was general agreement that this should be done, and it is surely a mistake to describe this in terms of a victory for any of the parties concerned, as is sometimes done.[70] It had indeed been a sad imbroglio, from which probably most people emerged with relief.

The policy of 1472 (however motivated) was deprived of its logical simplicity twenty years later when in January 1492 Pope Innocent VIII yielded to a campaign from Scotland conducted in the name of the young James IV, and by another constitutional re-arrangement divided the Scottish church into two ecclesiastical provinces instead of one. Glasgow was erected into a second metropolitan see with four suffragan sees all withdrawn from the province of St. Andrews.[71] There seems to be no justification for tracing this development back to the 1470s, with the implication that the overweening authority of St. Andrews was resented from the beginning. It is true that in February 1474 both king and pope agreed that Bishop Thomas Spens of Aberdeen might have personal exemption from the authority of the new archbishop for his lifetime;[72] but it should be noticed that this was justified on the two grounds that he was a senior figure in the Scottish church (he had been a bishop since 1459) and that he should not be subjected to someone with whom he was currently conducting a lawsuit. He may well have been the one crusty bishop in the country whom it was worthwhile to conciliate in order to establish the new metropolitan regime. Once Scheves became archbishop, Spens seems to have been formally subjected to St. Andrews again for the last year or so of his life.[73] But during the 1480s Scheves came to suffer for his personal loyalty to James III. As some of the younger generation of bishops began to push from below, the pope acceded in March 1487 to the king's request that the archbishhopric of St. Andrews be raised to the level of primate and legate *natus* on the model of Canterbury.[74] But Pope Innocent did not stick by his man at St. Andrews: when first Bishop Andrew Stewart of Moray and then Bishop Robert Blackadder of Glasgow sought personal exemption from the authority of St. Andrews, this was granted in April-May 1488.[75] Before these privileges can have been known in Scotland, the political revolution which caused the death of James III had taken place. Archbishop Scheves was now on the losing side, and Blackadder received official backing from the new king and parliament for his own elevation to metropolitan (though more on the York than the Canterbury model). The aim of both pope and king in 1472 that they should deal with the Scottish church through one leader was now frustrated under a different pope and a different king: as a result the country was to see much bickering between the two archbishops. An over-flexible papacy had allowed the personal rivalries of some of the local bishops to override the ideal of a well-disciplined branch of the church.

It seems right to emphasize yet again the note of co-operation between king and pope when we consider the broad picture of episcopal appointments over the century.[76] In the absence of a local metropolitan it had been the custom at least from the thirteenth century for Scottish bishops to seek confirmation of their election from the pope. The fourteenth century brought the papal practice of cancelling these elections as a matter of routine and substituting the formality of a papal bull of provision, with the concomitant charging of the fees known as the services in accordance with the supposed resources of the see. There was no challenge to this general system in the fifteenth century, when (as before) the form of election by the local chapter was usually in all likelihood a blind for the reality of royal nomination. In Archie Duncan's phrase, the fifteenth-century popes were 'able to resume broadly the comfortable working relationship with the monarchy which obtained before the Great Schism'.[77] Popes knew well that the king held the whip hand with his power to refuse to release the temporalities, and they must have been wary of trying to impose unwelcome candidates on him. It is interesting that the only appointment of an Italian papal familiar to a Scottish see in the whole of the Middle Ages (Prospero Camogli de' Medici of Genoa to the poor see of Caithness in 1478) is found in this period;[78] but it happened when pope and king (as it seems) had been working particularly closely over the problem of the lunatic Archbishop Graham, and appears to have been accepted obligingly by James III. There is on the other hand a long stream of royal familiars whom the pope accepted as bishops without apparent demur. The number of contested appointments outside the periods of schism was remarkably small: there are less than half-a-dozen affecting thirteen dioceses. Three of these attract attention because it would appear that the candidate supported by the crown was passed over by the pope in favour of someone else. In 1466 the pope's rejection of a royal nominee for Dunblane comes just after the taking of power by the Boyd faction, and may well reflect a change in the way patronage was exercised in the name of the young James III. Much more seriously the pope rejected two crown-supported candidates separately in 1483 – for Glasgow in March (when Robert Blackadder was provided) and for Dunkeld

in October (when George Brown was provided). But this was another exceptional period of political strife, when the crown's authority was in contention
between King James and his brother the Duke of Albany; and it has been
plausibly argued recently by Norman Macdougall that in fact James supported
Blackadder's mission to Rome to displace a bishop-elect who was Albany's
candidate rather than his own.[79] This makes it all the more remarkable that in
October Pope Sixtus hastened to appoint Brown to Dunkeld without waiting to
learn the king's wishes for this see (which as it turned out were strongly in favour
of someone else). It was an exceptionally rash move, which was probably
engineered by Cardinal Rodrigo Borgia,[80] and which was quite uncharacteristic
of papal practice throughout most of the century. It is even more surprising that
Sixtus and his successor Innocent VIII stuck to this choice despite fierce
opposition from James and his parliament; but a direct consequence (following
two visits to Scotland of an Italian papal legate and the sending of a Scottish
embassy to Rome)[81] was the famous bull of 20 April 1487, which in fact served as
a concordat for years to come.[82] The pope agreed to take no action to fill
vacancies in bishoprics and abbacies above a certain value for at least eight
months, to allow time for the king to nominate candidates of his choice. This
procedure had been requested by the king because of the importance of such
appointees in his parliament and council.[83] Thus the furore aroused by papal
flouting of the usual conventions produced a lasting written definition of the
joint responsibilities of king and pope (but not of local electors) in arranging the
most important church appointments in Scotland. Rather later in the century
than some other countries, Scotland in this way obtained its concordat, and the
uniformity of the papal procedures was eroded yet again in order to encompass
national aspirations.

We may note briefly how the headships of the larger Scottish monasteries
progressively became more and more subject to papal provision following royal
nomination in the course of the later fourteenth and fifteenth centuries, though
some important houses such as Melrose, Jedburgh, Dryburgh and Cambuskenneth escaped until quite late.[84] As with the bishoprics, less and less attention
was paid to the wishes of the community who were technically entitled to
choose their own head. Also more use was being made latterly of the device of
entrusting monastic headships to secular clerics *in commendam*. It is no doubt
correct to suggest that the papal attitude was becoming more concerned with
achieving a regular income from appointment fees and less with taking trouble
over the suitability of the appointees. Where the popes led, kings were in their
company. It is all too well known how in 1497 King James IV had no difficulty
in obtaining papal approval for his teenage brother James, Duke of Ross to hold
the archbishopric of St. Andrews *in commendam* along with the abbacies of
Holyrood, Dunfermline and Arbroath.[85] For royal cadets to be endowed with so
lavish an income from ecclesiastical benefices was a new trend: but it was just
the logical extension of what was common form in fifteenth-century attitudes to

the making of higher church appointments. There had been changes of emphasis, for James IV was no church reformer like James I, and Alexander VI was no Martin V. Yet it is fair to sum up papal attitudes to major church appointments in Scotland throughout the century as displaying a casual lack of concern for suitability, and an acceptance in most circumstances of the over-riding utility of co-operating with royal wishes. From the Scottish evidence at least the popes of the fifteenth century emerge more as followers than as leaders.

Notes

1. E.g. Walter Forrester (D.E.R. Watt, *A Biographical Dictionary of Scottish Graduates to A.D. 1410* [Oxford, 1977], 197–8).

2. N. Valois, *La France et le Grand Schisme d'Occident*, i (Paris, 1896), 197; Watt, *Dictionary*, 141, 472; *Copiale Prioratus Sanctiandree*, ed. J.H. Baxter (Oxford, 1930), xxxvii.

3. Watt, *Dictionary*, 442–3.

4. Ibid., 570, 671, 548.

5. *Fasti Ecclesiae Scoticanae Medii Aevi ad annum 1638*, second draft, ed. D.E.R. Watt (Scottish Record Society, 1969), under each diocese. At this time Orkney diocese still lay in the kingdom of Norway.

6. Watt, *Dictionary*, 539–42.

7. Ibid., 564–9.

8. Ibid., 237–9.

9. *Joannis de Fordun Scotichronicon cum Supplementis et Continuatione Walteri Boweri* (*Chron. Bower*), ed W. Goodall (Edinburgh, 1759), i, 374–5; *St. Andrews Copiale*, 23–29; Watt, *Dictionary*, 250, 482, 508.

10. This arrangement was confirmed by Pope Celestine III on 13 March 1192 (R.Somerville, *Scotia Pontificia* [Oxford, 1982], 142–4, no. 156). To the nine dioceses mentioned then Argyll came to be added (cf. A.A.M. Duncan, *Scotland: The Making of the Kingdom* [Edinburgh, 1975], 275–6).

11. Eugenius IV in 1436, when appointing a legate to visit Scotland (*Concilia Scotiae*, ed. J. Robertson [Bannatyne Club, 1886], i, lxxxvi, n. 3).

12. Ibid., ii, 3, 9–10.

13. *Calendar of . . . Petitions to the Pope*, ed. W.H. Bliss (London, 1896); *Calendar of . . . Papal Letters* (CPL), ed. W.H. Bliss and others (London, 1893); *Calendar of Papal Letters to Scotland of Clement VII of Avignon, 1378–1394*, ed. C. Burns (Scottish History Society, 1977); *Calendar of Papal Letters to Scotland of Benedict XIII of Avignon, 1394–1418*, ed. F. McGurk (Scottish History Society, 1977).

14. See *St. Andrews Copiale*, 9 for a list of these embassies.

15. *Chron. Bower*, ii, 449–51; *Acta Facultatis Artium Universitatis Sanctiandree 1413–1588* (Edinburgh and London, 1964), 12–13; cf. R. Swanson, 'The university of St. Andrews and the Great Schism, 1410–1419', *JEH*, xxvi (1975), 223–45.

16. *Cal. Benedict XIII*, 362–86, for graces issued Nov. 1417–Jan. 1419.

17. *Calendar of Scottish Supplications to Rome* (Scottish History Society, 1934–70), i, 1–231 for petitions granted Jan. 1418–Aug. 1420.

18. Ibid., 3, 8–9, 13–16; cf. *St. Andrews Copiale*, 18–20, 27–8.

19. Watt, *Fasti*, 268 (Ross), 175–6 (Teviotdale); Watt, *Dictionary*, 249, 357 (St. Andrews).

20. This useful phrase was coined by Ranald Nicholson in his *Scotland: The Later Middle Ages* (Edinburgh, 1974), chapter 12.

21. W. Brandmüller, *Das Konzil von Pavia-Siena*, ii (Münster, 1974), 356–9, 392, 394–5, 397–400, 430–3.

22. Full details in J.H. Burns, *Scottish Churchmen and the Council of Basel* (Glasgow, 1962); see index for Cameron.

23. Robertson, *Concilia*, i, lxxxvi, n. 3; CPL, viii, 229, 288–90; cf. *St.Andrews Copiale*, 461.

24. A.I. Dunlop, *The Life and Times of James Kennedy Bishop of St. Andrews* (Edinburgh and London, 1950), 27, 37.

25. See discussion in Nicholson, *Later Middle Ages*, 334–8.

26. Burns, *Scottish Churchmen*, index.
27. Ibid., 65–81.
28. Cf. J.H. Burns, 'The conciliarist tradition in Scotland', *Scottish Historical Review*, xlii (1963), 89–104.
29. *Formulary E: Scottish Letters and Brieves 1286–1424*, ed. A.A.M. Duncan (Glasgow, 1976), 31, no. 65; *The Register of Brieves*, ed. Lord Cooper (Stair Society, 1946), 47, no. 67.
30. *The Acts of the Parliaments of Scotland (APS)*, ed. T. Thomson and C. Innes (Edinburgh, 1814–75), ii, 14, c. 5.
31. *Chron. Bower*, ii, 508–9.
32. *Medieval Religious Houses: Scotland*, 2nd edition, ed. I.B. Cowan and D.E. Easson (London and New York, 1976), 86–7.
33. *St. Andrews Acta*, 34–5, 37–9; cf. xviii–xx.
34. *APS*, ii, 37–8, 61–2; *Registrum Magni Sigilli Regum Scottorum*, ed. J.M. Thomson and others (Edinburgh, 1882–1914), ii, No. 307; see discussion in G. Donaldson, 'The rights of the Scottish crown in episcopal vacancies', *Scot. Hist. Rev.*, xlv (1966), 27–35.
35. Cf. ibid., 34–5.
36. Robertson, *Concilia*, ii, 78–80, 282–3.
37. L. Macfarlane, 'The primacy of the Scottish church', *Innes Review*, xx (1969), 111.
38. *Cal. Scot. Supp.*, i and ii, passim; *CPL*, vii, passim; *The Apostolic Camera and Scottish Benefices 1418–88*, ed. A.I. Cameron (Oxford, 1934), passim.
39. E.g. *Cal. Scot. Supp.*, ii, 3, 32, 40; *CPL*, vii, 262.
40. *APS*, ii, 5, cc. 14–16; 14, c. 2; 16, c. 9.
41. *A Dictionary of the Older Scottish Tongue*, ed. W.A. Craigie (Oxford, 1937–00), *s.v.* 'barate', 'barratour', 'barratry'.
42. *CPL*, vii, 18–19; see generally Watt, *Dictionary*, 133–4; E.W.M. Balfour-Melville, *James I, King of Scots* (London, 1936), 177–9.
43. *CPL*, viii, 286–7, 344–5.
44. *St. Andrews Copiale*, 433.
45. Ibid., 369–72; Watt, *Dictionary*, 134; cf. Balfour-Melville, *James I*, 237–8.
46. Nicholson, *Later Middle Ages*, 293–4.
47. *Vetera Monumenta Hibernorum et Scotorum Historiam Illustrantia*, ed. A. Theiner (Rome, 1864), 465–8, no. 852.
48. *APS*, ii, 95, c.6.
49. D. McRoberts, 'The Scottish church and nationalism in the fifteenth century', *Innes Review*, xix (1968), 3–14, especially 12.
50. Nicholson, *Later Middle Ages*, 414–18. This ecclesiastical change must have been particularly welcome to King James III, who from 1470 onwards is thought to have shown some ingenuity in consolidating his newly acquired rights in the Northern Isles (ibid., 417).
51. Ibid., 460–2. See also Macfarlane, 'Primacy', 112,; N. Macdougall, *James III* (Edinburgh, 1982), 105.
52. McRoberts, 'Scottish church', 12.
53. See above, note 47. Dr. I.B. Cowan tells me that the related petition to the pope (which might have provided some background information) has not survived in the papal archives.
54. S. Ollivant, *The Court of the Official in Pre-Reformation Scotland* (Stair Society, 1982), 119; cf. 129–38, 159.
55. Ibid., 126; J.J. Robertson, 'The development of the law', in *Scottish Society in the Fifteenth Century*, ed. Jennifer M. Brown (London, 1977), 151.
56. For his biography see J. Herkless and R.K. Hannay, *The Archbishops of St. Andrews*, i (Edinburgh and London, 1907), chapter 1.
57. *APS*, ii, 85, c. 4.
58. Herkless and Hannay, *Archbishops*, i, 74: cf. 31–2.
59. He may well have been assisted in his mission by Henry, Abbot of Cambuskenneth, who was

commissioned as royal envoy to the curia on 25 June 1471 (*Reg. Mag. Sig.*, ii, no. 1034); cf. Nicholson, *Later Middle Ages*, 461.

60. Ibid. 462–3; Macdougall, *James III*, 106.
61. *CPL*, xiii, 202–6; cf. J.A.F. Thomson, 'Some new light on the elevation of Patrick Graham', *Scot. Hist. Rev.*, xl (1961), 82–8 for the argument that some influential vested interests in Scotland may have been aroused against Graham as a consequence of some of the powers and favours granted to him by the pope at this stage.
62. *Accounts of the Lord High Treasurer of Scotland*, ed. T. Dickson and Sir J. Balfour Paul (Edinburgh, 1877–1916), i, 67 (the king has been inquiring of a chaplain of St. Andrews 'anent certain matters anent the Bishop of St. Andrews'); cf. ibid., 44. It was only in Sept. 1476 that he is said specifically to have lost his reason (*CPL*, xiii, 555–6). His delusions are well vouched for in the bull ordering his deposition in 1478 (see below, note 67).
63. *Treasurer Accts.*, i, 46.
64. Ibid., 47: *The Exchequer Rolls of Scotland*, ed. J. Stuart and others (Edinburgh, 1878–1908), viii, 318–19; *CPL*, xiii, 38–9, 555–6; cf. Thomson, 'Some new light', 87–8.
65. Biography in Herkless and Hannay, *Archbishops*, i, chapter 2; *St. Andrews Acta*, 103, 111.
66. *CPL*, xiii, 33–4. He had made use of a dispensation granted by Archbishop Graham on papal authority. Thus was Graham's new status being recognized in royal circles in Scotland.
67. Ibid., 41.
68. Ibid., 555–6; cf. Cameron, *Apostolic Camera*, 252.
69. 'Instructions for the trial of Patrick Graham', ed. R.K. Hannay, *Miscellany of the Scottish History Society*, iii (1919), 171–8; Theiner, *Monumenta*, 478–81, nos. 862–3; *CPL*, xiii, 277. It was intended that Scheves should not claim unauthorised papal privileges as Graham had sometimes done.
70. Cf. Macfarlane, 'Primacy', 115; Macdougall, *James III*, 107.
71. *Registrum Episcopatus Glasguensis* (Bannatyne and Maitland Clubs, 1843), ii, 470–3; cf. *CPL*, xv, 564, no. 1448 for evidence that no copy of this bull has survived in the papal archives. See discussion in J.A.F. Thomson, 'Innocent VIII and the Scottish church', *Innes Review*, xix (1968), 29–30.
72. Theiner, *Monumenta*, 473–4, no. 858.
73. *CPL*, xiii, 68–9.
74. *CPL*, xiv, 152; Robertson, *Concilia*, i, cxix.
75. Cameron, *Apostolic Camera*, 223; *CPL*, xiv, 220–1; Theiner, *Monumenta*, 502–3, no. 885.
76. See Watt, *Fasti* for details.
77. W. Croft Dickinson, *Scotland from the Earliest Times to 1603*, 3rd edition, ed. A.A.M. Duncan (Oxford, 1977), 273.
78. Cameron, *Apostolic Camera*, xlvii–viii.
79. Macdougall, *James III*, 222–3.
80. Ibid., 224–5.
81. Ibid., 227–9.
82. Herkless and Hannay, *Archbishops*, i, 157–8; *CPL*, xiv, 4.
83. *APS*, ii, 171, c. 9.
84. Cameron, *Apostolic Camera*, xxxix; cf. Nicholson, *Later Middle Ages*, 459.
85. Herkless and Hannay, *Archbishops*, i, 184, 191–3, 197–8.

6

The Papacy and Ireland in the Fifteenth Century

J.A. Watt
University of Newcastle upon Tyne

The *Calendar of entries in papal registers relating to Great Britain and Ireland* reached the fifteenth century with volume IV, published in 1902. Volume XV, covering the years 1484–92, appeared in 1978. With twelve volumes summarising the contents of the Vatican and Lateran registers, and all containing large quantities of Irish material, so readily accessible, it can scarcely be said that the relations of Ireland and the papacy in the fifteenth century constitute a *terra incognita*. And yet surprisingly little has been written about that subject. Certainly not enough for anyone to feel confident that he might write the sort of essay of synthesis of the type so successfully produced in the collection edited by C.H. Lawrence, *The English Church and the Papacy in the middle ages*[1]. If a parallel Irish volume were to be attempted, there can be no doubt that despite the twelve volumes of the *Calendar of Papal Registers*, the fifteenth century would be the toughest assignment. By comparison, the twelfth and thirteenth centuries have attracted far more attention. And though the last decade or so has seen an enormous boom in the amount and quality of writing about medieval Ireland, ecclesiastical history seems curiously unfashionable and little enough of this new work has been about the Irish church. In that little, the papacy has not been prominent. Perhaps, then, this paper is a small attempt to begin the task of finding the papacy's proper place in the history of pre-Reformation Ireland.

Of course what can be accomplished in a short paper must be more restricted than my over-ambitious title suggests. The first limitation on my ambition (apart of course from ignorance) is our conference theme of politics and patronage. Patronage can mean different things. I am choosing to take it, for the most part, in its technical sense of right of presentation to benefice or office. How the papacy sought and was allowed to exercise that sort of patronage, assessed in the context of the roles of other patrons, is quite a big enough subject to be going on with. A second limitation is imposed by the nature of the material available for this study, a limitation which involves both chronology and a concentration on particular regions of Ireland. The *Calendars of Papal Registers,* and related papal material such as the *Libri Annatarum,* tell us a great deal about what the curia purposed in the way of ecclesiastical appointments, though so far it has remained largely unanalysed. But material from Ireland itself, to monitor the effectiveness of papal decisions, to trace the consequences of processes initiated in the curia, to assess the precise degree to which these decisions and processes were responses to events in Ireland, is very much less abundant. Indeed, the virtually complete absence of episcopal registers for all the Irish dioceses makes the two-way study of papal patronage, central and local, extremely difficult. The one diocese that does have surviving registers is Armagh. They begin in 1361 with the register of Archbishop Milo Sweetman and continue in broken sequence to Archbishop George Dowdall in the mid-sixteenth century. In the seventeenth century, when clearly there had already been fearsome loss of material, the registers were crudely bound in a way that did not ensure that all the material for an individual pontificate found a place in the correct collection and without any principle of arrangement, whether by subject or chronology or any other method of systematisation. Three of the registers have been calendared and one has been edited.[2] These textual studies relate to the period 1361–1456 with a gap for the period of Archbishop John Colton (1383–1404). Nothing of the fifteenth century after 1456 has been either calendared or edited, though in 1946 Fr A. Gwynn published a short book, *The Medieval Province of Armagh,* based on register material of the period after 1470.[3] For the purpose of this paper I have sought to integrate the papal and Armagh registers in the study of patronage, limiting myself to the first half of the fifteenth century; and I begin with Urban VI because of the interest and importance of the Great Schism period. Patronage and the papacy, then, 1378–1456, with particular reference to Armagh province and diocese. And one last limitation. Taking my cue from the dictum of Pope Innocent III and the Fourth Lateran Council (c.26): 'There is nothing more harmful to the Church of God than the elevation of unworthy prelates to the government of souls',[4] I have given rather more attention to the episcopate than to any other section of the clergy.

The province of Armagh, on the very edge of Latin Christendom, comprised a metropolitan who claimed, as the successor of St. Patrick, the primacy of all Ireland, and ten suffragan sees. Of these ten, three may be termed English or Anglo-Irish in that their bishops were either invariably or usually Anglo-Irish or English; and with *temporalia* taken into the king's hand, they were subject, more or less, to the same electoral procedures as bishoprics in England. These dioceses were Meath, one of the most strongly English parts of Ireland, Down, where the English presence was rather less uniformly dominant, and Connor (modern Co.

Antrim) where the English hold, by this period, was distinctly tenuous. In the Armagh diocese itself, there existed a formal administrative structure which recognised the reality of a distinction between an area *inter Anglicos* and an area *inter Hibernicos*. The latter comprised three deaneries: Tullaghoge, territory of the O'Neills, perhaps the single strongest Irish dynasty in the whole country; Orior, territory of the O'Hanlons; and Armagh city. *Inter Anglicos* lay three deaneries in an area constituted broadly by modern Co. Louth: Drogheda, Ardee and Dundalk. The archbishops, normally Anglo-Irish, but occasionally English, after the death of David O'Hiraghty in 1346, lived on their manors of Termonfeckin and Dromiskin in Co. Louth and very frequently, though by no means invariably, used St Peter's Drogheda as their cathedral. By trial and error, and with many a difficulty, the archbishops of Armagh had worked out a diocesan administration which administered the Gaelic section of the diocese partly directly, partly indirectly. It is the great fascination of the Armagh registers that they reveal, in all its detail, the nature of the ecclesiastical *modus vivendi* which bridged the cultural divide in this part of Ireland and transcended, often painfully and only partially, the basic ethnic division of the diocese. And having achieved or at least glimpsed the possibility of achieving such a *modus* within their own diocese, they were able to apply their experience to the province as a whole.

But the full story of how the *modus* worked, and failed to work, must be postponed.[5] My immediate concern is with the making of the episcopate in this culturally and politically divided province. Who were making the effective decisions about who became a bishop, and what sort of men were being promoted to Irish Armagh sees in the first half of the fifteenth century? That these questions were crucially important pastorally needs no further emphasis than the recalling of Innocent III's dictum already quoted. That they were also politically sensitive was made very clear in Rome in 1381–2, when the English embassy, led by Nicholas Dagworth and Walter Skirlaw, discussed church-state relations with the curia.[6] No doubt Ireland was not their first priority, but there was shown as much anxiety about the political reliability of bishops provided by the papacy in Ireland as in Aquitaine. What was being demanded from Urban VI was a papal instruction to all prelates in Ireland that they should command their clerical subjects to master the English language and ensure that no Irishman be promoted to any office or any benefice with care of souls unless he could speak and understand English.[7] It was claimed that the more powerful, better and greater part of the country (*'pocior, melior et maior pars terre'*) used that language and that experience had shown lack of linguistic uniformity in Ireland to be a potent cause of war. The demand put thus starkly, as if it were to apply to all four provinces and all thirty-three dioceses, was quite unrealistic. But it had its basis in crown policy established earlier in the fourteenth century and finalised in the often-reiterated Statute of Kilkenny of 1366, with its clauses decreeing that all who ministered within the English part of Ireland should know

English and be subject to security vetting.[8] When Dagworth and Skirlaw asked the papacy to refrain from apppointing the politically suspect and not to promote anyone *ad prelaturam* who could not understand English, the request was not, from the government's point of view, quite as unrealistic as it seemed at first blush. In reply, the curia protested against any attempt to shackle its freedom of choice, issued no mandate about knowledge of the English language as a requisite for ecclesiastical promotion, and allowed the Irish dimension of the embassy's demands to be covered by its general declaration that the papacy would look and act with paternal affection on anything touching the king and his kingdom. Such evasive platitudes were easily uttered. But it does seem that whether by accident or design the papacy did manage to avoid, in our period, providing any bishop who proved a serious political embarrassment to the crown, and yet at the same time refrained from any attempt, no matter how remote its chances of success, to create and sustain a politically subservient episcopate.

The papacy had a hand in some seventy provisions to Armagh bishoprics within the period. The figure is inevitably somewhat imprecise because of gaps in the sources. There are errors and uncertainties, therefore, in the Irish episcopal succession lists in the *Handbook of British Chronology*. It is not easy to generalise about these provisions unless it be to say, rather expectedly, that most and perhaps all took too long, that some were effective and that too high a proportion was disastrously unsuccessful. When the papacy provided an English-man (by birth; no other outsiders were nominated) the result was almost always unfortunate. The most glaring example of this in Armagh province concerned the small diocese of Dromore in Magennis territory in modern Co. Down, held by absentee Englishmen for most of the fifteenth century. In provisions for this diocese the papacy showed astonishing irresponsibility: for example, in the years 1431-33 there were four English friars acting as suffragans in English dioceses all with papal authority to call themselves bishops of Dromore.[9]

But this is an extreme example and not really typical of the papacy's action. Other dioceses of Gaelic Ulster could organise themselves to work the system to their own advantage. The classic example of this was Clogher, a diocese broadly comprising modern Cos. Fermanagh and Monaghan and part of south Co. Tyrone. There the Maguires were the chief ruling family and in control of who became their bishop, at least in this period. The evidence[10] suggests that the chapter, containing relatives and clients, continued to elect. Not surprisingly, Maguires came to be chosen and these choices were ratified by papal provision. Art MacCawell, archdeacon of Clogher, went himself to Rome in 1389 to be provided by Boniface IX. In 1437 his successor, Pierce Maguire, was postulated by the chapter. He had to be postulated and not elected because he was the son of a priest and needed a dispensation before he could be appointed bishop. He was duly dispensed *super defectu natalium*, bound himself to pay the required tax on his provision, and ruled his see for the next ten years. When he resigned his diocese in 1447, Nicholas V accepted Ross Maguire, illegitimate son of Thomas Maguire, whom the Annals of Ulster call king of Fermanagh and English officialdom would call *capitaneus nacionis sue*. Ross was consecrated by Archbishop John Mey with great celebration in the English town of Drogheda in 1449.[11] The harmony between Anglo-Irish metropolitan and native Irish bishop here symbolized prevailed until Ross resigned into the hands of Sixtus IV in 1475. Here then in Clogher is a satisfactory series of local appointments: capitular selections, kinship affiliations, uncontested papal provision, good working relationships across the ethnic divide with the metropolitan. But then the twist: these bishops were all married men. Bishop Pierce Maguire, whose father was a priest, was grandson of Bishop Art MacCawell; and he himself was the father of a large family, as was Bishop Ross Maguire. Their progeny was powerful as canons of the Clogher chapter, as rectors in the diocese, as abbots. From the papacy they received dispensation for their illegitimacy and to the papacy they had to apply to avoid uncanonical title. But no question about their celibacy seems to have arisen at the curia and the position was apparently tolerated by the metropolitan. There was nothing about this state of affairs which confined it to Clogher: clerical dynasties were the norm throughout the Gaelic world. One well-known Annals of Ulster entry forms part of the evidence of its general acceptability in Irish society: in an obituary, Cathal Óg MacManus Maguire, father of a large family, is praised among other conventional clerical qualities, 'as a gem of purity and a turtle-dove of chastity'.[12]

The bishops of the neighbouring diocese of Meath came from and moved in the very different milieu of the Anglo-Irish establishment. Meath was a rich diocese by Irish standards and more often than not its bishops, from the first anglicisation of the see in the early thirteenth century down to the Reformation, held high office in the colonial administration. We may assume that Meath was one of the Irish dioceses in whose filling the crown continued to take an interest. This did not of course obviate local pressures of the traditional kind. The see's strong link with the Dublin government made it liable to be caught up in the political feuds of the Anglo-Irish world. In 1433, for example, the Meath clergy were 'constreyned . . . by a grete compainie to chose a bishop . . . to the impediment of the fre eleccion of the clergy'.[13] The perpetrators of the violence – the Berneville family – had both the council of Basel and Eugenius IV to contend with as decision makers. In the event, the pope accepted the clergy's own choice. Pressure of a less vigorous sort came after the death of this choice, William Silk, in 1450. Archbishop John Mey, who as a Meath priest had had much to do with the selection of Silk seventeen years earlier, wrote to Nicholas V urging the suitability of Edmund Oldhall for promotion to the see. In addition to the usual qualities – *mundicia vite* etc. – his especial suitability, wrote the archbishop, lay in his being the brother of the chamberlain of the lord lieutenant, who was then Richard, duke of York, the most powerful man in the whole of Meath, who had in his gift most of the richest benefices in the diocese wherefrom the bishop might be maintained: he was also at present the intimate and special *clericus* of the duke.[14] Oldhall was given the see.

The episcopal succession in Clogher and Meath show, in their very different ways, the papacy as responsive to the local situation. Provisions to Dromore show it as indifferent to local needs or at least unable to provide for them. What of the metropolitan see itself? Examination of Armagh appointments must begin with a complication in the patronage processes which so far I have not considered, namely, the effect of the Great Schism. Incidentally, the following discussion is perhaps of especial interest to English historians in the light of a recent suggestion that Richard II's expedition to Ireland in 1394–5 'took the form of a crusade against the Clementinist Irish'.[15]

Archbishop Milo Sweetman died in August 1380. Some six months later, Clement VII nominated an ambitious Franciscan called Thomas O Colman to Armagh. O Colman who described himself as *lector sacre pagine* of the Armagh Franciscan house and a theology graduate of Oxford, Cambridge and Paris, had already some years earlier obtained a papal dispensation from illegitimacy in order to pave his way for promotion within his order.[16] In 1375 he obtained another dispensation to make him eligible for promotion to the episcopate, telling Gregory XI how he had repeatedly risked his life in times of war on behalf of the rights and liberties of the churches in Ireland.[17] In 1383, Clement VII associated him with the bishop of Glasgow and the pope's nominee to the see of Cashel in support of the small knot of Clementinists in the west of Ireland: the archbishop of Tuam and the bishops of Kilmacduagh, Clonfert and Achonry. In the meantime the Armagh *temporalia* (the Louth episcopal manors of Termon-feckin and Dromiskin) had been entrusted to John Colton, English by birth, but who had served in Ireland since 1361, as dean of St Patrick's Cathedral, Dublin since 1374, and between 1372 and 1382 successively as treasurer, chancellor and justiciar of the Dublin civil administration.[18] A man of enormous experience in the colonial world, ecclesiastical and civil, he was provided to Armagh by Urban VI and consecrated in St Paul's in March 1383. He ruled Armagh actively until his resignation in 1404. Unfortunately his own register has not survived, though occasional documents from it occur in other registers. There is no evidence that O Colman ever put in an appearance in Armagh. But a surviving provincial council decree of Colton's asserting the legitimacy of Urban VI, condemning those who had sought appointments from Robert of Geneva and made appeals to him, and who 'returning to the province have drawn many with them in schismatic error', may refer to him.[19] There is a hint in a papal letter that there was some support for Clement in the Armagh diocese itself when in 1390 Boniface IX granted a dispensation from illegitimacy to a member of a prominent Armagh clerical family, Thomas O'Loughran, later to be dean of Armagh and a close associate of Archbishop Colton's, which described Thomas as 'a great combatant of schismatics in his diocese'.[20] But nothing more is heard from Armagh about allegiance to Avignon. And after the early 1380s, the

Clementinist support in Connacht also disappears from the record. Papal and Armagh registers, native Irish Annals, crown records of various sorts, not least those concerned directly with Richard II's two Irish expeditions, are all silent about continuing Irish support for the Avignon allegiance. One must conclude that such support was highly localised and short-lived. There is nothing in the evidence to suggest that Gaelic Ireland as a whole, from political hostility to the English, gave its support to Clement VII; and also nothing, I suggest, to support the view that Richard II had an anti-Avignon crusade in mind when he went to Ireland.

John Colton resigned his see a few months before his death. Resignation of course needed papal permission and brought automatic reservation of the provision to the see. But this procedure allowed the resigning prelate and/or his clergy to send to Rome as proctor the man locally designated for provision. Very likely too, he picked up royal consent as he passed through England. Colton sent Nicholas Fleming to Rome with his resignation and he was given the see in 1404. Archbishop Swayne sent John Prene, his archdeacon and *officialis* of his court, in 1439 and he too was appointed. Swayne's own appointment had been rather less straightforward. He was an Anglo-Irishman from Kildare with Meath and Armagh connexions but he was not even the locals' second choice. When Fleming died in 1416, the chapter of Armagh, all native Irishmen, with the Anglo-Irish bishop of Meath and the abbot of the Cistercian abbey of Mellifont represented by a single proctor, elected Robert Fitz Hugh, chancellor of St Patrick's Cathedral, Dublin. The notarial document[21] recounting his election contains the information that they had earlier elected Richard Talbot. Talbot was the brother of the John Talbot who was to become the first earl of Shrewsbury and was then serving in Ireland as lord lieutenant, a man whom the *Annals of Ulster* were to describe as the most evil man since Herod. But Richard Talbot was the choice of Gaelic Armagh and he consented to his election. Before he could be provided, however, Dublin fell vacant. He was elected by the chapter and then papally provided to it. For Armagh the Council of Constance chose John Swayne. Holder of many benefices in Ireland, including the treasurership of St Patrick's Dublin, he had been, since the early years of the century, a papal chancery official (*abbreviator de curia*) and *secretarius* of John XXIII.[22] He described himself once as rector of the University of Siena.[23] He was to rule Armagh with some distinction for twenty-one years. The Armagh choices of Talbot and Fitz Hugh are a warning to historians against making too quickly judgements that equate Gaelic opinion with an inevitable anti-English stand. Especially when, to make the warning even clearer, it transpires that on the death of Prene in 1443, the Armagh chapter, this time vigorously supported by O'Neill, Ulster's most powerful Gaelic king, again attempted to make Richard Talbot their archbishop. Again Talbot gave his consent and actually described himself as archbishop-elect.[24] But it was John Mey, who as *officialis* of Meath was experienced in the affairs of Armagh province, whom Eugenius IV provided in 1444. He was to make an interesting contrast to Richard Talbot. Talbot was very much the colonial administrator, serving for long spells as chief or deputy chief governor, something of a warrior-prelate.[25] Mey was very much the dedicated pastoral bishop, as we can now see in some detail thanks to the edition of his register which Dr Quigley and Professor Roberts produced in 1972, a prelate who sought to avoid, on his own protestation,[26] attempting political solutions to pastoral problems.

Full acceptance of the pope's special position in relation to the episcopate was virtually complete throughout Ireland in this period: it included dispensations from canonical impediments to promotion to a bishopric, provisions to bishoprics, translations from one see to another, depositions, resignations. This special position also extended to diocesan structures, to such matters as the status of cathedral clergy, organisation of chapters, relations of suffragans with their metropolitan, union of dioceses. This is not the place to explore all these different occasions for papal intervention, every one of which can be found in this period. But I would like to examine one diocesan union, that of Down with Connor, partly because closer study of the Armagh registers tidies up the details of the unions, some of which in the accepted version summarised in the *Handbook of British Chronology* are confused and erroneous, but more importantly, for the light it throws on politics, patronage and the papacy in another part of the province of Armagh in the first half of the fifteenth century.

Down, a monastic cathedral, had provided to it in 1413 its then prior, John Sely. His somewhat chequered reign was to last to his death in 1445. It is from the 1430s that there comes to us, by way of Archbishop Swayne's register, evidence that the bishop's conduct was causing disquiet to his metropolitan. In 1430, Swayne threatened Sely with excommunication for not wearing his Benedictine habit as canon law required of him.[27] In 1434, he warned him to get rid of his concubine, one Letys Thomb.[28] Apparently after a period of cohabitation, Letys had left him to marry, but had subsequently returned to live with him. At the same time Swayne warned the prior of the cathedral, William Stauley, who was also living in concubinage.[29] It seems, incidentally, that the registers suggest that archbishops of Armagh operated a double standard in their province: tolerating episcopical concubinage (though not sexual promiscuity) *inter Hibernicos* (in dioceses such as Clogher, for example) but condemning it *inter Anglicos*. Nevertheless Sely and Stauley survived. In July 1438 Henry VI granted licence to Sely to ask the pope to unite his diocese with Connor, the agreement of John Fossade, bishop of Connor having been obtained. A year later Eugenius IV ordered that the union should come into effect on the death of either bishop. Before that happened, however, Sely again fell foul of his metropolitan. Archbishop John Prene, making visitation of Down in 1440, found him still cohabiting with Letys Thomb and guilty of simony and other crimes. It would seem that he had been excommunicated and suspended by Swayne but had continued in office, *in contemptu clavium*. When Sely failed to present himself at the metropolitan court, Prene went seriously to work to get rid of him. He supplied the pope with an account of Sely's trial and requested his deposition. Indeed he took his deposition for granted. Even before Prene had sent his certificate of process for deposition to Eugenius IV, he had chosen Sely's successor, William Basset O.S.B., and had begun to lobby support for him from the king, his chancellor and from the duke of York. He also persuaded James Butler, earl of Ormond and deputy lieutenant, to write personally to the pope asking for Basset to replace the soon-to-be-deposed Sely. Linked integrally with his efforts on Basset's behalf was a campaign to revoke the projected union of Down and Connor. Prene urged that the clergy of the two dioceses had not been consulted, were unlikely to agree to union, and that such a union could only enhance the power of the hostile Irish of the region. With his letter to the chancellor (Bishop John Stafford), went presents of Irish mantles and other garments and a promise that next Michaelmas he would send him a horse.

Sely was not deposed. He died before the pope got round to taking action against him. Basset did not get the see. Prene withdrew his opposition to the union. In November 1442, as *custos spiritualitatis* during the Down vacancy, he ordered John Fossade, bishop of Connor, to implement Eugenius's union of the dioceses. So far as Ireland was concerned, then, the bull took effect, as the pope had instructed, with the death of one or other of the incumbents. But the papal curia, in apparent ignorance of its own mandate, produced a successor to Sely in the Down see. He was an English Augustinian canon, who, like so many other English religious nominated to Irish sees in the fifteenth century, spent his episcopal career in England. Worse muddle was to follow. Two years later, in 1447, ignoring or being unaware that it had already appointed both a bishop of Down and Connor and a bishop of Down, the curia appointed to Down an English Carthusian, Thomas Pollard. He was not content to find a post in England, or perhaps he could not. For in 1448 he appeared in Downpatrick, showing his 'appostell provisyoun'. He attracted sufficient support from the Down clergy (probably hostile to the union, as Prene had anticipated), including the disreputable William Stauley still prior, to be able to take possession of the episcopal residence in the town. The harassed bishop, John Fossade, invoked the help of the seneschal of the liberty of Ulster and of his metropolitan, Archbishop John Mey. Mey excommunicated Pollard and Stauley but suspended the sentences *sub spe concordie*. All parties met in Downpatrick at the end of 1449. There is no record of what happened at the meeting. But when Fossade died in the course of 1450 Pollard was given custody of the temporalities of Down and Connor. His ministry, if indeed it was ever actually exercised, was to be brief; by December 1451 he was dead.

An appropriate provision to the united see would have put an end to confusion. But again the curia muddied the waters. In April 1451, Archbishop Mey recommended to Rome the appointment of an Anglo-Irish Dominican and made efforts too with the cardinals on his behalf. Nicholas V instead appointed

an Englishman, who spent the next twenty years working in the dioceses of
Lichfield and Worcester. In August 1453, Nicholas V tried again and provided
Thomas Knight, prior of the Daventry Benedictines. Eventually, in May 1456,
Mey was able to announce to the clergy and people of Down and Connor that
Knight, having exhibited his bulls of provision, was to be accepted as true
bishop of Down and Connor. Knight's rule was to last until 1469, despite his
grumble that the see was inadequately endowed and that it was situated where
homines indomiti et quodammodo silvestres commorantur. With Knight's pontificate
the union of Down and Connor was fully consummated.[30] The curia's record in
bringing about its achievement needs no gloss.[31]

I have so far tried to glimpse patronage in an important part of the Anglo-Irish
world – Meath, Armagh, Down, Connor. I have preceded it with an even
briefer glimpse of patronage in the Gaelic world of the diocese of Clogher. In
this last section of my paper I wish to return to that Gaelic world, but not this
time at the level of the episcopate. I spoke earlier of clerical dynasties and tried
to show their significance in Clogher. I want now to look at a clerical family
which was not, like the Maguires, of the lay ruling dynasty and did not supply
bishops, but was prominent on the next level of office in the Gaelic ecclesiastical world. From the Armagh registers and papal letters several families of
Armagh diocese *inter Hibernicos* suggest themselves for scrutiny. To put their
careers together would give real insight into how the Gaelic world supplied itself
with its clergy and how that clergy worked out a *modus vivendi* with its Anglo-
Irish prelates and, more marginally, with the papacy. I have only time to
concentrate on a single family. We have already met one of the family very
briefly:– Thomas O'Loughran dispensed from illegitimacy as the son of a priest in
1390 and papally commended for his opposition to the supporters of Robert of
Geneva.

In the first half of the fifteenth century members of the O'Loughran family can
be found in most of the important positions in Armagh diocese *inter Hibernicos* –
as deans of Tullahoge and Orior, abbots of Sts. Peter and Paul, Armagh, officials
and members of Armagh chapter, *officiales* of the city of Armagh itself. The
rectory they tried to keep as their hereditary possession was Donaghmore, near
Dungannon, the 'great church', *dominica magna*, which claimed Patrician
foundation. With the rectory went the office, common to the Gaelic world, of
erenagh, steward of ecclesiastical lands. From this ecclesiastical and territorial
base, a member of the O'Loughran family could look to further his career (or
widen his pastoral horizons) by service to his O'Neill *rí* and to his archbishop.
The career of Thomas O'Loughran, the antagonist of schismatics, exemplifies
this very neatly. He became O'Neill's secretary (*clericus secretus*) and as such
played a key role when Richard II was in Drogheda in 1395 to receive the
O'Neills' submissions. O'Loughran was the official interpreter.[32] Two years later
he is found as a member of Colton's *familia* when that archbishop went to Derry
on a famous occasion to vindicate his right as metropolitan to be *custos*

spiritualitatis et temporalitatis during vacancy.[33] From *c.* 1406 to his death *c.* 1417, he was dean of Armagh Cathedral. As such, for ten years he was the archbishop's most trusted official in Armagh diocese *inter Hibernicos*, especially in visitation.[34] This position, however, made him no less vulnerable to Rome-running than any other benefice holder in Gaelic Ireland. In 1414 Denis O'Cullen complained against him in Rome that as dean he had been guilty of simony and had held Donaghmore with another rectory (Aghaloo) without dispensation.[35] The dean warded off the threat, though his challenger was to succeed him and gain at last the title to Donaghmore after his death.

Another Thomas O'Loughran was to make himself equally indispensable to his archbishop. Apparently the son of an abbot of Sts. Peter and Paul, he became canon of Armagh and between 1426 and 1444 was very active as archbishop's commissary in the areas *inter Hibernicos*.[36] In his role as receiver of rents and tithe due to the archbishop he was at once a key figure in the Armagh ecclesiastical machinery and a man of influence in the Gaelic world. Thomas seems to have achieved and kept his position without benefit or harm from the papacy.[37] But for one of his relatives Rome had much to offer. Patrick O'Loughran, rector of Carnteel and vicar of Donaghmore, went to Rome in 1426, partly on pilgrimage, partly on business. His business was to keep his benefices. They were under threat because Patrick was married and Archbishop John Swayne had decreed a purge of concubinical priests, the penalty being forfeiture of benefices. Patrick returned from Rome armed with a papal letter of rehabilitation and permission to keep his benefices.[38]

Towards the end of our period the O'Loughrans continued to fall out of favour with their archbishops: Hugh O'Loughran, dean of Tullahoge *c.* 1430–40, repeatedly censured for failure to present the deanery's accounts; John O'Loughran, deprived by Archbishop John Bole of the same deanery and Donaghmore in 1462, after complaint at Rome, for concubinage, holding in plurality without dispensation and other irregularities; William O'Loughran, deprived of Donaghmore in 1463 for sexual offences and perjury. But these clerical families were nothing if not resilient. The O'Loughrans and their like would weather their occasional crises in the fifteenth century. Such families were not to be finally uprooted until the Plantation of Ulster; they had kept Gaelic Ulster Catholic through the Reformation.

Notes

1. F.R.H. Du Boulay, 'The Fifteenth Century', in *The English Church and the Papacy in the middle ages*, ed. C.H. Lawrence (1965), 197–242.

2. H.J. Lawlor, 'A calendar of the register of Archbishop Sweteman', *Proceedings of the Royal Irish Academy* xxix sec. C, no. 8 (1911), 213–310; id., 'A calendar of the register of Archbishop Fleming', ibid., xxx sec. C. no. 5 (1912), 94–190; *The register of John Swayne archbishop of Armagh and primate of Ireland, 1418–1439* ed. D.A. Chart (Belfast, 1935); *Registrum Iohannis Mey: The register of John Mey, Archbishop of Armagh 1443–1456* ed. W.G.H. Quigley and E.F.D. Roberts (Belfast, 1972). There is a typescript calendar of Prene's register (by W. Reeves) in the National Library of Ireland, Dublin. I am grateful to Dr. A. Cosgrove for drawing it to my attention.

3. A. Gwynn, *The medieval province of Armagh, 1470–1545* (Dundalk, 1946).

4. 'Nihil est quod ecclesiae Dei magis officiat, quam quod indigni assumantur praelati ad regimen animarum': *Conciliorum oecumenicorum Decreta*, ed. J. Alberigo et al. (1962), p. 247.

5. I have made a preliminary examination of the division in a paper read to the Joint Meeting of the Royal Irish Academy and British Academy (July 1982) now published as '*Ecclesia inter Anglicos et inter Hibernicos*: confrontation and coexistence in the medieval diocese and province of Armagh', in *The English in Ireland*, ed. J. Lydon (Dublin, 1984), 46–64.

6. E. Perroy, *L'Angleterre et le grand schisme d'Occident* (Paris, 1933), 177–8, 278–81.

7. Ibid., 394–5.

8. J.A. Watt, *The Church and the two nations in medieval Ireland* (Cambridge, 1970), chapter 10.

9. HBC, 317.

10. M.A. Costello, *De annatis Hiberniae* (Dublin, 1912), 54–5.

11. *Annals of Ulster* ed. W.M. Hennessy and B. MacCarthy (Dublin, 1887–1901), 3, 162–3.

12. C. Mooney, *The Church in Gaelic Ireland: thirteenth to fifteenth centuries* (Dublin, 1969), 60, citing *Ann. Ulster*, 3, 428, 430.

13. M.C. Griffith, 'The Talbot-Ormond struggle for control of the Anglo-Irish government 1414–47', *Irish Historical Studies*, 2 (1941), 395; R.D. Edwards, 'The kings of England and papal provisions in fifteenth century Ireland', in *Medieval Studies presented to A. Gwynn, S.J.*, ed. J.A. Watt, J.B. Morrall and F.X. Martin (Dublin, 1961), 272.

14. *Reg. Mey*, ed. cit., no. 282. On Sir William Oldhall, York's chamberlain, see J.S. Roskell, *The Commons and their speakers in English parliaments 1376–1523* (Manchester, 1965), 242–3, 360–1.

15. Cf. A. Tuck, *Richard II and the English nobility* (1973), 170.

16. CPL, iv, 206.

17. CPL, iv, 242.

18. References and further details of his career are provided in my 'John Colton Justiciar of Ireland (1382) and archbishop of Armagh (1383–1404)', in *England and Ireland in the later middle ages (Essays in honour of Jocelyn Otway-Ruthven* ed. J. Lydon, Dublin, 1981), 196–213.

19. *Cal. reg. J. Swayne* (ed. D.A. Chart), 15.

20. CPL, iv, 340.

21. *Cal. reg. J. Swayne*, 32–4.

22. CPL, vi, 374–5.

23. CPL, vi, 143.

24. *Reg. Mey*, nos. 283, 287–9.

25. J.H. Bernard, 'Richard Talbot, archbishop and chancellor, 1418–1449'. *Proc. Royal Irish Acad.*, xxxv (1918–20), sec. C, no. 5 (1919), 218–29.
26. *Reg. Mey*, no. 141.
27. *Cal. reg. J. Swayne*, 123.
28. Ibid., 151.
29. Ibid., 151.
30. *Reg. Mey*, nos. 23, 37, 136, 166, 195, 213, 221, 280, 281, 309; *Cal. reg. J. Preyne*, 58, 59, 141, 173, 188, 190, 191, 214, 215, 259; Costello, *De annatis*, 121–2, 124; *Rotulorum patentium et clausorum cancellariae Hiberniae calendarium* (Dublin, 1828), 265b.
31. Except to add that Pius II provided an English Dominican to Connor in 1459. He was to be suffragan in Salisbury and Exeter: Costello, *De annatis*, 142.
32. As well as O'Neill's go-between with Richard II and, presumably, writer of O'Neill's letters to the king: E. Curtis, *Richard II in Ireland, 1394–5, and submission of the Irish chiefs* (Oxford, 1927), 69, 136 (instr. viii; ep. 13).
33. See my 'John Colton', cited above, note 18.
34. *Cal. reg. Fleming*, nos. 10, 44, 58, 127, 147, 161, 172, 191. In this tightly-knit society, ecclesiastical duty might clash with family loyalty:– in 1411 Archbishop Fleming ordered Dean Thomas O'Loughran to proceed canonically for seizure of ecclesiastical lands against certain 'filios spurios moderne abbatis'. These illegitimate sons of the recently appointed abbot of Sts. Peter and Paul, Armagh are named as Thomas and Adam O'Loughran in T.C D. MS 557/2, pp. 213–14. The vacancy of the deanery by his death is mentioned in a document dated 30 Oct. 1417: *Cal. reg. Swayne*, 32.
35. *CPL*, vi, 421, 477.
36. His area of operation was usually Armagh itself both as collector and visitor: *Cal. reg. Swayne*, 44, 46, 65, 81, 90, 92, 105, 113, 120, 121, 123, 159. His death had occurred by 1444: ibid., 192.
37. Though a relative had by recourse to Rome obtained restitution of the rectory of Donaghmore in 1428; *Cal. reg. Swayne*, 97–9.
38. *CPL*, vii, 497. The departure of the Armagh pilgrimage is noted in *Cal. reg. Swayne,* 43.

7

English Bishops as Educational Benefactors in the Later Fifteenth Century[1]

Helen Jewell
University of Liverpool

Between 1450 and 1500, some fifty-nine different individuals held the seventeen English sees. As eight of these died, and another one had been removed from the bench, before the end of 1457, and seven were elevated only in the last five years of the century, only the forty-three prelates whose terms of office were more central to the period under review will be considered here. The details of their episcopates appear in the appended table. It should of course be remembered that episcopal incomes themselves varied greatly, which naturally affected the patronage at a bishop's disposal: Winchester and Canterbury were the two richest sees, followed by Durham, Ely, and York.[2]

This paper will begin with a very brief survey of the levels of educational achievement of the bishops themselves, a subject which can be dealt with summarily here, since it has already received considerable treatment elsewhere. Then attention will be focused on the normal, *de cursu*, involvement of bishops with educational facilities in their own dioceses or elsewhere, this involvement being illustrated with examples from the period. In this area of activity it is often difficult to tell from the formal records whether a bishop acted on personal motivation or was merely performing a duty. Thirdly, consideration will be given to what may be seen as an interest in education beyond the bounds of duty, shown by bishops in various activities, including the founding, endowing, or building of university colleges and schools, acting as major benefactors to such institutions, bestowing books on educational institutions, paying scholars' fees or contributing to their maintenance, and pursuing humanistic studies themselves, or encouraging others to do so. In these areas of activity it is more often possible to detect a degree of personal interest. Finally it will be asked whether participation in educational activities varied in relation to the date of elevation, and which bishops excelled as educational benefactors and what sort of men these were.

By the mid-fifteenth century, bishops were recruited predominantly from the university-trained clergy, and indeed mainly from the graduates of the higher faculties. The first decade of our period falls within the adult kingship of Henry VI, when there was a swing from the promotion of lawyers to that of theologians: this trend was reversed with the Yorkist accession in 1461, and preference for lawyers was also maintained by Henry VII.[3] Over the whole century (1399–1499) Cambridge provided twenty-nine bishops (21%) and Oxford ninety-eight (70%).[4] All the forty-three bishops considered here appear in Dr. A. B. Emden's *Biographical Registers*, though in one case, that of William Booth, the entry is to deny his university education: he was trained at Gray's Inn, or as Thomas Gascoigne put it with his usual acerbity, '*nec sciens nec graduatus in aliqua facultate in aliqua universitate sed cupidus legista juris regni*'.[5] Forty-two, then, were university men, and most had entered the higher faculties, with law in the overall lead and particularly prominent in the later part of the period. The bishops' university experience included study abroad in some cases, various individuals having been at Padua, Bologna, Cologne, Paris, Orleans and Louvain. In some cases their passage through one or more universities had been a prolonged one which included office holding in one or more colleges or universities.

Whether or not they were personally interested in education as individuals, medieval bishops were the leading officials of an institution which theoretically provided a coherent educational system under provincial and diocesan legislation.[6] Within the clerical body certain standards of literacy were desirable, and there were points in the career structure at which some testing was deemed appropriate. Ordinands had to be examined, among other things, in literacy, by the archdeacons of the diocese or other clerical examiners appointed by the bishop; and ordination could be refused for lack of learning, or made conditional upon further attendance at school. Some bishops' registers prove that the educational standards of the ordinands coming before them were examined, by either the bishops in person or their proxies. The names of candidates for ordination rejected on account of illiteracy are not preserved. But the ordination of one who was scarcely satisfactory may be seen in Thomas Beckington's register, where, among the priests ordained in September 1460, was entered the name Thomas Popham of Stogumber (Somerset), with the comment, 'memorandum that on the day of his ordination he swore on the Gospels to do his utmost to attain a better knowledge and understanding of grammar, and to present himself for examination by Master Hugh Sugar or any other commissary of the bishop once a year in the week of the next Consistory of Wells following the Exaltation of the Cross, until he be found capable'.[7]

Those aspiring to the cure of souls might undergo further examination, and acccordingly institution to a benefice might also be conditional on further learning. Beckington, apparently unlike his immediate predecessors, was careful to scrutinise the educational attainments of clerks presented to him by patrons, and insisted on priests 'understanding Latin and having some acquaintance with the Scriptures'.[8] Beckington's biographer Judd states that 732 institutions were made during Beckington's episcopate and that thirty-seven were cases where institution was conditional on the candidate attaining an improved standard at a specific date.[9] Though the defects were obviously similar (knowledge, letters, and scripture being mentioned, separately or together, as the deficient factor) the prescriptions vary, suggesting realistic application to the case. Sir John Brice, on being instituted as rector of Weston-in-Gordano (Somerset) in April 1453, was 'in view of his present lack of knowledge' to study 'for two whole years in the schools at Wells', and to offer himself for examination in Easter week each year; Sir John Burgeys, on being instituted as rector of Hornblotton (Somerset) in March 1456, was diligently to apply himself, for a whole year, 'to obtaining at the least a grammatical and literal understanding of the Holy Scriptures, and the daily round of divine offices', and to be examined before Easter 1457. He made rapid progress, being found competent and absolved from further examination in December 1456.[10] Sir John Greene, on being instituted as perpetual vicar of Puriton (Somerset) in September 1456, was committed to apply himself 'diligently, under the instruction of some well-informed person'; Sir John Lord, on being instituted as rector of Babington (Somerset) in July 1460, was to study 'for two whole years in some grammar school'; Sir William Rowle, whose admission as perpetual vicar at Compton Dundon (Somerset) in June 1462 was postponed because of his unfitness, was saved by the later advent of Master John Hobbes, perpetual vicar of Butleigh (Somerset), who came to the bishop and bound himself 'diligently to teach Sir William a better knowledge of letters, and to present him for examination within two years'.[11] Even a backslider might improve. In August 1450 Sir John Roberd, rector of Kilve (Somerset), arrived late for his examination, and it appearing 'that he had made hardly any progress in grammar during the last two years, the bishop enjoined on him once more that he should attend some grammar school for a year' and submit to examination at the end of the year, on pain of being deprived of his benefice. Happily, in September 1451, he was found 'to have a competent knowledge of the rules of grammar, and understanding of the scriptures' and was exempted from further examination and indeed given two years' leave of absence to study.[12] At the end of the century, Bishop Fox's Durham register contains a bond requiring the rector of Knaresdale (Northumberland), John Walys, who had just been instituted, to appear before the vicar-general within a year 'to read and construe adequately the first ten pages of the missal according to the use of Sarum'; and another entry admonishes a chaplain not to officiate within the diocese until he had been better instructed in grammar.[13] Even after institution a cleric might have his deficiency in letters probed in a diocesan visitation; half a century beyond our period, Bishop Hooper found nearly one-third of the parish clergy of the diocese of Gloucester educationally deficient.[14]

Individual bishops were well aware that educational standards were not all that was desirable. In 1455 Archbishop Bourchier recognized that there were in his diocese among the secular clergy *'idioti et indocti, litterarum imperiti ac pene prorsus ignari'* dangerously entrusted with the care of souls.[15] Unfortunately, evidence relating to clerical education is, as Mr. Heath has commented, 'extremely fragmentary'; and we have in the end what Mrs. Bowker has called 'a picture of clerical education which relies partly on figures and partly on inference'.[16] Statistics are not available for the education of those ordained and instituted, particularly if they were not university men. Of the graduates we can know a little more. Eighty-nine of those instituted under Beckington already held degrees, and some of these were allowed to absent themselves to university (usually Oxford if any is specified) for further study. Master Stephen Alva, bachelor in decrees, was given licence to study for two years in any university in 1459, Master William Stevyns, bachelor in laws, to study in any university in England for three years in March 1462, and Sir Philip Puttesham, bachelor of arts, to study three years at Oxford University in September that year.[17] Of the clergy instituted or already beneficed within the diocese of Canterbury and its jurisdictions in Archbishop Bourchier's pontificate, about 21% were university graduates, as Professor Du Boulay has shown.[18]

As a conscientious bishop thus surveyed the educational standards of the secular clergy ordained and instituted in his diocese, so too he might routinely concern himself in the educational provision maintained within abbeys and priories. In 1452 Beckington's register contains a post-visitation injunction to the prior and convent of Bruton (Somerset) that 'the lesser canons are to be intructed in grammar daily at suitable hours'.[19] William Grey's visitation injunctions of 1466 to the prior and convent of Ely included the reminder that the novices should have a master to instruct them, an injunction based on the constitutions of Ottobono, chapter 39.[20] Bishop Goldwell's visitations in the diocese of Norwich in the early 1490s revealed some educational deficiencies: at Wingfield College (Suffolk) in 1493 he found the school neglected, and there were no schoolmasters at Butley Priory (Suffolk), St. Mary's Walsingham and St. Benet's of Holme in 1494.[21]

Clearly a conscientious bishop regularly had the educational standards of churchmen in the diocese before his eyes. Such bishops would also be well aware of the diocese's institutional provision towards such an education, and indeed towards wider educational ends. The Fourth Lateran Council of 1215, enlarging on the 1179 decree, required cathedrals, and other churches with sufficient resources, to maintain schoolmasters to teach clerks and poor scholars freely, a provision followed in England, in Dr. Orme's opinion, in spirit rather than according to the letter.[22] Canon law encouraged clerks to teach children as well as adults elementary articles of the faith in order to save souls.[23] Intermittently, various aspects of the licensing of schoolmasters, constitution of new schools, and reformation of old ones came before the bishops. To cite Beckington's register again, in 1463 licence was given to John Faukeys, clerk, 'to hold a grammar school in Bristol during the bishop's pleasure, to teach all who come to him for instruction, receiving the fees etc. usually pertaining to such instructors'; and only the next month Master Roger Fabell, who held the degree of master in grammar, and was rector of Beckingon (Somerset), was allowed, because of the ruinous state of the rectory, to take up residence at Westbury College at Bristol for four years, to keep a grammar school there, the bishop of Worcester [John Carpenter] choosing him to instruct boys there in grammar.[24] In John Stanbury's register in 1454 the foundress's revised regulations for the chantry at Newland (Gloucestershire), which provided grammar teaching facilities, involved the bishop in ratifying the new statutes and admitting the chaplain, and if necessary visiting and correcting him: in 1465 the bishop ratified further changes.[25] By 1476 the fees for the various types of scholar at Ipswich had been fixed by the bishop of Norwich.[26]

These then are a few examples of aspects of educational business a conscientious bishop would find coming before him: testing the abilities of priestly candidates, investigating the teaching facilities in an abbey or priory, licensing men to teach in particular places, approving the regulations touching ecclesiastical foundations. Beckington's ordinances and statutes for the boy choristers at Wells provide an attractive instance of a bishop involving himself with the statutes of an existing foundation. These Wells ordinances were issued in February 1459–60 with Beckington's approval and commendation for the future. They had been instituted by Sir Robert Catur, teacher and master of the choristers, during whose period of office Beckington had found them diligently kept. The regulations concern four main matters: the character and duties and oath of the master; the like of the undermaster; the removal of obstacles to discipline; and the choristers' behaviour in church, school, refectory, and bedchamber. The statutes can be read in Watkin's *Dean Cosyn and Wells Cathedral Miscellanea*.[27] Here it is sufficient to comment not on the regulations themselves, but on the understanding of children revealed within them. Three aspects of the educational psychology here revealed deserve attention: teaching methods, what are called 'obstacles to discipline', and the use of pupils as prefects for disciplinary purposes. The recommendations made concerning teaching methods were that the head and undermaster were to conform in their manner of teaching, and were to be plain and 'brief yet full of matter'. They were to teach morally, and 'in mature fashion, which teaching is best to be done by manifold repetition'. Obstacles to discipline were defined as three. The first was bad behaviour, which if 'tolerated even for a little while, in a short time goes from bad to worse and is with the more difficulty uprooted'. This included vulgarity, swearing, lying, strifes, brawls, fights, rivalries, bursts of raucous laughter and 'derisions', and was to be treated with vigilance. The second obstacle was lack of concentration, which was to be pitied if a matter of natural disposition, but not if coupled with lack of application. The treatment was to be short firm lessons, and taking in hand by a keener pupil. 'The third hindrance to progress in learning' was defined, not unreasonably, as 'neglect of study': this was to be treated by kindly warning, progressing to sharp rebuke, and if necessary to flogging. Two choristers of the week were enrolled on the disciplinary staff to keep watch on the choristers' defects, and two others who were more skilful singers were to report delinquents to one of the masters. The statutes end by promising forty days' indulgence, under appropriate conditions, to those of the diocese who helped the choristers, one ingenious way of financing an educational system.

That Beckington was interested in education beyond the bounds of duty seems clear. But other bishops who shared this commendable interest did not necessarily reflect it so well in their formal registers; and on the whole bishops in England seem to have intervened surprisingly little in education in their dioceses, or left little record of it. Beckington's successor at Bath and Wells, Robert Stillington, an absentee bishop whose memory is not hallowed in his diocese, granted Sir William Fitzherbert seven years' leave of absence in November 1472 'for study'; Master William Buckett, bachelor in decrees, seven years 'for the purpose of studying at some university' in February 1473; and Thomas Stenying, subdeacon, seven years to study 'at the university of Oxford' in November 1474: these references provide no indication at all of his broad and utilitarian attitude to the education of boys in his native Acaster Selby (Yorkshire, W.R.).[28] The only references to anything educational in the first published volume of Archbishop Rotherham's register are numerous letters dimissory to men described as scholars, or in one case as an acolyte, 'of the schools of York', and three licences of absence to study. The archbishop's own collegiate foundation at Rotherham is mentioned in the register but not in its educational capacity.[29]

Certain bishops had educational responsibilities of a more demanding kind. The bishops of Lincoln and Ely were the diocesan bishops whose sees geographically contained the by this time largely autonomous universities of Oxford and Cambridge; and this gave them a degree of involvement in, and some responsibility for, those educational institutions, much increased of course in years when the diocesan bishop was also the university's chancellor. We may find, for example, Thomas Rotherham, while bishop of Lincoln, writing in 1476 to Oriel College, Oxford, of which he was visitor, about the method of electing the provost, and an elected provost of Oriel seeking his confirmation and admission; William Smith, also as bishop of Lincoln, confirmed new statutes made by Oriel in 1504 and 1507.[30] Simple practical matters might need to be settled: in 1489 the then bishop of Lincoln, John Russell, wrote to Oxford ordering that the old library seats and desks be used in the new school of canon

law.[31] At Cambridge Bishop Alcock of Ely visited the nunnery of St. Mary and
St. Radegund as its diocesan before ultimately dissolving it into his Jesus
College, where his Ely successor Bishop Stanley issued the earliest surviving
statutes in 1514.[32] The bishop of Lincoln's university responsibilities were not
confined to Oxford: he was also visitor and ordinary of King's College,
Cambridge.[33] Moreover, the bishops of Lincoln and Ely were not the only two
members of the episcopal bench who had responsibilities in the universities.
Their position was matched in regard to particular colleges by bishops who for
various historic reasons were visitors of those academic communities. The
bishops of Exeter were the official visitors of Exeter College, Oxford, the
foundation of their predecessor, Walter Stapledon.[34] Magdalen College, the
foundation of William Waynflete, bishop of Winchester, was from 1480 exempt
from Lincoln's jurisdiction and under that of the bishops of Winchester.[35] Thus
it came about that John Dowman was sent as commissary of Bishop Fox in
January 1507 to visit Magdalen, then in considerable disarray, partly at least
because the president had become bishop of Hereford and absented himself too
frequently. The gist of this visitation is printed in translation in Macray's *Register*
and makes entertaining, but not edifying, reading. Fifty-one articles of inquiry
were investigated, and on the more narrowly educational ones it was reported
that the speaking of Latin was not kept up, that lecturers were negligent, and
the care of undergraduates and choristers not observed. Four fellows were
identified as making little progress 'and no wonder since they do not attend
lectures'.[36] In the subsequent injunctions they were enjoined to attend, and
Latin speaking was ordered. Happily we may observe that misbehaviour at
Magdalen was not a deterrent to Fox's own educational plans, and that his
commissary Dowman lived to be a major benefactor to Pocklington (Yorkshire,
E.R.) where he founded the school in 1514, endowing five scholarships to St.
John's College, Cambridge for its boys.[37] Finally it should be noted that the
archbishops had certain supervisory powers at the universities: for example the
archbishop of Canterbury had the selection of the warden of Canterbury College
from three nominees of the Canterbury chapter, and the nomination of the
warden of Merton College from three put forward by the college; similarly the
archbishop of York had the right to confirm the election of the provost of
Queen's College, Oxford.[38] These examples are sufficient to show that bishops
could, of routine, have involvement in education within and beyond the bounds
of their dioceses.

   Next for consideration comes involvement in educational activities to an
extent which might be regarded as beyond or separate from the bounds of duty.
The first area of activity for investigation is the founding, endowing, or building
of schools and university colleges. Any such activity could be costly, and one
such project might be thought sufficient even for a bishop; but it is impressive
that bishops undertaking such patronage managed to spread it, in several cases,
over both schools and colleges. Waynflete founded a hall at Oxford in 1448,

dedicated to St. Mary Magdalen, and converted it into a college in 1457; by the first statutes, dating from 1480, there was already provision for grammar teaching by a master and usher within the college, and in 1484 Waynflete erected a second school, with a chapel, at Wainfleet in Lincolnshire.[39] John Alcock endowed the grammar school at Hull in 1479, and founded Jesus College at Cambridge in 1496.[40] William Smith secured the endowment of the grammar school at Lichfield in 1495, by a re-foundation of St. John's Hospital there, allocating support for a master and usher out of the hospital revenues; it seems significant that the grammar school at Banbury (1501), also a hospital foundation, emerges from obscurity while Smith was bishop of Lincoln, and he was definitely the founder of the grammar school at Farnworth (Lancashire) in 1507, and was co-founder of Brasenose College in 1508.[41] Richard Fox, founder of Corpus Christi College in 1516, built the schoolhouse at Taunton in 1523, and also built the school at Grantham and added to its endowment.[42] Others who founded schools were substantial benefactors to colleges, for example John Carpenter, called by Orme 'a notable patron of education', who founded the grammar school at Westbury-on-Trym and was a benefactor to Oriel, and Thomas Rotherham, who founded Rotherham grammar school and was a benefactor to Lincoln College, and to Pembroke College, and indeed to Cambridge University as a whole.[43]

As school founders, few bishops expressed their intentions as clearly as Rotherham, who, grateful for the fortuitous grammar instruction which had set him on the road to great things, wanted to establish at his birthplace a teacher of grammar 'for ever' together with a teacher of song: 'because that country produces many young men of great sharpness and ability and not all wish to take Holy Orders, that such people may be prepared for technical and mundane work, we have ordained a third Fellow, skilled in the art of writing and computing' (*in arte scibendi et computandi scientem et peritum*).[44] Not many miles away, at his birthplace of Acaster Selby, Robert Stillington established for the school attached to his college a triple curriculum comprising grammar, music together with song, and scrivener craft.[45] It seems well worth noting that two bishops who had reached the top of the civil service (both were chancellors of England), and were university men themselves, were not so exclusively academic, or pious, that they closed their eyes to the practical, unacademic, and non-religious aspects of education: they provided technical training under the same roof. It is, however, less surprising when an episcopal founder concentrates more obviously on Latin grammar, like Waynflete, who believed 'as experience proves, a weak foundation betrays the superstructure, and grammar is acknowledged to be the mother and basis of all science': Magdalen Grammar School rapidly became 'the seedbed of English grammarians'.[46] Among other things, Bishop Waynflete's priest-schoolmasters at Wainfleet were to pray for the increase of 'good morals and knowledge'; and the combination of 'good learning and manners' was carried on as a founding purpose into the next century by

Bishop Oldham at Manchester, and by Archbishop Holgate at York, Hems-
worth (Yorkshire, W.R.) and Malton (Yorkshire, N.R.), where the 1546 letters
patent relating to the foundations mention education 'as well in good manners
as in grammar and other liberal sciences'.[47] It is true, as Dr. Davies has recently
pointed out, that among the best known episcopally founded schools were some
which were 'only a small ancillary part of a much larger pious project intended
primarily for the commemoration of the founder', and Rotherham and Acaster
schools fit this description; nonetheless, the indications of the founders' grasp of
educational possibilities make them rather more important in educational
developments than regarding them merely as additions to chantries might
suggest.[48] Initially, £2,457 was poured into Rotherham's foundation, and £704
into Stillington's, both being more than just schools.[49] To found a college
needed considerable resources, or manipulative power over ecclesiastical funds.
As Jacob expressed it, 'foundation is a lengthy and developing process which has
to be sustained both by the flow of ready money and by an administrative
dexterity which in many cases arouses admiration for the tenacity and application shown'.[50] Bishop Alcock utilised the resources of a Cambridge nunnery, the
first indigenous house of religion in England to be suppressed, to found Jesus
College; by contrast the historian of Corpus Christi boasts that that college was
built 'from private resources, not ecclesiastical spoils', Fox and Oldham being
the great benefactors.[51]

The particular personal leanings of the founders may sometimes be traced in
actual statements in the earliest statutes, or by inference from the balance of
studies prescribed for the foundation fellows, or from their geographical
provenance. Waynflete's original emphasis was on the study of divinity and
philosophy; and he appointed readers in theology, natural philosophy, and
moral philosophy or metaphysics. Fox desired Corpus to advance knowledge and
maintain religion: rigid programmes were mapped out for the public lecturers in
Greek, the Humanities (Latin) and Theology, the last appointment not being
filled.[52] It was not uncommon for founders and benefactors to stipulate the
geographical catchment areas for their college members: this was a long
established practice by the later fifteenth century and outlived the middle ages.
Undoubtedly the fact that county or diocesan allocations can often be made
intelligible in terms of the careers of the founders or benefactors shows that this
was an act of favour, to promote scholars from a preferred area. Lincoln College,
founded by Bishop Richard Fleming in 1427 to train theologians, had its statutes
revised in 1479/80 by its munificent patron Thomas Rotherham, who inserted
the provision of a fellowship tied to the Rotherham area. Bishop Smith
apparently wished to found fellowships for men from Lancashire (his native
county) and Lichfield (his previous diocese), but the Lincoln fellows demurred
from altering their constitution so quickly, and Smith effected his projects by
co-founding Brasenose.[53] How precisely the geographical restrictions were
applied is a matter of disagreement; but one cannot imagine from the evidence

that founders meant them to be disregarded, or that college bodies expected to be able to ignore them with impunity. Geographical restrictions may also be seen as ways of widening or keeping open a catchment zone, in the interests of balance. At Corpus, where the distribution of scholarships and fellowships was quite clearly apportioned, when particular regions failed to fill their quota, the vacancy could be passed on within the favoured areas, but not so that any county got more than one extra scholar thereby.[54] At Cambridge in the last quarter of the fifteenth century Queens' College ruled that no more than one fellow should come from any county: and Peterhouse required fellows to be chosen equally from two regions, roughly representing north and south.[55]

Some episcopal founders of schools however required the teaching to be freely available to pupils from all parts. Archbishop Rotherham's school was to teach grammar freely to any scholars, and music freely to students from anywhere in England, but 'especially from the diocese and province of York'; Stillington's was to teach to 'all manner of persons, from whatsoever country they be within the realm of England'.[56] Archbishop Rotherham and Bishop Alcock included exhibitions for the maintenance of poor scholars at school,[57] thus acknowledging that there are more costs to education than school fees alone.

From the founders of schools and colleges, let us turn to the greater number of episcopal benefactors to schools, colleges, and universities. To deal first with donors of money or property, Edmund Audley gave his old college (Lincoln) £400 to buy lands in 1518, and had already given 200 marks to Chichele's chest at Oxford in 1509; earlier still he had defrayed the cost of restoring the old Congregation House in 1507–08.[58] Thomas Beckington left plate, vestments and a four-volume bible to New College; Merton and Lincoln also benefited from his executors' decisions, and ten honest priests were left £5 p.a. each, to study at Oxford and say daily mass.[59] Lawrence Booth was a liberal benefactor to Pembroke College, of which he had been Master for thirty years, 'to all appearance on his own merits'; and while Chancellor of Cambridge he started the movement for building an arts school and civil law school.[60] Thomas Bourchier left money for loan chests at both universities.[61] John Carpenter, once Provost of Oriel, left that college money to establish exhibitions, some tied to the school at St. Anthony's Hospital, London, which had been founded while he was Master.[62] James Goldwell gave money to All Souls, his old college.[63] William Grey contributed to the building of the library and other buildings at Balliol.[64] John Hales gave lands to Oriel, where he had been Provost.[65] Thomas Kempe gave Merton £400 for the annual provision of fellows' gowns, and also gave 1,000 marks for the completion of the Divinity School and building of the library at Oxford.[66] Thomas Langton, a Provost of Queen's College, Oxford, was also a benefactor to that college, paying for the building of rooms, founding scholarships for twenty years, and leaving money for loan chests there and at Pembroke College, Cambridge.[67] Walter Lyhert left vestments, books, and money variously to Oriel, Exeter, All Souls, and Gonville and Trinity Hall.[68]

John Morton repaired the school of canon law at Oxford, and left £128 6s 8d for twenty exhibitions at Oxford and ten at Cambridge.[69] Thomas Rotherham was a great benefactor to both universities, completing the Schools and library at Cambridge, and being a benefactor to Lincoln College, Oxford.[70] John Russell provided the site for the new canon law school at Oxford, and gave New College £100; he also favoured New College men in the appointments he made to cathedral dignities and canonries.[71] Edward Story is still remembered as a 'considerable benefactor' to Pembroke, to which he gave lands and vestments.[72]

This sort of benevolence was positively expected. The University of Oxford boldly solicited help with various building projects from bishops who were former students. No modern appeals organiser can match fifteenth-century Oxford for persuasive flattery. The principle is enshrined in a letter to Richard Hill, bishop of London, written in 1490 on the strength of reported benevolent intentions. 'To a mother involved in many cares and troubles, every act of kindness on the part of a good son is justly most acceptable'.[73] The fulsome phraseology reaches a peak in a letter to the bishop of Salisbury (Richard Beauchamp) in 1481; in Anstey's paraphrase, 'the daily and manifold instances of your beneficence to us cannot be dealt with in epistolary form; they need volumes to record them, that, when we have departed this life, those that come after may tell how there never was a prelate so good to us as you have been. You promised us the sun, and you have given us the moon also.'[74] The university wanted ever more: a letter to Bishop Lyhert of Norwich in 1470 referred to his 'numerous exhibitions for maintaining poor scholars' and went on to seek aid for completing the new school of theology, and for providing a new library to house Tiptoft's books; a similar letter to Milling of Hereford mentioned his exhibitions to students, and asked for aid for St. Mary's Church in 1490.[75] This importunity had an indecent haste about it. Bishop Kempe of London, who had been a generous supplier of building funds for the previous ten years, was sent a letter in 1487 which raced on from fulsome thanks to new business. 'We have been informed, from a source of unimpeachable veracity, that you propose to present us with some very valuable books. If this be so, we offer our heartfelt thanks, and beg that the books may be entrusted to Master Richard FitzJames who is our accredited agent for this purpose'.[76]

Clearly graduate bishops were expected to be generous to their old universities. The moral obligation was indeed sometimes pressed beyond death. In 1465 Oxford University begged the executors of the bishop of Bath and Wells (Beckington) to give money to rebuild the school of canon law; and in 1490 the same university wrote to the executors of the bishop of Coventry (John Hales) soliciting funds for the rebuilding of St. Mary's, pointing out that the late bishop expressed approval of the design, 'and said, as we are assured by trustworthy persons, that he would give £20 at the least towards that object'.[77] Oxford seems to have been the primary centre for such begging letters in the fifteenth century. Cambridge University at least knew how to deliver fulsome thanks, as a well-known letter to Rotherham shows.[78]

In the giving of manuscripts and books to Oxford and Cambridge college and university libraries, Audley was a donor of manuscripts and printed books to Lincoln, Beckington left a four-volume bible to New College (to be chained in the library for those wishing to study it), Fox gave over a hundred books and manuscripts to Corpus, and Goldwell gave manuscripts to All Souls and Gonville. Bishop Grey bequeathed his notable library to Balliol, Kempe gave ninety volumes to the University of Oxford to be chained in the new library in 1488, George Neville gave manuscripts to Balliol and secured Tiptoft's bequeathed books for the university library at Oxford. Rotherham gave manuscripts and printed books to the university library at Cambridge, to Pembroke College, and also 105 manuscripts to Jesus College, Rotherham. Russell's gift of 105 manuscript and printed books to New College was acknowledged in 1482; Smith gave manuscripts and printed books to Brasenose, and Waynflete manuscripts to Magdalen.[79] Other bishops passed on books to other learned libraries: of the regular bishops, John Low left books to the Austin friars at Oxford, and founded the fine library of the London Austins; Richard Bell, whom Professor Dobson has described as a man of conventional intellectual interests, passed on books to younger monks and the common library at Durham; Reginald Boulers left theology books to Gloucester Abbey.[80] In the Worcester diocese, John Carpenter projected a couple of libraries to be open daily in the cause of learning, at Worcester and at Bristol.[81] The disposal of other episcopal libraries, great and small, is little known. John Shirwood's library was an impressive humanistic collection: some of the books passed through Fox to Corpus, others remained at Bishop Auckland (County Durham) to be rediscovered there in the sixteenth century.[82] From the accounts of the executors of Archbishop Thomas Savage one finds that the king took all the antiphoners, grails, processionals, missals, copes, vestments and altar cloths, amounting to the value of £167 6s 8d, and what is described as 'all the lybrary, to the valor of £14 6s 9d.'[83] Savage was not a marked educational benefactor, though his own education, and his family connections, might have led one to expect so. From Oxford he had proceeded to Bologna and Padua, becoming a Doctor of Civil Law and jurist rector. He was a grandson of the first Lord Stanley, and was apparently involved in the foundation of the grammar school at Macclesfield (Cheshire), even if only in an encouraging capacity.[84]

The paying of scholars' fees, or maintenance of scholars in an episcopal household or elsewhere, is a more private activity, and so less likely to be publicly recorded than the making of a financial endowment. Nevertheless, there are some bishops who can be positively identified with this kind of benefaction. The University of Oxford's letter to Lyhert, cited above, acknowledged that he had provided 'numerous exhibitions for maintaining poor scholars'. Richard Pace, in his *De Fructu* (1517), recollected that Langton of Winchester, whose secretary he had been, sent him 'to pursue the study of literature, into Italy, to the school at Padua, which was then at its greatest prime, and benevolently supplied the annual expenses, as he showed wonderful favour to all men of letters, and in his day played the part of a second Maecenas . . . also he so highly prized the study of Humanity that he had boys and youths instructed in it at a school in his house, and was vastly delighted to hear the scholars repeat to him at night the lessons given them by the teacher during the day.'[85] According to Roper, Sir Thomas More was a product of similar benevolence, having been in Cardinal Morton's household and sent by him to Oxford.[86] Morton's own household schoolmaster soon afterwards was John Holt, author of an elementary Latin grammar, Lac Puerorum.[87] Stillington helped his nephews, the Nikke brothers, in their studies abroad.[88]

A final category of activity – the encouragement of, or participation in, humanistic studies – is again more difficult to trace with certainty. The extent to which those of a humanistic bent made efforts to share their riches with others varied greatly. The bibliophile Bishop Grey, who had manuscripts transcribed for him and supported English and foreign scholars, bequeathed his valuable library to Balliol; whereas Shirwood, in the circle of Neville, Langton, Milling, Selling and Linacre, seems accurately described by Weiss as a man of humanistic relaxations, but one who 'kept his learning to himself'.[89] Beckington's scholarship was put to practical use in application to correspondence and diplomacy: as the king's secretary he was influential in introducing humane values into official epistolography. He corresponded with other humanists and collected ancient and modern texts; he also wrote a legal treatise on the right of the English kings to the kingdom of France. In Bath and Wells he promoted Wykehamists, including Hugh Sugar and Thomas Chaundler, a leading promoter of humanism in Oxford, who dedicated works to Beckington.[90] Neville, a 'Maecenas and connoisseur', kept a household which was a reputed centre of men of letters; and he also fostered the fashion for studying Greek in the country.[91] Russell was described by More as one of the best learned men of his time, and his grant of a Lincoln prebend to William Grocyn, 'the first outstanding English humanist' as Professor Storey has recently called him, helped to finance Grocyn's studies in Italy.[92]

Bishop Fox, after being persuaded by Oldham to abandon the idea of a monastic foundation, provided Corpus with 'liberal and enlightened statutes', installing a public lecturer in Greek. Linacre gave Fox a copy of his printed translation of Galen's De Sanitate tuenda, and Fisher dedicated to him his treatise De Veritate Corporis. Fox was himself fully alert to new methods of literary dissemination. It was at Fox's request that de Worde compiled the Contemplaycion of Sinners of 1499; and Fox edited the Sarum Processional printed at Rouen in 1508, and later translated the Benedictine Rule into English for religious women, printed by Pynson in 1517.[93] A generation earlier Bishop Russell had collected printed books. The copy he owned of Cicero's De Officiis et Paradoxa, published at Mainz in February 1466, survives with a note of its purchase at Bruges in April 1467.[94] Printed books were among the above-noted gifts made by

Audley to Lincoln, Rotherham to Cambridge and Pembroke, Russell to New College, and Smith to Brasenose. Bishops who embraced the new technology so enthusiastically put to shame those academics who today falter before the computer terminal.

This somewhat lengthy review of various episcopal activities in educational patronage is now complete; and it is time to draw some conclusions, firstly on any chronological variations. Episcopal inclinations towards, or opportunities for, educational benefactions do not in fact seem to have undergone much change in the course of the period under review. In the case of the forty-three bishops surveyed here, the only two surviving from the 1430s were Bourchier, who was a direct benefactor to Oxford, and Low, who though less directly associated with educational benevolence, left books to institutional libraries, as noted earlier. Of the seven bishops who survived from the elevations of the 1440s, Beckington, Lyhert, Waynflete and Carpenter were benefactors by any definition; and Beauchamp, most fulsomely thanked by Oxford for his generosity to the university, was involved with the building of the divinity school at Oxford. Stanbury, a Carmelite, was a prolific writer whose works are lost; he oversaw the Newland school arrangements of 1455 and 1465 but only in a *de cursu* capacity. The only non-graduate bishop, William Booth, was on the original commission to draw up the statutes of Queens' College, Cambridge.[95] Of the nine bishops elevated in the 1450s who survived long enough to be considered in this survey, Lawrence Booth, Grey, Neville, Chedworth and Kempe were active in various fields in the cause of education, and Boulers left his theology books to the abbey library at Gloucester. Two of the six bishops elevated in the 1460s, Stillington and Rotherham, were major educational benefactors in their birthplaces, and Story was also involved in education and endowed the cathedral school at Chichester.[96] Five of the eight bishops elevated in the 1470s definitely exercised some beneficial influence on education, namely Morton, Milling, Russell, Goldwell and Alcock, as did three of the seven from the 1480s, namely Fox, Audley and Langton. Two others elevated in this decade may have had some influence, if we credit Shirwood's humanism as extending beyond his own personal entertainment, and if Hill's believed intentions were accurately reported. Two out of the four elevated before 1495, Smith and Savage, were also friends of educational causes, though only in Smith's case to a really sizeable extent.

It accordingly does not emerge that episcopal interest or participation in educational projects changed markedly in the course of the later fifteenth century, and individual bishops of like mind in the immediately earlier and later periods are not hard to find. William of Wykeham, founder of Winchester and New Colleges, Richard Fleming, founder of Lincoln College, Henry Chichele, founder of All Souls College and the school at Higham Ferrers (Northamptonshire), John Kempe, founder of Wye School (Kent), and Thomas Langley, endower of 'educative' chantry priests at Durham, all leap to mind as notable educational patrons; and Dr. Davies has commented recently on episcopal bequests to universities and colleges.[97] At a slightly later date Richard FitzJames, elevated to the episcopal bench in 1497, founded Bruton Grammar School; and bishops appointed in the early sixteenth century certainly carried on the good work, for example Hugh Oldham, John Fisher, William Warham, and, later, Robert Holgate, to name a few.[98]

Although his intentions may be as sincere, a benefactor who is only known to have presented one book, or one small sum of money, to an educational cause, can hardly be compared with a benefactor who founded a college and a couple of schools. There can be no doubt at all that some of the bishops were very much more important as educational patrons than others, and indeed had more patronage at their disposal. Those who really did the most for educational causes, men such as Waynflete, Rotherham, Alcock, and Fox, were worldly careerists and busy politicians. Alcock, Rotherham and Waynflete were chancellors of England, as were Lawrence Booth, Bourchier, John Morton, Neville, Russell and Stillington. Beckington, Lawrence Booth, Fox, Hales, Rotherham, Russell and Stillington had all held the Privy Seal; Grey had been treasurer; while secretarial, diplomatic, and ambassadorial tasks claimed the attention of Beckington, Goldwell, Grey, Langton, Lyhert, and Milling. The crown was still using rich bishoprics to reward servants; but as Dr. Cross has pointed out, by the end of the fifteenth century such prelates were probably taking their pastoral duties much more seriously.[99] The politics of the Wars of the Roses made life eventful for many of these civil servants: Stanbury was imprisoned after the battle of Northampton, and Neville spent three years in prison at Guisnes; Morton and Rotherham were in serious trouble in 1483, and Stillington spent several years in gaol.[100] Active patronage of, and involvement in, education went with active career participation; and it was not the backwater bishops (compare, for example, the poor showing of the successive holders of the comparatively impoverished see of Carlisle) who much indulged in encouraging the young to learn. It was, it may be noted in passing, to Waynflete among others that the four-year old Prince Edward, son of Henry VI, was assigned for tutorship in 1457, according to Waynflete's biographer; and it was to Alcock, then bishop of Rochester, that Prince Edward, son of Edward IV, was committed in 1473 at the age of three.[101]

The bishops most active in educational causes also prove to have been well known to one another. Beckington and Waynflete were friends of long standing. Waynflete was appointed with Chedworth, founder of Cirencester Grammar School, to revise the statutes of Eton and King's Colleges; and Stanbury left Waynflete a bible believed to have belonged to St. Louis.[102] Stillington was Beckington's chancellor.[103] Alcock and Rotherham shared the chancellorship of England in 1475; Alcock's Jesus College may have been partly inspired by Rotherham's, and Alcock was the supervising executor of Rotherham's will.[104] Fox was a friend of Oldham and Fisher, and Smith and Oldham were old acquaintances. These friends were well aware of each other's activities, and in some cases contributed to them, giving money or books or simply doing the occasional good turn. Because of these collateral interests, the bishops were not acting *in vacuo* themselves. This is most clearly demonstrated when a founder recommends a friend's foundation as the exemplar for his own: Oldham recommended Manchester Grammar School to follow Banbury's grammar teaching; Banbury school was Smith's inspiration. By *c.* 1524 the President of Corpus, the college founded (with Oldham's advice and support) by Oldham's friend Fox, had the nomination of the master and usher at Oldham's Manchester school.[105]

It would of course be reasonable enough to argue that there is little significance in the interest in education shown by the bishops who reached the top of the ecclesiastical and administrative professions, since they were in any case likely benefactors to educational institutions, given their and the contemporary situation. At the tail end of what Jacob called 'the age of the pious founder'[106] these essentially childless men had either the inherited or acquired wealth, or the manipulation of ecclesiastical funds, with which to be generous; they were highly educated themselves, they were professionally pious, and the prayers of scholars were highly valued at the time. Episcopal benevolence to educational causes was, however, more than a subscription to a church-controlled approved charity. At times an episcopal benefactor can be seen to have been acting with conviction and understanding. Langton is known to have bestirred himself to hear at night what his household boys had learnt in the day time, and was remembered as doing this with 'vast delight': does not this show sympathetic patience, if not positive enthusiasm for promoting pupils? Beckington's statutes at Wells, with their insight into educational psychology, seem based on real understanding of the young. Rotherham's concern for a technical stream to teach the worldly arts is also worthy of admiration. Alcock's foundations, and the St. Paul's boy bishop's sermon now associated with him, certainly suggest genuine personal interest.[107] These cannot all be dismissed as routine, *pro forma* expressions of good will to a fashionable cause. It may be concluded that episcopal patronage of educational causes, dominated by a few giants in generosity, but supported in less spectacular ways by perhaps two-thirds of the forty-three bishops reviewed, forms one of the most practical and promising aspects of the church hierarchy's activities in the late fifteenth century. (Non-episcopal higher clergy, it should be remembered, were also important patrons in this area.) Moreover, it may be argued that this was an area of activity embraced deliberately, sincerely, and with some very real appreciation of the consequences which might accrue.

Appendix
The Bishops of England, 1450–1500

Bishops are listed in *chronological order of consecration*, grouped by decades; and dates of subsequent translation and death are also recorded (where the processes of election spanned the end of a calendar year, the later year is given). Names are normally spelt as in *HBC*, which also provides more precise dates. Not included in this list are the bishops whose pontificates ended before 1458 or began after 1494.

1430–39
1. John Low   St. Asaph (1433); Rochester (1444)   d. 1467
2. Thomas Bourchier   Worcester (1435); Ely (1444); Canterbury (1454)   d. 1486

1440–49
3. Thomas Beckington   Bath and Wells (1443)   d. 1465
4. John Carpenter   Worcester (1444)   d. 1476
5. Walter Lyhert   Norwich (1446)   d. 1472
6. William Booth   Coventry and Lichfield (1447); York (1452)   d. 1464
7. William Waynflete   Winchester (1447)   d. 1486
8. John Stanbury   Bangor (1448); Hereford (1453)   d. 1474
9. Richard Beauchamp   Hereford (1449); Salisbury (1450)   d. 1481

1450–59
10. Thomas Kempe   London (1450)   d. 1489
11. Reginald Boulers   Hereford (1451); Coventry and Lichfield (1453)   d. 1459
12. John Chedworth   Lincoln (1452)   d. 1471
13. William Percy   Carlisle (1452)   d. 1462
14. William Grey   Ely (1454)   d. 1478
15. Lawrence Booth   Durham (1457); York (1476)   d. 1480
16. George Neville   Exeter (1458); York (1465)   d. 1476
17. John Arundel   Chichester (1459)   d. 1477
18. John Hales   Coventry and Lichfield (1459)   d. 1490

1460–69

19. John Kingscote	Carlisle (1462)	d. 1463
20. Richard Scrope	Carlisle (1464)	d. 1468
21. John Booth	Exeter (1465)	d. 1478
22. Robert Stillington	Bath and Wells (1466)	d. 1491
23. Thomas Rotherham	Rochester (1468); Lincoln (1472); York (1480)	d. 1500
24. Edward Story	Carlisle (1468); Chichester (1478)	d. 1503

1470–79

25. John Alcock	Rochester (1472); Worcester (1476); Ely (1486)	d. 1500
26. James Goldwell	Norwich (1472)	d. 1499
27. Thomas Milling	Hereford (1474)	d. 1492
28. John Russell	Rochester (1476); Lincoln (1480)	d. 1494
29. William Dudley	Durham (1476)	d. 1483
30. Richard Bell	Carlisle (1478)	d. 1496
31. Peter Courtenay	Exeter (1478); Winchester (1487)	d. 1492
32. John Morton	Ely (1479); Canterbury (1486)	d. 1500

1480–89

33. Edmund Audley	Rochester (1480); Hereford (1492); Salisbury (1502)	d. 1524
34. Lionel Woodville	Salisbury (1482)	d. 1484
35. Thomas Langton	St. David's (1483); Salisbury (1485); Winchester (1493)	d. 1501
36. John Shirwood	Durham (1484)	d. 1494
37. Robert Morton	Worcester (1487)	d. 1497
38. Richard Fox	Exeter (1487); Bath and Wells (1492); Durham (1494); Winchester (1501)	d. 1528
39. Richard Hill	London (1489)	d. 1496

1490–94

40. Oliver King	Exeter (1493); Bath and Wells (1496)	d. 1503
41. William Smith	Coventry and Lichfield (1493); Lincoln (1496)	d. 1514
42. Thomas Savage	Rochester (1493); London (1496); York (1501)	d. 1507
43. John Blythe	Salisbury (1494)	d. 1499

Notes

1. I am most grateful to Professor R.B. Dobson whose helpful comments on the penultimate draft of this paper enabled me to improve the final version before I read it at York.
2. A table showing the wealth of the English bishoprics in 1535 is supplied in W.G. Hoskins, *The Age of Plunder* (1976), 127.
3. R.G. Davies, 'The Episcopate', in *Profession, Vocation and Culture in Later Medieval England*, ed. C.H. Clough (Liverpool, 1982), 53–65; J.R. Lander, *Government and Community: England 1450–1509* (1980), 121.
4. T.H. Aston, G.D. Duncan and T.A.R. Evans, 'The Medieval Alumni of the University of Cambridge', *Past and Present*, 86 (1980), 69. In Aston's earlier article, 'Oxford's Medieval Alumni', ibid., 74 (1977), 28, the figures are given as 19% and 72%.
5. *BRUC*, 73. I am grateful to my colleague Dr. A.B. Cobban for clarification of certain technical terms used in *BRUO* and *BRUC*.
6. R.M. Haines, 'Education in English Ecclesiastical Legislation of the later Middle Ages', in *SCH*, vii (1971), ed. G.J. Cuming and D. Baker, 161–75.
7. *The Register of Thomas Bekynton, Bishop of Bath and Wells 1443–65*, ed. H.C. Maxwell Lyte and M.C.B. Dawes, II (Somerset Record Society, 1, 1935), 256.
8. Ibid., I (Somerset Record Society xlix, 1934), xxi.
9. A. Judd, *The Life of Thomas Bekynton* (Chichester, 1961), 129.
10. *Register of Bekynton*, I, 203, 267, 275.
11. Ibid., I, 273, 347, 372–3.
12. Ibid., I, 148–9, 170.
13. *The Register of Bishop Fox of Durham*, ed. M.P. Howden (Surtees Society, cxlvii, 1932), 27, 45.
14. Haines, 'Education', 175; N. Orme, *English Schools in the Middle Ages* (1973), 20–1; C. Cross, *Church and People, 1450–1660* (Hassocks, 1976), 95–6.
15. *Registrum Thome Bourgchier Cantuariensis Archiepiscopi AD 1454–86*, ed. F.R.H. Du Boulay, (CYS, liv, 1957), 21.
16. P. Heath, *The English Parish Clergy on the Eve of the Reformation* (1969), xii; M. Bowker, *The Secular Clergy in the Diocese of Lincoln* (Cambridge, 1968), 2.
17. Judd, *Life of Bekynton*, 129; *Register of Bekynton*, I, 314, 369, 375.
18. *Registrum Bourgchier*, xxxix.
19. *Register of Bekynton*, I, 180.
20. 'Ely Chapter Ordinances and Visitation Records 1241–1515', ed. S.J.A. Evans, *Camden Miscellany* xvii, (CS, 3rd series, lxiv, 1940), 58–9; *Concilia*, ii, 16.
21. *Visitations of the Diocese of Norwich, AD 1492–1532*, ed. A. Jessopp (CS, new series, xliii, 1888), 52, 54, 59, 61.
22. A.F. Leach, *Educational Charters and Documents, 598–1909* (Cambridge, 1911), 143–5; M. Gibbs and J. Lang, *Bishops and Reform, 1215–72* (1934), 157; Orme, *English Schools*, 174–5.
23. Haines, 'Education', 161–75 *passim*; Heath, *English Parish Clergy*, 6–7, 93.
24. *Register of Bekynton*, I, 393, 400–01.
25. *The Register of John Stanbury Bishop of Hereford 1453–74*, ed. A.T. Bannister (Hereford, 1918), 21–33, 105–10.
26. *VCH, Suffolk*, ii, 326.
27. A. Watkin, *Dean Cosyn and Wells Cathedral Miscellanea* (Somerset Record Society, lvi, 1941), 98–109.
28. *The Register of Robert Stillington, 1466–91, and Richard Fox, 1492–4*, ed. H.C. Maxwell Lyte

(Somerset Record Society, lii, 1937), 95, 96, 102; A.F. Leach, *Early Yorkshire Schools*, II, (Yorkshire Archaeological Society, Record Series, xxxiii, 1903), 89–90.

29. *The Register of Thomas Rotherham Archbishop of York 1480–1500*, I, (CYS, lxix, 1976), *passim*; 207, 34, 196, 63, 249.

30. *Oriel College Records*, ed. C.L. Shadwell and H.E. Salter (Oxford Historical Society, lxxxv, 1926), 64–7.

31. *Epistolae Academicae Oxon.* II ed. H. Anstey (Oxford Historical Society, xxxvi, 1898), 556.

32. A. Gray and F. Brittain, *A History of Jesus College Cambridge* (revised edition, 1979), 15–16, 10.

33. *VCH, Cambridge*, iii, 377.

34. C.W. Boase, *Register of the Rectors, Fellows and other members on the Foundation of Exeter College, Oxford, with a history of the College and illustrative documents* (Oxford Historical Society, xxvii, 1894), lii–vi.

35. R. Chandler, *Life of William Waynflete Bishop of Winchester* (1811), 143; *VCH, Oxford*, iii, 194, n. 11.

36. *A Register of the Members of St Mary Magdalen College Oxford*, ed. W.D. Macray, New Series, I (1894), 35–61.

37. *BRUC*, 192–3, 674; W.K. Jordan, *The Charities of Rural England 1480–1660* (1961), 307, 352.

38. *Registrum Bourgchier*, 15–16, 357; *Register of Rotherham*, 197.

39. *VCH, Oxford*, iii, 193–4; i, 472; *VCH, Lincoln*, ii, 484.

40. J. Lawson, *A Town Grammar School through six centuries* (1963), 25–8; Gray and Brittain, *Jesus College*, 21. The training of scholars in grammar was part of the original college plan: ibid., 23.

41. *VCH, Stafford*, iii, 281; *VCH, Oxford*, i, 461; W.K. Jordan, *The Social Institutions of Lancashire* (Chetham Society, 3rd series, xi, 1962), 33; *Brasenose College Quatercentenary Monographs*, I, (Oxford Historical Society, lii, 1909), Monograph IV, part I, 7; *VCH, Oxford*, iii, 207–8.

42. T. Fowler, *The History of Corpus Christi College with lists of its members* (Oxford Historical Society, xxv, 1893), 1, 21–2; *VCH, Somerset*, ii, 444; *VCH, Lincoln*, ii, 479. Fox was also a benefactor to Pembroke College, but not as generously as the college hoped: A. Attwater, *Pembroke College Cambridge: A Short History*, ed. S.C. Roberts (Cambridge, 1936), 20, 26.

43. N. Orme, *Education in the West of England 1066–1548* (Exeter, 1976), 182; *BRUO*, i, 360–1; Leach, *Yorkshire Schools*, II, 110; *BRUO*, iii, 1593–6; *BRUC*, 489–91.

44. Leach, *Yorkshire Schools*, II, 110, translated in E.F. Jacob, 'Founders and Foundations in the later middle ages', in *Essays in Later Medieval History* (Manchester, 1968), 173.

45. Leach, *Yorkshire Schools*, II, 89.

46. Chandler, *Waynflete*, 200; Heath, *English Parish Clergy*, 83.

47. Chandler, *Waynflete*, 199; A.A. Mumford, *The Manchester Grammar School 1515–1915* (1919), 10; *Letters and papers of Henry VIII*, xxi (2), no. 332 (72), cited in E.N. Jewels, *A History of Archbishop Holgate's Grammar School York, 1546–1946* (York, 1963), 10; H.M. Jewell, '"The bringing up of children in good learning and manners": a survey of secular educational provision in the north of England, c 1350–1550', *Northern History*, xviii (1982), 6.

48. Davies, 'Episcopate', 77.

49. Jordan, *Rural England*, 304, 305.

50. Jacob, 'Founders', 156.

51. Gray and Brittain, *Jesus College*, 2; Fowler, *Corpus Christi*, 21–2.

52. Chandler, *Waynflete*, 49, 201; R.S. Stanier, *Magdalen School* (Oxford, 2nd edition, 1958), 8; Fowler, *Corpus Christi*, 37–40, 58.

53. V. Green, *The Commonwealth of Lincoln College, 1427–1977* (Oxford, 1977), 6, 40, 72; Leach, *Yorkshire Schools*, II, 103–4.

54. Fowler, *Corpus Christi*, 46.
55. *VCH, Cambridge*, iii, 411, 336.
56. Leach, *Yorkshire Schools*, II, 115–16, 89–90.
57. Ibid., 122; Lawson, *Town Grammar School*, 27.
58. *BRUO*, i, 75–6.
59. Ibid., 157–9; Judd, *Bekynton*, 163.
60. 'The Register of the Archdeacons of Richmond 1422–77', ed. A. Hamilton Thompson, *Yorkshire Archaeological Journal*, xxx (1931) 12; *BRUC*, 78–9; *DNB*, ii, 49–50; Attwater, *Pembroke*, 21–3.
61. *BRUO*, i, 230–2.
62. Ibid., 360–1; Orme, *English Schools*, 200.
63. *DNB*, viii, 96–7.
64. *BRUO*, ii, 809–14.
65. Boase, *Exeter College*, 34.
66. *BRUO*, ii, 1032–4.
67. Ibid., 1101–02; *BRUC*, 352–3.
68. *BRUO*, ii, 1187–8.
69. *BRUO*, ii, 1318–20; *DNB*, xiii, 1048–50; Aston, 'Cambridge Alumni', 44.
70. *BRUO*, iii, 1593–6; *BRUC*, 490–1.
71. *BRUO*, iii, 1609–11; G.F. Lytle, 'Patronage Patterns and Oxford Colleges *c*. 1300–*c*. 1530' in *The University in Society*, ed. L. Stone, I, (Princeton, 1975), 143.
72. Attwater, *Pembroke*, 20, 26.
73. Anstey, *Epistolae*, ii, 602.
74. Ibid., 468–9.
75. Ibid., 390–1, 583.
76. Ibid., 532–3.
77. Ibid., 377, 579–80.
78. Leach, *Yorkshire Schools*, II, 102–3.
79. *BRUO* and *BRUC*, *passim*, and *Somerset Medieval Wills 1383–1500*, ed. F.W. Weaver (Somerset Record Society, xvi, 1901), 203; J. Tait, 'Letters of John Tiptoft Earl of Worcester and Archbishop Neville to the University of Oxford', *EHR*, xxxv (1920), 570–4; Leach, *Yorkshire Schools*, II, 162–6; R.W. Hunt, 'The Medieval Library', in *New College, Oxford*, ed. J. Buxton and P. Williams (Oxford, 1979), 326, 328.
80. *BRUO*, ii, 1168–9; R.B. Dobson, 'Richard Bell prior of Durham (1464–78) and bishop of Carlisle (1478–95)', *Transactions of the Cumberland and Westmorland Antiquarian and Archaeological Society*, new series, lxv (1965), 194, 193; *BRUO* i, 229.
81. R.F. Haines, 'Aspects of the Episcopate of John Carpenter, Bishop of Worcester 1444–76', *JEH*, xix (1968), 11–40.
82. P.S. Allen, 'Bishop Shirwood of Durham and his Library', *EHR*, xxv (1910), 452–3.
83. *Test. Ebor.*, iv, 312.
84. *BRUO*, iii, 1646–7; Orme, *West of England*, 176.
85. R. Pace, *De Fructu*, cited in F.J. Furnivall, ed., *The Babees Book*, EETS, OS 32 (1868), xix–xx.
86. W. Roper, *Life of More*, cited in Furnivall, *Babees Book*, ix.
87. Orme, *English Schools*, 110; *BRUO*, ii, 953.
88. R.J. Mitchell, 'English Student Life in Early Renaissance Italy', *Italian Studies*, vii (Manchester, 1952), 64.
89. *BRUO*, ii, 809–14; iii, 1692–3; R. Weiss, *Humanism in England during the Fifteenth Century* (3rd edition, Oxford, 1967), 152.
90. Ibid., 71–5; R.L. Storey, 'The Foundation and the Medieval College' in *New College*, op. cit., 25–6.
91. Weiss, *Humanism*, 141–8.

92. *BRUO*, iii, 1609–11; Storey, 'Foundation', 27–8.
93. Fowler, *Corpus Christi*, 21–5.
94. J.C.T. Oates, *A Catalogue of fifteenth-century printed books in the University Library of Cambridge* (Cambridge, 1954), 65, (no. 28). I am grateful to my colleague Dr. C.H. Clough for his assistance in clarifying the early Mainz printings of *De Officiis*.
95. *BRUO* i, 137–8 (Beauchamp); A.C. Reeves, *Lancastrian Englishmen* (Washington DC, 1981), 280–1 (Booth); *CPR, 1446–52*, 143–4.
96. Orme, *English Schools*, 215; *VCH, Sussex*, ii, 402–3. A fourth bishop, Kingescote, was apparently in Chaundler's circle, but I know too little of him to claim him as a humanist or fosterer of humanists: *BRUO*, ii, 1073–4.
97. Davies, 'Episcopate', 74–6.
98. *BRUO* ii, 691–2; Orme, *English Schools*, 69; *BRUO*, ii, 1396–7; *BRUC*, 229–30; *BRUO* iii, 1988–92; A.G. Dickens, *Robert Holgate Archbishop of York and President of the King's Council in the North* (St. Anthony's Hall Publications, 8; York, 1955), 22.
99. Cross, *Church and People*, 45.
100. R.J. Knecht, 'The Episcopate and the Wars of the Roses', *University of Birmingham Journal*, vi (1957–8), 112–13, 116, 120–2, 128.
101. Chandler, *Waynflete*, 71; *CPR, 1467–77*, 401.
102. Chandler, *Waynflete*, 21; *DNB*, iii, 175–6; Orme, *West of England*, 128; *BRUO*, iii, 1755–6.
103. A. Judd, 'The Episcopate of Thomas Bekynton, bishop of Bath and Wells 1443–65', *JEH*, vii (1957), 156.
104. *HBC*, 85–6; Gray and Brittain, *Jesus College*, 21–5.
105. Mumford, *Manchester Grammar School*, 471, 17.
106. Jacob, 'Founders', 154.
107. Lawson, *Town Grammar School*, 23.

8

Clerical Taxation in Fifteenth-Century England: The Clergy as Agents of the Crown

A.K. McHardy
University of Aberdeen

The role of the clergy in English central government during the fifteenth century is well known. Apart from those members of the higher clergy who were essentially politicians, two groups were important in central administration: firstly, the civil lawyers, active both in diplomacy and in the courts of chancery, admiralty and chivalry; and secondly those men of less specialised training who are usually known by the term 'king's clerks'.[1] However, in addition to these professional crown servants, there were other clerics whose part in government is less well known and less strongly emphasised. They were the clergy who executed the royal will in the localities: occasional, part-time, unpaid agents of the crown. While executing direct or indirect royal commands these clerical commissaries continued with their normal ecclesiastical duties, and though their work on behalf of the crown often involved some travelling, it rarely took them outside the diocese in which their benefices lay.

The duties which clerics performed in the localities on the orders of the lay power fall into two categories. One consists of miscellaneous business undertaken as a result of direct commands. These were issued by writs or by letters patent, and they instructed the clergy concerned – usually either a bishop or the head of a religious house – to undertake a variety of tasks: swearing in local officials, raising loans on behalf of the crown, repairing bridges, serving on commissions – of the peace, of array, of dykes and ditches – or chivvying recalcitrant clerics into obeying the orders of the royal courts.[2]

The other category of business performed by the clergy in the localities was by far the more important: this was the collection of taxes granted by the clergy to the crown, and here the collectors were acting only indirectly as crown agents, for the commissions to act were issued through ecclesiastical channels.[3] Clerical taxation has not received the attention it deserves; and this neglect of the subject, it may be suggested, has led to an unbalanced picture of the relations between church and crown in late medieval England. Discussions of interesting clashes of jurisdiction and principle have tended to obscure both that the crown was able to get its own way, as a matter of course, in vast numbers of church appointments, and also that it drew large sums of direct revenue from the English church. Indeed, the crown's interest in the church can be crudely summarised as 'money and patronage', and patronage was often a form of currency.

While Professor Storey's recent very important work on the decline of the clerical civil servant during the fifteenth century has shown that the crown's concern with patronage became less pressing,[4] its interest in money remained strong, as the clergy knew to their cost. During this period (1401–1496) the convocation of the northern province voted thirty grants of taxation to the crown – almost one grant every three years. Four of its grants were of two tenths, fourteen were tenths, ten were moieties (half tenths), and one was of only a quarter tenth. The total voted was twenty-seven and a quarter tenths. In addition, one subsidy of 6s. 8d. from every secular chaplain was voted, together with a tenth of two-thirds of the value of unassessed benefices.[5]

During the same period the southern province's convocation made forty-seven grants – that is almost one every two years. Five were of two tenths, eight of one-and-a-half tenths, twenty-four tenths, one of three-quarters of a tenth, and nine were moieties – a total of forty and a quarter tenths. One other vote was of a specified sum of £25,000.[6] Some of these grants also included poll taxes on certain members of the clerical estate who would otherwise have been immune; and nearly half the taxes granted were raised on the basis of tenths levied not only from the benefices traditionally assessed for taxation but from the unassessed as well. Occasionally additional, punitive taxes were voted on those who had incurred the displeasure of convocation. Lists of these taxes, granted by both convocations, and printed in the Appendices to this paper, show that the highest level of taxation was, as one would expect, paid between 1415 and 1420, and that (again not surprisingly) the 1420s were the leanest years for the exchequer.

How much money did the crown gain from these grants? A precise answer to this question could be given only after comprehensive study not only of the Enrolled Accounts, but pursuit of the debts onto the Pipe Rolls. But some rough and ready figures may be hazarded in an attempt to provide some idea of the theoretical sums involved. The value of a tenth from the northern province was about £2,000. This should have produced a total for the exchequer of some £54,500 in our period. However, the amounts brought in by the constituent parts of the province were not constant. The diocese of Carlisle does not figure in the Enrolled Accounts after 1416, and reappears only in 1512. Valued at less than £40, the loss of a tenth from Carlisle was more than offset by the sharp rise in the value of the archdeaconry of York. A moiety from there was worth £273 in 1410, £400 in 1418, and £411 three years later.[7] It may be that the figure of £54,500 is conservative. But the York convocation exercised wide powers of exemption, excusing all religious houses and benefices over a wide area allegedly devastated by the Scots. In addition, every grant carried exemptions, either total or partial, granted by convocation to named houses or benefices. Inevitably certain places figured often among the privileged; but examination of the lists of the exempt – to be found in the *Calendars of Fine Rolls* – shows that they changed, if only slightly, every time. It does seem that the exemptions reflected, albeit imperfectly, the impact of war, flood, fire or the sudden collapse of church buildings.[8] Convocation's generosity accordingly means that the value of a grant from the northern province was subject to some variation according to the exemptions which it granted.

In the province of Canterbury the sums involved were, of course, much greater. A tenth there was worth about £15,200.[9] This means that the theoretical value of the forty and a quarter tenths voted by the Canterbury convocation was £611,800. To this we must add the £25,000 voted to Henry VII in 1489, which brings the total to £636,800. Additional grants tacked on to some tenths, such as partial poll-taxes voted on five occasions in the course of the first half of the century (1406, 1419, 1430, 1436, 1449) and tenths levied on benefices previously unassessed, swelled this total. However, the yields of the poll taxes were unpredictable, and the unassessed benefices were not regularly taxed until the second half of the century.

The sums given above in connection with the southern province are drawn wholly from the English parts of it. The Welsh dioceses of the province made a negligible contribution to the crown's income, according to the evidence of the Enrolled Accounts. The accounts, it is true, are not infallible, but the Welsh dioceses figure so little in these documents that we are forced to conclude that they made only occasional, and then very incomplete, payments.[10] Therefore, when we talk of the importance of clerical taxes we mean, by and large, those raised in the English dioceses of the southern province.

By the fifteenth century the form of clerical taxation and the machinery for collecting it were already well-established. The property of the English church was assessed for taxation purposes by order of Pope Nicholas IV in about 1291 (the *Taxatio*);[11] and, while the effects of warfare necessitated a reduced valuation of the northern province in the early fourteenth century (the 'new assessment' of 1318),[12] the wealth of the southern province was not to be systematically surveyed again until the sixteenth century. The collecting machinery was also well developed by 1400. The process of collection during the years 1327–1336 has been described by W.E. Lunt in *The English Government at Work*,[13] and it remained basically unchanged during the fourteenth and fifteenth centuries. The changes which did occur between 1336 and 1500 all tended to the same result: they made the work of the collectors more difficult.

Who were the collectors of clerical taxes? They were very largely drawn from among the heads of religious houses, sometimes in association with their convents. The task of collection of clerical tenths was a traditional one for these religious superiors, for they had performed it during the fourteenth century[14] and were to do so throughout the fifteenth. They were chosen for the duty by the bishops, to whom the crown sent mandates ordering the appointment of collectors; but they were accountable to the exchequer. In making his selection a bishop was limited in a number of ways. He could not normally call on the services of the heads of Cluniac houses, for these were exempt from episcopal control,[15] nor of alien priors (a declining band) since their houses were in the king's hands on account of the war with France: however if these priories became denizen their priors were fair game.[16] The heads of poor houses which lacked the initial resources, both of men and of money, necessary to undertake the collections were not so employed. From the exchequer's point of view, the head of a house with too little property which could be seized as surety for payment was unsatisfactory. Cells of certain houses were rarely involved in tax collecting, because their priors argued that they were removable at any time at the whim of the head of the mother house. Cells of Sempringham, St. Albans and Reading usually escaped in this way.[17] Certain houses which would, in the normal course of events, have been on the bishops' lists for providing collectors became on occasion temporarily unsuitable. Thus houses whose administrations were so unsatisfactory that they had to be put into the hands of royal commissioners,[18] as well as those (rare, fortunately) torn by violent strife, as was Buckland Abbey, in Devon, between 1469 and 1473,[19] were not considered suitable to bear the responsibility of collecting. Further complications were added when convocation stipulated from time to time that those who had attended meetings of the lower house were not to be commissioned as collectors.[20]

All these restrictions left the bishops with limited room to pick and choose. The problem became more pressing in the fifteenth century when grants were more frequent than in previous times, so that the problem of rotating the commissions, to spread the burden as widely as possible, became increasingly important. There were several ways in which bishops could legitimately help to lighten this load on collectors. One was by altering the areas in which collectors operated. A bishop could subdivide large areas, as happened late in the century in the archdeaconries of Lincoln and Stow,[21] and thus hope to bring the task within the capability of smaller houses which could not have tackled revenue gathering over a wide area. By contrast, in the diocese of Bath and Wells, previously divided into two or three areas for collection purposes, it became the practice to employ only one collector.[22] This may have lightened the bishop's load for it gave him greater choice when issuing his commission, but it meant more work for the man selected. Some commissions included the head of more than one religious house;[23] while commissions which linked an abbot or prior with one or more secular clergymen seem to have been a speciality of the diocese of Hereford.[24] When convocation granted subsidies from the unbeneficed or from benefices not previously assessed, bishops could appoint two parallel sets of collectors, and this expedient was particularly noticeable in the earlier years of the century.[25] Bishops had a further option: they could appoint the heads of houses which were outside their diocese. This ungentlemanly device was sometimes successful. Examples from the archdeaconry of Leicester show houses from outside Lincoln diocese being used because they had appropriated churches in Leicestershire;[26] while in 1481 Breedon priory, in Leicestershire, was commissioned together with the prior of Nostell, in Yorkshire, which was Breedon's mother house.[27] Bishops who used this ruse were not always able to get away with it. In 1455 Bishop John Stanbury of Hereford appointed the prior of St. Oswald's, Gloucester, to act as a collector in the archdeaconry of Hereford. The prior and convent, knowing that they would be unable to collect the grant and fearing lest they should be penalised by the exchequer, successfully petitioned the crown for an order to compel the bishop to appoint another candidate for the task.[28]

Despite all these expedients there was an undeviating regularity with which, for example, the priors of Durham were committed as collectors in Durham diocese, the abbots of Ramsey in the archdeaconry of Huntingdon, the abbots of Peterborough in Northampton, the priors of Newnham in Bedford, the priors of Bermondsey in Surrey, the abbots of Muchelney in Bath and Wells diocese, and the priors of Bodmin in the archdeaconry of Cornwall. In other words, the headships of some religious houses carried the periodic collection of royal revenues as an inevitable and inescapable duty.[29]

The bishop, however, once he had appointed collectors, was free of direct responsibility for sums due from his diocese, save for the payment of his own contribution which he did directly to the exchequer.[30] This left the fifteenth-century collectors standing alone vis-à-vis the king's government. The outline of the process by which they executed their commission is clear: they publicized the grant; gathered the money due, in accordance with a copy of the *Taxatio* supplied by the exchequer; issued receipts to those who paid; and conveyed either cash or tallies (or a mixture of the two) to the exchequer. The details, however, are not so clear. For lack of evidence the work and names of subcollectors and their agents remain almost entirely a matter of conjecture. Only at Durham, thanks to Professor Dobson's work, can we see something of the process of collection and learn the names and status of those who carried it out.[31]

In contrast, little doubt exists in most cases about the attorneys who represented the collectors at the exchequer, for usually their names are recorded in the Enrolled Accounts. The type of person who acted as attorney changed in the course of our period. In the fourteenth century the attorney was usually a fellow-monk or fellow-canon of the collector; in the sample used in the present study (Lincoln diocese) these outnumbered non-religious attorneys by between three and four to one.[32] But from the beginning of the fifteenth century this situation rapidly changed. In 1401 religious outnumbered the others by only a proportion of five to four. In 1412 the non-monks, who were almost always laymen, outnumbered the religious by four to one; in 1422 this ratio had risen to six to one. Thereafter only stray examples of the use of the religious can be found. One can but speculate on the reasons for this change. Was there, perhaps, a national shortage of monks suitable for the task? Were laymen becoming so prominent in the management of monastic business that religious attorneys were simply shouldered aside? Was the nature of the attorney's job changing, because of increased lawlessness, from one of bank clerk to that of security guard? Some support for the suggestion that a strong man was needed to protect the money on its journey is given by the fact that the collectors in the archdeaconry of London – those with the shortest distance to travel – used their fellow-religious when this practice had been largely abandoned by others; but of course, this argument is not conclusive.[33]

Ideally, the attorney arrived at the exchequer on or before the appointed day bearing cash, tallies, and a list of exemptions and allowances which together equalled the total amount he owed. In practice this did not happen. Accounts were always rendered in instalments, usually two or three, and these could be spread over a few months or, quite commonly, over two or even three years. When the Enrolled Accounts were drawn up the outstanding debts were transferred to the appropriate Pipe Rolls. The fortunate collectors were those then described as 'quit'.

One item which was set against the total owed was the allowance which every collector could claim for expenses. The sums involved were considerable; they covered the cost of travels within his area and journeys to Westminster, sometimes payments to agents, and the large sums expended on parchment, ink and wax. For everyone within a collector's area who paid up was given a receipt; and the number of such receipts could run into scores and even hundreds. Survivals of these receipts are rare; but two issued in 1432 to the prior of Modbury in Devon do exist among the archives of Eton College.[34] Allowances for expenses varied between 1s. in the £ and 8d. in the £. The more unfavourable rate was given in the 1490s and was laid down by convocation.[35]

Legitimate expenses were not the only moneys which collectors paid out. Sometimes, when faced with recalcitrant clergy, they found it advisable to pay the defaulters' taxes out of their own pockets and then to apply for the aid of the secular power in recovering their outlays.[36] This expedient was a new and ominous development in our period, and symptomatic of the increasingly unwelcome nature of the chore of tax collection.

For the collectors found themselves ground between the growing demands of the crown on the one hand, and the increasing reluctance of the clergy to accede to them on the other. The crown's demands were growing in two ways. It no longer confined its tax demands to wartime. During earlier phases of the Hundred Years War periods of peace had been accompanied by lulls in taxation, but there was no such relaxation after the peace of 1396. Here was a financial expedient of Richard II's which Henry IV was glad to copy. Tax demands were made more frequently in his reign than at any other time during the fifteenth century though they were not answered more generously. This period from 1397 to 1413 established the demanding of clerical taxes as a routine matter of government which scarcely needed justification.

The other way that the crown put pressure on the church was by devising taxes designed to make good the deficiencies of the *Taxatio*. For in a number of ways the *Taxatio* was seriously out of date. It did not include property acquired by the church since 1291, for on that the clergy paid lay taxes. This was unsatisfactory to all: to the crown, because it wanted the clergy to pay taxes at a higher rate than did the laity; and to the clergy, who were disgruntled at being asked to pay two sets of taxes. Moreover, since 1291 new benefices had been created – colleges and perpetual chantries, for example – and there had been shifts of wealth which affected the value of temporalities and tithes. Perhaps least acceptable of all, a tax based on property allowed the many unbeneficed clergy to get off scot-free.

The crown, therefore, set out to exploit what it saw as this untapped wealth of the clerical estate, and once again it had models from the fourteenth century to warn and guide it. The fiasco of the 1380–1 poll tax (the third in a series levied on the clergy as well as on the laity) made all parties wary of similar ventures; but in 1406 convocation was induced to grant, in addition to a tenth, a tax of 6s. 8d. to be levied from every chaplain, stipendiary or salaried, every chantry chaplain or warden, from vicars and clergy beneficed in cathedral or collegiate churches, and from every other beneficed person who commonly escaped payment of clerical taxes. Despite the proviso that this was not to be used as a precedent, a similar grant of 6s. 8d. a head from the unbeneficed was made in 1419. In 1430 collection began of an ambitious subsidy which charged the unbeneficed at three rates (6s. 8d., 13s. 4d., and 20/-) according to income. Six years later a two-tier grant was made, its rates being 6s. 8d. and 13s. 4d., while in 1449 the one original rate of 6s. 8d. was used to gather revenue from the unbeneficed and stipendiaries.[37]

It is obvious that these poll taxes caused the ecclesiastical establishment a tremendous amount of extra work. Surviving tax assessments listing by name those bound to pay (in PRO.E.179) are a monument to the industry of their compilers, who were almost certainly secular clergy working on the instructions of the bishops. The religious were not, indeed, the most appropriate agents to administer these grants, which were being levied on the most mobile section of the clerical community. This point was eventually borne in on the bishops, and seculars were increasingly used as collectors of these subsidies from 1419 onwards.[38] By 1435 such taxes were being gathered, almost entirely, by archdeacons and their officials.[39] They were eminently suitable for this laborious chore.

It would seem to be a reasonable suggestion however that these clerical poll taxes were abandoned after 1449 not because they gave pain to the assessors and collectors, but because they did not bring sufficient pleasure to the exchequer. This was seen first in the northern province, where in 1406 the tax of 6s. 8d. levied from all those (whether beneficed or unbeneficed) not accustomed to pay was worth only £687 6s. 8d. With expenses and debts at the time of enrolment totalling upwards of £60,[40] the profit was evidently so modest that the experiment was not repeated in the province of York.

In the southern province the results of the subsidies were, at first, much more encouraging. Nevertheless, the Enrolled Accounts illustrate the essentially unsatisfactory nature of these clerical poll taxes and show how changing ecclesiastical conditions frustrated attempts to gather revenue. By way of illustration we may take two sequences of accounts. The sums due from the archdeaconries of Lincoln and Stow (which together covered Lincolnshire) for the five poll taxes were as follows:– 1406: £454 6s. 8d; 1419: £188 13s. 4d; 1430: £48 10s; 1436: £75 18s 8d; 1449: £121 13s. 4d.[41] More modest sums were to be raised from the archdeaconry of Oxford:– 1406: £52; 1419: £32 13s. 4d; 1430: £3 13s. 4d; 1436: £10 6s. 8d; 1449: £22 13s. 4d.[42] A similar pattern is evident in all the figures from this large diocese, with sharp falls being recorded in the sums due for the second tax, and further, though less dramatic, declines being seen in 1430. In some areas the amounts collectable were higher in 1449 than in 1436;[43] but in no instance did these modest gains bring the amounts which were due anywhere near to the high level of 1406.

Probably more than one reason accounts for the fluctuations and overall fall in the value of these extraordinary clerical taxes. One explanation lay in the different terms of the grants. In 1406 collectors were responsible for raising money not only from the unbeneficed but also from those who were beneficed but normally exempt from taxation. Thus in the archdeaconry of Nottingham the collectors raised money from one rector, twenty-eight chantry wardens, four mendicant brothers, and from the twenty-one vicars of Southwell college, as well as from 231 secular chaplains.[44] In the southern province the numbers of the beneficed who contributed were, in some areas, substantial: nineteen rectors and 125 vicars in Lincolnshire; one dean, twenty-four rectors, and eighty-one vicars in the archdeaconries of Northampton and Leicester;[45] forty-four rectors and eighty-four vicars in the diocese of Hereford.[46] In 1419 and 1436 the poll tax subsidies were collected concurrently with taxes of the conventional type which were levied not only on assessed benefices but also on unassessed benefices worth more than certain specified amounts.[47] The gathering of taxes from unassessed benefices was done by different collectors and the sums raised appeared in different accounts. This partly explains the fall in the amounts raised by the poll tax subsidies in those two years.

The introduction of higher rates of contribution for more highly-paid chaplains in the subsidy of 1430 was counter-productive; in one area after another collectors reported that they could find no one whose income (12 marks and over in the case of parochial and stipendiary chaplains, £10 and over in the case of chantry priests) qualified them to pay the top rate of 20s. The entire province produced only a score of such men:– a dozen in the archdeaconry of London, five in Canterbury archdeaconry, one each in the archdeaconries of Winchester and Northampton and the jurisdiction of St Paul's cathedral. These last three were considered such notables that they were named by the collectors in their accounts.[48]

In 1436 the grade of 20s. was not used, but the higher of the two rates fixed, 13s. 4d., was paid by only a small proportion of the chaplains resident outside London.[49] The employment of the higher tax rates in 1430 and 1436 was thus a serious miscalculation based, we may suggest, on a popular misconception concerning the wealth of chantry priests and other chaplains. However, the overall numbers of those paying these two poll taxes fell sharply. Yet because they rose again in 1449 it may be suspected that the taxes of 1430 and 1436 were marked by widespread exemption or evasion, as well as by official miscalculation.

The increase in the number of chaplains in 1449 (according to the Enrolled Accounts) was not sufficient to bring their numbers anywhere near to those recorded in 1406. There were, in most areas, only one-third of the chaplains recorded in 1449 that there had been in the first poll tax of the century.[50] This evidence supports Professor Storey's finding that the numbers of those entering holy orders was tending to fall in the fifteenth century;[51] and we can see the slack being taken up, as it were, by observing the fall in the numbers of the unbeneficed. This change in the size and composition of the clerical estate, coupled with the difficulties of collection, made clerical poll taxes an unattractive proposition to governments in the second half of the century.

After clerical poll taxes were discontinued, the crown concentrated on the taxation of previously unassessed benefices. In the first half of the century the inclusion of the unassessed in a grant was exceptional (1404, 1416(i), 1417, 1419, 1436, 1450, 1453); from 1461 it was standard practice. But to the end of the century and beyond the accounts covering the unassessed were presented separately at the exchequer from those of the standard tenth. This allowed the bishops to appoint different collectors if they so wished, though they used the opportunity with decreasing frequency.

To the constant and increasingly all-embracing tax demands of the crown the clergy of the southern province in their meetings of convocation responded by imposing conditions and exceptions when they made a grant. These are worth examining for they indicate the areas of friction and distrust which existed between the secular power and the ecclesiastical estate. Traditional stipulations that poor nuns and benefices ruined by disasters should not be taxed were joined, in the early fifteenth century, by exemption for benefices ruined by the Welsh rebels.[52] References to Welsh devastation cease before 1420; but between 1425 and 1440 a number of sundry exemptions was added to the concession of taxes, and, once added, they remained to become part of the regular process of tax granting. Blanket exemptions (preferred by the southern province to the individual exemptions of York) were granted to benefices which were vacant because of their low value,[53] as well as to those worth less than 12 marks a year if their holders were either residents or students.[54] In these matters the bishops' certificates were to be accepted without question. Beneficed clergy recently indicted for any felony who could produce a certificate of previous good character were also excused – surely an indication that the clergy felt themselves being harassed by the common law.[55] Most important, perhaps, was the provision that if a collector certified on oath that he was unable to raise the sum due from a particular benefice, the money was to be removed from his account and its collection to become the responsibility of the lay power.[56] All these exemptions made the collectors' work more complicated, and their accounts grew correspondingly longer.[57]

It was not therefore surprising that likely candidates for the commission to collect clerical taxes sought exemption from this labour. This was traditional practice.[58] What was new and perhaps surprising was the resentment which this expedient roused. Complaints against these 'buckpassers' started early in the century, for in 1404 convocation stipulated 'that no collector . . . be excused from the collection thereof by privileges of the king'.[59] Similar injunctions were made in 1406, 1416, and 1417.[60] By 1429 the warning had become a routine element in the conditions of a grant. It was evidently ineffective, because in 1449 an additional quarter-tenth was to be paid 'by all persons exempted by royal letters from the collection of tenths'.[61] A similar punitive quarter-tenth was imposed the following year.[62] Worse was to come. In 1453 convocation granted two tenths, with an extra moiety from those who had obtained letters of exemption from collection, 'provided always that if the religious thus exempted from the collection of tenths expressly renounce for ever their letters of exemption in the Chancery by Assumption next, and cause such letters of exemption to be cancelled there, so as not to use hereafter the same or other like letters of exemption, then they shall not be bound to pay anything beyond the two tenths aforesaid'.[63] The same penalty was imposed in 1472.[64]

Probably the number of those exempted from collection by the crown was not large; but royal meddling in the delicate mechanism of appointment clearly enraged both regular collectors and the bishops, already hard-pressed when it came to allocating collectors' duties fairly. Pity, for example, poor Richard Clifford, bishop of London, who in 1416 appointed the dean and chapter of St Paul's cathedral to collect the recent grant of two tenths in London diocese. The dean and chapter went to the king wailing that 'This has never been done before'; and the king, agreeing that this break with tradition was undesirable, ordered Clifford to appoint another collector.[65] We can perhaps understand from this example something of the resentment which caused these royal favourites to have no friends.

Royal meddling in the bishops' (already restricted) choice of collectors was but one feature of fifteenth-century tax gathering which made the role of the episcopate more difficult and complex. For, ironically, just as the bishops' responsibility for collecting the money was withdrawn, their involvement with tax gathering became greater than before. Assessments of the unbeneficed, a feature of the period 1371 to 1449, was one cause of this involvement.[66] Another was the need, particularly noticeable in the later fifteenth century, to reassess some benefices in the light of changed economic conditions.[67] A third cause of greater responsibility was the condition imposed on some grants that bishops should supply information about individuals, for example those accused of felony, which would exempt them from a particular tax.[68] This was in addition to the bishops' traditional privilege of certifying those individuals and houses whose poverty allowed their tax exemption. The increasing episcopal involvement in the administration of clerical taxes is often reflected in the memoranda sections of their registers, which in some cases became a record of clerical taxation and little else.[69]

Despite these increasing complexities we must conclude this preliminary study by noting the essential strength of the collecting machinery. The tax grants made in convocation, which usually followed meetings of parliament, did often reflect political opinion, particularly during the war with France.[70] But the success or failure of collectors did not, I would suggest, reflect the political state of the country; quittances and surpluses cannot be equated with times of domestic peace, nor debts with upheaval and turmoil.[71] Wild fluctuations in the success of collectors within particular areas there certainly were, from surpluses – some of them embarrassingly large[72] – to huge deficits.[73] But no recognisable pattern emerges at this stage, though an authoritative judgement must await further study.

What is noticeable is the way that the machinery of collecting taxes from the clergy carried on stolidly right through the century. It was so well-developed, and, despite some outside interference, so independent, that it could survive violent fluctuations in political fortunes, even changes of dynasty. Of course, not all collectors were equally competent, and some of the large debts recorded at the exchequer are surely attributable to sheer inefficiency. But, as a group, the collectors, together with their deputies and associates (and the assessors) must be reckoned among the unsung heroes of fifteenth-century government.

Appendix 1

Clerical Taxation Granted in the Province of York, 1401–1504

Mand. = mandate to appoint collectors.
Names = the date by which collectors' names were to be notified to the Exchequer.

All taxes were payable by equal parts unless otherwise stated.

1. Tenth. Granted, 26 July 1401. Mand., 20 Aug. 1401. Names, 30 Sept. 1401. Terms, 26 March 1402, 2 Feb. 1403.
   CFR, *1399–1405*, 134–5.

2. Subsidy of 6s. 8d. from every secular chaplain. Granted, 12 July 1406.
   PRO, E. 359/20 m. 3d.

3. Tenth. Granted, 10 Dec. 1408. Mand., 19 Jan. 1409. Names, 15 April 1409. Terms, 3 May and 11 Nov. 1409.
   CFR, *1405–13*, 140–1.

4. Moiety. Granted, 20 Jan. 1412. Mand., 1 July 1412. Names, 1 Aug. 1412. Term, 30 Nov. 1412 (complete).
   Ibid., 242–3.

5. Tenth. Granted, 27–28 July 1413. Mand., 17 Nov. 1413. Names, 25 Dec. 1413. Terms, 2 Feb. and 1 Aug. 1414.
   CFR, *1413–22*, 51.

6. Two tenths. Granted, 9 x 11 Jan. 1415. Mand., 30 Jan. 1415. Names, 1 March 1415. Terms, 14 April 1415 (tenth), 19 April 1416 (moiety), 29 Sept. 1416 (moiety).
   Ibid., 98–9.

7. Two tenths. Granted, 12 Jan. 1417. Mand., 28 Jan. 1417. Names, 1 March 1417. Terms, 11 April and 11 Nov. 1417.
   Ibid., 188–9.

8.   Tenth. Granted, 20 x 26 Jan. 1418. Mand., 19 March 1418. Names, 22
     May 1418. Term, 2 Feb. 1419 (complete).
     Ibid., 235–6.

9.   Moiety. Granted, 13 x 18 Jan. 1420. Mand., 27 Jan. 1420. Names, 25
     March 1420. Term, 1 May 1420 (complete).
     Ibid., 324–5.

10. Tenth, on conditions. Granted, on or after 22 Sept. 1421. Mand., 27
     Oct. 1421. Names, 12 April 1422. Terms, 24 June 1422, 24 June 1423.
     Ibid., 410–11.

11. Moiety. Granted, 7 Aug. 1428. Mand., 10 Dec. 1428. Names, 20 Jan.
     1429. Term, 2 Feb. 1429 (complete).
     CFR, 1422–30, 255–6.

12. Tenth. Granted, 8 Aug. 1430. Mand., 16 Dec. 1430. Names, 25 Jan.
     1431. Terms, 2 Feb. 1431, 2 Feb. 1432.
     HBC, 561; CFR, 1430–7, 23–4.

13. Quarter tenth. Granted, on or after 3 Oct. 1433. Mand., 13 Nov. 1433.
     Names, 13 Jan. 1434. Term, 2 Feb. 1434 (complete).
     Ibid., 180–1.

14. Moiety. Granted, 11 June 1436. Mand., 15 Jan. 1437. Names, 2 Feb.
     1437. Term, 2 Feb. 1437 (complete).
     Ibid., 309–10.

15. Moiety. Granted, 11 June 1436. Mand., 24 Nov. 1437. Names and term,
     2 Feb. 1438 (complete).
     CFR, 1437–45, 8–9.

16. Tenth. Granted, on or after 4 Oct. 1442. Mand., 12 March 1443. Names,
     31 May 1443. Terms, 24 June 1443 (moiety), 24 June 1444 (quarter), 24
     June 1445 (quarter).
     Ibid., 257–8.

17. Tenth. Granted, 30 Sept. 1445. Mand., 10 Nov. 1445. Names, 2 Feb.
     1446. Terms, 24 June 1446 (moiety), 24 June 1447 (quarter), 24 June
     1448 (quarter).
     CFR, 1445–52, 7–8.

18. Moiety. Granted, 12 June 1452 x 29 Jan. 1453. Mand., 12 June 1453. Names, 1 Nov. 1453. Term, 2 Feb. 1454 (complete).
    CFR, 1452–61, 40–1.

19. Moiety. Granted, 30 April 1460 x 23 March 1462. Mand., 16 Oct. 1462. Names, 14 Jan. 1463. Term, 2 Feb. 1463 (complete).
    CFR, 1461–71, 89–90.

20. Moiety. Granted, on or after 1 Sept. 1462. Mand., 26 Oct. 1463. Names, 14 Jan. 1463. Term, 2 Feb. 1463 (complete).
    Ibid., 119–20.

21. Tenth. Granted, on or after 8 Aug. 1463. Mand., 24 Oct. 1464. Names, 20 Jan. 1465. Terms, 2 Feb. 1465, 2 Feb. 1466.
    Ibid., 135–7.

22. Tenth. Granted, on or after 14 June 1468. Mand., 27 Oct. 1468. Names, 16 April 1469. Terms, 3 May 1469, 3 May 1470.
    Ibid., 225–7.

23. Two tenths. Granted, on or after 6 Feb. 1475. Mand., 10 March 1475. Names, 3 April 1475. Terms, 9 April and 28 May 1475, 2 Feb. 1476, 2 Feb. 1477.
    CFR, 1471–85, 115–18.

24. Moiety. Granted, on or after 17 Feb. 1479. Mand., 2 Sept. 1479. Names, 25 Nov. 1479. Terms, 11 Nov. 1479, 21 May 1480.
    Ibid., 189–92.

25. Moiety. Granted, on or after 27 Oct. 1478. Mand., 2 Sept. 1479. Names, 25 Nov. 1479. Terms, 11 Nov. 1479, 21 May 1480.
    Ibid., 192–4.

26. Tenth. Granted, on or after 29 Oct. 1481. Mand., 25 Feb. 1482. Names, 17 May 1482. Terms, 7 July and 8 Dec. 1482.
    Ibid., 226–9.

27. Tenth. Granted, on or after 19 Feb. 1487. Mand., 10 Sept., 1487. Names, 3 Nov. 1487. Terms, 11 Nov. 1487, 11 Nov. 1488.
    CFR, 1485–1509, 74–6.

28. Two tenths. Granted, on or after 27 Jan. 1489. Mand., 12 May 1489. Names, 20 June 1489. Terms, 24 June 1489 ('before 1 August following'),

11 Nov. 1489 ('before 1 Feb. following').
Ibid., 110–12.

29. Tenth. Granted, on or after 1 March 1492. Mand., 1 April 1492. Names
     and term, 1 May 1492 (complete).
     Ibid., 177–9.

30. Tenth. Granted, on or after 16 May 1496. Mand., 17 June 1496. Names,
     6 Oct. 1496. Terms, 11 Nov. 1496, 11 Nov. 1497.
     Ibid., 237–9.

31. Tenth. Granted, 5 x 14 Aug. 1504. Mand., 28 March 1505. Names, 2
     May 1505. Terms, 23 March ('payable by midsummer') 1505, 25 Decem-
     ber 1505 ('payable by Easter following', 12 April 1506).
     Ibid., 363–6.

Appendix II

Clerical Taxation granted in the Province of Canterbury, 1401–1495

1. Tenth plus moiety. Granted, 26 Jan. 1401. Mand., 12 April 1401. Names, 22 May 1401. Terms, 29 May and 30 Nov. 1401, 24 June 1402. *CFR, 1399–1405,* 123.

2. Tenth plus moiety. Granted, 21 Oct. 1402. Mand., 2 Feb. 1403. Names, 1 March 1403. Terms, 25 March and 24 June 1403, 2 Feb. 1404. Ibid., 197.

3. Moiety. Granted, 6 Oct. 1403. Mand., 12 Oct. 1403. Names, 11 Nov. 1403. Term, 18 Nov. 1403 (complete). Ibid., 225.

4. a) Tenth (2s. in the £) from unassessed benefices worth more than 100s. *p.a.*
   b) Tenth.
   Granted, 21 April 1404. Mand., 17 May 1404. Names, 17 June 1404. Terms, a) 24 June 1404 (complete); b) 11 Nov. 1404, 1 May 1405. Ibid., 246–7; E.359/20 m.1.

5. Tenth plus moiety. Granted, 24 x 28 Nov. 1404. Mand., 6 Dec. 1404. Names, 25 Dec. 1404. Terms, 2 Feb. (tenth) and 25 Dec. (moiety) 1405. *CFR, 1399–1405,* 292–3.

6. a) Tenth.
   b) 6s. 8d. 'from every chaplain, stipendiary or salaried, even in mendicant orders, from every chaplain or warden of chantries, and from every other beneficed person unaccustomed to pay the tenth, and also from all vicars or others beneficed in cathedral or collegiate churches'.
   Granted, 10 May 1406. Mand., 17 June 1406. Names, 1 July 1406. Terms, a) 25 Nov. 1406, 25 March 1407; b) 8 July 1406. E.359/20 m.2d; *CFR, 1405–1413,* 35.

7. Tenth plus moiety. Granted, 28 Nov. x 10 Dec. 1407. Mand., 20 Dec.

1407. Names, 27 Jan. 1408. Terms, 15 April and 1 Nov. 1408, 7 April 1409.
Ibid., 94–5.

8. Tenth plus moiety. Granted, 17 March 1411. Mand., 2 May 1411. Names, 22 May 1411. Terms, 13 Oct. 1410 ('in the quinzaine of Michaelmas last'), 24 June 1411, 2 Feb. 1412.
    Ibid., 209–210; HBC, 560.

9. Moiety. Granted, 1 x 19 Dec. 1411. Mand., 2 June 1412. Names, 1 Aug. 1412. Terms, 11 Nov. 1412.
    CFR, 1405–1413, 243–4.

10. Tenth. Granted, 6 March x 8 May 1413. Mand., 27 Sept. 1413. Names, 13 Oct. 1413. Term, 11 Nov. 1413 (complete).
    CFR, 1413–22, 31–2.

11. Two tenths. Granted, 1 x 20 Oct. 1414. Mand., 24 Nov. 1414. Names, 25 Dec. 1414. Terms, 2 Feb. 1415, 2 Feb. 1416. (see also no. 12).
    Ibid., 90–1.

12. Two tenths on assessed benefices and on unassessed benefices worth £10 p.a. and more. Granted, 18 Nov. x 2 Dec. 1415. Mand., 10 June 1416. Names, 24 June 1416. Terms, 11 Nov. 1416, 11 Nov. 1417. The term of the last tenth previously granted was now to be 24 June 1416.
    Ibid., 157–8.

13. Two tenths. Granted, 9 x 23 Nov. 1416. Mand., 28 Nov. 1416. Names, 25 Dec. 1416. Terms, 2 Feb. 1417 (tenth plus moiety), 18 April 1417 (moiety). The tenth granted 18 Nov. x 2 Dec. 1415 whose term had been 11 Nov. 1417 was now deferred until 24 June 1418.
    Ibid., 185–6.

14. Two tenths on assessed benefices and on unassessed benefices worth £10 p.a. and more. Granted, 26 Nov. x 20 Dec. 1417. Mand., 22 Dec. 1417. Names, 14 Jan. 1418. Terms, 2 Feb. 1418, 2 Feb. 1419. The tenth payable by 24 June 1418 is to be deferred until 2 Feb. 1420.
    Ibid., 218–19.

15. a) Moiety on all assessed benefices and on unassessed benefices worth £10 p.a. and more.
    b) 6s. 8d. from every chantry chaplain and unbeneficed chaplain whose income or stipend is 7 marks p.a. and more or 40s. p.a. plus food.

Granted, 30 Oct. x 21 Nov. 1419. Mand., 29 Nov. 1419. Names, 7 Jan. 1420. Term, 2 Feb. 1420 (complete).
Ibid., 309–10.

16. Tenth. Granted 5 x 27 May 1421. Mand., 17 July 1421. Names, 6 Oct. 1421. Terms, 11 Nov. 1421, 11 Nov. 1422.
Ibid., 401–2.

17. Moiety. Granted, 23 April x 18 July 1425. Mand., 23 July 1425. Names, 29 Sept. 1425. Term, 11 Nov. 1425 (complete).
CFR, *1422–30*, 105–7.

18. Moiety. Granted, 15 x 27 April 1426. Mand., 18 Nov. 1426. Names, 25 Dec. 1426. Term, 2 Feb. 1427 (complete).
Ibid., 149–150.

19. Moiety. Granted, 5 July x 20 Dec. 1428. Mand., 1 July 1429. Names, 29 Sept. 1429. Term, 11 Nov. 1429 (complete).
Ibid., 269–271; E.359/20 m.8.

20. a) Tenth plus moiety.
b) 6s. 8d. from all priests, celebrants of anniversaries, and stipendiaries who receive 100s. *p.a.* or the equivalent.
c) 13s. 4d. from all parochial chaplains and stipendiaries who are not members of a college, who receive 9 marks *p.a.* and more but less than 12 marks *p.a.*
d) 20s. from all parochial priests and other stipendiaries who receive 12 marks *p.a.* or the equivalent.
e) 13s. 4d. from all chantry priests whose chantries are unassessed and whose income is usually 10 marks *p.a.* but less than £10 *p.a.*
f) 20s. from priests whose chantries are worth £10 *p.a.*
Granted, 5 July x 20 Dec. 1429. Mand., 20 Feb. 1430. Names, 25 March 1430. Terms, a) 1 May 1430 (tenth), 1 May 1431 (moiety); b)–f) 1 May 1430.
CFR, *1422–30*, 306–8.

21. Tenth. Granted, 19 Feb. x 21 March 1431. Mand., 26 Sept. 1431. Names, 28 Oct. 1431. Terms, 11 Nov. 1431, 11 Nov. 1432.
CFR, *1430–37*, 62–4.

22. Moiety. Granted, 15 x 24 Sept. 1432. Mand., 3 Aug. 1433. Names, 28 Oct. 1433. Terms, 11 Nov. 1433, 11 Nov. 1434.
Ibid., 159–61.

23.   Moiety plus quarter tenth. Granted, 7 Nov. x 21 Dec. 1433. Mand., 12
       Jan. 1435. Names, 1 May 1435. Terms, 24 June and 11 Nov. 1435, 11
       Nov. 1436.
       Ibid., 227–9.

24.   a) Tenth plus moiety on assessed benefices and on unassessed benefices
       worth 12 marks *p.a.* and more.
       b) 13s. 4d. from all chantry chaplains who usually pay neither clerical nor
       lay taxes and whose chantries are usually worth 10 marks *p.a.* If their
       chantries are worth more than 10 marks *p.a.* they are to pay a whole tenth
       'proportionally'; but if they are worth 100s. *p.a.* or more, though less than
       10 marks *p.a.*, they will pay only 6s. 8d.
       c) 6s. 8d. from all stipendiary priests and all collegiate and other chaplains
       earning 100s. *p.a.* and more but less than 10 marks *p.a.*; 13s. 4d. if they
       earn 10 marks *p.a.* and more.
       Granted, 12 Nov. x 23 Dec. 1435. Mand., 31 Jan. 1436. Names, 24 Feb.
       1436. Terms, a) 24 March 1436 (tenth), 24 June 1437 (moiety); b) and c)
       24 March 1436.
       Ibid., 269–72.

25.   Tenth. Granted, 29 April x 8 May 1437. Mand., 20 Dec. 1437. Names, 9
       Feb. 1438. Terms, 25 March 1438, 25 March 1439.
       CFR, 1437–45, 12–14.

26.   Tenth. Granted, 21 Nov. x 22 Dec. 1439. Mand., 18 April 1440. Names,
       6 May 1440. Terms, 23 June 1440, 11 Nov. 1441.
       Ibid., 135–7.

27.   Tenth. Granted, 16 x 26 April 1442. Mand., 10 Nov. 1442. Names, 20
       Jan. 1443. Terms, 25 March 1443, 25 March 1444.
       Ibid., 244–6.

28.   Tenth. Granted, 19 x 26 Oct. 1444. Mand., 4 March 1445. Names, 7
       May 1445. Terms, 24 June 1445, 24 June 1446.
       Ibid., 310–312.

29.   Tenth. Granted, 22 June x 8 July 1446. Mand., 17 April 1447. Names, 19
       May 1447. Terms, 24 June 1447, 24 June 1448.
       CFR, 1445–52, 61–4.

30.   a) Tenth.
       b) 6s. 8d. from all secular chaplains, friars and other religious serving
       parish churches or receiving stipends and yearly payments or who have
       chantries which are not assessed.

c) A quarter tenth, additional to a), payable by all who have royal letters exempting them from being collectors.
Granted, 1 x 28 July 1449. Mand., 18 Oct. 1449. Names, 6 Dec. 1449. Certificate of the names of those exempt from payment, 1 Feb. 1450. Terms, a) 25 March 1450, 25 March 1451; b) and c), 25 March 1450. Ibid., 139–42.

31. a) Tenth on assessed and unassessed benefices.
b) A quarter tenth, additional to a), payable by all who have royal letters exempting them from being collectors.
c) 2s. in the £ on all benefices usually exempt (with a very few named exceptions.).
Granted, 14 Nov. 1449 x 17 July 1450. Mand., 1 Aug. 1450. Names of collectors and those exempt from payment, 30 Sept. 1450. Terms, a) 25 March 1452, 25 March 1453; b) and c) 'immediately'. The two archbishops and the bishops of London and Winchester were to be the receivers and treasurers of this grant.
Ibid., 163–7.

32. a) Two tenths on assessed and unassessed benefices.
b) A moiety, additional to a), payable by all religious who are exempted from collection of any tenth in the diocese in which they are situated, unless they renounce their exemption.
Granted, 7 Feb. x 3 March 1453. Mand., 14 July 1453. Names, 30 Sept. 1453. Terms, a) 11 Nov. 1453, 11 Nov. 1454, 11 Nov. 1455, 11 Nov. 1456; b) 11 Nov. 1453.
CFR, *1452–61*, 37–40.

33. Tenth on assessed and unassessed benefices. (The unassessed are always included from now on.) Granted, 15 July 1461. Mand., 28 July 1461. Names, 30 Sept. 1461. Terms, 25 March and 11 Nov. 1462.
E.359/34 m.3; CFR, *1461–71*, 29–33.

34. a) Moiety. Granted, 21 July x 2 Aug. 1462.
b) Moiety. Granted, 8 x 25 Nov. 1462.
Mand., 1 Dec. 1462. Names, 14 Jan. 1463. Terms, a) 11 Nov. 1463; c) 11 Nov. 1464 for those who attended convocation in person, 2 Feb. 1463 for those who did not.
Ibid., 81–9.

35. Tenth. Granted, 6 x 23 July 1463. Mand., 24 Aug. 1463. Names, 20 Jan. 1464. Terms, 25 March 1464, 25 March 1465.
Ibid., 116–19.

36. Tenth. Granted, 12 May x 3 June 1468. Mand., 16 Oct. 1468. Names, 2
     Nov. 1468. Terms, 11 Nov. 1468, 1 May 1469.
     Ibid., 222–5.

37. a) Tenth.
     b) Moiety additional to a) payable by any regular who obtained royal
     letters of exemption after being appointed a collector.
     Granted, 23 Jan. x 21 Feb. 1472. Mand., 23 July 1472. Names, 30 Sept.
     1472. Terms, a) 11 Nov. 1472, 11 Nov. 1473; b) 11 Nov. 1473.
     CFR, 1471–85, 48–52.

38. Tenth. Granted, 3 Feb. x 9 April or 11 Oct. x 15 Dec. 1473. Mand., 8
     Aug. 1474. (Names, not known.) Terms, 11 Nov. 1474, 11 Nov. 1475.
     Ibid., 97 (From Exchequer (King's Remembrancer) Memoranda Roll,
     Michaelmas Term, 14 Edward IV).

39. Tenth plus moiety. Granted, 9 Feb. x 16 March 1475. Mand., 1 April
     1475. Names, 23 April 1475. Terms, 5 May 1475 (tenth), 3 Feb. 1476
     (moiety).
     Ibid., 112–115.

40. Tenth. Granted, 10 April x 7 May, or 25 May x 26 June 1478. Mand., 30
     Oct. 1478. Names, 2 Feb. 1479. Terms, 2 Feb. 1479, 2 Feb. 1480.
     Ibid., 166–9.

41. Tenth. Granted, 21 March 1481. Mand., 1 May 1481. Names, 1 June
     1481. Terms, i) holders of certain named benefices in each diocese were to
     pay the entire tenth on 31 May 1481; ii) everyone else, 24 June and 11
     Nov. 1481.
     Ibid., 229–33; E.359/35 m.42.

42. Tenth. Granted 3 x 24 Feb. 1484. Mand., 5 March 1484. Names, 28 May
     1484. Terms, 24 June and 11 Nov. 1484.
     CFR, 1471–85, 278–81.

43. Tenth. Granted, 10 Feb. x 11 March 1485. Mand., 29 March 1485.
     Names, 13 May 1485. Terms, 24 June 1485, 24 June 1486.
     Ibid., 307–10.

44. Tenth. Granted, 13 x 16 Feb. 1487. Mand., 13 April 1487. Names, 25
     May 1487. Terms, 24 June and 30 Nov. 1487.
     CFR, 1485–1509, 61–5.

45. £25,000. Granted, 14 Jan. x 27 Feb. 1489. Mand., 28 Feb. 1489. Names, 15 March (moiety) and 15 Sept (moiety) 1489. Terms, 1 May and 1 Nov. 1489.
    Ibid., 109–10.

46. Tenth. Granted, 21 June x 8 Nov. 1492. Mand., 24 Feb. 1492. Names, 1 April 1492. Term, 23 April 1492 (complete).
    Ibid., 169–74.

47. Tenth. Granted, 19 Oct. x 21 Dec. 1495. Mand., 30 Jan. 1496. Names, 1 April 1496. Terms, 24 June and 11 Nov. 1496.
    Ibid., 233–7.

Notes

1. See *Profession, Vocation and Culture in Later Medieval England*, ed. C.H. Clough (Liverpool, 1982),Chapters 4 and 6 for helpful recent discussions of these two groups during the fifteenth century.
2. The *Calendars of Patent Rolls* record these commands *passim*, as do the royal writs entered in bishops' registers; see A.K. McHardy, 'Notes on a Neglected Source: A Register of Royal Writs in the Lincoln Diocesan Archives', *Lincolnshire History and Archaeology*, 16 (1981), 25–7.
3. The crown commanded the bishops to appoint collectors and to notify their names to the exchequer.
4. *Profession, Vocation and Culture*, 103–8.
5. These are listed in Appendix I.
6. These are listed in Appendix II.
7. PRO (Enrolled Accounts), E.359/17 mm. 10, 17d, 17.
8. York Minster was exempted from one of the two tenths granted in Jan. 1417 because it was 'notoriously burdened and disfigured by reason of the sudden collapse of the belfrey', *CFR, 1413–22*, 188.
9. The total is based on the amounts due, as recorded in the Enrolled Accounts. For other estimates see M. McKisack, *The Fourteenth Century* (Oxford, 1959), 287, and R.A. Griffiths, *The Reign of King Henry VI* (1981), 109.
10. The archdeaconry of Brecon was the only part of Wales to contribute frequently. Occasionally other small areas also appear in the accounts, e.g. the archdeaconry of St. Davids in 1412 (E.359/18 m. 31d); some deaneries in St. Asaph in 1453 (E.359/24 m. 42d); the archdeaconries of Carmarthen and Cardigan in 1484 (E.359/37 m. 10d). In 1436 there were accounts for the subsidy from the diocese of St. Asaph and from the archdeaconries of St. Davids, Cardigan and Carmarthen, but not from Brecon (E.359/20 m. 10d).
11. *Taxatio Ecclesiastica Angliae et Walliae Auctoritate P. Nicholai IV circa A.D. 1291* (RC, 1802).
12. McKisack, op cit., 287.
13. Vol. II, *Fiscal Administration*, ed. W.A. Morris and J.R. Strayer (Cambridge, Mass., 1947), Chapter VI.
14. Ibid., 233–5; A.K. McHardy, 'The Crown and the Diocese of Lincoln during the episcopate of John Buckingham, 1363–98' (Oxford University D.Phil. thesis, 1972), Appendix B.
15. *CFR, 1377–83*, 43.
16. Thus Tywardreath (Cornwall), denizen *c.* 1400, and St. Andrew's, Northampton, denizen in 1405, were both commissioned as collectors in 1453; D. Knowles and R.N. Hadcock, *Medieval Religious Houses: England and Wales* (2nd edn., 1971), 57, 97; E.359/24 mm. 30d, 35d.
17. *CPR, 1388–92*, 380; *CFR, 1377–83*, 199; *CCR, 1381–85*, 363.
18. E.g., Coventry in 1401: *CPR, 1401–05*, 23.
19. *CPR, 1467–77*, 171 (1469), 408 (1473).
20. E.g., in 1468, 1475: *CFR, 1461–71*, 225; *CFR, 1471–85*, 114–15.
21. The divisions were made partly in accordance with the civil boundaries: the city of Lincoln with the parts of Kesteven and Holland; the archdeaconry of Stow with the parts of Lindsey, in 1484, 1496; E.359/37 mm. 2d, 10d, 53d, 54d. Early in the century one collector was commissioned to act in both archeaconries; later, separate collectors were used, one for Stow (small), another for Lincoln (large).
22. The change came in 1398; see R.W. Dunning, 'The Administration of the Diocese of Bath and Wells, 1401–1491', (Bristol University Ph.D. thesis, 1961), p. 257. Thanks are due to Dr. Dunning for allowing me to make use of his thesis. Moreover, it was he who, by drawing

my attention to the class of Enrolled Accounts (Clerical Subsidies) some years ago, made possible the writing of this paper.

23.   E.g., two in the archdeaconry of London in 1401, two in the archdeaconry of Leicester in 1411, four in the archdeaconry of Lincoln in 1419; E.359/18 mm. 2d, 26d, 53.

24.   In 1401, for example, the collectors for the whole diocese were the priors of Wenlock and Bromfield together with the rectors of Rushbury and Pembridge; E.359/18 m. 3.

25.   The three different types of tax – tenths on assessed benefices (E.359/18, mm. 22–6, 34–5, 37–8); on the unassessed (E.359/21, m. 36); and poll tax subsidies (E.359/20) – were presented separately. See also n. 73. The only exception was in 1406; see below.

26.   In 1453 the responsibility for gathering most of the grant of two tenths on the assessed and unassessed benefices in the archdeaconry was committed severally to the abbot of Lilleshall (Salop) 'proprietor' of Ashby de la Zouche church and to the prior of Upholland (Lancs.) 'proprietor' of Whitwick church: E.359/21 mm. 23d, 24d; E.359/24 mm. 39d, 42d. In fairness to the bishop of Lincoln it should be added that the abbot of St. Mary de Pratis, Leicester, who would otherwise have been a most suitable commissary, was committed by the bishop of Worcester to collect all parts of both taxes in the archdeaconry of Coventry: ibid., m. 36d; E.359/21 m. 23d.

27.   E.359/35 m. 45d.

28.   *CFR, 1452–61*, 130.

29.   R.B. Dobson, *Durham Priory 1400–1450* (Cambridge, 1973), 174–83; E.359/17–38 *passim*.

30.   Dunning, op. cit., 253.

31.   Dobson, op. cit., 179.

32.   McHardy, 'The Crown and the Diocese of Lincoln', Appendix B.

33.   London collectors were still using their fellow-religious in the ealy 1460s; E.359/34 mm. 8, 34.

34.   Receipt by John Combe, deputy for the prior of Pilton, collector in Devon, from William Beuselyn, prior, (of Modbury) of 12s. 2d. being a moiety of a tenth for the priory, 11 Jan. 1432; receipt by Thomas, abbot of Buckfast, collector of the second moiety of a tenth granted in the penultimate convocation, of 12s. 2d. from the prior of Modbury by the hand of Andrew Chalvedon, 8 Oct. 1432: Eton College Records 1/280,284.

35.   E.359/20 mm. 4, 6d (1419, 1430); E.359/37 m. 54 (1496); *CFR, 1485–1509*, 236.

36.   Between 1399 and 1407 writs of aid were issued to enable collectors to recover moneys owed to them for this reason. See, for example, *CPR, 1399–1401*, 141; *CPR, 1401–05*, 223, 484, 250, 318; *CPR, 1405–08*, 92, 270, 271. The dioceses involved included Salisbury, Winchester, Hereford, Lincoln and London.

37.   *CFR, 1405–13*, 35; *CFR, 1413–22*, 309–10; *CFR, 1422–30*, 306–8; *CFR, 1430–7*, 269–72; *CFR, 1445–52*, 139–42. The accounts of these experimental subsidies are enrolled on E.359/20.

38.   In 1419 the collectors in 12 out of 38 areas were seculars.

39.   In 1435 the collectors in 41 out of 46 areas were seculars.

40.   Not all the expenses and debts were enrolled.

41.   E.359/20 mm. 2, 4, 5, 6, 8–11, 11d.

42.   Ibid., mm. 2, 4, 6d, 9, 12.

43.   But not in Bedford, which remained the same, nor in Buckingham; ibid., mm. 10, 11, 12.

44.   Ibid., m. 3.

45.   Ibid., m. 2.

46.   Ibid., m. 2d.

47.   £10 and more in 1419, 12 marks and more in 1436: *CFR, 1413–22*, 309; *CFR, 1430–7*, 270.

48.   William Raunston, Nicholas Bateman, and Walter Cheseman respectively: E.359/20 mm. 8, 7d, 6d.

49.   Some examples of ratios of those taxed at the lower rate to those at the higher (by archdeaconry) are: Oxford 31:0; Lincoln 190:4; Northampton 99:1; Huntingdon 56:0; Buckingham 45:2; ibid., mm. 9,10.

50.   The number of chaplains in the archdeaconries of Leicester and Northampton fell from 813 in

1406 to 301 in 1449; in Lincoln and Stow from 1,211 to 365; in Buckingham from 141 to 46; ibid., mm. 2, 2d, 9d, 10.

51. See *Profession, Vocation and Culture*, 102–3 and n.72.

52. CFR, *1399–1405*, 123, 197, 225.

53. 1425; CFR, *1422–30*, 106.

54. 1428–9; ibid., 270.

55. 1429–30, ibid., 307.

56. 1481; CFR, *1471–85*, 231–2.

57. At the beginning of the century there were usually six accounts on each face of membrane; by the end there was room only for one.

58. See, e.g., CPR, *1385–9*, 45, 123, 506.

59. CFR, *1399–1405*, 293.

60. CFR, *1405–13*, 35; CFR, *1413–22*, 186, 218.

61. CFR, *1445–52*, 142.

62. Ibid., 165.

63. CFR, *1452–61*, 39.

64. CFR, *1471–85*, 51–2.

65. 26 June 1416: CFR, *1413–22*, 160.

66. The assessment of the unbeneficed is still a somewhat mysterious process, but the collectors of the 1381 poll tax in the archdeaconries of Lincoln and Stow were issued with a list of the unbeneficed by the bishop; PRO E.179/35/22d. It was the bishops who also made returns of estimates of the value of unassessed benefices, and who, in addition, certified the names of resident incumbents. See, e.g., the returns for the archdeaconry of Berkshire, 1468–9; E.179/53/231.

67. The problem can be seen in the registers of John Morton, archbishop of Canterbury, and of Thomas Langton, bishop of Salisbury, which are being edited for the Canterbury and York Society by Dr. Christopher Harper–Bill and Mr. David Wright.

68. Requests for exemption made by the bishop of Lincoln, for this reason, late in 1468 included the names of the abbots of Thame and Missenden among those indicted for felonies; E.179/39/403, nos. 1–5.

69. See, for example, *Registrum Roberti Mascall, episcopi Herefordensis, A.D., MCCCCIV –MCCCCXVI*, ed J.H. Parry with introd. by C. Johnson (Cantilupe Society, 1916 and CYS, xxi, 1917).

70. R.A. Griffiths, *The Reign of King Henry VI*, 382–4, 391.

71. It seems likely that variations in the success of revenue-gathering were caused by local circumstances including the competence of the collectors.

72. Most were a matter of pennies, but the prior of St. Frideswide, Oxford, had a surplus of 32s. 3 d. on his account as collector in Oxford and Buckingham in 1412; E.359/18 m. 31. When one collector was commissioned to gather the sums due from two concurrent taxes a surplus on one account could be set against a deficit on the other. Two examples from the archdeaconry of Leicester demonstrate this practice. In the 1430 poll tax the abbot and convent of St. Mary de Pratis had a surplus on their account of 7s. 4d. which they set against their liabilities as collectors of the tenth granted in the same year: E.359/20 m. 7d. In gathering the tenth on the unassessed voted in 1461 the abbot and convent of Croxton showed a surplus of 8d. which they set against the sum owed for the assessed benefices: E.359/ 34 m. 9d.

73. For the tax of 1481 the prior and convent of St. Katherine without Lincoln (collector in Kesteven and Holland) owed £276 out of their total of £511 at the time of enrolment: E.359/35 m. 46d.

9

Religion and the Fifteenth-Century English Gentleman[1]

Colin Richmond
University of Keele

On page seventy-nine of a recent book on *The Parish Churches of Medieval England* there is a photograph of a church. The caption beside it reads: 'George Brudenell's church at Quinton, Northamptonshire, neglected in the early sixteenth century while Brudenell, a miscreant member of the local country gentry, was rector.'[2] There was something queer about this, I thought, for had I not seen the rebus 'G bru denell' carved on the screen in the sitting room of what had been the rectory at Quainton, Buckinghamshire? The reference the author of the book on parish churches gave for his George Brudenell was Peter Heath, *The English Parish Clergy on the Eve of the Reformation*, page 137. I quote: 'Others [other incumbents of gentry origin that is], like Master George Brudenell, rector of Quinton in 1519 and a member of the Buckingham family of that name, showed only unwarrantable arrogance towards their flock: through his neglect the vestry roof was in need of repair; in his rectory Katherine Hows had conceived; he violated his parishioners' rights of common and seized many of their cattle; to the church, the record adds laconically, he owed 40s.' Mr. Heath's reference was to the diocese of Lincoln visitation records. It shortly became clear that George Brudenell had indeed been rector of Quainton, Buckinghamshire, for fifteen years; it was he who had put the ceiling, fireplace, and screen of the screens passage into the hall of the rectory there.[3] This story of a misprint becoming a *mis*photograph would have been enjoyed by a later incumbent of Quainton rectory – though (I rush to add) after it had become the thoroughly secular Quainton House – K.B. McFarlane. It has also enabled me to dispose of two birds with one devious stone: to include McFarlane's name in the first paragraph of this paper, which I had assumed was obligatory on such an occasion, and to raise one aspect of religion and the fifteenth-century English gentleman which I do not want to make my main theme. George Brudenell, gentleman rector, miscreant or typical of his class, might be used to illustrate any number of themes, but chiefly he represents that exterior face of religion which I do not want to concentrate on here. And, while it may be true that his class is coming to dominate that side of religion in England by the fifteenth century, and dominate it for centuries to come, it is not the gentry's domination of religion, but their determination of religion itself that I wish to discuss.

Allow me, in my second paragraph, to drop another name, more directly than in the first. Dom David Knowles in 1924 when he was a callow twenty-eight – if Dom David ever was callow – published in the *Downside Review* a paper called 'The Religion of the Pastons'. He concluded: 'In short, though the letters reveal nothing to suggest that a religious revolution was inevitable or even probable, there are certain characteristics in the religion of the Pastons and their circle which help to explain how the change, which did in fact come, was made possible'.[4] I think he is right: 'certain characteristics in the religion of the Pastons', and let them for the moment stand for the gentry at large, do 'help to ex-plain' the Reformation in England. They are not, however, the characteristics which Dom David singled out. He considered such things as 'an absence of warmth and fulness', 'the truths of the Old Testament' obscuring 'the love and grace and light of Christianity', the rare appearance of our Lady's name, the infre-quent allusion to the Mass, to the Holy Eucharist, to the Sacrament of Penance, and the lack of reference to new or newer devotions, for instance 'to our Lord's Passion', as revealing which way the wind was blowing – a chilly one according to Dom David, for whom (as he wrote) 'it is impossible not to remember how completely East Anglia lost the faith within the following sixty or seventy years'.[5]

That begs many questions, some of which we may come to later, as does his *not* discovering certain things in these fifteenth-century letters; after all, one did not then waste precious paper, time and energy in discussing such familiar or personal matters as the Mass, the Sacrament of Penance, or our Lord's Passion. It is entirely incidentally that we learn, for example, that 'the more part of al the parisch' were at mass one Easter Eve, that William Worcester received 'the blissed Sacrament' at Easter (because he swore by it),[6] that Sir John Hevenin-gham, having heard three masses by nine a.m., went into his garden to 'sey a lytyll devocion'.[7] This is not to deny that there is a degree of coolness in the Pastons' religion, the male Pastons' religion that is; for Margaret Paston, while it is difficult to think of her quite as Dom David does as 'worthy of a high place among her devout countrywomen of all ages'[8], was by any definition a warmly pious lady. On some matters indeed she could be fiery. When her son Edmund Paston's servant Gregory, as Edmund described it:

'happyd hym to haue a knavys loste, in plaeyn termes to swhyve a quene; and so dyd in the konynere-close. Yt foretunyd hym to be a-spyed be ij plowemen of my modyrs, whyche werene as fayne as he of that matere, and deseyerd hym to haue parte; and as kompany requereyd, seyd not nay, jn so myche that the plowemen had here alle a nythe in there stabylle and Gregory was clene delyuerd of here_and, as he swhereys, had not a do wyth here wyth-in my modyres place. Notwyth-standdyng my modyre thynkkys that he was grownd of that matere, where-fore there is no remedy but he most a-voyde.'

And so Edmund had to get rid of him.[9] If, therefore, true religion has to show itself in right action, Margaret, who was having no fornication in her farmyard, here displayed her religiousness at Gregory's expense.

If it is actions which count then it is over Judge William Paston's chantry that the Paston menfolk show not just their coldheartedness but also their lack of true religion. And, we may add, over John Paston's tomb. William Paston's intended perpetual chantry was never established by his son and grandsons; for this neglect there may have been pressing financial reasons – or so they might have excused themselves.[10] The *unfoundation*, however, remains a fact. So does that of Sir John Fastolf's college of priests and poor men at Caister, which was the preoccupation of his declining years and (we must assume) to ensure whose foundation he gave – if he did give – that splendid mansion to John Paston in the first place. Whatever the eventual and alternative arrangements made for Fastolf's soul at Magdalen College, Oxford, they were not an adequate substitute for daily prayers of seven priests and seven poor men at Caister College.[11] As late as 1477 Sir John Paston's intentions were still that four priests should sing at Caister for the souls of Fastolf and his friends.[12] The destination to which good intentions lead us is well known. Could the Pastons have been as casual about Hell as they were as careless – so far as relatives and friends were concerned – about Purgatory? Certainly they were not prone to morbidity, being about as opposite as one could readily imagine to those psychological wrecks with whom some historians populate the late Middle Ages. That, however, is another issue, one which there is not time to develop here; I merely offer you the Pastons as folk not oppressed by the so-called burdens of late medieval religion. Anxiety, *angst, maninconia* is not to be detected in them. Yet their casual attitude towards Purgatory does concern our theme. Purgatory's almost instantaneous disappearance less than a hundred years later and at the hands of the descendants of men just like the Pastons, suggests that it had for them as little critical reality as it had for the Pastons. Here then may be one characteristic of the Pastons' religion which could help explain how the religious revolution of the sixteenth century was made possible.

It cannot, however, be that simple. For when it came to John Paston's tomb they showed none of that family pride which is reckoned a striking characteristic of their class and, if anything, even more striking of those sixteenth-century gentlemen who made the English Reformation. In 1478, twelve years after his death, John Paston's tomb at Bromholm was still unmade; Sir John was all promises: by Michaelmas, he wrote to his mother, 'ther shalle noone be lyke it in Norffolk'.[13] Margaret's reply was to the point: 'My cosyn Clere dothe as meche coste at Bromholm as whylle drawe an c li. vpon the deskys in the quere and in othyr placys, and Heydon in lyke whyse; and yf there xulde no thyng be don for zour fadyr, yt wolde be to gret a schame for vs alle, and in cheffe to se hym lye as he dothe.'[14] If anything got done it probably was not a great deal, for Sir John Paston in his will drawn up at this time,[15] left only £20 for 'a closette [to be] made . . . ouer my faders body', hardly enough to construct a mausoleum unique in the county. Margaret in her will of 1482 left not a penny to Bromholm for any purpose; her tomb, to judge from her detailed instructions and if they were carried out, would have cost rather more than £20; it was to be at Mautby.[16] This parsimony over John Paston's tomb probably did reduce or help keep depressed the family's standing in Norfolk society, as Margaret had predicted it might; it was in sharp contrast to the lavish expenditure there had been on the actual funeral of John Paston in 1466, which was a grand, indeed a deliberately ostentatious, affair.

Here the Pastons were attempting to show that they had arrived and, as is usually the case in such circumstances, they overdid it. At St. Peter Hungate, the Pastons' parish church in Norwich, John's body on its journey from London to Bromholm, accompanied all the way by a priest and twelve poor men with torches, lay overnight beneath the roof John himself had paid for;[17] thirty-eight priests, thirty-nine choir boys, twenty-six clerks, four torchbearers, the Prioress of Carrow, her maid and the anchoress of that house, as well as an unknown number of friars surrounded it there. As for the costs, both here and especially at the funeral at Bromholm, they were extravagant: on the hearse over £30, for mourning clothes more than £18, on food and drink another £30, on candles and torches £11, and on alms in gold and silver a surely prodigious £50, as well as £16 worth of copper.[18] If the family was intent on making an impression, it appears to have succeeded: John's final departure from his native Norfolk was a splendid show.

Post-Reformation funerals are a mystery to me, but I understand lavish doles were frowned upon as being the wrong sort of charity. The Pastons in 1466 were surely characteristic of an age and patterns of behaviour which were passing. Moreover, if the mode and manner of John's funeral were religion in the sense of 'social relations' then the Pastons cannot be regarded as representatives of new habits of behaviour or of mind, for religion as 'social relations' was by 1466 an ageing phenomenon. Their sort of funeral show, and that particular way of showing off, were not going to contribute to the making of the English Reformation.

Nor were their unexceptional attitudes towards pilgrimages, saints, and images. Yet, therein may lie the principal reason all three, as aspects of a single approach, disappeared at the Reformation. They had departed from that part of the minds of the Pastons where critical or active beliefs were located, and were now lodged amid that mental lumber which is dispensible and which can therefore be removed without loss or pain. This is not to say that all English men and women were so disposed; many, possibly most, were not, but many, perhaps most, of the English gentry may have been. One other thought on saints may be worth voicing. Is there an increasing Englishness about that sort of devotion? Given the chauvinism the Hundred Years War had produced it would be strange if there had not been. Saints George and Christopher seem fashionable;[19] Walsingham's popularity appears to have been growing (though John Paston III went to Compostella and Canterbury)[20] at the expense of continental shrines, Rome always excepted; the writer of the prologue of the *Nova Legenda Anglie* maintained that there was no need for anyone to go on pilgrimage in foreign parts for the merits and examples of English saints were sufficient for all;[21] and Osbern Buckenham, a friar of Stoke-by-Clare who wrote Saints' Lives for a number of Suffolk gentry patrons, advertized his *Mappula Anglie* as a source book of the English past.[22] In many other ways too, secular rather than religious, the Pastons were typical of that Englishness which helped (and helped a great deal) to make the Reformation, just as the making of the Reformation contributed (and contributed a great deal) to make that Englishness. The Anglican Church is nothing if not English.[23]

There is, nonetheless, one matter where saints are concerned which I do want to dwell on, and which carries me from what in modern jargon we could call the public sector of religion to the private, and thus to my main theme. That is the matter of relics. Fifty years ago, commenting on the Emperor Sigismund's installation as a Knight of the Garter at Windsor and his gift to St. George's Chapel of a relic of St George in May 1416, J. H. Wylie wrote 'To the modern historian St George's heart is less interesting than the statutes promulgated at this Chapter, which are our earliest authority for the regulations of the Order'.[24] Not anymore. Now we all know that, in another quotation, 'the Bollandists' chaff may . . . prove the social historian's grain'.[25] Sir John Fastolf, prudent Knight of the Garter, may not even figuratively have had the heart of St. George, but he did have one of his arms. He gave it to the Guild of St George at Norwich of which he and the Pastons were members.[26] Sir John also had a finger of John the Baptist, valued at £40, but it is the cross and chain (presumably of gold) containing a piece of the Holy Cross, which he wore 'dayly aboute hys nek' and worth £200, that interests me more.[27] Elizabeth Paston also had 'a pece of the Holy Crosse, crossewise made, bordured with silver aboute',[28] while the Pastons' friends and connections also had relics: John de Vere, earl of Oxford, for instance, another two or possibly three pieces of the Holy Cross, his second wife Elizabeth Scrope yet another piece, which she also wore daily about her neck,[29] and William Haute (the father of Sir John Paston's fiancée Anne) among a varied collection a piece of 'that stone on which the Archangel Gabriel descended when he saluted the blessed Virgin Mary'.[30]

To discover the function of these relics is not my purpose here, although in passing I offer the observation that they were more than tastefully mounted charms;[31] the will of Sir Robert Radcliff of Hunstanton, Norfolk, who died in 1486, shows that.[32]

> Also I wull that all suche Reliques as be within a purse brodered with golde and perle with all other Reliques thereby hanging be in the keping of my saide doughter Anne so that she deliver it and them to gedres to my saide doughter Elizabeth in tyme of nede whanne soever she requirith to have theme. And so in tyme of nede to be comen to theme bothe as they wolle have my blessing.

Sir Robert had no sons. Relics were not simply valuable heirlooms, they were not 'simply' anything. Of course, some of their power had gone. In the tenth century the Holy Lance had won a great battle – the equivalent of the British halting a war in Ceylon in the nineteenth century by seizing the Buddha's tooth[33] – and king Athelstan had hung his relic pouch about his neck. Now, in the fifteenth century, no knights (that I know of) had relics in their swords as Roland had had, the Holy Lance prevented pains in the side,[34] and it was ordinary gentlefolk who used relics in their personal jewellery. The popularization of Christianity in diffusing relics had reduced or altered their potency, or so it seems at this distance. More certain is the conclusion that this popularization, this personalization of relics is a feature of the privatization of religion; relics had come off the streets into the home, out of the grand and public reliquary into the coffer on the dressing-table or its fifteenth-century equivalent. It is this privatization of religion for the gentry, its becoming for them non-communal, even anti-populist, which seems to me the most important development in later medieval English religion. It leads directly to the English Reformation. The Pastons are, in this respect, typical.

In Paston church, for instance, they had their private pew. Agnes Paston was in it after evensong on the Sunday before St Edmund one November around 1450 when two other parishioners came up to reopen the argument about the wall she had had built which, according to them, blocked both the king's highway and their processional way, and 'all that tyme Waryn Herman lenyd ouyr the parklos and lystynd whatt we seyd'.[35] The private pew or 'closett' as Agnes called hers[36] may not have guaranteed privacy, but it may have reduced (temporarily at least) the number of quarrels over precedence, like that between Thomas Rode and William Moreton 'concerning which of theym should sit highest in churche', though it would not have helped them settle – as their neighbour William Brereton had to settle for them – which should 'foremost goe in procession'. That was in 1513 in the church of a great Cheshire parish, Astbury, where more than one gentleman worshipped.[37] Almost one hundred years before in the not too distant church of Ashton-under-Lyne in south Lancashire, when the seating was allocated for women of the parish no provision was made for the wives and daughters of the leading local gentlemen, Sir Ralph

Ashton, Sir John Byron and Ralph Staveley; presumably those families already had their own private accommodation in the church.[38] Did the private pew and ultimately the private chapel also curtail the discord about precedence when the pax was taken around to be kissed?[39] Perhaps the gentry had excluded themselves from this communal exercise. They often had, as Sir John Fastolf had, a pax in their domestic chapels:[40] within the ordered circle of their households the private pax going its rounds could cause no disharmony, but its original purpose had been wholly removed.

Pews themselves, whether private or not, engender privacy or at any rate introspection and non-participation. They, it seems to me, are a manifestation of the interiorization of religion, a corollary of its personalization, its becoming in the later Middle Ages what the Church since at least the twelfth century had taught it as, an occupation for the individual as well as, if not more than, the preoccupation of the community. What the literate and educated gentlefolk got up to in their private pews was part of that process. They looked at or read books as well as saying their prayers and reciting their rosaries. Whether they followed the Mass in the liturgical books or in a paraphrase and devotional commentary, or they read something unconnected with the service, they were, so to speak, getting their heads down, turning their eyes from the distractions posed by their fellow worshippers, but at the same time taking them off the priest and his movements and gestures.[41] Such folk, in becoming isolated from their neighbours, were also insulating themselves against communal religion, possibly even religion *per se*, for how can you be religious on your own?

It was an obvious next step to have even the Mass at your own home, in your own chapel, conducted by your own priest, at your own altar.[42] The Pastons had chapels in their houses at Paston and Mautby, and there was of course one at Caister.[43] These do not survive. Others do: the Hautes' (or the Clements') at Ightham Mote, Kent; the Stonors' at Stonor, Bucks, where in the 1470s among 'the stuffe of the chapelle . . . wyche must be left fro Eyur unto Eyur' were a number of alabaster panels but no relics;[44] Sir Robert Harcourt's at Stanton Harcourt, Oxfordshire; Sir Richard Edgcumbe's at Cotele, Cornwall. The last is tiny, more like those oratories or closets where the more devout of the gentry might go to escape from the household to pray, to read,[45] or to pore over those books of hours which, as Joan Evans once remarked, were 'both a cause and a consequence of the development of castle chapels'[46] and in which they could (on certain pages) observe themselves in postures of adoration.

It is not easy to imagine the first John Paston in any such posture nor, for that matter, his prosaic and businesslike chaplain and clerk, James Gloys. They were well suited and James served the family for twenty-five years until his death in 1473. If a surviving Whitsun sermon of his was preached before John Paston in the 1460s one wonders what meeting of the eyes there may have been between them as James declaimed, 'A man joyth sumtyme in gold and syluer and in gret substaunce of erdly godes . . but this joy is not parfyght, but this ioy is not stabill, but is mutabill as a shadow'.[47] Gloys' own earthly goods were substantial rather than showy; they included, as one would expect, a sword as well as a silver cross and among the books a book of Statutes as well as the Lives of the Fathers.[48] There was not the intriguing variety of another private chaplain's, Thomas Nandyke's possessions: a handsaw, a little gun of brass, two crossbows, a melting ladle, a fire rake, two astrolabes, a lute, a great desk to write upon, a glass to look in, and books of physic and astronomy. To some a private chaplain needed to be more than priest, clerk, and estate officer: Thomas Nandyke, Cambridge M.B., was also both doctor and astrologer to Henry, duke of Buckingham.[49] It was only the very grand who could afford to retain a doctor or an astrologer, or, as Anthony Woodvill may have had at Grafton Regis, a hermit in the family hermitage, thus anticipating those Gothic Revival landowners who hired hermits to occupy their grottoes, caves and oratories.[50]

The Pastons steered clear of such extremes. Their religion was as uncomplicated as their private chaplain seems to have been. No hairshirts for him or them. No books on our Lord's Passion, like that of a Norfolk neighbour of theirs, Sir Miles Stapleton of Ingham, either;[51] the majority of Sir John Paston's English books were secular: he enjoyed lighter reading than that, as no doubt he preferred watching Robin Hood to a mystery play.[52] There was a 'Preyer to the Vernycle'; it, however, is not evidence of a particular devotion to Jesus. In contrast to the Plumptons, who towards the end of the fifteenth century were interested in the new devotion of the Holy Name of Jesus, the Pastons were unresponsive to the most recent cults. In that respect they were also unlike Henry VI who was a devotee of the cult of the Five Wounds and who had received relics of St. Bernardino himself. If Henry was a model of lay piety it was a model the Pastons, like most English laymen, did not seek to emulate.[53] Dom David is right: 'If a concordance were made to the Paston Letters, the name of God would be found to occur very many hundreds of times, but that of our Lord much more seldom'.[54] Whereas, for example, Edward Plumpton in the 1480s ends his letters, 'our Lord preserve you' or more frequently, 'Jesu keep you',[55] the Pastons almost always end with 'God' or 'the Trinity keep you', that is, in the case of John Paston I and Sir John Paston, if they end with a devout sentiment at all. John Paston III invariably closed with 'God save you' except twice in March 1477 when he used 'Jesu preserve you'.[56] Twice also did Margaret's letters have the name of Jesus at the head; that was on the same day, 28 January 1475,[57] and was probably due to the unidentified scribe rather than to her. As, however, the young Walter Paston in the 1470s did in two of his three surviving letters end 'Allmythy Iesus have yow in hys kepyng' and 'Iesu preserve yow to hys pleswr',[58] in this matter the question of changing conventions needs to be considered: God or Jesus may not have come other than literally into it.

Except for Margaret. She wrote to her husband in 1448 when they were enduring Sir Robert Hungerford, Lord Moleyns' occupation of their estate and house at Gresham:[59]

'I pray zw hertyly here masse and other servys that ze arn bwn to here wyth a devwt hert, and I hope veryly that ze xal spede ryth wele in all zwr materys, be the grase of God. Trust veryly in God and leve [love] hym and serve hym and he wyl not deseve zw.'

The connection she makes here between doing the right religious thing and, through the consequent supply of God's grace, the success of one's endeavours, she also makes elsewhere. To her son Sir John, for example, she wrote when he became engaged, 'be as trew to here as she were maried on-to you in all degrees and ye shall haue the more grace and the better spede in all othere thynges',[60] or again to Sir John: '. . . and yf any thyng haue be a mysse any othere wyse than yt howte to haue ben be-fore thys, owthere in pryde ore in laues expencys ore in any othere thyng that haue offendyd God, amend yt and pray hym of hys grace and helpe, and entend welle to God and to zowr neybors . . . and God xale send zow the more grace to haue zowr entente in othere thynggys.'[61] We take note of 'and to zowr neybors', as we do also of Margaret's sense of obligation to her ancestors when she writes that until she fulfils her responsibility to 'the dede and . . . them that I haue my goodes of . . . I know for certeyn that I shall fayll grace and displeas God':[62] as we have seen, she knew there was no prosperity that way. Such seems to me a thoroughly religious attitude towards life because it is a practical one. It is for that reason not at all incompatible with the notorious advertisement for the vacant Paston living at Oxnead ('the parsonage stant be a fresch ryuer syde', 'there is a good markett town callyd Alysham with-in ij myle', 'the cyte off Norwych is with-in vj myle', 'the see is wyth-in x myle', and 'it is butt an esy cure to kepe, for ther ar nott past xx persons to be yerly howselyd'[63]) which superficially appears to be as much about religion as the Conservative Party is about compassion.

Let me begin to pull some strands together. The first point is that the Pastons, including the religious Margaret, were not like that Throckmorton for whom his confessor drew up such a formidably pious programme for the day, nor had they, as has recently been written of Sir Richard Empson (mistakenly I would have thought), 'inclinations towards the devout'.[64] Unlike either Henry VI or Richard III, also recently described, somewhat unnervingly, as 'a genuinely pious and religious man'[65] – which is like calling Joseph Stalin a genuinely devout Marxist – the Pastons were more like Edward IV: not extremist.

If they were not religious specialists nor were they – and this is, I think, a less obvious and more important point – nor were they very much, if at all, given to what used to be termed superstitious practices. They, on the evidence which survives, were not preoccupied with the exact size of the wound in Christ's side, or the precise number of drops of blood He shed, or in carrying about with them, for the benefits it would bring, the correct length of the nails of the Crucifixion. Pieces of paper with the different names of God written upon them or incantations for making angels appear on the thumbnail of a child did not

interest them, as they did Robert Reynys, churchwarden of nearby Acle in the
1470s.[66] Nor can I imagine them sticking in their book of hours one of the
parchment picture cards of the Holy Rood of Bromholm as a member of the
Lewknor family of Sussex did in theirs,[67] or pasting up at Paston or Caister any of
those inexpensive woodcuts available at shrines or booksellers' shops, or
covering their hats in pewter badges, or putting on Henry VI's hat to cure their
headaches – the list could be extended.[68] If what has been thought of as 'lower
class magic' was not their style nor was that astrological variety increasingly
found tempting by the upper classes – like Henry, duke of Buckingham and
Henry VII.[69]

Was it education which made the difference? Not, I hasten to say, in terms of
the astrology, which in its various branches had such a varied appeal, but where
popular religion was concerned? Was it literacy, not in particular bible reading,
which detached men and women from what by the 1530s would be called
idolatry and superstition, just as it certainly set them apart from the 'rude
people'?[70] Scripture reading specifically was important, not least for some of the
'rude people', but there is also a distinct frame of mind engendered by books and
a bookish education; it includes a lack of spontaneity, a confidence in the
efficacy of reason and logic and a dependence on that sort of knowledge, and if
not a contempt for non-readers a feeling of difference from them. When this is
allied to other frames of mind, which arise from differences created by income,
occupation, custom, taste – class differences they might be called – [71] then
religion, hitherto for the laity a cohesive leveller because it comprised shared
experience in the behaviour of worship, breaks apart, becomes two-layered:
religion of the people, religion of the governing or determining classes, the latter
by c. 1500 largely literate, secular, and, to return to an earlier theme, privatized.
If, therefore, religion does fall apart in England after this fashion at this time,
male lay literacy was a cause: education, in other words, was divisive.[72] It is the
literate and well educated male Pastons of the fifteenth century who were, so to
speak, potential and proto-Erasmians. It seems appropriate that there was to be
an early sixteenth-century Erasmus Paston.

Education, however, was no more than one begetter of Erasmian attitudes, as
it was of the Reformation itself. There were other causes of that religious
revolution. If it was most revolutionary in the respect I am suggesting, namely of
the elimination of a great part, certainly the popular part, and surely the most
important part of religion, then the religion of the Pastons embodies those
causes too. There is detachment in John Paston III's advice to his mother to take
his unmarried sister Margery to pray to the Holy Rood at the North door of St
Paul's 'that sche may haue a good hosbond or sche com hom ayen.'[73] I detect
that here we are not distant from Thomas More's tolerant and amused attitude
to those other women who also went to St Paul's, but to offer to the image of St
Uncumber that she might unencumber them of their cumbrous husbands.[74] The
trouble came when educated men did *not* take such things lightly. That occurred

when such things were no longer understood; the prelude to non-comprehension was the not doing them oneself,[75] and the coming to feel they were vulgar things to do. In other words, the other phenomenon of the religion of the late medieval gentry, of withdrawal into their private chapels, into their books of devotion, and into their own heads,[76] was crucial to the anti-communal nature of the English Reformation. Boy bishop ceremonies, for instance, became indecorous, irreverent, occasions of bad taste[77] at the same time as images became idols. 'Decorum' and 'gentility' are (like 'condescension'[78]) new sixteenth-century words for new late medieval things. If they excluded (as they did) such items as 'offering of money, candles, or tapers to images or relics, or kissing or licking the same, saying over a number of beads, not understood or minded on'[79] we are bound to ask 'not understood or minded on' by whom? Religion was being re-defined and in its re-defined and exclusive form was imposed by one group, a minority group of laymen, upon another. For the majority of English folk, therefore, the religious revolution of the sixteenth century was as great a fraud as for the mass of the Russian people the Bolshevik revolution was to be.[80].

Notes

1. I would like to.thank Peter Jackson and Carolyn Busfield for their help during the writing of this paper, and (among others) Professor John Bossy, Margaret Aston, and Caroline Barron for their stimulating thoughts after it had been read.

2. Colin Platt, *The Parish Churches of Medieval England* (1981). For his reference see p. 78.

3. See McFarlane's pamphlet on the house for a description of it and of George's modifications. I am grateful to David Morgan for sending me a copy of this little known work of the master's.

4. Volume xlii (new series, xxiii), 143–63. The quotation is from p. 163. Again, I am most grateful to David Morgan for telling me of this paper and for sending me a copy of it.

5. Ibid., 162–3.

6. Norman Davis, ed., *Paston Letters and Papers of the Fifteenth Century* (Oxford 1971), Part II, 199, 205.

7. Ibid., Part I, 39; cf. Colin Richmond, *John Hopton* (Cambridge, 1981), 235–6.

8. Op. cit., 162.

9. Davis I, 635.

10. Davis I, 44–5; Davis II, 609; cf. Richmond, op. cit., 123, n.74.

11. A.D.K. Hawkyard, 'Some late medieval fortified manor houses: a study of the building works of Sir John Fastolf, Ralph lord Cromwell, and Edward Stafford, third duke of Buckingham' (unpublished University of Keele M.A. thesis, 1968), 65–7.

12. Davis I, 507.

13. Davis I, 510.

14. Davis I, 380.

15. Davis I, 507. He specified the same sum for his own tomb which he wanted to be beside his father's.

16. Davis I, 383–4.

17. He was (according to Rachel Young and Geoffrey Goreham, *St Peter Hungate* [Norwich, 1969], 5) the builder of nave and transepts also. The Pastons' town house was on Elm Hill. John acquired the advowson of St. Peter's in 1458. The church's remodelling was completed in 1460.

18. James Gairdner, ed., *The Paston Letters* (Library edition, 1904), iv, 226–31. Contrast the £71 spent on the funeral of Thomas Stonor twelve years later: C.L. Kingsford, ed., *The Stonor Letters and Papers*, i, CS, 3rd series, xxix (1919), 143–4, 162.

19. Sir John's will: Davis I, 506.

20. For Walsingham see Davis I, 218, Davis II, 198. For John III's pilgrimages see Davis I, 465, 560–1.

21. Cited by H. Maynard Smith, *Pre-Reformation England* (1938, reissued 1963), 168.

22. Samuel Moore, 'Patrons of Letters in Norfolk and Suffolk, c. 1450', part II, *Publications of the Modern Language Association of America*, xxviii (1913), 92.

23. See also the somewhat neglected paper of Denys Hay, 'The Church of England in the Later Middle Ages', *History*, liii (1968) 35–50.

24. *The reign of Henry the Fifth* (Cambridge, 1914–29), iii, 14.

25. Sergei Hackel, ed., *The Byzantine Saint* (1981), 2.

26. Mary Grace, ed., 'Records of the gild of St George in Norwich, 1389–1547', *Norfolk Record Society Publications*, ix (1937), 23, 31.

27. Magdalen College, Oxford, Fastolf Paper 70. It was no doubt very like the Clare reliquary in the British Museum, a chain and a cross of gold which on its discovery in 1866 during the construction of a railway station on the site of Clare Castle, Suffolk, still contained its piece of

the True Cross: *The British Museum Quarterly*, no. I (1936), plate I and p. I. Clare belonged to Richard duke of York, with whom Fastolf was closely connected.

28. Davis I, 211.
29. Sir William St John Hope, 'The Last Testament and Inventory of John de Veer, thirteenth Earl of Oxford', *Archaeologia*, lxvi (1915), 313, 314; *Transactions of the Essex Archaeological Society*, new series, xx (1933), 15–20.
30. N.H. Nicholas, ed., *Testamenta Vetusta* (1826), 300.
31. Which seems the view expressed in Joan Evans, *Magical Jewels of the Middle Ages and Renaissance, particularly in England* (Oxford, 1922), 134–6. When King Egfrith of Northumbria imprisoned St. Wilfrid, his queen Iurminburg 'took away the reliquary of the man of God which was filled with holy relics and (I tremble to say it) she wore it as an ornament both in her chamber at home and when riding abroad in her chariot. But this brought nothing but evil upon her . . .': B. Colgrave, ed., *The Life of Bishop Wilfrid by Eddius Stephanus* (Cambridge, 1927), 71. I offer this interesting quotation without comment; I am grateful to Miss Barbara Raw for supplying me with it.
32. PRO, Probate 11/11, fo. 185.
33. V.G. Kiernan, *European Empires from Conquest to Collapse, 1815–1960* (1982), 118. Was it perhaps the Brecbennoch of St Columba, carried by the monks of Arbroath, which helped the Scots to victory at Bannockburn in 1314?
34. H. Maynard Smith, op. cit., 182.
35. Davis I, 36.
36. Hers was no doubt like those John Pympe in his will of 1496 wished to be made in Nettlestead church, Kent: *Archaeologia Cantiana*, xxviii (1909), 276.
37. Christopher Rowell, *Little Moreton Hall* (The National Trust, 1979), 29. Men being what they are, disputes about the positioning and distribution of pews continued to disturb the peace in the sixteenth and seventeenth centuries. I owe that information and these references to Professor John Bossy: David Hey, *An English Rural Community: Myddle under the Tudors and Stuarts* (Leicester, 1974), 219–20; M.J. Ingram, 'Communities and Courts: Law and Disorder in Early Seventeenth Century Wiltshire', in J.S. Cockburn, ed., *Crime in England 1550–1800* (1977), 126. Women being what they are too, the Wife of Bath might be remembered:

> 'In al the parisshe wif ne was ther noon
> That to the offrynge bifore hire sholde goon;
> And if ther dide, certeyn so wrooth was she,
> That she was out of alle charitee'.

For a Yorkshire gentry dispute of the 1470s about where they (and their wives) were to sit in church, see A.J. Pollard, 'Richard Clervaux of Croft: a North Riding squire in the Fifteenth Century', *Yorkshire Archaeological Journal*, I (1978), 162. I am grateful to Dr. Pollard himself for this reference.

38. W.M. Bowman, *England in Ashton-Under-Lyne* (Altrincham, 1960), 167–8. The document dates from before 1422; do any other such records survive? The movement towards worshipping in church (as well as at home) as a family and household was perhaps a cause and consequence of such new seating arrangements, as Margaret Aston suggested to me. There is both a 'sociology' and a 'geography' of folk in church which is beginning to come to light. Somewhere, for instance, I have seen benches for servants which fitted into the ends of the pews of the families they served, and which pulled out for them to sit alongside their masters and mistresses during services. Alas, I cannot recollect where.
39. H. Maynard Smith, op. cit., 97.
40. Gairdner, op. cit., iii, 188.
41. W.A. Pantin, 'Instructions for a Devout and Literate Layman', in J.J.G. Alexander and M.T. Gibson, eds., *Essays presented to R.W. Hunt* (Oxford, 1976), 404–5. Compare *A Relation . . . of the Island of England . . . about the year 1500*, CS, old series, xxxvii (1847), 23: '. . . they all

attend Mass every day and say many Paternosters in public (the women carrying long rosaries in their hands, and any who can read taking the office of our lady with them, and with some companion reciting it in the church verse by verse, in a low voice, after the manner of churchmen) . . .' On the matter of private religion I am indebted to Gail Simmons' 1982 Keele B.A. dissertation, 'Public and Private Devotion in the Later Middle Ages', esp. 17–18, 21, 27 et. seq.

42. There is, of course, the whole question of the 'private' mass, which 'more and more preempted the field. It gradually determined the very form of the solemn Mass': Handbook of Church History, ed. H. Jedin and J. Dolan, vol. iv, From the High Middle Ages to the Eve of the Reformation (1970), 570–4.

43. Davis I, 27, 374–5; Hawkyard, op. cit., 34–5.

44. C.L. Kingsford, ed., The Stonor Letters and Papers, i, CS, 3rd series, xxix (1919), 146.

45. W.A. Pantin, op. cit., 406.

46. Art in Medieval France, 987–1498 (Oxford, 1948), 201.

47. Davis II, 597.

48. Davis II, 360.

49. PRO, Probate 2/48, inventory dated 1491; BRUC, 418; he was described as a 'Nigromansier' when attainted for his part in the rising of October 1483; he was pardoned in 1485: Carole Rawcliffe, The Staffords, Earls of Stafford and Dukes of Buckingham, 1394–1521(Cambridge, 1978), 34, 227.

50. Geoffrey Parker, 'The Medieval Hermitage of Grafton Regis', Northamptonshire Past and Present, 1981–2, 247–52, esp. 251.

51. P. Lasko and N.J. Morgan, eds., Medieval Art in East Anglia 1300–1520 (Norwich, 1973), item 44, p. 33.

52. Davis I, 517–18. For Robin Hood see ibid., 461, and R.B. Dobson and J. Taylor, Rymes of Robyn Hood (1976), 203–4.

53. Roger Lovatt, 'John Blacman: Biographer of Henry VI', in R.H.C. Davis and J.M. Wallace-Hadrill, eds., The Writing of History in the Middle Ages: Essays presented to Sir Richard Southern (Oxford, 1981), esp. 434–441. For the relics, A.G. Little, 'Introduction of the Observant Friars into England', PBA, x (1921–3), 455; they were sent to restore Henry's health in 1454 by no less than St. John of Capistrano. Did they?

54. Op. cit., 162–3.

55. Thomas Stapleton, ed., Plumpton Correspondence, CS, old series, iv (1839), 88 et seq. It was Sir Richard Plumpton's wife who was interested in the feast of the Holy Name of Jesus in 1499: ibid., 130. Cf R.W. Pfaff, New Liturgical Feasts in Later Medieval England (Oxford, 1970), chapter 4.

56. Davis I, 606–7.

57. Davis I, 371, 373.

58. Davis I, 645–6.

59. Davis I, 225.

60. Davis I, 338.

61. Davis I, 346.

62. Davis I, 351.

63. Davis I, 178.

64. M.R. Horowitz, 'Richard Empson, minister of Henry VII', BIHR, lv (1982), 49.

65. Charles Ross, Richard III (1981), 128.

66. Dom Louis Gougard, Devotional and Ascetic Practices in the Middle Ages (1927), 101–2; Berndt Moeller, 'Religious Life in Germany on the Eve of the Reformation' in G. Strauss, ed., Pre-Reformation Germany (1972), 38; C.L.S. Linnell, 'The Commonplace Book of Robert Reynys of Acle', Norfolk Archaeology, xxxii (1958–61), 111–127 esp. 114, 117, 125, and text figure. This interest in precise measurement is interesting and understandable: devout folk wished to know exactly what the objects associated with Christ were like; see, for instance, among the

'Goodys of Master William Wey ys lefte to the chapel made to the lyknes of the sepulkyr of owre Lorde at Jerusalem' at Edington, Wilts., the 'borde byhynde the qveer the lengthe of oure Lorde ys sepulkyr, wyth the hythe of the dor, the brede of the dore, the lengthe of oure Lordys fote, the depnes of the morteyse of the crosse, and the rundeneys of the same': G. Williams, ed., *The Itineraries of William Wey*, Roxburghe Club, 1857, p. xxviii. William Worcester's passion for measuring everything (see his *Itineraries*, passim) seems to me a related aspect of this preoccupation.

67. Francis Wormald, 'The Rood of Bromholm', *Journal of the Warburg Institute*, i (1937–8), 32–34 and plate 7b; M.R. James and C. Jenkins, *A Descriptive Catalogue of the Manuscripts in the Library of Lambeth Palace* (Cambridge, 1932), 747–50.

68. B. Spencer, 'King Henry of Windsor and the London pilgrim', in J. Bird, H. Chapman, J. Clark, eds., *Collectanea Londiniensia* (London and Middlesex Archaeological Soc. 1976), 247.

69. For William Parron at Henry VII's court see John Armstrong, 'An Italian Astrologer at the Court of Henry VII', in E.F. Jacob, ed., *Italian Renaissance Studies* (1960), 433–54.

70. See the Ten Articles of 1536, Cromwell's Injunctions of 1536, and the royal Injunctions of 1538: C.H. Williams, ed., *English Historical Documents, V, 1485–1558* (1967), 803, 806, 812.

71. Viewed from above – by the increasingly literate upper classes (in town and country) – urban workers and rural yokels appear to be as far beyond the pale of salvation as they are those of 'courtesy', reason, and civilization. Isn't this the same as telling someone you don't like 'to go to Hell!'? As Dante did. See Alexander Murray, *Reason and Society in the Middle Ages* (Oxford, 1978), 237–42; Natalie Zemon Davis, Charles Trinkaus, and Heiko Oberman, eds., *The Pursuit of Holiness in late Medieval and Renaissance Religion* (Leiden, 1974), 308–9; Richard C. Trexler, *Public Life in Renaissance Florence* (New York, 1980), 107–8. In England the comic literary 'class' convention is displayed within 'The Tale of Beryn' in the contrasting behaviour of the pious knight and irreligious pardoner, miller and 'othir lewde sotes' in Canterbury Cathedral: lines 135–192. It was in England too that these 'noble' and 'Christian' attitudes were shown up for what they were by Thomas More in *Utopia*: see the valuable comments of J.H. Hexter, *The Vision of Politics on the Eve of the Reformation* (1973), 194–8. Thomas also saw through the Reformation; it was part of that 'conspiracy of the rich aiming at their own interests under the name of Commonwealth'.

72. Godparentage and confraternities may have run counter to this divisiveness. Professor Bossy suggested the former, Caroline Barron the latter. So far as confraternities as meeting places for all ranks of society are concerned, the ordinances of the Gild of St. Michael on the Hill, Lincoln, should be borne in mind: '. . . whereas this gild was founded by folks of common and middling rank, it is ordained that no-one with the rank of mayor or bailiff shall become a brother of the gild unless he is found to be of humble, good, and honest conversation . . . And none such shall meddle in any matter . . . nor shall such a one take on himself any office in the gild': J. Toulmin Smith, ed., *English Gilds*, EETS, OS xl (1870), 178–9. This topic (the social composition of English confraternities) is a promising one.

73. Davis I, 529.

74. Maynard Smith, op. cit., 157.

75. Compare the doing of different things by the two groups, Catholic and Protestant, at Regensburg in Holy Week 1541; their not doing the same things was the measure of the gap between them, *was* the gap between them: Peter Matheson, *Cardinal Contarini at Regensburg* (Cambridge, 1972), 87–8. The sharpest illustration of the difference different behaviour can make is provided in another, albeit religious, context; Helene Deutsch remembers Poland between the first and second world wars: 'I often saw the same priest on the streets, on his way to administer extreme unction to a dying soul . . . the sight has lasted in my memory all my life: the priest in his white lace surplice holding before him the viaticum, followed by a hunch–backed altar boy carrying the censer and a shrill little bell . . . All the passersby would sink to their knees like wheat stalks in the wind. I alone, the Jew, would remain standing in solemn silence. I felt marked by a stigma and full of shame. I did not belong': quoted in Celia J.

Heller, *On the edge of destruction: Jews of Poland between two world wars* (New York, 1977), 70–71.

76. The idea of a later medieval – early modern shift away from materiality and into abstraction, from action into cerebration (which might be termed 'religion and the decline of sensuality') occurred to me while reading Marina Warner's novel *In a Dark Wood* (Penguin Books, 1980), esp. 158–9, 222–3. As it was no more than an idea I left it alone. However, as Professor Bossy (not knowing of my thoughts) has subsequently written to me of 'an increasing tendency to formulate abstractly the things you are praying about (e.g. adversaries/adversities)', I have the temerity to mention this apparently anti-Incarnational movement of the Reformation era.
77. H. Maynard-Smith, op. cit., 139–40.
78. W.A. Pantin, op. cit., 413.
79. *English Historical Documents*, V, 812: the Royal Injunctions of 1538.
80. See Thomas More quoted in note 71 above.

10

Urban Piety In The Later Middle Ages: the Evidence Of Hull Wills*

Peter Heath
University of Hull

Popular religion in later medieval England is still relatively unexplored. There have, indeed, been some notable historical studies of limited groups or areas, and literary and theological scholars have illuminated various devotional texts and liturgical practices; yet nearly a quarter of a century after Jacques Toussaert anatomised religion in fifteenth-century Flanders, England still lacks any study comparable in scale and detail.[1] One reason for this lacuna may be the difficulty of the subject, what Berndt Moeller called its 'particular elusiveness', or its resistance, as Malcolm Vale pointed out, to measurement and quantification.[2] An even more potent explanation may be the very success of the English Reformation and of Protestant and Erasmian propaganda, which together have largely discouraged extended investigation into the doomed pieties and practices of the orthodox. English medievalists and Reformation scholars alike have tended to approach later medieval religion with Wycliffite and Lollard denouncements and survival in the forefront of their minds. And yet in the fifteenth century the ordinary religion of the townsmen and villagers of England becomes more accessible to the historian than at any time previously, for it is from this century that wills begin to survive in significant numbers, not least in the archives of the diocese and province of York. To test the value of this evidence, to assess the problems which it poses,[3] and to complement the work of Dr. Vale on the Yorkshire gentry, the present study is focused on the religion of the community of Hull from the beginning of the fifteenth century up to the eve of the Reformation, from 1400 to 1529.

The only substantial industry in medieval and early Tudor Hull was shipping and this ought to make it a particularly interesting community for the study of late medieval piety. Its trading connections extended from Portugal and Spain to Lübeck and Danzig.[4] If much of the Baltic trade was carried in Hanse ships, this resulted in North Germans, Pomeranians and Lübeckers being frequent – if not perhaps always welcome – visitors to Hull. Possibly of more significance was the trade – the main part of Hull's business – with the Low Countries whence there might have filtered back, not so much through the seamen as through the merchants, some traces of the *Devotio Moderna*. The English coastal trade involved contacts with Boston and Lynn as well as with London and Newcastle. Inland and family connections extended to Lincolnshire, Holderness, Doncaster, Pontefract, Beverley and York. So Hull could be a melting pot of different European and English traditions – orthodox, as Gordon Forster has said,[5] but in a variety of interesting ways.

Ecclesiastically the structure of Hull was simpler than one might at first expect in a city of its kind. It was, for one thing, too recent a growth to have within its walls the institutional variety of York, Norwich or Bristol. It had no great monastic house, no Benedictine or Augustinian foundation. It was even too late to attract the Franciscans and Dominicans, who were already established in Beverley; instead, the Carmelite and Augustinian friars colonised Hull. Even its two parish churches were strictly speaking chapels with parochial attributes: Holy Trinity, the principal one, a chapel of ease of Hessle, itself appropriated to, and served by, the Augustinian canons of Guisborough; and St. Mary Lowgate, appropriated to the nearer house of Augustinian canons at North Ferriby and served by a stipendiary chaplain. As well as the parochial chaplains at each of these, there were several chantry priests; and at Holy Trinity twelve of the latter with a clerk were, from 1409 at least, organized into a college; living in houses in the churchyard, they were known as the Priests of the Table and each was appointed jointly by the mayor of Hull and the vicar of Hessle.[6] A mile north of the city wall stood the Charterhouse founded in the late fourteenth century by the De La Poles. Together, these institutions served a community of over – probably well over – 2,000 souls. In terms of aggregate taxable wealth Hull citizens lagged behind the burgesses of Lavenham and were well down the national list; nevertheless, among them were some comfortable merchant families, if none with quite the De La Poles' flair for opulence.[7]

The wills of Hull testators were usually proved in the exchequer court of the archbishop of York, and overwhelmingly the texts were entered in that court's probate registers.[8] Very frequently, although the will was registered there, probate itself was conducted in Hull by the dean of Harthill, or else in the vicinity of Hull by some other official specially commissioned to act for the exchequer court: thus in 1448 John Burnham's will was proved at Cottingham by the rector there, who was also receiver of the archbishop's exchequer.[9] Although the series of probate registers is extensive, there are some notable gaps: the registers contain no wills – from any part of the diocese – from October 1408 to March 1417 and from January 1418 to May 1426; other lapses in the registers for the rest of our period amount to some two and a half years.[10] Moreover, some twenty-five wills which were proved on commission by the dean of Harthill are unrecorded at York; they are noted in the dean's act books which begin to survive only from the early sixteenth century. Even in the exchequer registers there are some notes of probate unaccompanied by texts of the wills concerned. Eight other Hull wills are recorded in the archiepiscopal registers between 1409 and 1425, but none thereafter.

No probate jurisdiction pertained to the office of the archdeacon of the East Riding, and the competence of the dean and chapter of York did not extend to Hull. Nor did anyone else execute probate there except on *ad hoc* commissions from the exchequer court. Nevertheless, Hull wills are to be found in other courts. As many Hull merchants had far-flung business and property interests, it is not surprising that a few – four in all for this period – had their wills proved in the Prerogative court of Canterbury; two of these were also registered at York.[11] At least one Hull man even had his will proved before the dean and chapter of St. Paul's, London, and we would have known nothing of this but for the Hull city records.[12] Sometimes, when the terms of a will conferred extended responsibilities upon the mayor and aldermen of Hull, the original probated text was handed over to the city authorities either to be kept in their archives or to be copied into their Bench Books. Three original wills, two with notes and seals of probate, are still extant, though no trace of them is to be found at York; and one other, also unknown at York, is copied into a Bench Book.[13]

From all these sources, for a city of more than 2,000 souls over a period of 130 years, a mere 355 wills have been studied. Extrapolating from the extant material and records, it is probable that altogether no more than 500 wills were proved in this period; others were probably made but not submitted for probate. The occasional intestate records prove that not everyone made a will;[14] but that a larger proportion of the populace was doing so, and having them proved, at the end of our period than at the beginning is not entirely clear. While 120 will texts survive for the first three decades of the sixteenth century, 103 are extant from the years 1450 to 1480. The 1490s, however, yield only fourteen texts, and no gap in the records accounts for this apparent decline. Behind these fluctuations in the number of registered and known wills, there may lurk an alternation of energetic and feckless registrars or deans or receivers. More probably, changes in the mortality rate are operating, but without firm census figures this is impossible to calculate; moreover, there is not a single reference in these wills to plague or to the English sweat, and few indeed of the testators confess to being sick at all.[15] One hazard of these fluctuations is that certain features of piety may seem more common in one decade than in another simply because wills are more common then.

Clearly, Hull wills allow us access to the religious norms of a minority of the inhabitants only, and this minority is a social and economic élite. Not till the 1530s does a Hull testator describe himself as a labourer: our men are merchants, traders, craftsmen and mariners; our women are their wives and widows. A corollary of this is that no change in the social status of the testators can explain the difference in language between the earlier and later wills. A third of the wills – 119 out of 355 – are in English, but there is no vernacular will before 1453, and there are only six in the next three decades; the last twenty years of the fifteenth century yield eleven more English wills, the first thirty years of the sixteenth no fewer than 101.[16] These bare figures mask the steep rise which took place in the 1480s, for whereas in each of the previous three decades English wills had formed about 5% or 6% of the total, in the 1480s the ratio rose to 24%, and in the 1490s to 43%; in 1500–10, 68% are in English, and in the next two decades over 90%.

It seems uncertain that this transformation reflects a change of scribe. We know that around 1500 John Dalton, Thomas Dalton, and William Goodknape wrote their own wills in English, and that Robert Bere, the common clerk of the city, and John Yoele wrote a number of wills – in the 1450s and 1480s respectively – in Latin; but very few other wills record who penned them.[17] In any event, the change of language was not accompanied by any innovation in the form of the will or in the pattern of bequests. If many more people wrote their own wills as English became an acceptable medium, it still seems probable that they enlisted some guidance – from a cleric or notary or scrivener or directly from a written formulary – for the shape and agenda of the will. It is precisely the problem of evaluating the resultant commonplaces and the occasional eccentricities which makes will-evidence as treacherous to use as it is beguiling to cite. The historian who exploits wills must evade the dangers of being deluded on the one hand by statistics and on the other by impressions.

So far as the reliability of individual texts is concerned, there are few records by which one may test this; the best opportunity is in the will drawn up by William Goodknape in 1502, for a notarially attested copy of this was produced in evidence in a lawsuit thirteen years later and is still extant.[18] The copy differs from the registered version in a number of respects. Firstly, place-names, of which there are several, have clearly been standardized (not modernized) in the probate register. Secondly, no reference appears in the notarial copy to the will being written, as the register asserts, in Goodknape's own hand. Thirdly, the notary's copy includes a bequest – not in the register – of his soul to Jesus. Finally, the notary's copy also records an addition, dated 7 May 1503, granting the executors discretion if the money proved inadequate for the bequests – the very point then at issue – and praying mercy from Jesus and Mary, St. Michael and all the saints in heaven. Clearly some revealing clauses may be missing from the York register, where signs of carelessness abound, but the omissions appear to be too limited to alter significantly the overall picture which emerges from the wills. What perhaps is more worth remarking in the Goodknape example is the discrepancy between bequest and reality. Not only were executors sometimes unreliable, but testators were sometimes so unrealistic about the extent of their wealth that one suspects they readily subscribed to the maxim that 'it's the thought that counts'. Even where bequests were fulfilled, details could be posthumously changed or an unconscionable, and now inexplicable, delay elapse before fulfilment; thus the chantry provided for in the will of John Tutbury, who died in 1434, was only established, as we learn from the city records, in 1453.[19] And not only do wills sometimes tell us of plans which in the event were not realised, but of course they sometimes say nothing of important matters which did happen; for example, two perpetual chantries endowed in the fifteenth century are unmentioned in our wills.[20]

In the light of all these qualifications, what follows is not a definitive account of religion in late medieval Hull, but simply a picture seen through one particularly large, though undoubtedly limited, aperture.

What impelled most testators to make a will is seldom explicitly stated and even then few ventured beyond the briefest common form. When John Wardall, for example, spoke in 1521 of 'this transitory life', he was voicing an apprehension no doubt common enough among the merchants and mariners commuting between Hull and the Continent.[21] In 1480 John Hardy, merchant, had made his will '*proponens visitare terram Seland causa mercandisi*'; and in 1517 another merchant, John Gegges, made his, 'considering myself oftentimes to be in peril both by water and land'.[22] Richard Doughty, in 1485, probably spoke for most when he compiled his will, 'considering the unstable estate of man and what chance ensueth daily in every age for the inconstant demeanour of man, providing always that wisdom is a man always to be ready and prest when he shall be called upon'.[23] Four other men were more expansive. In 1487 John Dalton, merchant, began his will with these words:

'I considering and remembering think in my heart that the days of men in this mortal life be but short and that the number of death is in the hand of Almighty God; and that he hath ordained the terms that no man may pass; remembering also that God hath ordained man to die, and there is nothing more certain than death and nothing more uncertain than the hour of death, I seeing daily die princes and great estates and men of all ages end their days, and that death gives no respite certain to living creatures but takes them suddenly. For that consideration, I being in my right wit and mind (loved be God), whole and not sick, beseeching Almighty God that I may die the true son of holy kirk, of heart truly confessed, with contrition and repentance of all my sins that ever I did since the first hour I was born of my mother into this sinful world unto the hour of my death; of which offences I ask and beseek

Almighty God of pardon and forgiveness. And in this I beseech the Blessed Virgin Mary and her blessed son Jhesu our Saviour that suffered for me and all sinful creatures, and all the holy company of paradise to pray for me etc., for these causes aforesaid. I doubting to die intestate, I being of live and whole mind and memory (loved be God), I dispose and ordain such goods as God hath lent me, moveable and immoveable, my testament devise and ordain of this my last will in the form and manner that followeth.'[24]

Ten years later, in 1497, a year after John's death, his brother, Thomas Dalton, repeated almost verbatim John's words cited above.[25] The identical words were used again twenty-three years later, in April 1520, by another merchant, Robert Harryson, who had formerly been an apprentice of John's, had married John's widow and left 10s. to each of the four sons of Thomas Dalton.[26] The next year, in April 1521, another merchant, Henry Walker, began his will with almost the same words; his connections with Dalton have yet to be established.[27] All four men explicitly stated that they had written their wills themselves – but their independence clearly had its limits. These are the only wills which break away from the standard formulae and they may be taken to reveal a shared family concern about the fate of their souls and a keen sense of the need for redemption.

Whatever the reason for making a will, the first task of the testator was to dispose of his soul. Almost all commend their soul to Almighty God, the Virgin Mary and all the saints – or the celestial company and court – of heaven. In a dozen wills God is described as 'my creator', and in five as 'my saviour'. John Kyme in 1408 and William Dene in 1446 each commended his soul to Almighty God 'who redeemed it with his precious blood'.[28] Otherwise there is very little explicit acknowledgement of redemption, least of all through Christ. Indeed, only in eight wills is the soul committed to Christ, and only in one of these – where Richard Russell in 1445 offers his soul 'into the hands of Jesus Christ' – does the emphasis or expression justify allusions to a Christocentric piety.[29] John Dalton, in 1487, mingled his appeal to Christ with too many other invocations:

'I recommend in humble devotion, contrition and very repentance of my defaults and sins, praying and crying to our saviour, Jhesu Christ. And in this I commend and will my soul to our Lord Jhesu Christ when it shall depart from my body and to Our Lady Saint Mary, St. Michael, St. John Baptist, St. John the Evangelist, St. Katherine, and St. Barbara and all the holy company and saints of heaven.'[30]

Thomas Dalton, in 1497, using identical terms, added a few more saints by name: St. Peter, St. Thomas, St. Antony, St. Sebastian, and St. Ursula.[31] Robert Harryson, in 1520, omitted St. John the Baptist and Thomas Dalton's additions, but added St. James.[32] Henry Walker, in 1521, simply entrusted his soul to Jesus, St. Mary, St. Michael, St. John the Baptist, St. John the Evangelist, and all the company of saints in heaven.[33] With Peter Burton, who, in 1460, called upon St.

Katherine and St. Agatha, and William Goodknape, who, in 1502, named St. Michael, these are the only testators who commend their souls to specific saints.[34] Perhaps it is significant that they are clustered towards the end of our period, but the Dalton circle is really too intimate to justify any generalisations about changing attitudes in Hull piety. What is notable is the individuality within that group of men; they were not just mindless plagiarists.

Surprisingly in a city whose principal church was dedicated to the Holy Trinity, souls rarely were. Margaret Chery in 1401 commended her soul to 'Almighty God, Father, Son and Holy Ghost'; and Thomas Beauchamp, a chaplain, dedicated his soul in 1428 'to the high and most holy Trinity' as well as to the Blessed Virgin and all the saints.[35] In 1460 Thomas Johnson began his will with an invocation of the Holy Trinity, but left his soul conventionally to God Almighty, the Blessed Virgin and all the saints.[36] Only one other testator left his soul to the Trinity, William Tailour in 1509, and he added the Blessed Virgin and sought the prayers of the holy company of heaven.[37] Usually the Virgin supplants the second and third persons of the Trinity, and she is often described by the ancient Christian formula as mother of God ('his mother').

Fourteen testators simply commended their souls to God Almighty alone. However, to read any Protestant tendencies into this would be absurd since they all ante-date 1517; one cannot even be sure that they reflect Lollard or other radical and austere influences.[38] In three of the wills there are bequests to various guilds, and in one of these wills there is also provision for a pilgrimage to Rome; four others are patently brief and hurried, one a nuncupative will. There are no references to saints or guilds or shrines in the remainder, but masses, obits and trentals do occur. That six of these fourteen wills date from the 1450s seems less significant when three of them contain references to guilds and one other is very brief. Hasty composition or careless registration, rather than any theological re-orientation, is the more likely explanation of these commendations.

After the commendation of the soul came the disposal of the body. The vast majority of the testators – over 200 of them – wished to be buried inside Holy Trinity church, usually in the south aisle of the choir before or next to some specific image or altar. Some sixty-four sought burial inside St. Mary's church. Twenty-four were content to be buried in the churchyards. Nine wished to be buried in the Austin Friars, two in the Carmelite house, and two in the Charterhouse. Most of the rest – often travelling as mariners or merchants – left it to executors to secure for them some sort of Christian burial wherever they should die. Burial within the parish churches was socially prestigious and usually £1 or £2 was paid for the privilege or ostensibly for the work involved. Those to be interred inside the churches were ex-mayors, sheriffs, aldermen, chamberlains. Holy Trinity in particular must have seemed like a Council Chamber of deceased civic officers and their wives. Just as the nobility and the gentry had their family vaults in neighbouring churches and abbeys, so the burghers of Hull had their civic or corporation vaults in Holy Trinity and, to a lesser extent, in St. Mary's.[39]

It is no wonder, then, that the building of these churches was a major preoccupation of our testators. During this period the nave of Holy Trinity was being extended and completed.[40] In 1401 and 1404 money was left for the hire of a mason, respectively for one year and for half a year; in 1406 and 1408 quantities of lead were bequeathed.[41] Alan Wilcox left £5 for glazing in 1408, and in 1412 John Birkyn assigned £4 to the making of the great window in 'le Westgavell' (the west gable); a further 6s. 8d. was donated, by John Wysdom in 1419, for the making of a window in the west part of Holy Trinity.[42] At the same time other money was being given for paving the church. Half a century on, in 1458, John Dalton left £1 for work newly built on the north side of the church, and in 1460 John Adam earmarked £1 for the new construction.[43] The great bell tower of Holy Trinity, though begun in the fourteenth century, was only completed at the end of our period. Between 1518 and 1529 it attracted no fewer than seven specific bequests amounting in all to £18. 10s.[44]

During the fifteenth century a succession of donations was also made for completing and adorning the high altar. In 1427 William Hedon left the proceeds of the sale of land towards the construction of the reredos; Alice Bilton in 1441 bequeathed £1 for painting an image of the Blessed Virgin which was newly completed at the side of the high altar; four years later William Proktour gave £1 for painting an image over the high altar, and in 1448 William Yonge left 6s. 8d. for painting of the angels above it, a further 10s. for which was given by Elizabeth Harwod in 1474.[45] In the next decade Roger Busshell set aside £8 for a canopy for the holy sacrament on the high altar.[46] Other testators left various lengths of cloth – linen and twill – and towels, and Agnes Ellis in 1505 gave her best beads of coral (her rosary, presumably) to be hung about the skirts (sic) of the same altar.[47]

In addition to these donations for the fabric and fittings of Holy Trinity, some £130 was given towards liturgical needs. Five pounds was left for a new antiphoner in 1448, but more money was lavished upon vestments than books.[48] In 1437 John Gregg bequeathed £50 for four red copes, an example not wasted on some of his successors: William Proktour in 1445 provided £13. 6s. 8d. for a cope of the same colour and pattern as Gregg's; in 1479 John Whitfelde and in 1483 Roger Busshell each left £20 for a cope.[49] Fortunately, William Clederow had left £3 in 1454 to provide a cupboard in which to keep the copes.[50]

Other altars, of which there were many, and various lights in the church and its chapels attracted a total of £90 in legacies over the whole period. However, excluded from all these figures are the additional and unspecified sums which the executors of wills may have given from the residue of the estate; nor do they include sums donated – and often originating from the same citizens – by the guilds. The guild of St. Mary, for example, one of only two for which we have extant accounts, assigned during this period £10 to the church rebuilding and nearly £20 for the renewal of the organs in the Lady Chapel of Holy Trinity.[51]

St. Mary's church, a much smaller structure, fared scarcely less well in this time. Over £200 was given towards its building. At least £26 of this was intended for the bell tower, which was begun in the 1450s, and for the bells. Twelve testators remembered the building of the steeple in their wills, six others made bequests explicitly for the bells. In addition £100 was left in cash or kind towards the vestments; but less than £10 was bestowed upon the altars, of which St. Mary's had far fewer than Holy Trinity.

It is clear from other sources that a very imperfect record of the money given for the building and adornment of the parish churches is to be found in the wills; nevertheless, one can count bequests amounting to at least £800, quite apart from the undisclosed sums set aside for this purpose by executors. The scale of this expenditure bears eloquent witness to the communal pride and personal enthusiasm which were invested in the town's churches; in particular, the bell tower was a prominent landmark of parochial *amour propre* and, as we shall see, a valued facility in the ritual of death.

The fabric and fittings were important for accommodating suitably not only the deceased's body but also the funeral and the ensuing commemorations. Indeed, almost of more concern than where one was buried was how one was buried. Several testators wanted priests – even on occasions all the priests and friars of the town – and the poor, in varying numbers, to be present at their interment. Many specified that the twelve Priests of the Table and their clerk should attend the funeral and the great bell be rung 'as is accustomed for the souls of notable men of the town', and the bellman 'to go about according to the use and custom of the town' on the day of the funeral, and on the seventh day and the month's day and year's day as well.[52] Henry Paty in 1504 required the Priests of the Table and their clerk to sing *dirige* and mass at his burial 'according to the custom of the church', but it was not only in Holy Trinity that they operated: Isabell Obsam in 1517 wanted them to attend her burial in St. Mary's.[53]

In the early years of the fifteenth century – there appears to be a marked decline in the latter part – funerals were often accompanied by extravagant expenditure on wax torches and crosses to surround the hearse. In 1405 Agnes Styllyngflet provided 32 lbs. of wax for this purpose; William Fyrsmarsk in 1431 and John Hesill four years later were each content with a mere 20 lbs.[54] John Garton in 1456 left not only £2 to buy twelve torches but also 12 lbs. of wax for two candles and a candle cross to burn about his body on the day of his burial.[55] All this was surpassed in 1438 by widow Gregg who arranged for no fewer than eighteen torches to burn about her body: altogether she set aside £40 for the torches and for doles to each priest, friar and pauper at her exequies.[56] John Swan in 1476 left £30 for the expenses of his funeral, seventh day and anniversary.[57] William Goodknape's inventory records the expenses after his death: £17. 11s. 4d. for the day of his burial, £10. 17s. 10d. for his twelve-month day, and £5. 19s. for his second-year day – in all a sum which would have kept a chantry priest going for seven years.[58]

Of all Hull's testators, only one expressly scorned this ostentation: John Fitlyng, burgess, in 1434 empowered his executor to provide for his funeral and the octave, but to do only what was necessary for the praise of God and to avoid all appearances of vainglory, remembering the Apostle's words, 'Conform not to this world'.[59] The alms which Fitlyng bequeathed included 5d. to be given each Friday for one year to five poor and sick men in honour of the five wounds of Christ (a devotion unique to this will in Hull): 5d. to five poor women each Saturday for one year in honour of the Blessed Virgin Mary; and 3d. to three poor men each Sunday in honour of the Holy Trinity. Fitlyng's words and arrangements are a revealing commentary upon his fellow burgesses.

Most testators who prescribed the detailed form of their funerals also made some provision for commemoration on the octave of their burial, sometimes even for the month's mind, and frequently for the anniversary in one or more successive years; a few made perpetual arrangements. John Scalys in 1467 stipulated that a perpetual obit for his own soul, and those of his wife, daughter, parents and benefactors, was to be performed by the clergy and chaplains of the Table in the choir of Holy Trinity: on the evening preceding the anniversary of his death exequies were to be observed; on the day of the anniversary itself a mass for the dead was to be celebrated; and the great bell was to be rung for the exequies and the mass 'as is the custom in that church or chapel for the more noble and distinguished of the town'.[60] William Ripplingham in 1464 wanted his obit to be celebrated in Holy Trinity in perpetuity by the vicar and the Priests of the Table and the clerk, with the great bells being rung first, as was the custom, and the bellringer going through the town.[61] Elizabeth Garner in 1513 insisted on an obit for her late husband and herself 'solemnly as for an alderman'.[62]

On occasions, for the obit as for the funeral, the tomb was ostentatiously adorned. Asselia (?Alice) de Malton in 1402 left to the guild of Corpus Christi a baldaquin of silk to cover her tomb and that of her husbands on the day of the obit.[63] Similarly Agnes Styllyngflete in 1405 left her bed-cover to the guild of St. Katherine; Thomas York forty years later, in 1445, left his best bed-cover to his son 'to be placed over my tomb when my exequies are celebrated'; Alison Wynder in 1506 arranged for her bed 'to cover the hearse over my husband and me every year during the space that he and I have mass and dirige' within the Austin friars.[64] Display reached its pinnacle with Joan Thurscrosse in 1523: a baldaquin of black velvet was to be made specially to cover the hearse in St. Mary's; on the cloth an image of the Holy Trinity was to be wrought in gold, and a dead man in a winding sheet was to be depicted lying before the Trinity, while at the sides there were to be four angels, in gold and needlework, with candlesticks in their hands as though they were giving reverence to the Trinity, and at the feet of the dead man was to be written, 'for a memorial'.[65] That Joan should speak not of a woman in winding sheet but of the generic man seems to deprive this representation of any morbid egotism and to leave it as a visual representation of the cliché about transient life. In total some fifty-seven testators requested obits at fees ranging from 2s. to 6s. 8d. per annum; thirty-four of them were to be perpetual and seven others were to last for twenty years or more. About this recurring obit with its display and the social awareness of its founders, there was prominent a concern for the esteem of this world, whatever anxieties about the next may have been implied.

When we turn to trentals, the celebration of thirty requiem masses in quick succession after death, a much greater concern with the next world is evident. Only thirty-nine testators made bequests for trentals and only for 102 – less than an average of three apiece – at that. The cost of a trental varied from 5s. to 6s. 8d. or even on rare occasions up to 10s.; the more expensive, twenty-four trentals out of the 102, were usually those of St. Gregory. Most bequests were for two trentals – one at each of the friaries in Hull – but sometimes four were specified, the Dominicans and Franciscans of Beverley also being enlisted; occasionally a fifth in Holy Trinity was requested. A few testators were content with merely one, usually in Holy Trinity and with the Priests of the Table. William Clederow in 1454 was unusually extravagant in requiring nine and also unusually independent in his choice of form: he specified that three trentals of the Father, Son and Holy Ghost, three of Our Lady, and three Requiem trentals should be performed, three (one of each, presumably) at the Charterhouse, three at the Austin and three at the Carmelite friaries.[66] Although it was common for testators to want their trentals completed immediately after death, as did William Gelyot in 1449 and Hans Martyn in 1453, some were less urgent; John Garton in 1456 was content to have his within a year of his death, but in his case there were other insurance policies to realise.[67] In any event, thirty or sixty or 120 masses or, as with Clederow, 270 masses express urgency simply by their numbers. What seems worth stressing here however is that only a small rump of the social élite which constituted Hull's testators sought trentals at all, cheap though they were (cost-efficient, one might say); and few of these few exceeded moderation.

Other testators, not necessarily with more means, and some testators who had purchased trentals, invested in daily masses over a period of years. That barely a dozen contemplated the establishment of a perpetual chantry is possibly explained by the expenses that would be incurred for the required inquisition and licence, but there were undoubtedly people of considerable resources who positively preferred to organize their piety round different priorities. Three testators – in 1460, 1464, and 1497 – provided for perpetual chantries only if their heirs in the second generation should become extinct, which evidently did not happen.[68] On the other hand, the bequest of Robert Holme in 1449 for a perpetual chantry to be established at the altar of St. Anne in St. Mary's church and to be administered by the mayor and aldermen seems to have failed for some reason which is now obscured.[69] In the event, a mere seven perpetual chantries materialised between 1400 and 1529, though two of these – Aldwyke's, in 1448, and Alcock's, in 1482 – find no mention in our wills.[70] Two perpetual chantries were located in St. Mary's church – Aldwyke's at the altar of St. James, and Geoffrey Thurscrosse's at the altar of St. Anne – and all the rest were sited in Holy Trinity church.[71] They were each served, except perhaps Aldwyke's, by one of the Priests of the Table, and they were all administered by the mayor and aldermen, although Haynson's was only indirectly in their control as the guild of St. Mary took responsibility for his foundation.[72] John Tutbury in 1432 and John Bedford in 1450 each itemised service books and vessels and vestments in their wills for the use of their chantries; it is likely that for the other foundations the executors provided these items.[73]

Apart from the perpetual chantries envisaged and realised, money was assigned by 122 testators to pay priests to celebrate masses for a year or more, almost exclusively in the parish churches and usually at a rate of £4. 13s. 4d. or £5 per annum. The average duration of the endowment was about three years, but while one can point to examples of twenty years, few in fact exceeded ten and most were much less. For the most part, the details of performance were left to the executors to spell out in foundation deeds; John Ryddesdale, in 1479, was unusual in specifying in his will that the priest, who was to celebrate for his soul for one year at the altar of St. John the Baptist, in Holy Trinity church, should come 'immediately after the mass to my tomb and say the psalm *de profundis* and the accompanying prayers and sprinkle holy water'.[74]

Altogether some 164 testators, almost half the total, made bequests for one or more of these commemorations of the soul. Just over fifty invested in two types of provision, and only a handful in all three. In total these bequests conferred well over £1,000, and probably nearer £2,000, upon the clergy in payment for masses. Although much of this money would be transferred by annual instalments, sometimes over a long period, a high proportion was undoubtedly transmitted within the lifetime of the first heirs, and overwhelmingly this money was assigned to the secular clergy of the city.

The friars attracted regular, but not invariable, legacies, and most of these were for trentals. A total of 139 testators left an average of slightly over 15s. each to the Austin friars, £107 in all, while 163 testators left the Carmelite house an average of just under 10s., or a total of £70. Nearly all those who contributed to the Austin friars also remembered the Carmelites. Both houses elicited as well certain gifts in kind: barrels of honey, fothers of lead, saltfish, rosaries, towels and a bed. The difference in the totals of money left to each house, and hence the difference in the average legacy, is explained by the largest donation of all, given by Thomas Prestone to the Austin friars in 1451.[75] He bequeathed £33. 6s. 8d. for the purchase of lead and wood and for the hire of labourers so that the north aisle of their church, in which he wished to be buried, could be properly roofed. Although barely a handful of people sought burial in the friaries, a number of others requested and rewarded their presence at funerals and commemorations elsewhere. For example, William Hapsham, in 1521, left 6s. 8d. to each house of friars in Hull provided that 'they come and do *dirige* and mass according to the old custom of the town', and he was buried in Holy Trinity;[76] three years later, James Haull left 3s. 4d. to each order of friars in the town 'as they do the custom of the said town'.[77] (It is not clear whether this custom concerns the friars principally or the form of the *dirige* and mass.) In 1527 John Cokett, who was to be buried in the Charterhouse, bestowed 6s. 8d. on each friary in Hull so that their inmates should attend his burial and octave and anniversary.[78]

Although in all this period prayers and obits and trentals were sought from the friars with considerable frequency, there are only three instances of people establishing chantries in these houses. In 1453 Hans Martyn provided for masses from the Austin friars for three years and left it to his executor to agree on the stipend to be paid.[79] In 1503 John Johnson gave £2. 6s. 8d. to the prior of the Austin friars to sing for his soul for a half a year.[80] And in the same year Beatrix Bellard, who was to be buried in the Carmelite chapel of the Blessed Virgin, requested masses there for as long as funds lasted.[81] Whether this reluctance to entrust chantries to the friars resulted from deliberate discouragement by the friars or from a suspicion on the part of the laity that those orders, or at least those communities, might not be relied upon to sustain a daily obligation, or even from some notions of the relative spiritual worth of the suffrage of the various clergy in the city are questions unanswerable from the evidence available.

Perhaps the most surprising feature of Hull's testators is their seeming indifference to the nearby Carthusians. In sharp contrast with the friaries, the Charterhouse was virtually ignored by the will-makers. Carthusians figure in only twenty-three wills, and three of these contain no bequest to them: in one the prior and convent were appointed trustees for a chantry and an obit to be established in Holy Trinity; in two other wills the prior was named as supervisor.[82] Of the meagre total of £42 which was assigned to the house throughout the period, no less than £33. 6s. 8d. came in two legacies, one, in 1449, of £20 for a perpetual obit, the other, in 1420, of twenty marks for their daily prayers over four years.[83] A century later the Carthusians might have gained £300 by the will of Geoffrey Thurscrosse if the mayor and aldermen had reneged on a trust, but this unlikely contingency was anyway overtaken by the events which extinguished the Charterhouse altogether.[84]

Of the two men who sought burial in the Charterhouse, Robert Goldyng in 1453 and John Cokett in 1527, Goldyng tells us that his uncle was the prior at that time.[85] Goldyng's will is all the more interesting because it contains the sole reference that we have to the iconography of some of the glass of medieval Hull. He left £4 towards a window between the chapels of the Holy Trinity and St. Hugh in the Charterhouse; it was to have three lights, depicting the Blessed Virgin flanked by St. John Baptist and St. Thomas of Canterbury, and at her feet was to be the donor genuflecting.

These items apart, there is no evidence to show that the Hull Charterhouse exercised the sort of influence and attraction upon its immediate neighbours which Mount Grace and London did upon theirs. Nor is there any firm evidence of intellectual or spiritual distinction in this Charterhouse (or, indeed, in the friaries).[86] More than that, the house was perhaps too readily associated with the De La Poles to elicit the interest of Hull's burgesses. Most of all, however, until 1518, when Wolsey patched up a typically ingenious agreement, the Charter-house and the city were in chronic dispute over the exercise of jurisdiction in the area, known as the Trippett, between the city walls and the monastery precincts.[87]

Against this background, it looks as if Sir Ralph Ellerker was pleading a special cause rather than recording fact when he reported to Cromwell in 1536 that the Charterhouse was 'well favoured and commended by the honest men of Hull' who 'also desire this house may be continued'.[88] It is true that someone paid over £200 for its continuance beyond 1536, but that perhaps reflects a fear that a new landlord there, especially if he were a courtier, might upset the arrangements so skilfully wrought by Wolsey.[89] The friaries, on behalf of which no protest is recorded, offered an opportunity for Hull merchants to extend their holdings, but monasteries were apt to fall into the hands of Londoners and courtiers.

It was not only from the parish and chantry clergy and from the religious that prayerful support was enlisted by our testators; they also turned to anchorites and fellow laymen. In 1418 John Sandyrson left 6s. 8d. to Dominus William Raskyll, chaplain and recluse of Hull.[90] By 1438, however, Joan Gregg, and in 1464 John Grene, apparently had to resort to Beverley to find a hermit.[91] No Hull ankerhouse figures in these wills, and though one is heard of in city leases of 1467 and 1481, it is in terms which do not conclusively suggest a hermit's abode.[92] There does not appear to have been in Hull anything like the succession of recluses encountered throughout this period in Norwich.[93] Although there were certainly two widow-vowesses in the sixteenth century, Dame Joan York and Dame Joan Thurscrosse, no close parallel with Dame Julian of Norwich should be drawn.[94] They attracted no bequests and elicited no mention in the wills of others: if Dame Thurscrosse refers in her will to 'those for whom I am bound to pray', she was not alone in this; Edmund Riddalle, a merchant, remembered in his will of 1517 'all those I am bounden to pray for'.[95] In fact, a number of testators asked for the prayers of their fellows (and not simply of the poor, though this was common enough). In 1486 William Davell left 3s. 4d. to William Hambleton for his prayers, and, in 1490, Edmund Copyndale bequeathed an identical sum to William Haryngton for an identical purpose; Laurence Swattok, two years later, left his best primer, as well as 6s. 8d., to Thomas Fisher with the same request.[96] However, the most notable example of this practice occurs in the will of Alexander Wharton, merchant, in 1506: not only the poor, but his brother, his son-in-law, his friends and associates, even his servants received their legacies – amounting in all to £44. 10s. – in return for their prayers, which were in addition to those of the town's friars and of a mass priest for three years.[97]

Most obviously layfolk prayed for each other in the guilds, membership of which was enjoyed by many testators. There were at least twelve religious confraternities attached to Holy Trinity church and three more in St. Mary's, and there were others elsewhere in the city: the guild of St. Ninian, for example, seems to have been located in the Carmelite house, and in mid-century Holy Trinity guild acquired its own separate chapel in Beverleygate and was identified primarily with seafarers; the guild of St. Nicholas the Bishop, mentioned only in the wills of two priests and probably, therefore, a clerical brotherhood, is of uncertain location.[98] While some confraternities were intended for specialised membership, many were open to all, and some testators were cetainly members of several guilds. John Gregg, in 1437, left £1 to each of guilds of Corpus Christi, Holy Trinity, St. Mary, St. Giles, St. Katherine, and St. Anne, all in Holy Trinity church; his wife repeated these bequests in her will a year later.[99] Francis Bukk, in 1453, made gifts to seven of these guilds and to the guilds of St. Christopher in York, and St. John in Beverley.[100] In 1521 Arthur Welles left 12d. 'to each of the guilds that I am brother in' and then named the confraternities of the Resurrection, the Blessed Virgin, and St. George.[101] Dame Joan Thurscrosse, in 1523, assigned 3s. 4d. to each of the guilds of St. Mary's church and named those of Jhesu, St. James, and St. Helen.[102] By membership, of course, the testators shared in the spiritual profits of the masses and obits sponsored by the guilds, but not all of these maintained their own priest. When John Swan left 6s. 8d., in 1476, to each guild in the city having a priest he reckoned on a total sum of £2.[103] The other guilds no doubt employed one of the Priests of the Table *ad hoc*.

Confraternities, of course, were dedicated to particular saints or feasts, and many of them had their own altar and image or light. There were also a number of altars, images and lights seemingly unattached to a guild: we hear, for example, of the altar of St. Lawrence in Holy Trinity church, and of the altar of St. Antony and the image of St. Christopher in St. Mary's church.[104] It was before or near these images and altars that many testators asked to be buried. At the turn of the century the altar of Corpus Christi particularly attracted bequests. In 1497 Thomas Dalton left £8 for the purchase of a table of 'oversea work' to be set at this altar, and in 1502 William Goodknape bequeathed £20 for a table for it.[105] Perhaps these provisions were not realised, for in 1520 another merchant, Robert Harryson, also left £10 for a table of 'oversea work', and he stipulated that it was to depict the Corpus Christi story.[106] What evidently is intended in these bequests is the sort of carved retable so common on the continent, especially in the Low Countries and the Rhineland where our testators so often travelled and traded. The repetition of the same bequest by men so closely linked in other ways suggests perhaps that the last two were under some obligation to fulfil Dalton's original legacy. No other shrine attracted such substantial gifts; of the rest, the images of the Trinity and of Our Lady of Pity seem marginally the most popular in our wills.

Other indications of the cult of saints are few. Souls, as we have seen, were rarely commended to particular saints. Nor can private images be said to abound, if their occurrence in the wills is a true reflection of their numbers; a ring with an image of the Trinity on it was left by Margaret Hansford in 1447; a head of St. John the Baptist by John Bedford in 1450; a chain with a cross of gold by Richard Bille in 1451; a silver ring with a Katherine wheel by Agnes Bedford in 1459; a St. John's head and a St. James's shell by Elizabeth Gilliott in 1460; a painted cloth 'de vita Job' by Katherine Chereborough in 1477; and a 'covering of Arras having the picture of Our Lady riding into Egypt wrought on it' by Joan Thurscrosse in 1523. [107]

This restrained devotion to the saints is reflected again in the few references to pilgrimage. Only two testators, John Welles in 1445 and Richard Bille in 1451, left any money for a pilgrimage to be made posthumously. [108] Very few indeed left money to shrines elsewhere. The will of Richard Wilflete in 1520, with its bequests to Our Lady of Walsingham and to the Holy Blood at Wilsnack, as it is printed in the Testamenta Eboracensia is apt there to give a quite misleading impression that Hull citizens were prone to subscribe to these remote and glamorous shrines. [109] So far from that being so, even the nearer and less exotic shrines of St. John of Beverley, St. John of Bridlington, St. William of York, St. Wilfrid of Ripon and St. Robert of Knaresborough emphatically lacked support in Hull. John Welles alone left money to Beverley's saint, 4d. to be offered by a pilgrim on his behalf. [110] John Harpham left 3s. 4d. each to the fabric of the churches, rather than to the shrines, of York, Beverley, Southwell, Ripon and Knaresborough. [111] Rome attracted slightly more attention. Richard Bille left £5 to Master Nicholas Bubwith to go to Rome and pray specially for him on the journey there and back, presumably at shrines on the route. [112] In three other wills modest sums were bequeathed to the English hospice which accommodated pilgrims in Rome: 2s. from John Rathby in 1431, 3s. 4d. from John Harpham in 1451, and 2s. from Peter Burton in 1460. [113] It can safely be said that the Holy City did not loom large in the thoughts of Hull men and women, and that Europe's and England's saints aroused no great fervour in most of them.

If we measure the priorities of our testators by the consistency of certain bequests, then the poor must have stood very near the top of the list. [114] Nearly every legacy can be given some spiritual connotation, but none more so than those to the poor and needy. Many testators left money to be distributed among the several almshouses in the city; some people left coal or firewood for them; others provided a dole for the poor who attended their funeral or subsequent memorials or who simply prayed for them; a few remembered prisoners; several more provided for the marrying of maidens. In 1437 John Gregg left £43. 6s. 8d. to be distributed to the poor and needy of Hull over a period of ten years, as well as £21. 13s. 4d. to the poor of Beverley over five years. [115] His widow, in 1438, stipulated not only that ½d. should be given to each pauper at her first dirige and 1d. to those at her funeral mass and at her octave but also that twelve gowns should be bought for the poor on her burial day; 6s. 8d. was also left by her to the leper house in Beverley; she bequeathed £20 to buy woollen cloth for bedding and clothes for the poor, and another £20 to buy linen for smocks and sheets for them; a further £6. 13s. 4d. was left for distribution among them at the discretion of Richard Pountefrete; £10 was to be spent by her executors to redeem prisoners, and £1 was specifically left to the prisoners in York gaols.[116] Besides all this, however, Joan Gregg bestowed in perpetuity upon the mayor and commonalty of Hull the reversion of lands from which they were to provide annually £5. 4s. to the house for thirteen paupers which she had lately built in Aldkyrklane, the thirteen to share 2s. each week. The Gregg maisondieu was still receiving bequests at the very end of our period. The connection between legacies to the poor and good works for the soul's welfare is plain enough when the poor were to be remembered, as by Robert Holme in 1449, on his funeral day and its commemorations; but John Osay, in 1429, left nothing to chance when he spelt out that his £10 for diverse prisoners and the £20 for the neediest of the poor, blind and lame were 'for my soul and the souls of all my benefactors.'[117]

Some burgesses, of course, looked outside Hull for additional suffrages. The neighbouring religious houses of Swine, Meaux and Haltemprice naturally attracted some attention. Guisborough and North Ferriby, proprietors of Hessle and St. Mary's, understandably figure in these wills from time to time; but only the Franciscans and Dominicans of Beverley, usually linked with legacies to the Hull friars, appear with anything approaching frequency. York Minster, the mother church of the diocese, was often remembered by testators – or by those who guided their pens – but rarely for more than a shilling a time. Other places appear in the wills to witness to the birthplace of the testator, or to the presence of his relatives there, or to the scene of his trade: Newcastle-upon-Tyne, Grimsby, Pontefract, Thetford and London are in this list. One distant location, however, testifies to more than trade: in 1445 William Proktour, merchant, included among his bequests £5 which was to be delivered by Nicholas Stubbes to the abbey and convent of Veda[118] in Iceland for the purchase of a coloured woollen cloth 'so that the same abbot and convent would truly and charitably grant full absolution to me, now *in extremis* and seeking pardon for certain evils and offences which I have committed in time past; and so that this absolution shall be the more abundantly effective, they might wish to send as quickly as possible by Nicholas to the vicar of Holy Trinity or his deputy notice of this absolution under their common seal'.[119]

Not all devotional expression, of course, was *post mortem* and public; for some of the Hull burghers, at least, household or private prayers played a part in their spiritual life. Few, if any, of them, however, employed a domestic chaplain. In 1430 Agnes Tutbury left £2 to 'my chaplain', John Raper, who two years later was again so described by her husband, John Tutbury; indeed, the latter appointed Raper one of his executors and stipulated that he should be the first priest of the projected Tutbury chantry.[120] In 1509 William Tailour, merchant of the Staple, bequeathed £15 to Sir Richard Todd, 'my priest' to sing masses for three years.[121] Not long after this, in 1520, Geoffrey Thurscrosse insisted that the priest of the Table who was to sing for his soul should be called Geoffrey

Thurscrosse's priest 'after the common wise and usage of the said town', a requirement which may suggest that Tutbury's and Tailour's chaplains were serving chantries already for those families rather than serving in their households.[122]

It is the books mentioned in the wills which testify more surely to private piety. Altogether thirteen testators refer to books, and apart from the two volumes of 'physic' left by Laurence Swattok, apothecary, they overwhelmingly leave, or at least name, religious works. Four clerks predictably left service and song books, and laymen and women named primers more often than any other work. John Bedford, in 1450, listed in his will two portases or breviaries, one of them his largest book, more than one missal, and a small book with seven psalms and the litany and other prayers in it.[123] His widow, nine years later, left a new primer to Agnes Swan; and to John Swan, junior, she left the primer 'which I daily use'.[124] Thomas Seggefield in 1444 bestowed his primer upon his servant, and in the same year John Aldwyk directed his primer to his son, Geoffrey.[125] John Steton, in 1459, left 'my primer and the hours of the Virgin' to John Richard, junior, while John Scalys, eight years later, bequeathed his best primer to Thomas West.[126] Richard Doughty, in 1485, left his primer to his son, Richard.[127] As we have seen above, Swattok himself gave his best primer to his nephew, Thomas Fisher, with some money, in return for his prayers.[128] In a city which supported a grammar school, and some of whose citizens wrote their own wills, a good many other books were doubtless circulating, but their nature remains hidden in the wills. The mere naming of the primers as well as the multiple copies which were possessed and the care with which they were bequeathed suggest how much they were valued: Agnes Bedford was surely not alone in her daily usage.

The habit of private prayer is also attested, and far more commonly than by books, by beads. Although it is not always clear that the reference is to rosaries, the mention of beads with 'gauds' – often of silver gilt – establishes the frequency of this form of private devotion. Elizabeth Bukk, in 1455, left three rosaries: one to her daughter, one to her daughter-in-law, and one to another young woman.[129] Agnes Bedford, in 1459, also left her daughter-in-law a rosary, but this one had 'gauds' of gold.[130] It was not only women, however, who had rosaries, any more than primers were a sign of feminine rather than male devotion; in 1476 John Swan, merchant and former mayor, left two rosaries.[131]

Whatever the scale and intensity of these private devotions, they seem not to have contributed to any enthusiasm for sermons, for in all these wills there is not one single bequest for preaching. When the pulpit is mentioned, it is not in connection with sermons: one man, John Helme in 1510, wanted to be buried near the pulpit in Holy Trinity; another, John Langton in 1505, wanted his soul and the souls of his wives to be prayed for 'in the pulpit (in St. Mary's Church) by name every Sunday' for eighty years.[132] It may be that the secular clergy, and perhaps even the friars, of the city were too uninspiring to arouse any enthusiasm for sermons, though popular preachers – even now – are not always particularly learned or necessarily profound; certain it is that they elicited no funds from the testators of Hull.

What perhaps is more notably, though not quite so universally, lacking from these wills is anxiety. In very few does one meet that urgent or comprehensive provision of good works which borders on the frenetic and tells of a tortured soul. John Garton's will, in 1456, is almost unique in its well-nigh unquenchable thirst for assurance.[133] He wanted eighteen priests and two clerks to be present at his funeral and on his seventh day, and twelve torches were to burn about his body; £30 was to be disbursed among the poor on those days and £10 more – for his and his wife's souls – within forty days of his death; the five maisonsdieu of Hull were to receive £1. 10s. between them; the poor in Beverley were to get £20, and two almshouses there £1. 3s. 4d; £20 was set aside for the marriage of poor girls. In addition to all these bequests, two chaplains were to celebrate mass for his and his wife's souls daily for nine years; the priests who performed the Mass of Our Lady were given £12 to pray specially for John and his wife; the Carmelites were to celebrate four trentals for them within a year of his death, the Dominicans in Beverley another four, and the Franciscans there another four – 360 masses in all. The vicar of Welwick was to receive £5 for a new cope on condition that he ask his parishioners to pray specially for the Gartons every Sunday. The guilds of Hull were to get £1 each, and the guild of St. John Baptist a further £10 for the purchase of a cope immediately after Garton's death. A shilling was left to each light before an image in Holy Trinity church. For the fabric of Burstwick parish church and for the building of its bell tower £20 was earmarked, for Thorngumbald church £5, and for the steeple of St. Mary's in Hull £10. Probably the £25 left for the repair of the roads from Hull to Beverley, Anlaby and Bilton should be classed as alms as well. In total, for the welfare of his and his wife's souls, Garton assigned almost £300. Nevertheless, his will is devoid of extravagant confessions or reflections and shows no peculiar or morbid devotions.

To a far greater degree than the rest of the populace, the merchants and tradesmen of Hull had the opportunity and the capacity to express and to satisfy their spiritual needs. Richer, more articulate and far more travelled than most of their fellows, it was the aldermen and burgesses who endowed and sustained the community's religious institutions: they built the churches and adorned them with altars, images and lights; they commissioned services and provided them with books, chalices, vestments and organs; the guilds were manned and run by Hull's 'patricians'; they hired and fired most of the clergy of the city; finally, they reposed – ostentatiously surrounded by candles and surmounted by baldaquins – in the churches which they so lavishly enhanced and equipped. Religious initiatives and religious fashions in Hull rested with the burghers, more even than with the clergy. The self-revelations, therefore, of this governing élite have a significance which extends beyond their own numbers and class; the wills provide limits within which to locate the sentiments and priorities of the community at large.

The clergy, for their part, seem to have afforded no deep spiritual or meditative wells from which the people – of any class – might draw personal illumination or inspiration. The parish clergy were too simply educated – the two graduates who appear in the wills seem to have had no pastoral role – and many were remarkably transient.[134] That we know so little about the inmates of the friaries and Charterhouse suggests that they, too, had their limitations. In any event, the Charterhouse was isolated from most Hull citizens by a jurisdictional dispute which served to underscore its identification with De La Poles and the East Riding gentry. The deficiencies of the clergy were those of mediocrity rather than of scandal, and they perhaps reflect the complacency of the laity who employed and patronised them.

Despite contacts with the Low Countries, Hull's citizens yield no evidence of being touched by the *Devotio Moderna*. Some household prayers there undoubtedly were, and some literate lay piety, but few signs indicate that this activity was reflective, resourceful or independent: the books and the garrulous revelations in a few wills are commonplace, however earnest. Only one testator renounces pomp, none denigrates the flesh or expresses any loathing of it. Christ rarely appears in these wills and then but briefly. There is only one allusion to the new liturgical devotions, that to the Five Wounds of Christ, and this occurs in the same will which scorned pomp. Anchorites and anchoresses are scarcely known in Hull, apparently not at all after the early fifteenth century. Preaching attracts not one single legacy. In fact, throughout this whole period scarcely any shift in the pattern of pious bequests is detectable.

If, however, the Hull testators had no share in the new devotions and displayed no eagerness for change, their commitment to the familiar ones was remarkably low-key. Pilgrimages figure in very few wills and though the cult of saints was common enough, it was too diffused for any marked emphasis to be discernible and it certainly reveals no extravagances of feeling or of practice. Commemorative masses and good works abound, but they rarely approach, let alone reach, excess. Several bequests for chantries and obits are contingent upon the failure of heirs: in that event, what to do with the property but, *faute de mieux*, leave it to the undying and claim the spiritual interest? In very few wills indeed are there any signs of that torment about the fate of the soul and none of that morbid anxiety so long regarded as the late-medieval norm. The assumption that most medieval people were anguished by the prospect of the horrors awaiting them in the next world rests particularly upon the frequent and vivid portrayals of purgatory and hell in the literature, sermons, paintings and stained glass of the period; yet may not their frequency and intensity (as with all those statutes against livery and maintenance) simply testify to their futility and neglect?

All this may seem to imply condemnation of Hull men and women because they neither succumbed to *Angst* nor embraced novelty, because they neither clamoured at shrines nor read *avant-garde* works of devotion, because, in fact, they simply displayed tranquillity in their religion. What else, it may be asked, did they need to do or say in their wills to convince sceptical historians of the depth and sincerity of their beliefs? This very calmness and moderation could well be the sign of a sure and profound faith in the Christian gospel, for the abiding impression left by these wills is one of unclouded hope. Yet the bequests for obits, trentals, masses, and *pompes funèbres* ring still more clearly with confident investment and, above all, with social self-awareness: funeral and commemorative masses are to be 'as befits an alderman', or 'according to the custom of the town'. In these wills religion is overlaid with civic pride and is almost subsumed into civic ritual. Most of our testators were doubtless sincere in their faith, but they reveal few traces of misgivings or of introspection or of independent thoughts or even of independent emotions: their faith was remarkably insular, inert, and shallow, untouched by the new devotions, perfunctory almost in the old ones, uninterested in, and showing no deep acquaintance with, doctrine. When in 1559, through the agency of Melchior Smith,[135] Protestantism came to Hull, it came not as the climax of long or deep spiritual yearnings there, nor yet as release for tortured and fantasy-ridden minds, least of all as the heir of Lollardy and anticlericalism, but as rain to a dry land.

Notes

*   I am especially indebted to Dr. David Smith, Dr. Bill Sheils, and Professor Barrie Dobson for their help, suggestions, patience and encouragement during the preparation of this study. I am grateful also to Mr G.W. Oxley, archivist of Kingston upon Hull, and to his staff in the city record office. Throughout this paper, names, which are often variously spelt in the manuscript sources, have been standardized: the Latin of the wills has been Englished, and the English of the wills modernized.

1.   K.B. McFarlane, *Lancastrian Kings and Lollard Knights* (Oxford, 1972), 137–226; M.G.A. Vale, *Piety, Charity and Literacy among the Yorkshire Gentry, 1370–1480* (Borthwick Papers 50, York, 1976); N.P. Tanner, 'Popular Religion in Norwich with special reference to wills 1370–1532' (Oxford D.Phil. thesis, 1973); Hope Emily Allen's various works, but especially her notes to *The Book of Margery Kempe* (EETS, OS 212, 1940); R.W. Pfaff, *New Liturgical Feasts in Later Medieval England* (Oxford, 1970); J.T. Rosenthal, *The Purchase of Paradise* (1972); Sylvia Thrupp, *The Merchant Class of Medieval London* (Michigan, Ann Arbor Paperbacks, 1962), 177–90; Jacques Toussaert, *Le Sentiment Religieux en Flandre à la Fin du Moyen Age* (Paris, 1960).

2.   Berndt Moeller, 'Religious Life in Germany on the Eve of the Reformation', in *Pre-Reformation Germany*, ed. G. Strauss (1972), 14; and M.G.A. Vale, op. cit., 8.

3.   For a valuable discussion of evidential problems, though with particular reference to German sources, see Hansgeorg Molitor, 'Frömmigkeit in Spämittelalter und Früher Neuzeit als historisch-methodisches Problem', 1–20, in *Festgabe für Ernst Walter Zeeden*, ed. Horst Robe, H. Molitor and H.C. Rublack (Münster, 1976).

4.   For most of what follows in this and the next paragraph see *VCH, East Riding*, i (Oxford, 1969), particularly 59–70, 132–3 (for trade); 74, 157 (for population); 158 (for taxable wealth); 287–91, 294–6, 333–4 (for churches).

5.   Ibid., 90, where Mr. Forster speaks of the 'habitual piety' and 'conventional bequests' evident in the wills.

6.   Kingston upon Hull Record Office (henceforward KHRO), BRE 2, fos. 41v.–43r. This is a registered copy of letters patent of 8 January 1409 (new style) enlarging the endowment of the twelve chaplains.

7.   For taxable wealth see W.G. Hoskins, *The Age of Plunder: King Henry's England 1500–1547* (1976), 13. On the merchants of Hull, including some comments upon their religion, see J.I. Kermode, 'The merchants of three northern English towns', in *Profession, Vocation and Culture in Later Medieval England*, ed. C.H. Clough (Liverpool, 1982), 7–49.

8.   For the jurisdictional arrangements and consequent records, see David M. Smith, *A Guide to the Archive Collections in the Borthwick Institute of Historical Research* (York, 1973), especially 155–61; *Index of Wills in the York Registry 1389–1514* (Yorkshire Archaeological and Topographical Association, Record Series, vi, 1889), 199–204; *Index of Wills in the York Registry 1514–1553* (ibid., xi, 1891), 209–43. The wills of testators with substantial possessions in more than one diocese were proved in the prerogative court of the archbishop and recorded in the same registers which served the exchequer court.

9.   Borthwick Institute Probate Register (henceforward Prob. Reg.), 2, fo. 179r–v.

10. *Index of Wills . . . 1389–1514*, 199–202.

11. See J.C.C. Smith, *Index of Wills Proved in the Prerogative Court of Canterbury 1383–1558* (2 vols., The Index Library, London, 1893–95). These registers have not been consulted for this study.

12. KHRO, BRE 1, fos. 271–2 (registered copy), and BRA 69 (separate copy): the will of John Swynflete, drawn up on 4 September 1420 and proved five days later; registered in Hull in 1426.

13. KHRO, BRA 88/11, original will of Simon Berker (1438), with probate; BRA 87/47, original will of Richard Flynton (1491), without probate; BRA 87/40, original will of Peter Garner (1522), with probate; BRE 1, fo. 165, copy of will of John Snayth (1425). Three other extant original wills are registered at York: BRA 87/43, William Burgh (1460); BRA 87/45, Richard Flynton (1468); BRA 87/39, Alan Armestrang (1522). There are also extracts of the will of Margaret Darras (1469), not in the York registers, and of the will of her father, John Benne (1429), which is registered at York, both on one loose sheet in Hull, BRA 87/15.

14. These occur throughout the period in the probate registers and – in the early sixteenth century – in the deanery Act Books as well.

15. For a discussion of plague in Hull in this period, see J.M.W. Bean, 'Plague, Population, and Economic Decline in England in the later Middle Ages', *EcHR.*, 2nd series, xv (1962–63), 436–7.

16. Cf. Vale, op. cit., 4–6 for the vernacular wills of Yorkshire gentry.

17. Prob. Reg., 5, fos. 483v–485r; 6, fos. 51r–52r; 6, fo. 107r; 2, fo.305v; 2, fos. 350v–351r; 2, fo. 271v; 5, fo.57r.

18. Prob. Reg., 6, fo. 107r, and Borthwick Institute, Cause Papers G.72/4.

19. Prob. Reg., 3, fos. 371r–372r; KHRO, BRA 6 (foundation deed, dated Pentecost 1453).

20. Aldwyke's and Alcock's: see above, p. 219.

21. Prob. Reg., 9, fos. 144v–145r.

22. Prob. Reg., 5, fo. 95r–v; 9, fo. 76v.

23. Prob. Reg., 5, fo. 350v.

24. Prob. Reg., 5, fos. 483v–485r. Compare the not dissimilar words of Damoiselle Guillemette Coquillart of Rheims, in 1542, quoted by A.N. Galpern in *The Pursuit of Holiness in Late Medieval and Renaissance Religion*, ed. C. Trinkaus with H. Oberman (Leiden, 1974), 149.

25. Prob. Reg., 6, fos. 51r–52r.

26. Prob. Reg., 9, fo. 112r–v. For the ramifications of the Dalton family see J.I. Kermode, op. cit., 20–1.

27. Prob. Reg., 9, fo. 160r.

28. Prob. Reg., 3, fo. 281v; 2, fo. 152r.

29. Prob. Reg., 2, fos. 107v–108r.

30. Prob. Reg., 5, fos. 483v–485r.

31. Prob. Reg., 6, fos. 51r–52r.

32. Prob. Reg., 9, fo. 112r–v.

33. Prob. Reg., 9, fo. 160r.

34. Prob. Reg., 2, fo. 429r; 6, fo. 107r.

35. Prob. Reg., 3, fo. 70r–v; 2, fos. 539v–540r.

36. Prob. Reg., 2, fos. 443v–444r.

37. Prob. Reg., 8, fo. 31v.

38. Prob. Reg., 3, fos. 52v–53r (Robert Byset, 1401); 2, fo. 152r (William Dene, 1446); 2, fo. 233r–v (Richard Bille, 1451); 2, fo. 276r–278r (Francis Bukk, 1453); 2, fo. 271v (Hans Martyn, 1453); 2, fo. 325r–v (John Herryson, 1455); 2, fo. 362r–v (John Northeby, 1458); 2, fo. 372v (William Castelford, 1458); 4, fo. 177r (Nicholas Barbor, 1471); 4, fo. 103r–v (Henry Smyth, 1476); 5, fo. 132r (Nicholas Elesse, 1478); 7, fos. 1v–2r (Margaret Story, 1507); 9, fo. 24r (William Johnson, 1515); 9, fo. 28v (Thomas Taylor, 1516).

39. See, for example, on the gentry, Vale, op. cit., 9, and on the nobility, Rosenthal, op. cit., 4 and 5.

40. For a general account, and other details, of the building see the references in note 4 above.

41. Prob. Reg., 3, fos. 52v–53r (Robert Byset); 3, fo. 213r–v (Robert Rotherby); 3, fo. 256r–v (Matilda de Waghen); 2, fo. 575v (Alan Wilcox).

42. Prob. Reg., 2, fo. 575v; Borthwick Institute, Reg. 18 (Reg. Archbishop Bowet, vol. i), fo. 352r; Prob. Reg. 3, fo. 606v.
43. Prob Reg., 2, fos. 381v–382r; 2, fos. 433v–434r.
44. Prob. Reg., 5, fos. 493v–494r (Thomas Philippe, 1497); 6, fos. 51r–52r (Thomas Dalton, 1497); 9, fo. 73v (William Ryels, 1518); 9, fo. 240v (Geoffrey Thurscrosse, 1520); 9, fo. 218r (Arthur Welles, 1521); 9, fos. 272r–273r (Joan Thurscrosse, 1523); 9, fo. 447v (James Johnson, 1529).
45. Prob. Reg., 2, fo. 523r–v; 2, fo. 22r; 2, fo. 108r–v; 2, fo. 185r–v; 2, fos. 9v–10r.
46. Prob. Reg., 5, fos. 87v–88r.
47. Prob. Reg., 6, fo. 191r.
48. Prob. Reg., 2, fo. 179r–v (John Burnham).
49. Prob. Reg., 3, fos. 507v–508v; 2, fo. 108r–v; 5, fos. 148v–149r; 5, fos. 87v–88r.
50. Prob. Reg., 2, fo. 195r–v.
51. KHRO, M. 11 (account book of the guild of St. Mary). The other guild which has left accounts is that of Holy Trinity, for which see VCH, East Riding, i, 397–400.
52. See, for example, KHRO, BRA 87/15 (a chirograph, of 1481, concerning the obit of John and Margaret Darras). Compare also notes 60–62 below.
53. Prob. Reg., 6, fo. 128r–v; 9, fo. 65v.
54. Prob. Reg., 3, fo. 240v; 2, fo. 653r; 3, fos. 418v–419v.
55. Prob. Reg., 2, fos. 327v–328r and 341v.
56. Prob. Reg., 3, fos. 555v–556v.
57. Prob. Reg., 5, fo. 7r–v.
58. Borthwick Institute, Cause Papers G.72/5.
59. Prob. Reg., 3, fos. 284v–285r.
60. Prob. Reg., 4, fo. 242r–v.
61. Prob. Reg., 3, fo. 299v and 2, fo. 486r.
62. Prob. Reg., 8, fo. 105r.
63. Prob. Reg., 3, fo. 93r–v.
64. Prob. Reg., 3, fo. 240v; 2, fo. 113r–v; 6, fo. 161v.
65. Prob. Reg., 9, fos. 272r–273r.
66. Prob. Reg., 2, fo. 295r–v.
67. Prob. Reg., 2, fo. 194r–v; 2, fo. 271v; 2, fos. 327v–328r, 341v.
68. Christopher Welles (Prob. Reg., 2, fo.435r–v), John Spencer (2, fos. 486v, 489r), and Edmund Greveley (5, fo. 501r–v), though the last case is ambiguous and may refer to an obit rather than to daily masses.
69. Prob. Reg., 2, fos. 211v–212v.
70. The seven were those of Tutbury, Gregg, Aldwyke, Bedford, Haynson, Alcock and Thurscrosse. Aldwyke's will makes no mention of the chantry; Alcock's will is not among our 355 and seems to be unknown. For these two chantries see KHRO, BRA 87/34 (Aldwyke foundation deed) and J. Lawson, A Town Grammar School (Oxford, 1963), 25–30 (for Alcock's chantry and the attached school).
71. KHRO, BRA 87/34 (Aldwyke chantry foundation deed) and BRA 72/5 (Thurscrosse chantry foundation deed).
72. KHRO, BRA 72/5 makes clear that the Thurscrosse chantry, though located in St. Mary's church, was to be served by one of the Priests of the Table.
73. Prob. Reg., 3, fos. 371r–372v; 2, fos. 220r–221v.
74. Prob. Reg., 5, fo. 167v.
75. Prob. Reg., 2, fo. 225r–v.
76. Prob. Reg., 9, fo. 228r.
77. Prob. Reg., 9, fo. 288r.
78. Prob. Reg., 9, fo. 391r.
79. Prob. Reg., 2, fo. 271v.

80. Prob. Reg., 6, fo. 65v.
81. Prob. Reg., 6, fo. 99r–v.
82. Prob. Reg., 3, fo. 299v, and 2, fo. 486r (William Ripplingham, 1464); 2, fos. 443v–444r (Thomas Johnson, 1460); 8, fo. 105r (Elizabeth Garner, 1513).
83. Prob. Reg., 2, fos. 211v–212v (Robert Holme, 1449); KHRO, BRE 1, fos. 271–2 and BRA 69 (John Swynflete, 1420).
84. Prob. Reg., 9, fo. 240v.
85. Prob. Reg., 2, fos. 285v–286r; 9, fo. 391r.
86. E.M. Thompson, *The Carthusian Order in England* (1930), 330, could find no details of books at Hull Charterhouse and no other clues to its intellectual and spiritual worth.
87. KHRO, BRB 1, fos. 16r, 36r, 39 (1)r for evidence of disputes from 1450; and BRA 5 for Wolsey's arbitration, sealed 24 March 1518.
88. *Letters & papers of Henry VIII*, x, No. 980 – the basis of the assertion by D.M. Knowles that the Hull Charterhouse was venerated by its neighbours: see *Religious Orders in England*, iii (Cambridge, 1959), 308, 317. E.M. Thompson, op. cit., 206, while noticing the rarity of bequests from Hull testators, preferred to draw no conclusions from this, perhaps because she had consulted only the wills in print.
89. *Letters & Papers of Henry VIII*, xi, No. 385 (34); xiii(2), No. 457, i (3); xiv(2), No. 489.
90. Prob. Reg., 3, fos. 608r–609r.
91. Prob. Reg., 3, fos. 555v–556v; 4, fos. 230v, 235r. However, in 1435 Richard Russell of York had left money for two recluses in Hull: see p. 44, n. 129 of Kermode's chapter in *Profession, Vocation, and Culture*, ed. Clough.
92. L.M. Stanewell, *Kingston upon Hull: Calendar of Ancient Deeds, Letters and Miscellaneous Documents 1300–1800* (Hull, 1951), D. 437, D. 462.
93. See N.P. Tanner, 'Popular Religion in Norwich' (Oxford D.Phil. thesis, 1973), 116–29, 254–6.
94. Prob. Reg., 6, fos. 180v–181r; 9, fos. 272r–273r.
95. Prob. Reg., 9, fo. 44v.
96. Prob. Reg., 5, fo. 287v; 5, fos. 383r–384r; 5, fos. 410v–411r.
97. Prob. Reg., 6, fo. 216r–v.
98. See generally on the guilds VCH, *East Riding*, i, 84, 287–9, 295. For St. Ninian see Prob. Reg., 6, fos. 49v–50r (Cornelius Johnson, 1502); for Holy Trinity see VCH, *East Riding*, i, 397–400; for St. Nicholas see Prob. Reg., 5, fo. 274r (Richard Harwood, 1485) and 9, fo. 151v (William Porter, 1520).
99. See Prob. Reg., 3, fos. 507v–508v; 3, fos. 555v–556v.
100. Prob. Reg., 2, fos. 276r–278r.
101. Prob. Reg., 9, fo. 218r. Other wills refer to the guilds of St. Barbara and St. Erasmus: Prob. Reg., 6, fos. 49v–50r (Cornelius Johnson, 1502) for St. Barbara's guild; 2, fo. 315r (Elizabeth Bukk, 1455) for the guild of St. Erasmus; and 9, fos. 113v–114r (John Sharp, 1520) for the altar of St. Erasmus.
102. Prob. Reg., 9, fos. 272r–273r.
103. Prob. Reg., 5, fo. 72r–v.
104. See VCH, *East Riding*, i, 288–9, 295 for altars and images: and for these particular ones Prob. Reg., 6, fos. 180v–181r (Joan York, 1506) for the altar of St. Lawrence; 9, fo. 49r (Robert Bery, 1516), 9, fo. 144r (Henry Passmyer, 1520), and 9, fo. 170r (Joan Roclif, 1521) for the altar of St. Antony; 6, fo. 213r–v (Robert Langton, 1505) for the image of St. Christopher.
105. Prob. Reg., 6, fos. 51r–52r; 6, fo. 107r.
106. Prob. Reg., 9, fo. 112–v.
107. Prob. Reg., 2, for 158v–159r; 2, fos. 220r–221v; 2, fo. 233r–v; 2, fos. 418r–419r; 2, fo. 421r–v; 5, fo. 196v; 9, fos. 272r–273r. Of course, other images were in the possession of the guilds: thus Holy Trinity guild had statues of the Virgin, several pictures which included one of St. Anne, and a carved head of St. John the Baptist (VCH, *East Riding*, i, 398).

108. Prob. Reg., 2, fos. 115v–116r; 2, fo. 233r–v.
109. Prob. Reg., 9, fo. 117r and *Test. Ebor.*, v, 114.
110. Prob. Reg., 2, fos. 115v–116r.
111. Prob. Reg., 2, fo. 231r–v.
112. Prob. Reg., 2, fo. 233r–v.
113. Prob. Reg., 3, fo. 362r–v; 2, fo. 231r–v; 2, fo. 429r. It should be added that the fragmentary records of the English hospice in Rome name four Hull pilgrims who stayed there: John Andrew in 1479, James Browne and William Spencer in 1483, and John Monicor in 1514 (*The English Hospice in Rome* (The Venerabile Sexcentenary Issue, xxi, May 1962), 110, 123, 142). In 1509 the parishioners of Holy Trinity contributed 14s. 1d. in alms towards the rebuilding of St. Peter's in Rome (KHRO, M. 26, which is a chirograph recording the transfer of the money by the churchwardens to the dean of Harthill and Hull).
114. Compare the observations of Sylvia Thrupp on London in her *Merchant Class*, 174–80.
115. Prob. Reg., 3, fos. 507v–508r.
116. Prob. Reg., 3, fos. 555v–556v.
117. Prob. Reg., 2, fos. 211v–212v; 2, fo. 567r–v.
118. Presumably the Augustinian house of Videy (*The Catholic Encyclopaedia*, vii (1910), 626).
119. Prob. Reg., 2, fo. 108r–v.
120. Prob. Reg., 2, fo.667r; 3, fos. 371r–372v.
121. Prob. Reg., 8, fo. 31v.
122. KHRO, BRA 72/5 (foundation deed).
123. Prob. Reg., 2, fos. 220r–221v.
124. Prob. Reg., 2, fos 418r–419r.
125. Prob. Reg., 2, fo. 85v; 2, fo. 96r.
126. Prob. Reg., 2, fo. 394r–v; 4, fo. 242r–v.
127. Prob. Reg., 5, fo. 350v.
128. Prob. Reg., 5, fos. 410v–411v.
129. Prob. Reg., 2, fo. 315r.
130. Prob. Reg., 2, fos. 418r–419r.
131. Prob. Reg., 5, fo. 7r–v.
132. Prob. Reg., 8, fo. 52v; 6, fo. 213r–v.
133. Prob. Reg., 2, fos. 327v–328r and 341v.
134. The parish clergy will be the subject of a separate study.
135. On Smith see Claire Cross, 'Parochial Structure and the Dissemination of Protestantism in Sixteenth Century England: A Tale of Two Cities', in SCH, xvi (1979), ed. D. Baker, 269–78, and especially 274–6.

Index